The Chief

Ernest Thompson Seton in the woods near his DeWinton
estate in Connecticut.

The Chief

Ernest Thompson Seton and
the Changing West

By
H. Allen Anderson

Texas A&M University Press
College Station

Library of Congress Cataloging-in-Publication Data
Anderson, H. Allen (Hugh Allen), 1950–
  The chief: Ernest Thompson Seton and the changing West.
  Bibliography: p.
  Includes index.
    1. Seton, Ernest Thompson, 1860–1946. 2. Naturalists
—Canada—Biography. 3. Artists—Canada—Biography.
4. Authors, Canadian—20th century—Biography. I. Title.
QH31.S48A63 1986   574'.092'4 [B]   85-40751
ISBN 0-89096-239-1 **(cloth)**
ISBN 0-89096-982-5 (pbk.)

Manufactured in the United States of America
First Paperback Edition

CONTENTS

ILLUSTRATIONS

PREFACE

I first became acquainted with Ernest Thompson Seton's world of animals and Indians at a boys' camp in the mountains of northern New Mexico. That particular summer, our camp director had made arrangements to take us through Seton Castle, with the "Chatelaine" herself, Mrs. Julia M. Seton, as our tour guide. Certainly it was hard for me to envision a cupolaed European castle in the semiarid New Mexico foothills dotted with cedars and piñon pines. Nevertheless, we all sat with eager anticipation as the bus turned off the Old Pecos Road onto the dusty, half-mile drive leading to the castle. After passing several small adobe dwellings, the bus driver parked the cumbersome vehicle on top of a steep gravel incline. Filing out, we saw a large, many-roomed house that resembled, in part, the apartmentlike dwellings of Taos Pueblo. Built of native wood, sandstone, and adobe, this New Mexico "castle" blended perfectly with its surroundings. Only the television antenna on the highest point of the multilevel roof stood out as a reminder that modern technology had reached even this wilderness abode. In the rustic wooden doorway, overshadowed by a front porch supported by log columns, stood a bespectacled, red-haired lady in an embroidered Spanish-style dress. Mrs. Seton graciously bade us welcome.

Inside we found a rustic home, with a mixture of imported Eastern and native Southwestern styles apparent in the furniture and the rugs on the wooden living room floor. But what captured our eyes were the paintings and drawings of birds and mammals that covered the walls. Mrs. Seton, still lively despite her age, had us sit down in front of the hearth. Silence fell over the normally noisy group as she pointed out examples of her late husband's artwork, including the large oil of wolves feasting on the grisly remains of an unfortunate hunter. This controversial painting, she told us, was done while he was studying art in Paris. She also related several Indian legends, of how the demigod Nanaboujou took a scoop of mud and with his fingers painted the stripes on the sides of the naughty chipmunk and how he smoked up the Rio Grande Valley with his peace pipe, creating the haze of Indian summer. But the real highlight of her storytelling session was the tale of Old Lobo, the dreaded King Wolf, whose reign of terror among the New Mexico ranchers was ended by the young Mr. Seton when he rode the plains of the Currumpaw as a hired wolfer. We sat spellbound as Mrs. Seton directed our attention to the wall above the fireplace. Nailed there was Lobo's hide, a rusted wolf trap, and the torn noose of Seton's lasso that Lobo sheared in two as a last defiant act against his one great enemy, man. "Chief loved that wolf before it was over," she said, concluding this most requested of her husband's stories.[1]

After answering the questions of several eager listeners, Mrs. Seton took us through the library with its thousands of volumes, and the studio, which contained originals of the illustrations that the Chief (as she called him) used in his books. The Setons' private museum was also fascinating. Here were displayed countless Indian artifacts, as well as bird and mammal specimens. At the end of the tour, Mrs. Seton offered for sale a new hardback edition of her husband's most famous book, *Wild Animals I Have Known*.

That unforgettable experience sowed the seeds of my interest in this remarkable author of the wild. Ernest Thompson Seton was, in many ways, a strange mixture of the western frontiersman and the cultured eastern gentleman. Although he was born in a representative English industrial seaport and raised in the backwoods of the Canadian province of Ontario, Seton could never entirely shed the trappings of his alleged noble ancestry. It has been said that because of their frontier experience, "Canadians are not as optimistic, as volatile, as imaginative, as experimental, as assertive, as egotistic or energetic as are Americans. Those among them who have possessed such qualities have often become Americans."[2] Such a statement applies quite well to Seton, who spent most of his productive years in the United States and eventually became a naturalized American citizen. A man of many hats—naturalist, artist, author, poet, lecturer, social reformer, and above all, master storyteller—Seton sought the wilderness as his place of refuge and revitalization. The product of an unhappy home, he grew to scorn traditional religion and gradually adopted the nature pantheism of the native Americans, using the wilderness as his sanctuary. This "sanctuary," found first in the Ontario backwoods and the Manitoba prairies, slowly expanded to include the mountains and deserts of the American West.

Among other things, Seton observed and participated in the transition of the West from colony to pacesetter. While he was primarily concerned with its fauna, his encounters with the people of the region left a lasting impression both on him and on his readers. Westerners with whom he hunted and visited were incorporated into his quasi-factual tales and scientific works alike. In all his writings, the values of the Progressive Era are reflected in the attitudes and "homespun" dialogue of his characters. In a sense, Seton may be seen as a folk historian (or folklorist). Although Seton rubbed elbows with many of the rich and famous, he was concerned primarily with the grassroots individual. The most outstanding personalities he depicted were those who had risen not through business enterprise or book learning but through woodcraft—the ability to understand, commune with, and learn from nature. It is small wonder, then, that Seton was enamored of the American Indian and soon became an avid spokesman for Indian rights. Seton's Western experiences, in both Canada and the United States, served over the years to draw him further and further from his Eastern ties and the mainstream of American culture. An idealist with a towering ego, Seton's universalist viewpoints came into conflict with the martial, nationalistic atmosphere prevalent during World War I. After 1915, he was branded a radical by some and an eccentric by others. Subsequently, he became more closely identified with Western authors and artists. With their support, Seton reestablished his Woodcraft organization in the Southwest. While he maintained contacts with family and friends back East, his divorce from his first wife and marriage to another seemed to represent the completeness of his desire to start over in a new "frontier" environment more suited to his ideals. Yet throughout this transition he remained a popular figure, especially among America's youth, because of his eloquence as a public speaker. To many young people, the Chief was almost a folk hero. And in his own mind, Seton sought to build up that very image.

It is from the perspective of the changing West that this study of Seton's life, times, and works is written. Along with major events that shaped his early life, I place particular emphasis on his early field trips, contacts, and travels west, as well as on later events leading to the establishment of Seton Village in New Mexico. Though I examine his contributions to the worlds of art, science, literature, and youth work, my primary concern is with Seton as a people's man, family man, and social commentator. Above all, I attempt to present him as a Western man, part "Leatherstocking," part Eastern "dude," and genuine prophet of the outdoors. The years of his life (1860–1946) covered the most incredible epoch of rapid change in the history of Western civilization. A maverick in many respects, Ernest Thompson Seton remains a paradoxical, mysterious, and complex individual.

Several people deserve a special word of appreciation for their part in this project. First of all, my thanks go to Mrs. Dee Seton Barber, who gave me access to several files of her adoptive father's correspondence at Seton Castle. Likewise, Steve Zimmer, Bonnie Tooley, and other staff members of the Seton Memorial Library and Museum at Philmont Scout Ranch were very supportive and accommodating during the course of my research. Mrs. Ruth M. Christensen graciously allowed me to examine the Charles F. Lummis and F. W. Hodge correspondence with Seton at the Southwest Museum Library in Los Angeles. Ellen S. Dunlap of the Humanities Research Center at the University of Texas at Austin was instrumental in enabling me to work with the Seton materials there. Dr. Stan Hordes and others at the New Mexico Records Center and Archives also deserve thanks, as do the staffs of the Huntington Library, Bancroft Library, Yale University Library, Lilly Library (University of Indiana), Southwest Collection (Texas Tech University), and the Special Collections at the University of New Mexico. T. M. Pearce of the University of New Mexico, James G. Allen of Texas Tech University, Robert Sutton of Albuquerque, and Louise Wells of Clayton, New Mexico, provided interesting insights into Seton's life and character. John Henry Wadland's analytical study of Seton's role in the Progressive Era was of particular value in developing certain portions of my manuscript, especially Seton's achievements in art and science and his work with the Boy Scouts organization.[3]

My appreciation is also extended to professors Richard N. Ellis, Donald C. Cutter, Ferenc M. Szasz, Charles D. Biebel, and Richard W. Etulain for their advice, encouragement, and helpful criticism, and to Mrs. Eleanor L. Orth for the final typing of the manuscript. Last of all, special thanks go to my father and mother for their patience and support throughout the course of my research.

The Chief

CHAPTER 1

From England to Ontario:
A Backwoods City Boy

As a backwoods Canadian boy, Ernest Thompson Seton came to owe his allegiance not to his family but to the wilderness and the wild animals that inhabited it. However, he was also a city boy of Scottish background and had grown up in an environment of rapid urban and industrial development and the social problems associated with it. Such disparate elements produced a driven young man who longed for his own version of Camelot and a simpler way of life. He soon found his Camelot in the wilds, and even while living in Toronto, he sought out its few vestiges of nature. An artist-naturalist was thus born.

Young Seton's remarkable pilgrimage to his Camelot began at the English seaport town of South Shields in Durham. Located on the south bank of the River Tyne where it empties into the North Sea, South Shields was (and still is) the port for the great commercial city of Newcastle nine miles upstream. Here was the famous harbor where the first lifeboat was launched. Merchant ships from all corners of the globe lined the waterfront, as did fishing boats and trawlers from Cornwall, the Dogger Bank, and even far-off Newfoundland. Overhead, flocks of gulls screamed continuously.

In 1860, South Shields had a population of around 40,000. On the hills in the outskirts of town were the homes of miners, for under the slopes were some of England's largest coal deposits. The innumerable factories jammed along the river in the town's great manufacturing district took advantage of this cheap source of fuel and labor. Near the mouth of the river, facing the sea, were the abodes of a powerful clique—the shipowners, self-made merchants who owned one or more of the vessels that crowded the harbor and riverfront.

Among the more prosperous of these shipowners was Joseph Logan Thompson. Born in 1821, the eldest son in his family, Thompson faithfully carried on the business his father and grandfather had firmly established. By 1860 he owned a dozen sailing ships and was highly respected by his associates and the captains he hired. Many of his neighbors were related to him, either by blood or by marriage; in 1843, he had married Alice Snowden, daughter of a neighboring merchant family. Thompson's plain, solid, three-story brick dwelling at No. 6 Wellington Terrace was thus prominent in the merchant marine community.[1] From the third story, one could look out over the town, the wheatfields and meadows of the surrounding countryside and the often fogbound coast. To the north could be seen the somber ruins of Tynemouth Abbey, a silent reminder of the medieval church and Viking raids.

Almost immediately, numerous offspring, nearly all boys, began arriving at the Thompson house "in true Victorian succession." In the winter of 1859–60, Alice Thompson, once again with child, asked the family doctor what she should do to endow this one "with better gifts than common." The doctor told her to take care of her health, keep herself free from any "nervous upset," and fix her mind on lofty ideals. Therefore, Alice consulted her Bible daily and also began reading a popular romantic novel, *Ernest Maltravers*. A profoundly religious woman, she hoped and prayed that her child would be like the novel's hero, an outdoorsman, a hunter, and "in the field sense," a naturalist. Above all, so family tradition relates, Alice hoped he would inherit the courage and forbearance of a notable Scottish ancestor, Evan Cameron of Lochiel, who had helped rid Scotland of the fierce wolf packs that had devastated the livestock. When summer came, Alice began going to a nearby beach and taking a daily dip in the ocean. One particularly stormy day in July, she almost lost her life when an undertow pulled her from the shore, but "Old Ellen" Robertson, the family's nurse who always accompanied her, caught her by the hair. From this shock, so Ellen and others in the family believed, the baby was born prematurely—with a fear of water and a heavy crop of curly black hair. Ernest Evan Thompson, named after his mother's literary hero and distinguished ancestor, came into the world on August 14, 1860.[2]

The story of Ernest's claim to nobility is confusing, but there may be some truth to it. Throughout his life, he maintained that his family was descended from George Seton, fifth earl of Winton, a highland Scottish nobleman who had fled into exile in Italy with his Stuart retinue during the Jacobite uprising of 1715. Seton claimed that the earl had a grandson, George Seton of Bellingham, Northumberland, who as sole heir, legally received the title from the Bailies of Cannongate—Scotland's highest

tribunal—after the general amnesty of 1823. Although he died child-
less, this sixth earl of Winton allegedly named Joseph L. Thompson—
Ernest's father and supposedly the earl's first cousin—the only male sur-
vivor of the line, as the lawful heir to the title.[3] What Seton apparently
did not know, or at least failed to acknowledge, was that the fifth earl of
Winton had died in Rome unmarried and thus without legal issue.
Years later, a grandson of Ernest's brother Enoch said that an unsuccessful claimant had attempted to prove that the earl did leave a son
from whom the family was presumably descended.[4] Seton, however,
sought to prove his argument by saying that his great-grandmother Ann
Seton, on her deathbed, admonished Joseph to stand up for his rights as
titular heir. Since Scottish law permitted the earldom to be transmitted
through a female in the absence of a male heir, she could carry the surname. Therefore, Ernest concluded that his father was indeed the legitimate claimant to the title, even though he never used it. Instead, he continued going by the name Thompson, reportedly an assumed name
taken by his paternal grandfather, Alan Cameron; after the second Jacobite uprising ended with the debacle at Culloden in 1746, Cameron and
many of his fellow clansmen sought refuge in northern England, changing their names to hide their identities. An important man and a relative
of the Lochiel wolf hunter, Cameron was said to have had a price of a
thousand pounds on his head. But his mastery of the King's English,
which reflected his education, made his disguise complete, and the
Thompsons (or Camerons) and their kin began recouping their lost for-
tunes on the waterfront of South Shields as shipowners in the British
merchant marine.[5]

This migration of Seton's forebears marks the first recorded instance
of his family's attempt to seek a better life by pulling up stakes and moving. The legitimacy of his claim to the name of Seton, however, remained in question, as there was never agreement on the issue within
the family. Supposedly, his father was all for asserting his right at a "con-
venient date," but that date never came. All through his adult life, Seton
would be preoccupied with his alleged name and inheritance, an obses-
sion that would affect his career and cause him to aspire to greatness.[6]

Family claims and legends were momentarily forgotten on that August morning in 1860 when baby Ernest joined the growing brood of
Thompson children. During the next two years, two more boys, Walter
and Alan, arrived, making a total of ten sons. Over a period of eighteen
years, the Thompsons had eleven surviving children. Their only daugh-

ter died at the age of six, but her loss was partially eased when a niece, Polly Burfield, came to live with them.[7]

Joseph Logan Thompson had the outward qualities of a successful businessman and exemplary father. His honesty and high moral standards were reflected in his business dealings. He abstained from smoking and drinking and raised his children on strict Presbyterian principles. Grave and dignified, Thompson kept up with the latest advances in science, art, and literature, and he especially loved the classics. Overall, he seemed a well-mannered Victorian English gentleman—yet underneath the gentleman lay a paradox. For one thing, Joseph Thompson was indolent and never really liked having to work for a living. In addition, he had an extreme mania for "proper respect" and apparently thought of himself as next to God, never capable of doing wrong. Often, he was neglectful of business and inconsiderate of the needs and wishes of his family. More than once he bought fancy rifles, expensive greenhouses, and various scientific instruments with money that Alice had set aside for the boys' future. Worst of all, Joseph had a dangerous temper, which exploded whenever any family member showed what he deemed lack of respect; he often berated his sons or beat them with a riding crop or his slipper whenever they talked back, committed some other trivial offense, or failed to stand at attention when he entered. He rarely allowed his wife and children to make their own decisions, particularly those regarding money and careers. Far from being a loving, affectionate father (if Ernest's accounts can be trusted), Joseph was a despot, a terror to his household.

Joseph's tirades could probably be traced to the deep-seated frustrations of his own upbringing. His father had likewise been a hard taskmaster. Indeed, Joseph had aspired to a college education and a career as a civil engineer with the railroads that were just coming into use. But his shortsighted father, calling railways "a mere fad," insisted that Joseph succeed him in the shipping business. Out of the sense of duty bred by his Calvinist training, the son complied. Subsequently, Joseph's own tyrannical whims created permanent rifts with his household. It is small wonder that Ernest later regarded his father as "the most selfish person I ever heard of or read of in history or in fiction."[8]

Toward his mother, Ernest felt differently; indeed, Alice Snowden Thompson was the stabilizing force in the whole unhappy situation. Rigidly pious and conscientious, she read her Bible day and night and studied the works of leading clergymen and theologians. Unlike her husband, she practiced what she preached and more than made up for the affection he apparently withheld from the children. Oddly enough, along with her abiding Calvinist faith, Alice also believed in omens and endorsed many of the medieval Scottish folk superstitions, which she incorporated into her Christianity to entertain the children or to emphasize moral truths. Ernest praised his mother for her charity toward others as well as her constant care and concern for all her offspring, although admitting that while full of energy she was also "weak in character." Alice never desired such a large swarm of children but of course had no say in the matter; thus, as time went on, she adopted a martyr's complex and became a model of Biblical long-suffering. To divorce or separate was out of the question to this pious Victorian mother, although she came close to doing so on at least one occasion.[9]

It was in this often tense atmosphere that Ernest spent his early childhood. Even as a toddler, he was said to have had a fascination for wild things; whenever he fell and bumped his head, Alice could quiet his sobs by pointing out a bird in the trees outside or even a fly on a windowpane. One unusual way for Alice to get little Ernest to sit still was to prop him up next to a bedpost, wrap him in a Cameron tartan shawl, and tell him, "You are a tree. Trees do not move." Thus admonished, he would sit serenely for an hour or more.[10]

Ernest was possessed of a keen sensitivity, a strong curiosity, and a tenacious memory for details. He remembered certain events that occurred when he was only three—fishing trips with the family to Rothbury in Northumberland, fascination with sheep in the rolling farmlands, and a brother keeping a crippled sea gull as a pet—and recalled certain indignities he had suffered, as well.[11] He also had a vivid imagination that sometimes ran wild. Once, after he had turned five, Ernest and his seven-year-old cousin, Willie Snowden, were playing in the latter's backyard when some chickens belonging to an elder cousin, Harry Lee, strayed onto the scene. Imagining themselves mighty warriors, the boys chased the hens around the yard and then speared them with fishing irons. It was one of the few times Alice agreed that Ernest deserved a whipping from his father. Later, Ernest recalled that this was his first instance of succumbing to the bloodthirsty hunting instinct, followed by feelings of revulsion and remorse.[12]

Soon after that episode, a series of misadventures involving Thomp-

son's ships and business transactions suddenly reduced both his fleet
and the family fortune. When one of his ships was attacked and burned
by black pirates on Africa's Gold Coast, Thompson realized that his
position was becoming increasingly precarious. Consequently, he sold
the remaining ships and prepared to move his family across the vast Atlantic to Canada.

Ernest, then only a few months from his sixth birthday, remembered
the bustle of preparation for the move, the vast piles of boxes filled with
family heirlooms and necessities, and the cheap lodging at Glasgow before boarding the steamer *St. Patrick* for Quebec. From the three-week
transatlantic voyage, Ernest retained vivid memories of the rats that in-
fested the ship, particularly his family's stateroom. His first impression
of Quebec, where the *St. Patrick* docked in June, 1866, was that of "a big
rock that blocked the back windows" of the hotel in which the Thompsons stayed. Of the five-hundred-mile train trip from Quebec to their
new home in Lindsay, Ontario, Ernest recalled one memorable night
when his father pointed out the fireflies twinkling about the darkened
spruce and tamarack swamps. "It was one of those delicious rare moments when your dream fairy comes to you, and you know it is really
true," Seton later wrote.[13]

Although the Thompsons, for the moment, were probably little concerned with major happenings in their new homeland, 1866 was the year
Canada was transforming itself from colony to dominion. Canadian
leaders were seeking to formulate an orderly settlement of her vast western lands and to unite the developing provinces under one national government like that of the United States. In addition, they hoped to improve regulation of trade, obtain a more favorable trade balance with
their southern neighbor, and heal festering diplomatic wounds resulting from the recent Civil War. The Canadians knew that in order to
build up a politically and economically strong confederation, settlement
from overseas immigration and establishment of industry were necessary.[14] The Thompsons, however unwittingly, thus became part of the
movement to transform Canada, particularly Ontario, from an agrarian
state into an industrial one. Soon after they had settled in Lindsay, the
Dominion was formed with the passage of the British North America
Act in 1867. As "pioneers" seeking a better life, the Thompsons had arrived at the dawn of a new era.

Lindsay was one of several frontier townships founded during the
1850s in the outlying areas of upper Ontario, where the fertile soil gave

way to the rock and muskeg of the Canadian Shield.[15] Seton remembered vividly his impressions of the town:

Wooden sidewalks, huge pine stumps everywhere with vigorous young cedars growing about their roots; barefooted, bareheaded boys and girls scoffing at our un-Canadian accent. Apple trees laden with fruit to which we soon learned to help ourselves; tall rank weeds with swarms of grasshoppers everywhere; the coffee-colored river with its screaming, roaring sawmills; cows and pigs on the main street; great hulking, heaving oxen drawing loads of hay, with heavy breathings that were wonderfully meadowlike and fragrant; and over and above all, in memory as in place, the far pervading sweet sanctifying smell of newcut boards of pine.[16]

Even before he took his family to Canada, Joseph Thompson had envisioned himself as a gentleman farmer on a picturesque piece of land. Now, with his brood of sons and pious notions of filial duty, his dream seemed to be on the verge of realization. In that frame of mind, he bought a partly cleared hundred-acre tract in virgin forest on Stony Creek, about four miles east of town, giving the boys visions of living like wilderness hunters, a lifestyle similar to what they had read of in *Robinson Crusoe* and *Swiss Family Robinson*. In September, 1866, the Thompsons moved out to their new backwoods farm, settling in a three-room log shanty. This cabin, with a few similarly crude outbuildings, had been the handiwork of "Fightin' Bill" McKenna, who had first laid claim to the tract. Reputedly a sometime horse thief as well as horse breeder, McKenna and his exploits were almost legendary in the upper Ontario settlements. Later, Seton would feature him in one of his works.[17] Living in McKenna's crowded, rat-infested shelter was only temporary, however; by the following January, the Thompsons had moved into a two-story, eleven-room brick house that Joseph had built and dubbed "The Elms" after two large elm trees that grew beside the gate. Later that spring, to the joy of the family, Old Ellen, Alice's faithful nurse, arrived. She had remained behind when the Thompsons left England in order to look after her aged mother, who had soon passed on. Ellen, who was considered a member of the family, remained at The Elms until her own death in October, 1869. A hardworking domestic, she was always sympathetic to the children, fond of animals, and full of creative ideas for indoor activities.[18]

Ernest and his brothers stored up many lasting memories from their life on the farm. Among these were the lessons of pioneering and self-reliance, including carpentry and timber-cutting. With those skills, they

made their own toys: wood carvings, picture frames, even balls and
bats. Ernest began to show a knack for art and architecture when he
built a small model of The Elms and, along with his brothers, constructed tiny wilderness scenes—called "landskips"—in candy boxes;
these were fashioned out of twigs, grass, lichens, and other items from
the woods. Of course, there were always chores to be done, and Ernest
recalled many amusing experiences with the domestic farm animals, especially Old Duke, an ornery ram. There was also time to go to school,
and Ernest began his formal education in a one-room log schoolhouse
located about a mile from the farm and run by Agnes O'Leary, a bright
young lady still in her teens.[19]

What stood out foremost in Ernest's mind about those first four years
in Canada were his ventures into the woods and early contacts with the
wild things. He collected bird nests and eggs, and on occasion he kept
birds and small mammals as pets. One exciting moment in his young life
was a visit to the stuffed bird collection of Charlie Foley, a local hard-
ware merchant.

Even as a small boy, Ernest had mixed feelings about the killing of
wild creatures for mere sport. Once, he and some of his schoolmates
raided a red squirrel's nest and killed the mother squirrel; remorse followed as they discovered four young that she had been nursing. One
boy suggested feeding them to his cat, but the youngsters were in for a
surprise when they saw the old feline "adopt" them as her own. Though
the baby squirrels died soon afterwards, Ernest saw this incident as an
example of the animal instinct to help one another.

Ernest and his brothers also thrilled to the tales of their pioneer
neighbors. One especially outstanding personality was Charles Peel, a
veteran hunter, who was known and loved by the neighborhood youth
for his wild stories of wolf and bear hunts. Such tidbits of oral history
evoked in Ernest further sympathy for the wild creatures.[20]

While the Thompson boys soon learned the "ways and speech of the
woods," their parents had greater difficulty fitting into the neighborhood. As Ernest later put it, they were "too evidently gentlefolk to attract the rude pioneers." For one thing, it required considerable time
and hard work to keep up the homestead. Furthermore, the older sons,
apparently weary of maintaining their father's baronial aspirations, began one after another to strike out on their own. In 1870, Joseph, who
was nearly fifty, decided to sell the farm and move the remainder of his
offspring to Toronto, where he quickly secured employment as an ac-

countant. Ernest recalled that memorable day in April when the family bade farewell to the homestead and piled into the train for Port Hope, on the shore of Lake Ontario, some forty miles to the south. He described his first view of the lake, with its sailboats and flying gulls, as "one of those moments of supreme joy, fraught with the happy sense that fairies are real." After lunch at Port Hope, the Thompsons continued west to Toronto, where they soon found living quarters on Elizabeth Street near the lakeshore.[21]

Ever since Fort York's establishment on the Don River in the eighteenth century, it had been the nucleus of Upper Canada. Fought over by British and American armies during the War of 1812, York grew into the bustling, progressive community of Toronto, British in character.[22] Many important business and political leaders built their estates along the shore of Lake Ontario and later on the crest of the hill overlooking the town. At the time of the Thompsons' arrival in 1870, Toronto had become Canada's "rising star." The old lakeshore estates were already being replaced by the factories and smoke of industrialism brought on by the railroads. Palatial mansions degenerated into slums, brothels, and rooming houses as new residential districts sprang up farther inland.[23] At the same time, churches of various denominations grew rapidly throughout the city; they, in turn, became instrumental in bringing higher education and the fine arts to this former wilderness outpost. Overall, Toronto was a new western town possessed with a spirit of energetic optimism and "equipped with all the talents which it has pleased God to place in the Anglo-Saxon's keeping."[24]

It was into this growing urban environment that ten-year-old Ernest was suddenly thrust. Joseph's new position soon enabled the Thompsons to place themselves in a comfortable atmosphere similar to the one they had known in England. The older sons, who had gone into various occupations such as contracting and real estate, gradually drifted back into the family fold.[25] Yet while most of the Thompsons seemed enthusiastic about city life, Ernest longed for the simpler pastoral existence, the discoveries of the mysteries of the woods, and the lives of the wild creatures that he had left behind in Lindsay. Already, he valued nature study as a discipline and looked on it as his security blanket from the world's problems.[26]

Certainly, Ernest had reason to seek security. The Thompsons' first home, at 184 Elizabeth Street, was in a poor section of town. The young neighborhood toughs who attended the nearby school made life miserable for the new kid on the block by calling him "Squinty" because of his crossed eyes, the result of an early childhood accident in England. Eventually, that affliction corrected itself; in the meantime Ernest, despite his frail stature, learned to fight back and earn respect from the bullies. More than once, Ernest's elementary education was interrupted by his family's move for better housing to reflect its upwardly mobile social standing; in 1872, the Thompsons moved from Elizabeth Street to a house on Mutual Street, in a more respectable part of town. Nevertheless, in his writings Seton capitalized on the beatings he received from teachers and classmates alike; he mentioned little in regard to curriculum despite the fact that he was an excellent student.[27]

If schoolboy conflicts affected his sensitive spirit, Ernest's home situation had even greater consequences. Joseph Thompson had apparently learned little from his experience in Lindsay. Now that his older sons were again helping materially to maintain his authority, he more than ever sought to control his family through skillful manipulation of piety and guilt.[28] Coupled with their father's autocratic rule was the ultra-conservative Calvinistic atmosphere in which the boys were raised. After their move to Toronto, the Thompsons affiliated themselves with the local Presbyterian congregation and strictly observed the sabbath. Thompson apparently overlooked the idea of Christ's love for sinful man, for Seton later stated that "the one continual preachment was the fear of hell." As far as church leaders were concerned, anything human was considered "bad and born of the devil," a philosophy once applied when Ernest's older brother William and a friend, both of whom had been appointed church librarians, added two hundred volumes of secular and popular fiction to the Sunday school bookshelves. The idea was to attract more neighborhood youths to the church, and the plan worked—but when Joseph and other church elders found out, the "sinful" books were taken away, and Sunday school attendance rapidly decreased. Consequently, Ernest began to picture the Almighty as a "hideous child-devouring monster" and thus began to develop a distaste for churches.[29]

With his sensitive young mind thoroughly revulsed, Ernest sought avenues of escape. Certainly there were happy diversions during his growing years—games like marbles (or "mibs"), the summer trap shoots at Don Flat, and the annual fair at Toronto during the harvest season. But as he grew older, Ernest developed a persecution complex and a sense of isolation that followed him throughout his life. Longing to

break away from the clutches of city life, both physically and emotion-
ally, the boy began making solitary hikes through the Don Valley and to
Toronto Marsh near the lakeshore. These areas, among the few vestiges
of wilderness in Toronto, reinforced Ernest's love of nature and later
became the settings for some of his animal tales.[30] In city settings,
Ernest found happiness in observing the habits and anatomy of birds,
stray dogs, cats, and even rats that lurked about the streets, yards, and
alleys. The outstanding personalities he remembered from his early
Toronto years were those who shared his love for wild things. Among
them were Catfish Joe, a reclusive old fisherman who lived on a small
island in the middle of Toronto Marsh, and Dr. William G. Brodie, a
dentist who was also an amateur naturalist and often kept unusual pets.
It was Brodie's rattlesnakes that Ernest's rat so heroically killed before it
itself expired.[31]

Coupled with his love for animals was Ernest's inventiveness. Neighbors often took notice of his crude gadgets, which he was sometimes
able to sell for a few pennies. When his older brother George was ap-
prenticed to a printer, Ernest became interested in wood engraving, a
hobby further stimulated in 1871 when his grandfather in England sent
him a book on engraving techniques. This, in turn, led to the boy's decision to construct his own printing press out of discarded type and other
items from the *Toronto Globe* office. With ink made from soot and water,
the roller from a broom shank wrapped in muslin, and the newsprint
from grocer's paper, the *Toronto Times* was ready for business. However,
the newspaper ceased publication after the first issue, in which Ernest
attacked his schoolteachers and boasted of his Tom Sawyer exploits. Besides that, fire destroyed the workshop where his press was housed.

Thereafter, the boy's creativity was channeled in other directions.
After the Thompsons moved to their Mutual Street house, the younger
sons and their friends began playing Robin Hood, using as a hideout a
cave that Ernest helped dig under the house. Father put a stop to that
when he discovered that the cave dangerously undermined the foundation. Other memorable pastimes included Saturday afternoon "cir-
cuses" that Ernest and his friends sometimes staged, often at great
trouble and expense. For these productions, the boys employed their
various pets as well as their own talents. They sold homemade tickets
for five cents (ten cents for reserved seats) and rehearsed their acts after
school during the week for the scheduled performance on Saturday.[32]

A high point of Ernest's creative young life came when, at age fourteen, he built a secret hideout—a crude hut of logs, brush, and scrap lumber—in a ravine near the Don River. To this tiny touch of Eden, which he dubbed "Glenyan," Ernest often came to get away from his problems and to imagine himself an Indian living in harmony with the wild. This small interlude in paradise was brief, however; one summer day in 1875 after a brutal beating from his father, Ernest discovered, to his grief, that his secret shanty had been "desecrated" by tramps.[33]

One other escape valve that Ernest often employed was his books. He especially loved the romantic adventure classics of James Fenimore Cooper and other authors, as well as the western dime novels and similar popular fiction upon which his parents and teachers sometimes frowned. When he was sixteen, Ernest discovered that he had a knack for romantic poetry; he composed an epic entitled "The Kingbird," based on his observations and the stories of this bird's fighting prowess that he had seen and heard at Lindsay. The poem did not appear in its final form until 1879, but Seton always boasted that it marked the true beginning of his nature-writing career. Earlier, he had received his first introduction to ornithology when he saved up his scant earnings to buy a copy of Dr. A. M. Ross's *Birds of Canada*. Although this book proved to be incomplete and outdated, Ernest treasured it and found it a challenge to add information that Ross had left out.[34]

By 1875 the Thompsons had moved again, this time to South Pembroke Street. Ernest spent his high-school years at Toronto Collegiate Institute, considered one of the province's finest secondary schools, where he stood at the head of his class. With rigid determination to do better than his best and perhaps earn a college scholarship, Ernest immersed himself in his studies. Such intellectual overwork was more than his thin, underdeveloped body could stand, and eventually even his lungs were affected. Acting on the family doctor's orders, Alice Thompson sent Ernest back to the old homestead at Lindsay for a rest.

The farm on which the Thompsons had labored for four years was by then owned and occupied by the family of William Blackwell, the son of one of the area's pioneers. The Blackwells, who had six children, welcomed the ailing boy as one of their own; under their care, with plenty of food and opportunity to enjoy outdoor life once again, Ernest soon regained his health. He saw Blackwell as an ideal father figure and throughout his teen years looked forward to spending part of his summer vacations with him. It was during those happy times that Ernest and the boys of the neighborhood camped out in the woods in their homemade tepees, living and thinking like Indians and learning the ways of survival in the wild. Here he encountered such unforgettable characters as the old frontiersman Caleb Clark, and Granny de Neuville, an old crone known as the Lindsay Witch, who impressed Ernest with her folklore and herbal knowledge. Seton would later immortalize these personalities in his autobiographical novel, *Two Little Savages* (Sam Blackwell, who was about Ernest's age, was the second "little savage").[35] It was also during one of these country respites that Ernest, while staying at the cabin of a neighboring farmer, fell ill with malaria. In his weakened condition, he singlehandedly fought off a hungry lynx, using a fish spear as a weapon.[36]

Ernest's father scorned his son's longing to become a naturalist, fearing that such an occupation was unprofitable. But since Ernest's artistic talents were clearly evident from the time he began making woodcuts, Joseph determined that the boy should become a professional artist, with sufficient training at an established academy. During the summer of 1876, Ernest had taken a few lessons in oil painting from a neighbor who was an adept amateur artist and had painted his first real animal portrait, that of a dead sharpshin hawk he had found in the Don Valley and had rigged up on a homemade apparatus similar to that used by John J. Audubon. For the moment, however, Ernest succumbed to his father's desires and later that year enrolled as a portraitist's assistant. He also earned extra money by painting flesh tones over the blackened eyes of prizefighters and men injured in brawls. "I got my first financial start in life as operator in a beauty parlor," Seton later quipped.[37]

During the next two years, Ernest remained in the portraitist's studio, where he learned several new processes. Knowing that he needed quality instruction to become an expert artist, however, he enrolled in the night classes of the Ontario Art School, which had been established only a few years before by the fledgling Ontario Society of Artists (OSA). There he came in contact with such noted English-born artists as J. A. Fraser, Marmaduke Matthews, and T. Mower Martin. But the teacher in the OSA who inspired and influenced him most was Charlotte M. Schreiber. Impressed by Ernest's draftsmanship and realizing that his family environment tended to stifle his creativity, Mrs. Schreiber invited him to spend weeks at a time at her wealthy husband's country estate at Springfield-on-the-Credit, twenty miles west of Toronto, where she had a spacious studio. Seton ever after revered Mrs. Schreiber for her kindness and respect; she alone somehow managed to fill an emotional void and bolster his ego during those early years. Subsequently, he often referred to her as his "Aunt Schreiber" and sought to pattern not only the quality of his art but also his whole life after hers.[38]

His visits to Springfield also gave Ernest more opportunities to observe animal life. From the start, he never painted or sketched because he enjoyed the activity; his motive was always love for his subject. To him, art was merely a vehicle for other purposes; his themes were inevitably the wilderness and the creatures in it, never the pastoral or urban landscapes that were the norms of the OSA at that time. Under Mrs. Schreiber's guidance, however, Seton gradually effected a sufficient compromise with accepted Victorian parameters to win the gold medal at the Ontario School of Art in the spring of 1879.[39]

Delighted by his son's artistic achievements, Joseph consented to send him to the Royal Academy in London for at least a year. Ernest was to set sail in June. During the preparation period he made a brief visit to the Blackwells in Lindsay and, with his cousin Polly, had his first view of the spectacular Niagara Falls. The departure date, June 12, 1879, came quickly, and Ernest found himself on the deck of the *Algerian* in Toronto Harbor waving farewell to the people with whom he had spent his whole life. In a real sense, Ernest was bidding adieu to his childhood, "not without a sigh, yet with a vast sense of ever-growing relief and escape."[40]

Indeed, he was for the moment glad to be rid of family pressures. As a boy, he had often felt dominated by his older brothers, with whom he had little in common; his father's overbearing rule had become increasingly oppressive; and while he would do anything in the world for his mother, Ernest felt repelled by her religious orthodoxy. Burdened as she was by the complexities of her responsibilities, Alice at times seemed to neglect the needs of her gifted son, yet in times of crisis—especially those arising from Ernest's recurring illnesses—she lavished tenderness and affection on him. Confused and harried, Ernest rebelled in a subtle manner against both his family and the accepted religious conventions of his day by seeking refuge in fields, streams, and marshes.[41] Certainly his actions were not atypical for a teenage lad seeking to discover himself.

As the *Algerian* made its way down the St. Lawrence, with a stopover in Montreal, and then across the Atlantic, the young man seemed destined for a career as a major artist, living in the best environment that

Victorian England had to offer upcoming young people in that profession. But while Joseph Thompson thought that he had scored a victory for God and the church, he was doomed to disappointment. The young naturalist he had sought to discourage was soon to find legitimate means to pursue his nature studies.

CHAPTER 2

An Artist-Naturalist
in the Making

On June 28, 1879, Ernest arrived in London where he found lodging at the Regents Park apartments. As he stated, this was the beginning of "a new epoch in my life." At nineteen, Seton was "long-legged" and "lanky," having attained his full height of six feet at the age of sixteen. But now he was plagued by a new physical ailment. His physique still underdeveloped in other ways, Ernest had suffered a hernia while working out at the YMCA gymnasium in Toronto in 1876. Consequently, the family doctor had prescribed for him an iron truss, which he described as a "loathsome reptile . . . forever boring into my flesh," even though it did not hamper his running or walking.[1] Despite such minor discomforts, he eagerly set out to make the best of his new environment.

After getting settled in his living quarters, Seton spent the remainder of the summer visiting relatives in South Shields and London. On September 1 he began preparation for the competition entry piece that was required for admission to the Royal Academy. For his subject, he chose the *Hermes* statue at the British Museum. When that was rejected in December, he began a second piece the following March, Michelangelo's *Satyr*, which was not formally accepted until December 25, 1880. Therefore, January 18, 1881, was his first day as a student at the academy. Actually, the number of days Seton attended classes was small. Not until April 8 did he pass his probation exams, and by October he was on his way back to Canada. Nevertheless, he somehow made a strong impression on his instructors, for he was one of only six students awarded a coveted seven-year scholarship. His first public appearance as an artist was in June, 1881, for the Dudley Gallery of London. Among his most noted pieces of artwork from that first trip were his Byronic pen-and-ink self-portrait and the oil landscape on which he later superimposed the subjects for his *Goat Defending Her Kids from the Fox*.[2]

In all, Seton spent less than thirty months in England. His father sent him four hundred dollars to help cover expenses, but he was compelled to use his own resources for the rest; he therefore secured his first employment in the profession as an illustrator for the Cassell, Petter, and Galpin publishing firm, making black-and-white drawings on wood for book engravings. On Sundays, for his mother's sake, Seton visited several churches in London, but the services "never had any message for me; I found it more profitable to take a long walk into the country." If nothing else, daily walks helped strengthen his legs and keep him physically fit. Above all, his animal studies began to occupy his time, especially when he found that his scholarship allowed him free admission to the London Zoo. In addition, Seton embarked on a rigorous, self-taught program of animal anatomy, using dog cadavers and applying the artistic principles learned at the academy to his animal drawings.

The high points of Seton's studies in London were frequent visits to the library of the British Museum. Despite the fact that persons under twenty-one were normally not allowed a reader's ticket, Seton was able to gain admission by writing to the museum trustees—none other than Lord Beaconsfield, the archbishop of Canterbury, and the Prince of Wales—who soon awarded him a life membership ticket. Thus armed, Seton was introduced to the works of pioneer naturalists like John J. Audubon, Alexander Wilson, Thomas Nuttall, and Henry David Thoreau, as well as the early publications of Spencer F. Baird, Elliott Coues, Robert Ridgway, and John Burroughs. The realization that these men were able to make a living by studying wildlife inspired Seton all the more to pursue such a course.[3]

Seton's inner struggles as a "westernized Easterner" heightened during his stay in London. Certainly, he looked down upon the city as a "wasteland of shivering cold, gloom and starvation." In March, 1881, he penned a document of personal goals in which he made several imaginative predictions: "In 1890, I shall marry an English woman, or of English extraction. . . . In 1905, I shall *by God's help*, have made a comfortable fortune by my pen and pencil, also in part by judicious speculation. I shall then return to England, buy a small estate in Devonshire, and a house in London. *In 1915, I shall be knighted by the King* in recognition of my work as an artist-naturalist."[4]

Such fanciful prophecies, none of which materialized, illustrate the intensity of Seton's struggle for self-identity. Furthermore, his medical condition, in addition to his living in near poverty, was endangered by the unique demands he made upon himself. Blaming all his short-comings on his prudish Victorian environment, Seton pictured himself as a physical and mental flagellant. He began to dabble in Zen, and he became a vegetarian. Like an ascetic monk, he gloried in abstinence from sex by fasting, taking cold baths, sleeping on boards, and avoiding paintings and sculptures of nudes. Possibly because of his rigid, intro-spective lifestyle, Seton began to hear "voices," so he claimed, urg-ing him to go to western Canada and then to New York, where fame awaited him. Such a move, of course, meant forsaking his valuable scholarship and disappointing his father and art teachers in Toronto. But the cravings to go west and study the wild things grew stronger and soon eclipsed any negative considerations at home.[5]

Thus it was late in October, 1881, that Seton took passage on a cattle ship back to Toronto, traveling in the company of roughneck Irishmen whom he described as "brawling, blasphemous beasts." Stormy seas lengthened the normal eight-day voyage to sixteen, and the rough trip plus the ship's lice served to break his health. After several restful days at home, however, Seton regained his strength and was again exploring his old haunts in the Don Valley and Toronto Marsh, collecting, dissecting, and sketching bird specimens.

Soon after his son's recovery, Joseph Thompson, provoked at the ap-parent disaster of the London venture, called him into the study and there presented him with an itemized bill for $537.50 to cover the "dis-bursements that had been made for me since my birth." In later years, Seton dramatized the episode, using it to justify the hatred he felt to-ward his father. Throughout his life, he believed that Joseph used this ploy to coerce his sons who had come "of age" to go out and work on their own and at the same time continue to contribute to the family in-come. More recently, it has been argued that since Joseph had subsi-dized Ernest's art education to the tune of $400 and had gotten poor results, he probably asked his son, not unreasonably, to reimburse him. Be that as it may, the rift between the two was widened.[6]

Undaunted, Seton sought work in town. He was hired by Rolph Smith & Company to make bird drawings for a set of twelve Christmas cards; for these efforts, which he completed and delivered in six weeks, he was paid sixty dollars. In the meantime, other opportunities for him to study, paint, and write natural history were developing. In 1880, while Seton was still in England, the dentist, Dr. William G. Brodie and

Ernest Thompson Seton, age two, with his mother and father. (Courtesy Seton Memorial Library, Philmont Scout Ranch)

Ernest Thompson Seton, age fourteen, at his easel. (Courtesy Seton Memorial Library, Philmont Scout Ranch)

Ernest Thompson Seton, age seventeen. (Courtesy Seton Memorial Library, Philmont Scout Ranch)

Ernest Thompson Seton in 1901, from a cyanotype. (Courtesy Charles F. Lummis Photo Collection, Southwest Museum, Los Angeles)

The Thompson family in 1889. Ernest is seated in the center. (Courtesy Seton Memorial Library, Philmont Scout Ranch)

Ernest Thompson Seton, age forty-six, in his "camping outfit." (Courtesy Seton Memorial Library, Philmont Scout Ranch)

Seton with his daughter Ann (wearing large bow) and her playmate. (Courtesy Seton Memorial Library, Philmont Scout Ranch)

Seton's original Sinaway Tribe at Standing Rock Village, Wyndygoul, 1903. (Courtesy Seton Memorial Library, Philmont Scout Ranch)

Seton, Lord Baden-Powell, and Dan Beard at New York, 1910. (Courtesy Seton Memorial Library, Philmont Scout Ranch)

Seton laying the cornerstone of the first Boy Scout building, Baltimore, 1911.(Courtesy Seton Memorial Library, Philmont Scout Ranch)

Chief Scout, 1912. (Courtesy Seton Memorial Library, Philmont Scout Ranch)

POST CARD.

CORRESPONDENCE.   FOR THE ADDRESS ONLY.

[handwritten message] To the Boy Scouts of the Panhandle — Ho Scouts! — Some of my best days were spent riding in the Panhandle. It is a glorious country one of the best in the World for Scouting — So I hope you will rise to your chance and become the best Scouts in the World. — Greeting from Ernest Thompson Seton, Chief Scout

The message on a postcard written by Seton aboard the *Lusitania* to a Scout troop, 1915. (Courtesy Panhandle-Plains Historical Museum, Canyon, Texas)

The front of the postcard sent by Seton from the *Lusitania* to a Scout troop, 1915. (Courtesy Panhandle-Plains Historical Museum, Canyon, Texas)

Seton in the woods near his
DeWinton estate, ca. 1917.
(Courtesy Seton Memorial Library,
Philmont Scout Ranch)

A Woodcraft Council meeting at DeWinton, ca. 1918. (Courtesy Seton Memorial Library, Philmont Scout Ranch)

Seton the taxidermist, ca. 1921. (Courtesy Seton Memorial Library, Philmont Scout Ranch)

Seton displaying some of his artwork. (Courtesy Seton Memorial Library, Philmont Scout Ranch)

Seton, 1927. (Courtesy Charles F. Lummis Photo Collection, Southwest Museum, Los Angeles)

Seton (*front row, fifth from right*) with a group at a Woodcraft conference at his home, 1924.
(Courtesy Seton Memorial Library, Philmont Scout Ranch)

Seton, Charles F. Lummis,
and Clyde Fisher at Santo
Domingo, New Mexico,
1927. (Courtesy Charles F.
Lummis Photo Collection,
Southwest Museum, Los
Angeles)

Seton in his "woodcraft cabin" at DeWinton. (Courtesy Seton Memorial Library, Philmont Scout Ranch)

Mary Austin, whom Seton considered a "kindred spirit." (Courtesy University of New Mexico General Library, Special Collections, T. M. Pearce Collection)

Julia Seton in her lecture costume. (Courtesy Museum of New Mexico)

Seton shaking hands with a
young Woodcraft Indian
brave, ca. 1940. (Courtesy
Seton Memorial Library,
Philmont Scout Ranch)

Farolitas (*luminarias*) at
Seton Village at Christmas-
time. (Courtesy Museum of
New Mexico)

Julia and Ernest Thompson Seton at the University of New Mexico campus, August 14, 1946. (Courtesy University of New Mexico General Library, Special Collections)

A display of the Setons' Indian collection at the Philmont Museum. (Courtesy Seton Memorial Library, Philmont Scout Ranch)

Julia Seton unveils a portrait of her late husband, 1967. (Courtesy Seton Memorial Library, Philmont Scout Ranch)

The story of Old Lobo is told again at the Philmont Museum, 1967. (Courtesy Seton Memorial Library, Philmont Scout Ranch)

his son Willie, Jr. had organized the Natural History Society of Toronto. This group of amateur botanists and zoologists met periodically at the Canadian Institute, with which it was later affiliated. Of course, Seton eagerly joined the society, and he and the Brodies spent many enjoyable hours hiking through the bogs around Asbridge Bay, taking field notes and looking for new specimens. Before Seton had left for England in 1879, Dr. Brodie had advised him to keep a journal of his findings and activities. Now that he was back, the dentist showed him techniques of preparing and stuffing specimens.[7]

Having been formally introduced to the practical side of natural history, and faced with an increasingly uncomfortable home situation, Seton was more than anxious to fulfill his calling to go west. Ironically, it was through his father's farfetched dreams that the opportunity came. Still desiring to maintain patriarchal control over his family and retaining his vision of himself as a gentleman farmer, Joseph looked westward to the prairies of Manitoba. In 1876 he had sent his son Arthur, two years older than Ernest, to the frontier province to scout its agricultural possibilities. Arthur, who had started out as a carpenter's apprentice with his older brothers Joseph, Jr. and William, chose a tract of land near the new settlement of DeWinton, soon to become Carberry. In 1879 he began homesteading this 160-acre tract. Soon afterward another brother, Charles, joined him.[8]

Indeed, 1881–82 saw the peak period of the Manitoba land boom. In 1870, Manitoba had been made a province under the stipulation that all ungranted lands within its borders would be retained by the government and their resources utilized for the benefit of the nation as a whole. Two years later, the Canadian Pacific Railway was chartered. At the same time, the national government, under the leadership of Prime Minister John A. MacDonald, passed the Dominion Lands Act, the Canadian version of the U.S. Homestead Act. Hoping to divert immigrants from the United States, the Canadian Parliament allowed prospective settlers to fulfill residence requirements in three years (as opposed to five years in the United States) from the date of entry. Men over eighteen could claim a 160-acre quarter section as their own. In addition, depending on availability of funds, they could purchase contiguous quarter sections at market value.[9] Realizing that land prices in Manitoba were cheaper than in Ontario, Joseph figured that if he and each of his five youngest sons patented a free homestead, they could secure a foothold which, over time, might grow into their own family empire. By 1882, Arthur, having lived on his quarter section near Carberry for three years, was theoretically eligible to obtain title to it, but he had made few improvements and was still residing in his original claim shanty.

It was Arthur who invited his naturalist brother out to help build a frame house on the property. Seton not only had good reason to leave home but also saw an opportunity to study the vanishing Manitoba wilderness and its wild inhabitants. Armed with an etching device Charlotte Schreiber had given him, plus four geese, four turkeys, sixty chickens, five days' provisions, and twenty dollars in cash, he boarded the train for Manitoba on March 16, 1882. Accompanying him was Willie Brodie, who had laid claim to some choice farmland on the upper Assiniboine River near the new town of Brandon.[10]

The train trip was Seton's first real "western" experience. It took three days to reach St. Paul, Minnesota, where an approaching blizzard, the last of the season, delayed the train for two days. Sending Brodie on ahead by "the next through express" with half of the provisions, Seton opted to stay with the cattle car where he had stored his fowl. For the next few days, the slow train with its broken-down engine plodded through the howling snowstorm, more than once compelled to stop while Seton and his fellow passengers shoveled snowdrifts from the tracks. At Fergus Falls, they waited four days for a rescue engine and snowplow, but even then they still had to battle the drifts that continually piled against the train. In the meantime, Seton's provisions ran out, and he was reduced to eating the raw eggs laid by his hens. Finally, fifteen days after leaving Toronto, the train pulled into Winnipeg, the booming railway center and capital of the province. Here Seton waited for the storm to abate before catching the first westbound passenger train to DeWinton and then trudging through the snow to the half-buried log shanty where he was warmly greeted by his brothers and Willie Brodie. It was April 5, 1882. Looking back to that harrowing episode, Seton thought it wonderful that delicate snowflakes (nature) could stop trains (technology).[11]

After the weather cleared and the spring thaw set in, the four young men busied themselves at constructing a six-room frame house and various other buildings, including a chicken coop. Late in May, Joseph arrived with the rest of the family to determine how well this new setting suited his regal tastes. Responding to his desire to locate several homesteads, the sons frequently went off on a series of "land hunts." For Seton, these travels were opportunities to sketch and record field observations. In his journal he noted minute details of various species, including measurements, external features, coloration, and (for birds) the number of feathers. Seton marveled at the abundance of wild game in the sandhills and surrounding woods southwest of Carberry, and he was thrilled by the flocks of migrating birds on the broad plains of the Souris.[12]

At the same time, Seton recorded his impressions of the pioneers who, like his own family, had come to subdue this wilderness.

Each day we met others of our kind on the trail, in camp, or in their new sod houses, giving us a cheery salute as we passed; or, better still, helping each other to make the passage of some dangerous swamp or ford upon the trail. There was poverty writ on every wagon and team; there was scarcity of food and of essentials of life; there was dirt in the sordid cabins built of sods with tarpaper roofing. On wall and floor and roof there was dirt; there was every element that in the East would have made a horrid slum, a bed of wretched misery, of squalor, of gloom and yet, there was no slum, there was no gloom; for every eye was ablaze with the light of hope.

Young men there were with young wives; and a few with babies. Older men who had failed in the East were here with the newborn hope. Every furrow struck, every post-hole sunk, every sod house temporarily built, was prompted, planned and completed, roofed in with the glamor of glowing expectation for the future, a magic that turned their squalor into freedom, their hardships into a joke. The sun came up and sank each day on a world of newborn hopes.

While most of these pioneer farmers were found to be helpful to neighbors and strangers alike, giving without asking in return, some were not always honest in their dealings. During their first land hunt, Seton and his brothers bought a pair of oxen from a squatter who was about to be evicted from reserved school land. Farther along the trail, however, the Thompsons traded these to a passing party of settlers for a pair of thoroughbred mares. Too late, they discovered that these "Arab steeds," while ideal for saddle riding, were poor substitutes for oxen in pulling a wagon.[13]

Whenever Seton was not hunting land, he did more than his share of the chores necessary to develop the Carberry farm. His experiences in the optimistic frontier atmosphere led him to associate the West with the future. Yet unlike most settlers, he had personal hopes of a far different nature. Seton's idea of a perfect home out West was the primeval wilderness in the midst of an isolated wildlife sanctuary setting. The more he continued his field observations, the closer the bond he felt with the prairie landscape. As spring turned into summer, and summer into fall, he noted the effects of seasonal changes on wildlife behavior patterns. From such studies Seton formulated his own theories and compared them with those of other natural scientists. For example, he discovered that pocket gophers in Canada, like earthworms, functioned to loosen the fertile soil.[14]

Although the land hunts were beneficial to Seton in his pursuit of natural history, none of his brothers could locate another suitable homestead. Perhaps they were too accustomed to the rolling, wooded farmsites in Ontario to accept the flat, largely treeless Manitoba prairies. As the Christmas season of 1882 neared and the thermometer dropped to thirty degrees below zero, Joseph and Alice Thompson decided that this barbaric wasteland of wind and blizzards was too much; they abandoned the Carberry homestead and returned to Toronto, followed by the rest of the family except Arthur and Ernest.

For Seton, the winter weather was "good medicine." Now he had a chance to study closely the tracks and other signs of animals. Calling these signs the "alphabet of the woods," he learned how to interpret them and make deductions like a detective seeking clues.[15] Among the animals he trailed were the wolves and foxes that often lurked near the farms in winter, looking for easy pickings from poultry and livestock. It was during this time that Seton acquired from a neighbor, Gordon F. Wright, a black collie puppy, which he named Bingo. Bingo had been sired by Wright's collie, Frank, known locally for his courage in fighting off predators. Seton came to cherish Bingo as his intimate companion, and later he published the dog's unusual life story.[16]

Aside from nature studies, life on the farm throughout the long, hard winter was uninterrupted drudgery. Time and again, the brothers had to work to protect their livestock and chickens from the fierce blizzards. On days when the wind was not bad, they hauled wood from a spruce grove several miles away for lumber and fuel. In March, 1883, when signs of an early spring thaw appeared, Seton decided to see about a cure for his hydrocele, hoping to rid himself of his bothersome iron truss. Having heard of the surgical skills of a Dr. Moses Gunn in Chicago, he arrived there on March 15 and endured the operation at St. Joseph's Hospital five days later. After a six-week recuperation period at the hospital and at the home of his brother George, Seton returned to Carberry "strong now in body as in soul."[17]

By the time of his return in early May, spring had come to the Manitoba prairies, and Seton eagerly filled his journals with detailed observations and collected bird and small mammal specimens. One favorite spot was two miles southwest of Carberry, a shallow lake bordered by a marsh that attracted fifty species of birds. Neighbors half-jokingly began referring to this "ideal" patch of wilderness as "Seton's Kingdom." At the end of the month, however, Seton's springtime joy was dampened by word that his friend Willie Brodie, who had taken up residence on his own claim, had drowned in a canoeing accident in the Assiniboine's raging waters. For the next few days, Seton was beside himself with grief; years later, he said of young Brodie: "His superior knowledge was of continual value to me, and our united efforts resulted in ever increasing light on the wonders and beauties of the new world we were exploring together."[18]

As summer came on, Seton feverishly continued his explorations and land hunts. During July and August he had a new traveling companion, Robert Miller Christy, who was a naturalist from London. Seton had first met him in London, where Christy was working as a bank clerk, and together they had explored rural areas outside the city. The Englishman had thus come out for a return visit and to expand his own knowledge. Afterward, Christy published his account of that memorable summer journey.[19] In October, Seton and two companions set out from Carberry and went into the far northern section of the province near the present Saskatchewan border. A short distance from Fort Pelly and the Cotai Indian reserve, Seton found his "promised land," a beautiful plain near Duck Mountain.

Here was the "paradise" he had last seen at Lindsay. A lake lay in the midst of the property, fed by a swift stream coursing through a small valley. The monotony of the waving prairie grasses was broken in the distance by the sharp rise of Duck Mountain and the wooded areas beyond. Such a scene, in addition to agricultural possibilities, contained a wide diversity of animal life. It had changed little since the early frontier days when Hudson's Bay Company traders built their posts and established their lucrative fur trade with the Plains Crees, Assiniboins, and other Indians. Through this mixture of plains and woods, lakes and streams, the hardy French Canadian *voyageurs* had come in their birchbark canoes, seeking beaver and other fur sources. Here, too, not so long ago, the voyageurs' descendants, the half-blood Métis, had come up from the Assiniboine and Red River settlements in their wooden cart brigades to hunt buffalo. By 1883 the buffalo had disappeared, and many Métis had moved into the Saskatchewan plains ahead of the Ontario pioneers, with whom they often clashed. At their heels came troops of Northwest Mounted Police, sent to keep the peace and prepare the vast, untamed territory for the civilizing forces that were soon to come.[20] For Seton, this was a dream world where he could go back in time, maintain contact with the wild things, and live the isolated existence he had read of in Thoreau's *Walden*.

From the time of his boyhood exploits, Seton had looked upon the American Indian as his model for life in the wilds. In Manitoba he at last had opportunity to acquaint himself with members of the red race. In the summer of 1882 he had visited Fort Ellice, the old Hudson's Bay Company trading post on the Assiniboine, where he became acquainted not only with the traders but also with several of their Indian employees and customers. The stamina of one young Cree courier, who had carried dispatches on foot from Fort Qu'Appelle, 125 miles away, particularly impressed him.[21] On that visit, Seton had purchased an Indian "medicine bag" in which he stored valuable papers, including his British Museum ticket and his three letters of introduction. After staking his Duck Mountain claim, Seton performed a small "ceremonial" of his own by burning those papers, marking "the end of my London life." On the way to the land office at Birtle to register their claims, Seton and his companions spent a cold, rainy night camped near the Assiniboine River canyon. The next morning they shared their breakfast with a hunting party of Plains Crees who were camped nearby with their families. Seton was impressed with the honesty of these "wild pagan Indians" who "scorned to take anything that belonged to people with whom they were at peace."[22]

Although he had ceremoniously "burned his bridges" with the city, Seton at the same time instinctively rebelled at the thought of "civilizing" his homestead and making a living behind the plow. For one thing, he realized that he should maintain at least peripheral contact with the art world. More important, he knew that in order to be successful as a naturalist, he needed to be known as one. This meant seeking an outlet for his work, and New York City was the most opportune place to find it. With that in mind, Seton used his "hen money" for a train ticket and left Carberry on November 14, 1883.[23] On the way, he stopped overnight in Chicago to see his brother George, who had married and was beginning to make his own niche in the printing business. George graciously donated ten dollars to help his brother meet the remaining travel expenses.[24]

With less than three dollars left in his pocket, Seton arrived in New York on November 23. Since this was the weekend of the Thanksgiving holidays, which meant all businesses were closed, Seton spent the next three days eating sparsely and acquainting himself with the city's sights and sounds. Central Park with its zoo and birdlife quickly became one of his favorite haunts. After the holidays Seton sought a permanent job. The sketches from his portfolio soon attracted the attention of the Sacket, Wilhelm and Betzig lithography firm, who hired him as a commercial artist at a starting salary of fifteen dollars weekly, though he considered himself worth much more. The story of how his drawing of a raven for one of the firm's traveling agents resulted in a five-dollar pay raise was one of his favorites.[25]

In the meantime, Seton was happy to find several artist acquaintances from his OSA days in Toronto who, like himself, had come to New York to escape Victorian restraints. He shared an apartment with Charles Broughton, a promising Ontario watercolorist who later became a noted magazine illustrator. Through these associations Seton canvassed several likely job prospects. One contact was the brother of Toronto artist J. A. Fraser, W. Lewis Fraser, art manager of *Century* magazine, to whom Seton sold a drawing of a scarlet tanager for ten dollars. While this money went to pay his rent, the sale also established a dependable business connection.[26] Beginning in January, 1884, Seton attended evening classes at the Art Students' League. Under the tutelage of William Sartain, Seton picked up several pointers on illustrating and had his first exposure to "a life class with models," a teaching method of which the OSA disapproved. Here he first met the western artist Frederic Remington and also Daniel Carter Beard, whom he found to be "a clever draughtsman . . . jolly and full of good stories." In his spare time, Seton found a few occasions to attend the theater, and from "cheap seats" he saw performances by such leading thespians as Edwin Booth and Lillie Langtry.

Despite the novelty and variety of such activities, Seton again found himself dissatisfied with the urban environment: "New York life goes hard against the grain with me. In fact it is not life at all in my estimation." Certainly the winter weather, along with his confinement to an office desk six days a week, allowed him "little chance for bird study." Even worse, the museums were closed on Sundays, and he had to be content to sit through the sermons of famous clergymen like T. DeWitt Talmadge and Henry Ward Beecher. As the spring of 1884 came on, so again did the "call of the West."[27] And Seton was more than ready to answer it.

CHAPTER 3

The Golden Years

Already Seton's writings were beginning to gain public notice. While traveling around Manitoba, he had often sent letters about his discoveries to Dr. Brodie and the Toronto Natural History Society; at the same time, he began compiling his findings on various species in narrative, short-story form, and some of these were printed in Canadian periodicals as early as February, 1883. In December of that year, Seton learned from his colleagues in New York that Professor Goldwin Smith was starting a new periodical in Toronto called the *Week*. Its editor, a young nature writer and poet from New Brunswick named Charles G. D. Roberts, had seen a paper of Seton's on the prairie chicken and was hoping for contributions along such lines.[1] As a result, Seton spent many evenings alone in his living quarters, writing and perfecting several animal stories, although none of them was published until a few years later.[2]

Seton's bird studies also attracted the attention of America's leading ornithologists. On his return from England in 1881, he had secured a copy of Elliott Coues's *Key to North American Birds* (1872) and had used it as a guide in identifying and classifying his specimens in Manitoba. Early in 1883, Seton innocently wrote Coues, informing him of his findings and offering his "services as a correspondent in the line of natural history."[3] Coues, a cofounder of the infant American Ornithologists' Union (AOU) and editor of its official publication, the *Auk*, forwarded the letter to his colleague Spencer F. Baird. As secretary of the Smithsonian Institution in Washington, Baird was glad to know of someone who could help complete that museum's Canadian bird specimen collection. He not only accepted Seton's offer but greatly encouraged the young artist-naturalist's efforts, outlining for him his own methods of mounting skins and eggs.[4] Furthermore, Baird sent a letter of introduction on Seton's behalf to Clinton Hart Merriam, secretary-treasurer of the AOU. Merriam, later to become first chief of the U.S. Biological Survey, formally accepted Seton's original offer and invited him to join the union. Learning of Seton's artistic abilities, Merriam asked for a private preview.[5]

Seton had good reason, then, in addition to the "old spring fret," to return to the Canadian frontier. Not even an offer by Betzig to raise his salary to twenty-five dollars a week could hold him back. After leaving New York on April 14, 1884, Seton stopped over at Merriam's Locust Grove home in the Adirondacks. One look at a sample of the young naturalist's talent was all that was needed to convince Merriam to order fifty additional drawings at a high price as fast as Seton could find the animal subjects and produce them. At Toronto, Seton gave his first public address to the Natural History Society before rejoining his brother at the Carberry farm.

Seton considered 1884 the high point of his "golden years" in Manitoba. Not only was he in good health and back in his element, but he also had a legitimate and profitable means of sharing his discoveries. In June, after spring planting, he and Arthur went north via Fort Pelly to the Duck Mountain tract. The homestead laws required that before a settler could establish claim to the land, he must build a dwelling and plow a hectare during the first two years. The brothers therefore spent a week digging a well and erecting a claim shanty on the spot. After its completion, Seton carved his name and the date on the lintel over the door. On June 20, they returned to Carberry to check up on the crops. In fording the Assiniboine, their wagon became stuck in a hole, and they would have lost the whole outfit had a friendly Cree not helped them out. Grateful, the brothers accepted his invitation to dinner at his lodge in the Cotai Reserve.[6]

All during the summer, Seton divided his time between farm work and preparation of the drawings for Merriam. In his journal he recorded his ecstatic sense of discovery, and his collection of plant and animal sketches and specimens increased tremendously. From August through October the brothers were busy with the harvest, but whether threshing wheat or digging potatoes, Seton never failed to take note of all the forms of wildlife he found, even the field mice running in and out among the sheaves. After the first snows fell in late October, Seton resumed his studies of animal tracks. About that time the old hunting instinct stirred within him, and he decided to try for a deer in the Carberry Sandhills, where they were abundant. Accordingly, the brothers and some of their neighbors spent several days in the snow and cold, attempting unsuccessfully to bag their elusive quarry.[7]

It was during this hunt that Seton encountered an unforgettable character who would remain in his mind as his ideal man of the wilderness. This was Chaska, a Cree who was likewise stalking deer. Certainly, Seton's description of him does stir up images of James Fenimore Cooper's "noble savage":

> He was about six feet tall in his moccasins, straight and well-built, his features decidedly aquiline. His hair hung in two long black braids, ornamented with a bunch of brass rings and thimbles. He was dressed in the customary white blanket and leggings. A scarlet handkerchief covered his ears. He carried the usual fire-bag, knife and gun. He was a minor chief, and evidently a man of experience, for he spoke excellent English.
>
> We took to each other from the beginning. There was an indefinable charm about his quiet dignified manners—and I knew that he could teach me much about woodcraft.[8]

During the next two months, Chaska showed him many practical methods and tricks used by his tribe in hunting game. On these jaunts Seton felt himself one in spirit with the land, the animals, and the Indians. Nothing pleased him better than trudging into the scattered aspen and evergreen forests, feeling the crunching snow under his sometimes frostbitten feet. He thrilled at the Canadian sunsets and the wolves howling at night. Throughout the winter, Chaska and others of his tribe shipped the carcasses of deer they had killed by rail to Hudson's Bay Company officials at Brandon; with the proceeds, they obtained more supplies and ammunition for further hunts. Eventually, the Indians went back to their tribe, and Seton never saw Chaska again. But the memory of that representative of Canada's disappearing frontier lingered. In his guide's honor, Seton named his lake near Carberry "Chaska-Water."[9]

One thing Seton discovered in his contacts with the Indians of Manitoba was the enmity between the Plains Crees and the Sioux. Although Sitting Bull and his following had returned under pressure to reservation life in the United States in 1881, parties of Sioux hunters still frequented the area around Carberry in a desperate search for game. Neither the local Indians nor the whites were happy to see them; there was hardly enough game as it was without these intruders from south of the border. Even the "noble" Chaska expressed his discontent with their presence. Bitter rivalry ran deep.

Seton learned of the rivalry one day after he and a companion, Jim Duff, tracked and shot a huge bull moose in the vicinity of the Sandhills. The naturalist agreed to guard their kill while Duff went to notify the rest of the party and bring them back with the bobsleds and horse-drawn sleigh. While Seton was alone, a tall Sioux hunter came up and demanded at least half the carcass for himself. With rifle in hand, Seton firmly resisted the Indian's demands, and the two argued in sign lan-guage and broken English. Finally, the brave sullenly left, threatening to return with his fellow hunters. Fortunately, the timely arrival of Seton's companions prevented any further incident. A week later, in the Car-berry post office, that same Sioux brave, accompanied by his compan-ions, entered and shook hands with Seton in an apologetic gesture.

Seton dramatized the moose hunt in several of his writings. Although the ritual of the hunt was a challenge demanding an intimate knowledge of the wilderness, the killing itself brought him no pleasure; he declared afterward that never again would he lift a weapon against any big game "threatened with early extermination." [10]

While Seton obviously enjoyed his treks into the world of the pio-neer, he knew that it was impossible to commute between the city and the country while trying to hold down full-time employment. Certainly, good artists were in demand in New York. That, plus his contacts with the Smithsonian and the AOU, convinced Seton that fortune awaited him as a career writer, researcher, and illustrator, not as a frontiersman "in a log cabin rearing a swarm of half-breed children." [11] Furthermore, he decided that by engaging in free-lance work, he could determine his own hours and have the independence necessary to study at the library or take extended field trips. Such a course of action meant sacrificing not only Duck Mountain, but possibly Manitoba as well, yet at this point Seton was not afraid to take a gamble. The wilderness was deeply implanted in his soul, and through the pen and the brush he could give it expression. [12] As it turned out, Seton never returned to the claim shanty on which he had carved his name.

There were also historical factors influencing his decision. By 1883 the Manitoba land boom had suddenly run its course. Despite the efforts of syndicates and real estate promoters to buoy the boom by providing easy credit, the bubble burst, resulting in the abandonment of many homesteads and even proposed townsites. This was due, in part, to fed-eral tariff policies and to the monopoly of the Canadian Pacific Railway, which through a series of business and political maneuvers acquired ex-clusive rights to build Canada's first transcontinental railroad—a task it finally completed in 1885. The farmers, in 1883, sought to counter the resultant high shipping rates by creating the Farmers' Union, an organization similar to the Granger movement in the United States. But their attempts were largely unsuccessful.

Farther west, indeed not too far from Duck Mountain, the Métis were rallying under their charismatic leader, Louis Riel. Since their move west, their fears of Anglo settlement had spread to the Plains Crees, and the smoldering resentment of the two groups led to the outbreak of the Riel Rebellion in the summer of 1885.[13]

Although Seton surprisingly made no allusions to these dramatic events in his writings, his brother Arthur was to some extent a participant. In 1883 he had enrolled at the University of Manitoba Medical School in Winnipeg, dividing his time between his studies and the Carberry farm; he later abandoned the homestead altogether. During the Riel Rebellion, Arthur served as an apothecary with the Winnipeg Field Hospital, supplying medicines and drugs to the troops, who soon put down the uprising. Eventually he graduated with honors and set up practice in Winnipeg.[14]

At the end of January, 1885, Seton returned to Toronto and the "paternal domicile." There he spent the next seven months completing the commissioned illustrations for Merriam and preparing for his most ambitious project up to that time, a book on the birds of Manitoba. Meanwhile, in his role as a field correspondent for the AOU, he submitted notes on his bird observations to the *Auk*.[15] The tension between him and his father continued to grow, however, and in September Seton made his way back to New York to attend, at Merriam's urging, the annual meeting of the AOU at the American Museum of Natural History.[16] There he met the museum's zoology curator, Joel Asaph Allen, as well as several of the nation's leading ornithologists, including Elliott Coues, Robert Ridgway, and William Brewster. He also met Daniel Giraud Elliott, another noted zoologist and animal artist, who gave him valuable instructions on accurate measurement and reproduction of animal anatomy.[17]

Even more important were the contacts Seton made with potential publishers, especially the Century Company, whose magazine circulation had recently been boosted.[18] W. Lewis Fraser, the art editor, asked Coues to edit the biological material to be included in the forthcoming multivolume second edition of the *Century Dictionary*; Coues, in turn, promptly talked Fraser into hiring Seton to illustrate the text, and Seton found himself with a contract for one thousand drawings at five dollars each. Seton also contacted Mary Mapes Dodge, editor of *St. Nicholas*, the popular children's magazine published by Century.[19] A neighbor at his New York boardinghouse was Henry M. Steele, who within five years would become art director for *Scribner's* magazine.

In December, Seton made his first trip to Washington, D.C., to work closely with C. Hart Merriam on some illustrations for an upcoming Biological Survey report. There he met the "grand old man" of the Smithsonian, Spencer F. Baird, who eagerly accepted his information on and specimens of Canadian birds. Baird, in fact, was ready to take him on as a staff artist, but Seton had no desire to be tied down to a full-time desk job.[20]

Throughout most of 1886, Seton worked steadily on his *Century Dictionary* illustrations and submitted reports to the *Auk*. His confidence (and his ego) grew even more when Dr. Brodie requested that he send his findings to the Canadian Institute in Toronto. Even the government of Manitoba began to publish some of Seton's crude scientific hypotheses.[21]

For all the success he was beginning to enjoy in New York, Seton still considered Canada his home. "The lure of the West was overwhelming," and he wanted to experience more of the wilderness before technology did away with it. Accordingly, in September, 1886, Seton made preparations for another field trip. This time he planned a canoe voyage to the Lake of the Woods, following the old portage routes of the Hudson's Bay Company. By the 1880s the lake, located on the international boundary between Minnesota and Manitoba, was becoming popular as a summer resort.[22] On October 6, Seton left Toronto for the Lake of the Woods via Sault Ste. Marie—where he sketched the Soo Locks—and Port Arthur, on Lake Superior's western shore. He spent nearly a month collecting specimens and meeting with local Cree and Ojibwa residents. He picked up many of their terms for birds and beasts (for example, *müz* for moose, and *Mûc-kwĭ-té-pĭj-ĕ-ki* for buffalo, literally, "prairie horned beast"). Afterward, he returned to Carberry, where he did various odd jobs and resumed his hunting and trapping in the woods, using the techniques he had picked up from Chaska.[23]

Seton's days of "far tramping afoot" in the Canadian wilds during winter were numbered, however. Apparently, the hours and days spent in below-zero temperatures had affected his joints, for on November 23 an arthritic seizure crippled his right knee. Only years later, when he had a chance to visit a specialist, did the affliction respond to treatment.

In the meantime, he regarded this personal tragedy as the "end of my youth . . . I never again was the running athlete of my world."[24]

Seton's "youth" was ending in other ways as well. Many of his favorite meadows had been transformed into waving fields of grain, for despite the collapse of the land boom, Manitoba's immigrant population was gradually increasing, although at a much slower rate than that of the American West. While other settlers realized their dreams of turning the province into a fertile agricultural community, Seton felt that farming the land was merely a way of losing it, along with its marshes, flowers, birds, and beasts. Even the newly created Lake Dauphin district, which included his Duck Mountain tract, was attracting more settlers. This move was stimulated in part by exploration for oil in 1886; furthermore, the district was served by the Manitoba-Northwestern Railway, a subsidiary of the Canadian Pacific.[25] While Seton accepted the inevitability of progress, he often longed for the time when Indian and buffalo, hunter and hunted, lived in harmony with the open prairie. At the Lake of the Woods, he had lamented the fact that mining and timber interests, as well as the railroad, would soon destroy the pristine land of the Chippewas (Ojibwas). "The beauty of barbarism must pass away," Seton wrote, "and give place to the higher beauties of civilization and art."[26] The aftermath of the Métis uprising may also have influenced that attitude. Like the Plains Crees on their squalid reserves, Seton apparently felt that the sense of freedom he had experienced in the primeval wilderness was fast disappearing. The Indians and Métis, along with the wild creatures, were being chased from his beloved prairie.[27]

Once again Seton took up residence at the family abode in Toronto in January, 1887. During the next three years, he concentrated on his Manitoba birds project and continued making field observations in the area. In the spring his older brother Joseph, Jr. proposed buying a wilderness tract outside Toronto and developing it into a summer resort. Knowing Ernest's desire to be near wild things, Joe offered to set him up as the resident manager, complete with a cabin-studio in which he could do his artwork. Ernest eagerly took him up on the idea. Therefore, in May, Joe purchased an eighty-six-acre farm on Lake Ontario, about a mile from Port Credit and adjoining the Lorne Park resort. Seton immediately fell in love with this new arrangement; the woods and marshes abounded in foxes, raccoons, skunks, and numerous other species.[28]

Here for a short time the artist-naturalist lived a life that suited him.

There was time to visit "Aunt" Charlotte Schreiber, his former art teacher, at her Lorne Park cottage, as well as occasions to go raccoon hunting with George "Dod" Denison and his coon hound Ranger.[29] Neighbors who shared Seton's interests gladly helped add to his specimen collection. After learning that his old chum from London, R. Miller Christy, had opened a taxidermy studio in Winnipeg, Seton sent some of his specimens there to be mounted; at the same time, he took lessons in taxidermy to master the trade himself. Even his own nieces and nephews were eager to help their naturalist uncle by reporting interesting sightings.[30] The observations Seton made at the Port Credit farm became the basis for many of his most famous short stories, including "Raggylug," "Silverspot," and "The Springfield Fox."[31]

During this time, Seton submitted "The Drummer on Snowshoes," the first of his illustrated animal stories, to *St. Nicholas* for publication. "The Pintail," "Tracks in the Snow," "The Ovenbird," and others followed in rapid succession.[32] He also became a regular contributer to *Forest and Stream*, America's leading outdoor magazine, having met its editor, George Bird Grinnell, through association with the AOU. In this weekly periodical he related his hunting experiences in Canada, sometimes using biblical and classical allusions.[33]

While these early successes boosted Seton's reputation as a writer and illustrator, he also longed to be recognized as a natural scientist and thus prided himself, with a degree of arrogance, in being in the company of famous men. His desire to cultivate the ornithologists led him away from the Canadian colony to the American Museum of Natural History. There in the fall of 1888, J. A. Allen outfitted a special studio for Seton in which to complete the drawings for Coues. Next door was the office of Allen's newly appointed assistant, Frank M. Chapman, who would one day succeed him. The two men became fast friends. Another frequent visitor to the museum was the upcoming young bird painter, Louis Agassiz Fuertes, from whom Seton gained new ideas on anatomy and coloration. Together, the three young upstarts shared their findings and hypotheses, sometimes over the dinner table. One night, at the restaurant of New York's Endicott Hotel, they startled the other guests by calling lustily to each other in various bird "languages."[34]

Seton likewise sought to rub elbows with the men of the Smithsonian. From Robert Ridgway, the Institution's curator of birds, he occasionally sought advice on matters of coloration. In turn Ridgway solicited several of Seton's drawings for his own scientific research. Many of these were later featured in Ridgway's eight-volume *Birds of North and Middle America* (1901–19).[35] Another individual of note whom Seton met was William Temple Hornaday, then the Smithsonian's chief taxidermist. Impressed with Seton's understanding of animal anatomy, Hornaday commissioned him to make detailed drawings of buffalo for the monograph he was preparing on the threatened extermination of that animal. The artist-naturalist's knowledge of the effects that captivity and lack of exercise had on the buffalo's physical appearance—he used the bison at Central Park Zoo as his subjects—further served to bring Hornaday into his circle of friends.[36]

Despite all his contacts and commissions, Seton let nothing stand in the way of his main goal, the completion and publication of his two-hundred-page work on the birds of Manitoba. Believing that the bulky manuscript was the springboard for his scientific career, he attempted to sell it to several well-known Canadian publishers; when none expressed interest, he turned to the Smithsonian.[37] But Seton, with his limited self-training, had few adequate analytical tools. Robert Ridgway, who edited the text, sharply criticized the author's inability to keep emotional reactions from tinting his bird descriptions. Seton was coming closer to telling stories of bird heroes than presenting an objective, scientific record of bird habits. The controversy over the manuscript, which was blown out of proportion and created a rift between Seton and Ridgway, dragged on into 1891 after Seton had left for Europe.[38] However, the unwieldy work was printed as a monograph by the United States National Museum.[39]

It is ironic, indeed, that Seton never had the luxury of university training in science; with it, he would have been qualified to conduct field investigations for a salary in the service of the Canadian government. As it was, he had been appointed by the Ottawa government, through the endorsement of the Toronto Natural History Society, to be the naturalist of an exploratory expedition to Hudson Bay in 1884, but his move west before official approval of his appointment had prevented his accompanying the party.[40] Nevertheless, after Seton's controversial manuscript was published, Thomas McIlwraith, chairman of the AOU's Canadian Migration Committee, found it useful for his own research; so did John Macoun, naturalist for the Dominion Geological Survey, whose friendship, advice, and direction in matters of natural history Seton valued.[41]

Seton's apparent failure to prove his ability as a serious scientist led

him to the realization that art was his primary mode of expression and
source of recognition among his peers and the public. Not wishing to
spend his life illustrating other people's work, Seton was determined to
achieve greatness himself; therefore, his ambition demanded that he
channel all his energies into art.

Furthermore, his brother's Port Credit resort scheme was faring
badly, supposedly because the neighboring Lorne Park Company sought
to do its competitor "much mischief." At any rate Joe's financial condition worsened, and he was finally forced to sell out at a loss, with the
foreclosure of the mortgage completed by the end of 1889. As resident
manager, Seton got nothing out of the venture except the experience,
which he deemed valuable. In the meantime, he had invested in some
Toronto real estate with his brother Alan. As part of this scheme, they
built a store that Alan managed, and in the summer of 1890, Seton was
able to sell out his interest for sixteen hundred dollars. He paid four
hundred of this to his father as the last installment on his bill "for educating and bringing me up" and, with the remainder, sailed off to London and to new adventures in the Latin Quarter of Paris.[42]

Once again it appeared that Seton had given up his beloved western
wilderness for the refined, cultured world of arts and letters. However,
his struggle for identity in both worlds, reflected in his attempts to
combine art and science, was soon to heighten.

CHAPTER 4

The Wolf Man in Paris

Seton's love affair with the wilderness had deepened greatly during his "golden years," but his decision not to farm the Duck Mountain claim reflected his wish to keep it wild and untamed. To him, the wilderness contained an innate morality that humankind should emulate, not conquer and subjugate. Stung by the controversy over his Manitoba birds monograph, Seton sought refuge in his art. Over the next few years, his passions would rise again over the subject matter of his paintings.[1]

Having completed his *Century Dictionary* drawings, Seton (at the possible suggestion of Charlotte Schreiber) chose the summer of 1890 to join the exodus of OSA members to France. Since the studios in Paris were closed for the summer, Seton bided his time in London, "where at least I could study animals in the zoo." There he met three of England's most noted animaliers: John Swan, Archibald Thorburn, and their teacher, German-born Joseph Wolf. Like Seton, Wolf had had a lifelong interest in wildlife and had made his living as an artist illustrating scientific works. After analyzing his portfolio, Wolf greatly fortified Seton's interest in animal anatomy and gave him some pointers on bird feathering.[2] Certainly, here was a figure who had managed to bridge the gap between art and science.

Seton also called on the family of his old friend R. Miller Christy. Miller's brother Gerald became an important contact in England for the artist-naturalist, and their sister Eva, who was studying art herself, accompanied Seton to Paris via Calais in December.[3]

On January 19, 1891, Seton began his work at L'Académie Julian, a loosely organized art school made up of several expatriate artists from Canada and elsewhere, as well as those rejected by the more rigid, elitist Ecole des Beaux-Arts. In the midst of the sights and sounds of the French capital, he felt totally out of his element. Writing to his friend Henry M. Steele of *Scribner's* magazine, he admitted at times an "overpowering craving to be once more on the prairies and amid the Sandhills of Manitoba." Yet he adapted, learned French, and mingled with his fellow students, especially those from his home country. Classes at the academy consisted largely of painting the human figure from a live model posing nude on a dais. Naturally, Seton was shocked at this, as well as other liberal and sometimes permissive elements of Parisian life; however, he soon shed the vestiges of his Victorian prudishness.[4]

As time went on, Seton became affiliated with several American painters, notably the impressionist Robert Henri, whose radical beliefs in individual freedom Seton in part shared. Many of their evenings and weekends were spent discussing the political advantages of socialism and anarchy, and analyzing such controversial books as Edward Bellamy's *Looking Backward*.[5] Equally important were Seton's initial contacts with A. A. Anderson, the academic portraitist, known mainly for his searching paintings of public figures like Thomas Edison and Elihu Root. Having arrived in Paris in the 1880s, the independently wealthy Anderson had studied with several noted French artists before establishing his own studio in the boulevard Montparnasse. Here he brought together several aspiring young artists living in the Latin Quarter to organize the American Art Association. Anderson was himself a Salon gold medalist, and by the time Seton appeared on the scene, he wielded considerable influence.[6] His academic style appealed to Seton's conservative side and "to his instinct for scientific exactitude." In fact, Henri's left-wing philosophy, along with the liberal environment of the Latin Quarter, served to represent Seton's love for the wilderness, while Anderson's friendship depicted his need for security within society befitting his noble heritage.[7]

Seton's study of classical art forms only heightened for him the appeal of the contrasting world of nature. His idea that art was merely a representation of nature was reinforced; no mere copy of a bird could be as beautiful as the original. While other painters at the academy concentrated on human portraiture, Seton refused to limit himself to "perfect" forms of classical art (like the perfect squares of Manitoba's grain fields). Not even the advice of his most influential French teacher, Jean Léon Gérôme, to concentrate on human figures fazed him.[8] Under Gérôme's expert tutelage, Seton learned much in regard to color, light, and brushstroke, but his mastery of such techniques all wound up serving his desire to do justice to his animal subjects.

While most of his mornings were spent at the easel, the academy's informal structure allowed Seton to make daily excursions to the Jardin des Plantes Ménagerie to sketch its animals. He also took every opportunity to study the wildlife in Fontainebleau Forest and other wilderness areas outside Paris. During the spring and summer, Seton made several trips across the Channel to England to further his studies in bird and mammal anatomy. On one of these trips, Seton studied the sea birds and their nesting grounds on the Essex coast, and through the Christys he was able to publish some of his findings.[9] There were also times for recreation and sightseeing—bullfights at the Plaza des Toros (where to Seton's relief, no man or beast was killed), boat trips down the Seine, and visits to historic sites such as the cathedral at Rouen with its famous Bayeux tapestry.[10]

Seton's favorite mammal subject as a symbol of nature was the wolf. Even as a small boy, he was fascinated by the animal, and he had argued against its traditional "villain" image in literature.[11] During his Manitoba field trips, Seton had sometimes observed, hunted, and trapped wolves for scientific purposes as well as for bounty. He never forgot his glimpse of the scene from the window of his snowbound train near Winnipeg in 1882, where a huge wolf was holding a pack of dogs at bay. Nor did he forget the time during the spring of 1887 when, while hunting near Carberry, he was pinned to the ground, a hand and a foot each caught in a wolf trap. At that time, he might have ended up as wolfbait himself had it not been for the providential appearance of his faithful dog Bingo, who drove off the menacing pack and helped free his master.[12] Such episodes undoubtedly crossed Seton's mind as he pondered what he was going to do for the 1891 Grand Salon of Paris. To him, the wolf symbolized everything alien to the Parisian art world and all that he had left behind in Canada. While the dog, Gérôme's favorite animal subject, represented nature tamed by man, the wolf depicted that part of nature man could never tame.[13]

Accordingly, Seton chose for his subject a captive wolf at the zoo, which obliged him by taking afternoon naps at approximately the same location each day. Setting up his easel near the cage, Seton painted the subject from life on a two-by-four-foot canvas. In March, he delivered his *Sleeping Wolf* to the Grand Salon for adjudication by a jury of experts, including Gérôme. To Seton, the message of the painting was clear and simple: although the animal is asleep, he is still alert and ready, all wolf, all wild; here was a symbolic portrait of nature, which man should respect. While the jurors did not necessarily understand all of what Seton tried to say, he was pleased to learn that they had accepted the painting on the basis of its realism.[14]

Heartened, Seton declared that for the competition the following year, he would do a painting that more forcefully expressed his views on the relationship between man and nature. Gérôme suggested that he use the genre style, a painting that told a story. Furthermore, Henry Mosler, the American genre artist and another favorite instructor, advised him to "make it big" to achieve greater impact with his audience. About that time, in January, 1892, the Paris newspapers came out with reports of a woodsman in the Pyrenees who had profited from hunting sheep-killing wolves. One night during the winter, he failed to show up at his cottage. The next morning it was discovered that the wolves had gotten him; this was their hour of revenge. Having found an unproven but suitable wolf story and acting on his instructors' suggestions, Seton obtained a laboratory skeleton, peasant's clothes, wolf skins, and a bucket of cow's blood from the slaughterhouse. With these items, he made afternoon boat rides to snow-covered St. Cloud Park, five miles out of Paris, and proceeded to reconstruct the tragic scene for his painting, which was done on a four-and-a-half-by-seven-foot canvas. Once, when two gendarmes happened onto this gory panorama, they thought they had come upon a murder scene and arrested its supposed perpetrator. But after Seton politely explained the situation, they let him go on the basis that it was "some sort of American joke."

Seton originally titled his finished product *The Triumph of the Wolves*, but on the advice of friends, he changed it to *Awaited in Vain*, hoping that it would better appeal to the conservative Salon. He afterward regretted the change, since it made the human victim and his family in the distant cottage, rather than the wolves, the objects of sympathy. Even so, the altered title did little good; in April, 1892, Seton received the staggering news that his work had been rejected; indeed, the Salon had been shocked by the content and had paid little attention to the painting's technical qualities. The jurors accused Seton of being antihumanist, when he really meant to portray the message that man should respect, not seek to dominate, nature.[15]

Seton was crushed but, as usual, not ready to admit defeat. What he needed to do now, he decided, was to clear his head, which meant a return to his beloved Manitoba. Accordingly, Seton went to London and then took passage to New York, where he spent a few days visiting friends and submitting to George Bird Grinnell a series of articles on outdoor activities in France.[16] Late in May, he returned to Toronto and spent the remainder of the month collecting specimens in the vicinity of Erie, Pennsylvania.[17]

Arriving at Winnipeg on June 4, Seton spent a day at the taxidermy shop of Calvin Hine, the largest in the province. At Carberry, he visited familiar haunts and looked up his old hunting companions, including Jim Duff and Gordon Wright. In addition to his farm, Wright ran a boardinghouse in town, and it was with him that Seton spent most of the summer. Even as he stepped off the train, the artist-naturalist could not help noticing the changes the past decade had brought to his favorite frontier town. Not only had it grown, with new businesses thriving, but its once treeless setting was now shaded by various deciduous and evergreen species, "man-planted, every one." Even the old homestead was almost concealed by the trees he and Arthur had set out. The prairies, once laden with flowers, bird nests and gopher burrows, had been transformed into furrowed wheatfields. Fences lined with thistles and other weeds not native to the region ran parallel to the roads. The Sandhills were largely overgrown with spruce trees, and even his beloved Chaska-Water was gradually becoming a reedy marsh. Everywhere he looked, Seton noted these change with sadness. He compared them with the loss of his own youth; in addition to his arthritic knee, his eyes were worn from years of making minute drawings, compelling him to wear glasses whenever he worked at the desk or easel.[18]

Nevertheless, Seton was glad, even for a short time, to be back in his element. "Here I am in heaven," he wrote to Gerald Christy.[19] He wasted little time before making further wildlife observations. During his excursions, he discovered that while some species had disappeared from the area, others had increased in population. Along with his findings, he sketched in his journal the few vestiges of the Manitoba frontier, including old Fort Garry (from which Winnipeg grew), the lodges of the Sioux and Chippewa, and, of course, Chaska-Water.[20]

Seton's brief draft of wilderness tonic that summer was merely a prelude to his attempt at obtaining further recognition in his adopted country as an artist and naturalist. One way of achieving this, he decided, was through connection with high officials in the provincial government. Stopping over in Winnipeg in September, Seton called at the home of James Wickes Taylor, the American consul, whom he had first met in 1885 through Spencer Baird. Taylor's daughter, Elizabeth, had studied art with Seton in Paris, and he considered her a close friend,

especially after she had helped him obtain a six-month railroad pass
from Lord Strathcona, president of the Canadian Pacific Railway. During the summer, while Seton was in Carberry, Elizabeth had outfitted
an expedition to explore the Mackenzie River.[21] Through the Taylors, as
well as the Hine taxidermy firm, Seton met a certain W. Scott, the government officer in charge of preparing the Manitoba exhibit for the upcoming Columbian Exposition in Chicago. Impressed with the artist-
naturalist's achievements, Scott asked him to help the local taxidermists
label and select the mounted specimens from the government museum
for display at the fair. Seton agreed, and was able to extract from Scott a
letter of recommendation to the premier of Manitoba, Thomas Greenway. Seton made an appointment to see the premier, and Greenway subsequently made him "official naturalist to the Government of Manitoba,
without salary, except when on specially appointed missions, when I am
to have $5 a day and my expenses." In the end, Seton had only a second-
ary part in putting together the exhibit the following spring, but his
new "government official" status was complete.[22]

Back in Toronto, armed with his new political label, Seton sought to
exhibit his controversial painting, *Awaited in Vain*, at the Chicago Exposition. He had sent for his "big wolf picture" from Paris and, hoping
to attract a more favorable audience, opened it to public viewing in his
father's drawing room at 86 Howard Street. Almost immediately, the
crowds began coming. Public reaction to the portrait was mixed; it was
either a "masterpiece" or a "monstrosity." The local newspapers publicized the showing so highly that Seton had to move his exhibition
downtown to the back room of Ellis's Jewelry Store, where he could
better accommodate the crowds. One noted visitor was the Canadian
Indian poetess, Pauline Johnson, who also was known by her Iroquois
name Tekahionwake. She admired the painting, and when George Reid,
a local artist, introduced her to Seton, she reportedly exclaimed, "I
know that we are kin. I am a Mohawk of the Wolf Clan, and that picture
shows that you must be a wolf spirit come back in human form." They
became friends for life, and Tekahionwake always called Seton her "dear
Wolf Man."[23]

Gloating over the apparent success of his exhibition, Seton submitted
the painting to the Toronto Committee of Selection. This group, consisting of members of the Royal Canadian Academy (RCA), was dominated by the OSA, to which Seton had been officially elected in 1892,
likely on the strength of his *Sleeping Wolf*.[24] However, the jurors dis-

missed the painting "by a majority of one" on the grounds that it did not accurately portray life in Canada. For the moment, it looked as though public ambivalence worked against him. After all, a picture like *Awaited in Vain* that represented human limitations seemed out of place at a fair meant to show human achievements.[25]

Nevertheless, Seton refused to take the verdict sitting down, especially when he learned that the OSA members had voted in favor of the painting and that the dissenting ballots had been cast by a group of Montreal artists for strictly moral reasons; they considered the work "blasphemous." While Robert Harris, who had been given the task of mounting the Canadian art collection for the fair, was reluctant to take sides in the issue, several prominent OSA men, including former RCA president Lucius R. O'Brien, went to bat for Seton.[26] The mounting controversy, which spilled over into the newspapers, dragged on for weeks and caused one of Seton's artist friends, Robert Gagen, to jokingly label the portrait *Bones of Contention*.[27] Unable to get favorable results by direct appeal, Seton next traveled to Ottawa and used his political contacts—acquaintances from homestead days like John Macoun, Geographical Survey director Alfred Selwyn, and Sen. J. N. Kirchoffer of Souris—to influence the committee. These three civil servants petitioned John S. Larke, Canada's executive commissioner at the fair. When Larke refused to compromise his position, Seton then used his own government official status to appeal to Toronto senator Frank Smith and his colleague, Minister of Agriculture Auguste Angers, who was Larke's immediate superior.[28] Using Machiavellian tactics, Seton worked behind the scenes. He enlisted the support of jury member Homer Watson at the latter's home in Doon and even claimed that he had made alterations in the painting.[29]

The pressure exerted by the OSA and Seton's political connections gradually worked to soften the positions of Robert Harris and the Montreal group. Finally, the committee reconsidered and accepted the portrait, with only one negative vote; *Awaited in Vain* was displayed at the Columbian Exposition, although not necessarily in "a central place in the space assigned to the Canadian Exhibit," as Seton later claimed.[30]

By the fall of 1893, Seton's name had become familiar throughout most of Canada, while his readership and contacts in the United States continued to increase. The AOU paid him twenty-five dollars for bird drawings, and the U.S. Department of Agriculture awarded him two hundred dollars for drawings of certain rodent species. Seton's inventiveness, at the same time, reached Armour and Company of Chicago: he sent that meatpacking firm instructions for a new method of making pemmican that he had devised from the techniques of the Canadian Indians. He also sent out a slate of directions on tanning hides and furs. Even England, the land of his birth, was beginning to hear of Seton; the British Museum purchased a collection of his mammal skins.[31]

Whatever victory Seton gained in getting his painting into the Exposition collection, it was a hollow one. Despite the furor over the "masterpiece," it largely escaped public notice at the fair. While the criticism put forth by the Montreal group was on a moral basis, Seton's victory was merely political; the art of politics had prevailed over the art of the artists. Blind ambition had led him to compromise his views. In an indignant spirit, coupled perhaps with a sense of guilt, Seton gradually exiled himself from the RCA and Canada's artistic elite.[32] Under his persecution complex, he saw himself as a maverick once more.

Joseph Thompson, by then in his seventies and more irascible than ever, was not impressed with his son's "latest disaster." Their relationship disintegrated into open hostility, and for the remainder of Joseph's life, neither of them saw or spoke to the other.[33] Certainly, Seton was embittered, but he had no desire at that time to return to either Paris or Manitoba. What he needed was to escape into a new frontier where he could expand his horizons.

CHAPTER 5

The Plains of
the Currumpaw

Unknown to Seton at the time, the Columbian Exposition was the scene of the American Historical Association's annual meeting for 1893. At that meeting on July 12, a young Wisconsin historian named Frederick Jackson Turner notified his fellow Americans that the key to their democratic heritage was their westward expansion into empty land. His argument was accepted by his public; it made sense of their past and gave them "a national myth at the same time that they acquired a national history." The overall feeling was that in light of the vanishing frontier and the seemingly un-American technological changes occurring by the 1890s, it was the duty of the historian to revive and conserve the "great American tradition."[1]

From his experiences in Manitoba, Seton had seen Turner's theory in action as newcomers transformed the virgin prairie into a rural garden landscape. Like Turner, he mourned the passing of the untrammeled landscape. But unlike Turner, Seton did not identify himself with the pioneer settler who sought to eliminate the wilderness. Rather, his attitudes more closely paralleled those of the perpetual migrant who felt at home in the forests and "wide open spaces," lived like the Indians, and always tried to stay ahead of approaching civilization.[2] Instead of seeing the frontier as a permanent "escape valve," Seton came to be numbered among those who looked upon the West as a temporary place of refuge, where one could regain health, vitality, and peace of mind. Such a viewpoint was compatible with his own notion of the wilderness as a natural history field laboratory.

It was his interest in wolves plus his association with a wealthy family that gave Seton his initial acquaintance with the American Southwest and the world of that unique, partly mythical culture of the cowboy.[3] In Paris, he had met Virginia Fitz-Randolph, "a tall, fine looking girl of aristocratic manner," while attending a social gathering at a missionary's home in the Latin Quarter. Subsequently, they took in many of the sights of Paris together, and when Seton made his return voyage from Liverpool to New York in May, 1892, Virginia and her fiancé accompanied him. At the Hoboken Dock, Seton was introduced to her father, Louis V. Fitz-Randolph, who invited him to Virginia's homecoming reception at their estate in Plainfield, New Jersey. There he learned that Fitz-Randolph, in addition to other business interests, owned a large cattle ranch near Clayton, New Mexico. Throughout the spring and summer of 1893, as the fracas over his wolf painting boiled and then simmered, Seton's several trips to New York included frequent visits to the Fitz-Randolph home. Late in the summer, after having learned of his hunting experiences, Fitz-Randolph asked the artist-naturalist if he would go to New Mexico and help rid his ranch of the wolves that were taking a terrible annual toll among his cattle. Distressed over the turn of events in Canada and eager for a vacation from confining easel and desk work (and in compliance with his doctor's orders to rest his eyes), Seton accepted the assignment.[4]

According to arrangements, Seton was to stay for at least two months, do what he could to exterminate wolves, and influence the ranch hands to begin an organized war on the pests. Seton would keep the skins of the animals he killed, plus the bounties. Fitz-Randolph would foot the bill for ammunition, poisons, traps, and travel expenses, as well as room and board. A horse would also be furnished. Total expenses were estimated to be eighty dollars.[5]

The artist-naturalist traveled from New York via Toronto, where he purchased a revolver, to Chicago. There he spent a day at the Exposition, then in its closing weeks; among other attractions, he attended a performance of Buffalo Bill's Wild West show, his "earliest sight of high-class lasso work."[6] From Chicago, Seton took the Atchison, Topeka and Santa Fe line for Pueblo, Colorado. He described the farmlands of Illinois and Missouri as "beautiful countries of undulating rich land," while the sweeping prairies of Kansas reminded him of southwestern Manitoba. At one watering stop, Seton sketched a jackrabbit and took note of the old wallows, paths, and other traces of the bison that had once roamed there. In conversing with a weatherbeaten wheat farmer, Seton heard to his amusement that most of the notorious Kansas cyclones "originated in Eastern newspapers." Arriving at Pueblo, which he described as a "pretty little city," he saw for the first time the lofty peaks of the Rockies. Here, too, he had his first glimpse of the plant and animal life that characterized the southern plains. From Pueblo, Seton traveled the Fort Worth and Denver line via Trinidad and Barela to Clayton, where he arrived on the night of October 22, 1893.[7]

Clayton in the 1890s was a boisterous little "cowtown" with a population of around four hundred. Originally, it was the brainchild of Stephen W. Dorsey, cattle baron and ex-senator from Arkansas, who, with his associates, in 1887 established the town near the best water sources available to the approaching Fort Worth and Denver Railroad. They named the site after his son, Clayton Dorsey. The following year, when the railroad began accepting cattle for shipment, Clayton became a campground for the area cattlemen. Soon a permanent town sprang up after several small businesses moved in.[8] When Seton arrived on the scene, Union County had recently been created, and Clayton was engaged in a heated contest with neighboring Folsom over which town would become the county seat—an honor that Clayton would soon win.[9] Cattle and politics were the main items of conversation.

As the gangly thirty-three-year-old Seton stepped down from the train at the station, he saw a windswept frontier town not unlike those he had first seen in Manitoba. Yet this place had an atmosphere almost foreign to him. Here at the northernmost point of the region known locally as "Little Texas," the Anglo and Hispanic cultures intermingled and occasionally clashed. But Seton had come primarily to study a natural world fast being altered by the "civilization" that Clayton represented. Before leaving for New Mexico, he had set for himself a threefold goal: "to kill fifteen gray wolves . . . to ascertain accurately the weight of all large animals killed . . . to sketch the tracks of all the quadrupeds of the region."[10]

With that in mind, the young naturalist trudged down the dusty street to the Clayton House, the town's only hotel. Owned and operated by Harry J. Wells, the Clayton House doubled as the community social center, containing a barroom and a dancehall ("run on the most respectable lines") where a dance "in true Western style" was held every Saturday night.[11] Directly across the street was the general store operated by A. W. Thompson, who was also the town's postmaster.[12] About fifty yards behind the hotel was a small, muddy pond from which Seton would take several bird and mammal specimens. In the center of town stood a lone cottonwood, the only tree in the community. Always the sharp-eyed observer, Seton once spotted a ladderback woodpecker busying itself on the trunk, while all the cats in town stalked it from various directions. He also observed a large flock of sheep being herded into railroad cars for market and was surprised to learn that goats often served the same function as sheepdogs for this operation. In his journal, Seton made several sketches of the town, taking note of the volcanic rock areas, especially the twin peaks to the west known as the Rabbit Ears. One native plant that particularly attracted his attention was "the remarkable shrub called tumbleweed."[13]

After spending two days in Clayton, Seton left with the mail carrier for Louis Fitz-Randolph's L Cross F Ranch, where he was to be employed as a wolf hunter. Formerly a part of the Prairie Cattle Company's Cross L range, the L Cross F was located on Piñabetitos Creek, about twenty-five miles to the southwest. It was managed by the foreman, H. W. Foster, who was officially Seton's "boss." However, because the ranch was temporarily without a cook and the foreman was away on business for a short time, arrangements were made for Seton to board at the cabin of Jack Brooks, a neighboring rancher. Brooks's small holding was on Leon Creek, about seven miles from the L Cross F headquarters and close to the tiny community of Clapham, which had the nearest school and post office.[14]

For a few days after moving into the Brooks cabin, Seton carefully studied the terrain and observed the local fauna. Despite the fact that he was there during the late fall and early winter, many species of birds were still fairly plentiful. Seton noted his reaction to his first roadrunner, or "Mexican peacock," which resembled, in his thinking, an English pheasant. One cowboy called it "half magpie, half chicken."[15]

Among the native mammals, Seton was impressed with the abundance of prairie dogs, but because they were difficult to catch, he was able to bag only three.[16] Another fascinating rodent was the kangaroo rat. Seton later caught two of these creatures and kept them in a crude pine-box cage to study their habits more closely, but they did not remain captives long. The naturalist awoke one morning to discover that they had chewed through the half-inch thick box top and escaped.[17] One of Seton's most prized specimens was a bobcat, his first opportunity to study the "Texas wildcat" or "red lynx." Once, when he happened upon some bobcat and skunk tracks, he was able to determine that the inexperienced young cat had attempted to make prey of the skunk, with disastrous results for the former. In order to "keep tracks of any four-footed visitors that might call," the naturalist made it a nightly practice to sweep the dust smooth around the cabin.[18]

Beginning his wolf hunts in earnest, Seton quickly mastered many of the cowboy arts and skills such as throwing the lasso, flanking a steer, and shooting from horseback, but even then he knew that catching wolves was no easy task. He had learned from experience in Canada that these animals, once considered dangerous to man, had since been "educated by gunpowder to let man alone."[19] And trailing wolves with dogs was not always successful because of the arroyos that slashed the plains, often enabling a pack of wolves to elude and draw off their pursuers.[20]

The reason wolves were so destructive to sheep and cattle, Seton observed, was that man had deprived them of the buffalo, antelope, and deer, their main sources of food; without these, wolves had no choice but to prey on livestock. Consequently, local ranchers had declared all-out war against them, and "wolfing" came to be considered great sport, as well as a challenge, in many western ranchlands. Cowhands saw a chance to make extra money from the bounties (usually five to ten dollars) that were offered for each wolf pelt.[21] Traps and poisons, imported in vast quantities, were quite successful at first, but by the 1890s many wolf packs seemed to have learned to detect them. Seton believed that wolves, being social animals, somehow "passed on" information about man's weapons to others of their kind.[22] No wolf would go near a carcass that had any trace of human contact, and by their keen sense of smell, many could detect poisoned bait.

Seton began his campaign against wolves by using strychnine, which he had successfully used in Canada for specimen collecting, but not once did he get a wolf with it. It was fairly effective on coyotes, of which he later claimed to have bagged more than a hundred (some by poison and some in traps), whereas he caught only five wolves, all of them in steel, double-spring traps.[23] (Although he supposedly devised a method by which he could get at least two coyotes every night, he remarked, "I have changed from a coyote killer to a coyote protector; and the devilish secret of destruction shall perish with me.")[24] After one chilly November evening, when a played-out cowhand mistook strychnine for quinine, with fatal results, Seton abandoned the use of poisoned bait.[25]

In conjunction with his wolf hunts and animal observations, Seton associated with the populace of Clayton and vicinity, frequently participating in their activities. A. W. Thompson, the storeowner, recalled that one morning after a light snowfall when Seton took him to the edge of town and showed him some rabbit tracks, the naturalist followed the tracks, pointing out where the rabbit had stopped, gone on, jumped, and finally disappeared. Seton also let Thompson pick out a dozen coyote skins from a pile he had stored at Kelly's Feed Yard.[26]

Another building in which Seton kept his animal skins was a small adobe shed located behind the Clayton House. Mrs. Harry Wells, wife of the hotel owner, stored her eggs in this shed, which she kept locked so that passing cowboys would not steal them, and she was at first reluctant to allow the naturalist access to the storehouse. But he assured her that he would not so much as touch the eggs, and in later years Mrs. Wells recalled that Seton was "very much a gentleman."[27]

Seton was impressed by the fact that nearly every cowboy carried a rope and could use it skillfully. He commented in his journal on the cowboys as masters of the horse and lasso, as well as on their liberal use of certain terms, many of Spanish origin. He considered the "list of wild creatures in this country incomplete without the cows and the cowboys," but "the cowboy unfortunately is always at his worst when on public view—ie, when in the towns—then all his vices are rampant and his better parts forgotten or smothered in drink. At home, at sober work, I find him always good humored, rollicking, reckless, hardworking, courteous and hospitable to a degree that I never before experienced." Certainly, Seton often experienced firsthand the monotonous life of the cowboy at work, riding the ranges for days at a time and spending nights at various ranches and line camps.[28] Occasionally, he accompanied the L Cross F hands on roundups and gathered many of their campfire tales. It was on one such venture in December, 1893, that Seton claimed his first and only glimpse of a wild mustang herd led by the legendary black stallion later immortalized in his story "The Pacing Mustang."[29]

One notable cowboy was Billy Allen, considered the champion roper in the whole region. Before coming to the L Cross F outfit, Allen had worked on the vast XIT Ranch in Texas and had been among those who eradicated the last of the buffalo herds in the Panhandle.[30] So skilled was he with the lasso that he could rope a badger before the animal could get to the safety of its den. Once, while roping a "lumpy jawed" steer for wolf bait, Allen threw the animal over in a complete somersault, breaking its neck and both its horns at the roots.[31]

Seton commented favorably on the Winchester repeating rifle, the ranchers' favorite hunting weapon. He had brought both his Winchester and his new revolver to New Mexico; then, soon after his arrival, Charlotte Schreiber sent him a new breech-loading Marlin "that was guaranteed to put the Winchester out of business." However, after one close scrape with a particularly ornery "lumpy jawed" steer, during which the breech jammed because of the cold weather, Seton rated "the good old Winchester" superior to any other brand.[32]

Among the admirable traits that Seton noted in his cowboy colleagues was their love for parents and families. He recalled one Sunday morning when a circuit rider held a revival meeting in the Clapham schoolhouse, which doubled as a church building. Standing behind the teacher's desk, the preacher began his sermon to the predominantly cowboy audience by stating that "in SIN did our mothers conceive us." A tall Texan in the front row, unfamiliar with that passage of Scripture, immediately jumped up, pulled his gun on the clergyman, and sternly warned him not to slander his mother like that. Seeing this incident as representative of his own liberal thinking, which opposed his Calvinist upbringing, Seton felt that Christian doctrine should not condemn "every God-appointed natural human emotion and relationship" as sin. Indeed, this was a major step in his gradual shift away from conventional Christianity. As he later remarked, "I did much thinking those days. One has lots of time, riding all day on the hurricane deck of a bronc, at the tail end of a steer."[33]

In his acquaintance with the men and women of the West, Seton soon experienced the feelings of prejudice that occasionally flared between the Anglo and Hispanic populace. He also discovered that the law was loosely interpreted on the frontier and that small ranchers sometimes rustled cattle from their larger, more prosperous neighbors. Once, when Seton and his cabinmate Jack Brooks were slaughtering a steer Brooks had killed, the naturalist noticed that it bore a different brand. When Seton inquired about that, Brooks replied, "It don't do too much to know about brands in New Mexico." Soon afterward, an angry Mexican cowman came and searched the cabin, adding to Seton's suspicions.[34]

It was an unexpected encounter with rustlers that allegedly got Seton into trouble and forced him to cut short his wolf hunts. According to the story, Seton had arranged through Brooks a meeting with the brothers Joe and Charley Callis, who had a small holding near the Canadian River. Joe, an outlaw but also a successful wolfer, knew several hunting and trapping methods that Seton was eager to learn. While the three men were encamped on the river, the outlaw-wolfer sketched sev-

eral local cattle brands in the sand and asked Seton whether he could
alter them in any way. Unaware of his companions' true motives, the
artist-naturalist did so; only when he saw them alter the brands of cattle
they had rounded up in the canyon did he realize their intentions. Seton
promptly informed them that he wanted no part of their illegal activities, and the rustlers let him go only on his promise that he would keep
quiet about the affair.[35]

This escapade, Seton said, forced him to leave New Mexico earlier
than he had planned. On the evening of February 5, 1894, a deputy sheriff whom Seton had befriended came and told him that a week earlier
Joe Callis, while on a drunken binge in Clayton, had boasted openly
about Seton's "slick counterbrand." As a result, a warrant was out for
Seton's arrest. The deputy, fearing that his friend's testimony "could not
convince a Mexican judge and jury," advised him to take the midnight
train out of Clayton. Seton hastily packed his belongings and left for "a
place called New York."[36]

That is the way Seton told it in his autobiography, but his journal
contains no substantial evidence for what may have been either "a good
story" or faulty memory. In his diary, Seton merely told of spending the
night at the Callis brothers' abode, helping to load their chuckwagon
for an early start the next morning, and camping out the following
night in Alamosa Arroyo—near the old Francisco Gallegos Ranch—to
take refuge from a cold "northeaster." At the Gallegos place, he commented on the locoweed and its effects on livestock and also mentioned
that cow chips were the only fuel available. Two days later, the men
made the twenty-five-mile ride back to the Callis ranch "in the face of
driving sleet," and from there, the naturalist rode on back to Clapham.
Nowhere in the journal did Seton either affirm or deny that the Callis
brothers were rustlers. When he prepared to leave New Mexico, Seton
discussed final arrangements about his bounty money (seventy-two dollars in all); he then spent six months in Toronto before returning to
New York.[37]

Seton's first venture to America's vanishing frontier was, by his admission almost traumatic. Given his humanitarian philosophy toward animals, it is not easy to imagine him in the role of a hired wolf hunter.
While Fitz-Randolph may have hired him to participate in an experimental predator-control program, and while he undoubtedly joined the
group of exterminators dedicated to reducing the ranchers' financial
losses, Seton at the same time saw this experience as a golden oppor-

tunity to expand his knowledge of wolves and other wildlife in a region of North America he had never seen. In his journal, he analyzed the behavior of local species, and these notes were used in many of his later publications.[38] One memorable episode in particular proved to be a milestone—his capture of Old Lobo.

The Valley of the Currumpaw (or Corrumpa) River north of Clayton contained some of the best grasslands in eastern New Mexico, complete with water holes and shelter from the harsh winters. From its headwaters near Capulin Mountain, the often dry Currumpaw runs east toward the Oklahoma Panhandle, where it feeds the North Canadian. This valley was ideal cow country, but "plenty of cattle meant plenty of wolves," and that meant a loss of thousands of dollars annually to the local cattlemen and sheep ranchers.[39]

Soon after Seton arrived in the fall of 1893, he heard stories of a pack led by a huge killer wolf of devilish cunning. Some of the cowboys claimed that Old Lobo, as he was called, killed a cow or a sheep every night—not because he needed that much food but because his almost supernatural instinct warned him never to return to a kill, as it might be poisoned or surrounded with traps. The Currumpaw sheepmen and ranchers offered for Lobo's pelt a tremendous bounty, which gradually increased until it amounted to a thousand dollars.[40] But repeated attempts to snare him were in vain. Although he was seldom seen, people always knew when he was around by his distinct howl and huge tracks. One Clayton resident declared that since Lobo's kind was so difficult to kill, it was "not worth making a business of it."[41]

From the first, Lobo was number one on Seton's list. Seton established headquarters for this operation in an abandoned sheep rancher's adobe near the Currumpaw's sandy riverbed:

It was a rough, rock-built, squalid ranch-house that I lived in, on the Currumpaw. The plaster of the walls was mud, the roof and walls were dry mud, the great river-flat around it was sandy mud, and the hills a mile away were piled-up mud, sculptured by frost and rain into the oddest of mud vagaries, with here and there a coping of lava to prevent the utter demolition of some necessary mud pinnacle by the indefatigable sculptors named.

The place seemed uninviting to a stranger from the lush and fertile prairies of Manitoba, but the more I saw of it the more it was revealed a paradise. For every cottonwood of the straggling belt that the river used to mark its doubtful course across the plain, and every dwarfed and spiny bush and weedy copse, was teeming with *life*. And every day and every night I made new friends, or learned new facts about the mudland denizens.[42]

From these quarters, for nearly a month, Seton tried all kinds of devices to trap the King Wolf with the assistance of two cowboys, Charlie Winn and the roper, Billy Allen.[43]

The story of how Seton's ingenuity and persistence enabled him to snare the wily despot in January, 1894, remains one of the classic animal tales in the annals of the Southwest. In his story of "The King of Currumpaw," Seton ascribed to Lobo the adventures of several individual wolves observed or reported in the Clayton area and the XIT Ranch before narrating the events leading to the old marauder's capture.[44] He later spoke of the episode as "one of the turning points" of his life, and indeed it was.[45] When Seton's narrative was published in *Scribner's* magazine in November, 1894, it almost immediately received worldwide notice. Leo Tolstoy called it "the best wolf story I have ever read," while C. Hart Merriam was curious as to how much adorned it was.[46] William Hornaday wished he could have been there "to help dig holes and carry dirt." Furthermore, he wished that Seton "could have told verbatim just what Lobo said as those four traps sprang upon him one after another . . . his remarks would have been highly edifying."[47]

More important, the tale marked the beginning of a new style of nature writing for Seton and others. Before his New Mexico venture, Seton admitted to using the archaic method of making animals talk and giving them other obviously anthropomorphic qualities. According to Seton, it was one of his own earlier works, "The True Story of a Little Gray Rabbit," that inspired Rudyard Kipling to write *Jungle Book*. "The King of Currumpaw," however, was the earliest example of an animal story that adhered more carefully to scientific method.[48] Seton often used the episode to illustrate man's conflicts with the laws of nature. In time, Lobo's tragic death and that of his albino mate, Blanca, came to symbolize the extermination of wolves from the southern plains.

In addition to making its mark on his profession, the New Mexico venture had a significant impact on Seton's personal life and thought. Geographically he had "gone home." To some degree, the southern plains were an extension of the Canadian prairies even though this setting of sagebrush, cottonwood, and cactus was "more parched."[49] While the territory's frontier atmosphere was new to him, Seton agreed that any wilderness, regardless of its geographic location, provided an escape from the urban East. In Seton's view, however, the wilderness was not there just to provide an opportunity for the individual white man to prove his heroism. For him, the Indians in Canada and, to a lesser extent, the cowboys in New Mexico represented a collective ideal in that both groups demonstrated how men could live in harmony with other men and with their wilderness environment. In that respect, Seton identified more with the utopians and less with Turner—yet he had cast himself as a heroic wolfer with a job to fulfill.[50] When he had captured Lobo, Seton had not the heart to kill "his kindred" in cold blood. After the great wolf died "of a broken heart," the naturalist felt that he had killed his "Sleeping Wolf," the hero of his own imaginary world. He was obviously overwhelmed at the extent of an animal's loyalty to its mate; Lobo's undoing had been his devotion to Blanca, his "silly young wife." Certainly, this served to reinforce the naturalist's belief in the superiority of animal morality over human reason, especially men's murderous thoughts and actions.[51] Eventually, Seton began inserting a wolf track into his signature to express his symbolic "kinship" with Lobo's kind.

CHAPTER 6

La Poursuite and Marriage

While he had not attained his goal of "fifteen gray wolves," Seton's first trip to New Mexico ultimately proved to be a major springboard to success. During his six-month stay in Toronto, he kept busy writing and submitting more articles to his publishers (he first offered "The King of Currumpaw" to *Century* before it was accepted by *Scribner's* magazine). In March he sold most of his New Mexico wolf-trapping articles to the Oneida Community in upstate New York.[1] It was also during this time that Seton first dabbled in ethnological and archival history. Before leaving for New Mexico in October, 1893, he had written to ask Frederick Webb Hodge, head of the Smithsonian's Bureau of Ethnology, to edit and publish the Thomas Hutchins manuscript that had recently been found in the Hudson's Bay Company archives. This manuscript, written about 1770 at Fort York, contained much information on the Indians and wildlife of that era, subjects that immediately caught Seton's interest. Since Hodge had earlier helped edit a manuscript on Eskimo culture, Seton hoped that he would do the same for the Hutchins material "as the *ethnological part* . . . is the most valuable of all." Upon his return to Toronto in February, 1894, Seton learned that prior commitments had forced Hodge to decline the task for the time being. However, Hodge recommended Seton's old friend, R. Miller Christy, for the job. As it turned out, Christy's publishing business and other writing, plus the sudden death of his assistant editor, delayed preparation of the Hutchins manuscript for several years,[2] but the experience drew Seton and Hodge closer together through their mutual interest in Indian cultures.

On July 7, 1894, Seton boarded the S.S. *Spaarndam* at Jersey City for a return voyage to Paris, just barely making connections. Had he missed the boat, "the entire course of my history would have been changed in consequence," for among his fellow passengers on that cruise were Mrs. Albert J. Gallatin, wife of the noted California financier, and her twenty-two-year-old daughter, Grace. Seton was almost immediately smitten by Miss Gallatin's aristocratic manner. College educated, she had strong feminist views, yet her love for things cultural and her style of dress definitely betrayed her French ancestry.[3] The ship reached Boulogne on July 19, and by July 31, Seton was back in Paris boarding in the Latin Quarter. When the Gallatin ladies arrived a month later, following a tour of England, he found living quarters for them and, during his spare time, showed them the sights.[4]

Seton resumed his art studies in August. During the afternoons, he began preparations for an ambitious project designed to make up for his past failures in the eyes of both artists and scientists. Bothered by the fact that there were no publications on bird and mammal anatomy from the artist's viewpoint, Seton sought to remedy that deficiency by planning "a careful analysis of the *visible forms* and proportions of the *living* animal."[5] Having learned from the *Birds of Manitoba* fiasco, he was determined to prove that he could work within the controls of science without unleashing his imagination or moralism. Enthusiastically, he began measuring live specimens and dissecting dead ones. For his studies of wolf and dog anatomy, Seton used the cadavers of dogs that he bought at a pound just outside Paris. Upon reentering the city limits on the trolley, he was always stopped by customs officials, who became amused at the "dead dog man."[6]

In the text and illustrations of the resulting book, *Studies of the Art Anatomy of Animals*, Seton applied the principles he had learned from Elliott, Wolf, and other animaliers, as well as the techniques taught by Gérôme and his colleagues. As the project pregressed, Seton traveled to London to call on Wolf, John Swan, Frederick Leighton, and Britton Riviere (whom he described as a "decrepit old man"). All gave him favorable opinions of his manuscript and drawings, and by 1895 he had secured a contract with Macmillan and Company to publish the finished product.[7]

One of the items—in addition to weapons, strychnine, and traps—that Seton had taken with him to New Mexico was a Kodak box camera. When his traps caught Blanca and Lobo, he had "played the part of the Kodak fiend" and secured two photographs of each wolf.[8] He later noticed that Lobo resembled his *Sleeping Wolf*, which had been admired for its photographic realism. In compiling his *Art Anatomy*, Seton included new facts of anatomy that had been discovered as a result of recent developments in camera technology. He was especially interested in Eadweard Muybridge's 1878 theory on the way photography reveals a contrast between a "sun" and a "brain" picture. In his text, Seton carefully examined Muybridge's famous photographic series of a galloping horse, which revolutionized works of art containing animals in motion.[9]

Art Anatomy, published in early 1896, met with favorable criticism. Its success was due not only to Seton's analysis of the Muybridge photographs, but also to his elaborate drawings of various mammal anatomies designed to provide artists with scientifically accurate forms and proportions. Gérôme, who was fascinated with greyhounds, especially admired the dog studies. Indeed, Seton had come close to obscuring the line between art and science, but he let nothing detract him from his belief in nature's dominion over man.[10]

Seton's scientific emphasis on anatomy and motion carried over into the portrait he was preparing for the 1895 Salon competition. But here he allowed his emotions more freedom of expression. *The Pursuit* (or *La Poursuite*), which he submitted in January, 1895, depicts the view from a Russian sleigh of a pursuing wolf pack. This highly improbable though realistic scene was derived from a story that Seton later published in *Forest and Stream*.[11] Its message is rather ambiguous. Perhaps he meant to show wicked men pursued by vengeful wolves retaliating against man's destruction of nature. Or perhaps he expressed a continuing guilt in the death of Lobo: men chased by wolves in a snowy Russian woodland was the antithesis of the sunny New Mexico plains where men chased wolves.

The Pursuit was "highly approved" by Mosler, Gérôme, and others of the academy; to Seton's disappointment, however, the Salon rejected the painting itself but accepted six of his preliminary sketches of individual wolves. Although the jurors obviously liked the wolves in motion, they neither understood the message of the finished product nor liked the impressionistic treatment of the snowy landscape. This acceptance of the parts without the whole was an inadequate consolation for the growing failure Seton had felt since the controversy over *Awaited in Vain*.[12]

Although the subsequent success of *Art Anatomy* helped lift the burden of failure from Seton's shoulders, that very success in a sense contributed to his failure as a full-time artist. Art for art's sake could never be his goal. At the same time, the power and influence of the Julian Academy was waning. Robert Henri and others of Seton's impressionist friends had broken away from its stance on realism and genre, and had branched out on their own. Even Seton's later oils and watercolors show a definite trend toward impressionism.[13] An equally important factor was his increasing interest in photography; over the years, as camera technology improved, Seton would make more use of it than of sketching. After all, he reasoned, photographs demanded much less time and trouble to produce, and they represented wildlife more accurately than did paintings. Above all, he would no longer be required to sacrifice his scientific and moral considerations at the "artistic altar."[14]

Meanwhile, Seton's love life was taking a significant turn. Almost from the time he had first arrived at Paris in 1890, he had been a favorite among several respectable ladies in the Latin Quarter.[15] One particularly outstanding beauty was Caroline Fitz-Randolph, younger sister of Virginia, whom Seton had met when he visited their father's estate. Caroline had attended Wellesley College before becoming "a Bohemian of the Bohemians" while studying art in Berlin and Dresden, and she took a sincere interest in Seton's work, calling him her "kind old philosopher." She especially loved his characterization of Lobo; the wolf, she said, had a "Mr. Hyde sort of sneer."[16]

Nevertheless, Seton seemed to be most attracted to Grace Gallatin. Years earlier, as a gawky, ill-dressed nineteen-year-old in London, he had come to know a lovely, cultured London artist by the name of "Miss H. H. Hatten." He had met her when he was preparing his first competition entry for the Royal Academy in 1879. She was said to be "a very pretty girl of my own age" and reportedly "had a way of seeing and developing the best there was in me." Later Miss Hatten turned up in New York in company with Seton's Canadian art colleagues. Apparently, she was a person to whom the artist-naturalist felt free to express his feelings, but whether she was his "first love" or a mere personification of the ideal woman-on-a-pedestal in romantic fiction is uncertain.[17] Perhaps Grace posssessed many of the same qualities. At any rate, from the time she and her mother arrived in Paris in 1894, she and Seton were often together during the next two years. While he was working on *Art Anatomy*, he boasted of being "her guardian," and during the summers they frequently vacationed in both Paris and London. Grace, in fact, provided valuable aid in the preparation of *Art Anatomy* for the press. Her own literary gifts, in addition to her art appreciation, enabled her to sympathize with his aims. As Seton later remarked, "She recognized the elements of a success when she saw them." In April, 1896, they left Paris

and took passage on the *St. Paul* from Southhampton to New York. On
June 1 they were married at a Presbyterian church in New York, with
Rev. Norman Dix, pastor, officiating.[18]

At the age of thirty-six, then, Seton found his life greatly changed: he
was no longer a roving bachelor, he was seceding from the world of art,
and he was about to launch a whole new career with his pen and voice.
Having cut himself off from the OSA and RCA, as well as from his father, Seton had no compelling desire to go back to Toronto. Accordingly, he chose New York as a home for himself and his socialite bride
and as a base of operations for his wilderness field trips.

CHAPTER 7

Journey to the Yellowstone

As the nineteenth century drew to a close, the trans-Mississippi West became even more prominent in the American imagination. Beginning with the post–Civil War industrial boom, Eastern capitalists looked upon it as a promised land of raw materials to be exploited; other disenchanted Easterners saw a land of unfettered individualism and glorious expanse, the antithesis to their own crowded, elitist environment. Contrary to their antebellum counterparts, Americans in the 1890s believed that two such disparate societies could never coexist; consequently, they sought to reconcile East and West by identifying a nationalistic consensus of values. Their efforts gave the vanishing Wild West an inherent "Americanness," and they became exponents of Western frontier life.[1] Many prominent Eastern intellectuals saw the West in a state of rapid transition and attempted to capture a portion of it before it passed on. In 1892, Elliott Coues, after completing his part of the *Century Dictionary* project, won new fame by editing historic frontier travel journals, including those of Lewis and Clark, Zebulon Pike, Alexander Henry, David Thompson, Jacob Fowler, and Charles Larpenteur.[2]

Ernest Thompson Seton, too, can be listed among the influential chroniclers of the turn-of-the-century West. While his initial contacts with cowboys came a decade later than those of Theodore Roosevelt, Frederic Remington, and Owen Wister, Seton had experienced a small area of the West where cattle ranching was still dominant. Like Coues, he had seen portions of the unspoiled wilderness during boyhood and young manhood. Like Roosevelt, he at first enjoyed the thrill of the hunt (something Roosevelt never got over) but at the same time realized the need for wildlife preservation. Like Remington and Wister, Seton used both the pen and the brush to re-create scenes from the disappearing frontier. And like all of these contemporaries, he saw the West as a land of clean air and renewed vitality.[3]

Unlike most of his contemporaries, however, the values that Seton derived from his Western experiences were neither nationalistic nor based on Victorian morality or Anglo-Saxon supremacy. As a Canadian citizen he looked at American achievement from a slightly different angle; even more, his emphasis on animals rather than humans gave him an entirely new perspective on the West. Seton's all-American hero came to be not the cowboy but the Indian, the very race that the cowboy and his kind disposessed; consequently, many Americans would see him as more of an antebellum romantic, hearkening back to the days of Cooper, Irving, and Parkman.[4] Yet during the late 1890s, Seton's Western field trips—all made in the company of his wife and as a first-class tourist—served to propel him to international fame as a writer and speaker.

Seton's marriage into a wealthy family and subsequent rise as a member of the "new rich" Eastern establishment seemed particularly fitting for one of noble Scottish background. Yet almost from the first, there were major disagreements. While Grace preferred life in the city, "hobnobbing with artists and writers, among receptions and pink teas," he longed for the solitary life in "wildwood surroundings." They decided to compromise by looking for a country house within commuting distance of New York and settled on Sloat Hall, the ancestral home of the De Sloat family near Tappan, New Jersey. This 235-acre estate was located two miles from the Tappan railroad station, which was some twenty miles from New York. While Seton felt that the thirty-room colonial mansion was "ten times too much for my plans," he accepted it as a wedding present from his wealthy mother-in-law. Two days before the wedding, May 30, 1896, Seton gained title to the estate.[5]

Not wishing to live on Mrs. Gallatin's income, Seton sought "remunerative work." He continued to offer his services as a naturalist to the Smithsonian's bird publications and resumed his activities with the AOU.[6] In June, Frank Chapman commissioned him to do the illustrations for his *Bird Life*, a popular pictorial version of his successful *Handbook to the Birds of North America*. For this job, Seton was paid fifteen dollars a day, and it provided a steady income throughout the summer of 1896. The grounds surrounding Sloat Hall contained an orchard, which Seton called a "paradise for birds," and he and Chapman spent many pleasant hours bird-watching by the brook that flowed through the estate. Several of his finished products were displayed at the annual AOU meeting alongside those of Louis A. Fuertes. Seton, with an uncharacteristic show of modesty, declared Fuertes's works superior to his own, but Chapman felt that Seton's possessed "a greater artistic and spiritual quality."[7]

Although they enjoyed entertaining Chapman and other guests at Sloat Hall, the mansion, like their marriage, brought only temporary happiness to the Setons. Neighboring farmers began circulating the story of how twenty years earlier, when two Italian tenant couples shared Sloat Hall, one man was murdered when caught in *flagrante delicto* with the other's wife; the house was thus said to be haunted by the ghost of the victim, a musician, who on certain nights was heard to sing unholy songs. While the Setons shrugged off such superstitions, various noises in the house made it impossible to keep most of their hired help for more than a month. Eventually, Seton discovered a rattling window and other natural causes of the sounds, but by November, Grace in particular had decided that the place was more trouble than it was worth. Accordingly, they vacated Sloat Hall in favor of a fashionable apartment on New York's Fifth Avenue. They subsequently leased the house for a year, then sold it; not long afterward, Sloat Hall and its outbuildings mysteriously burned to the ground.[8]

In the meantime, Seton was enjoying his rise in New York's social circles. His studies on wolves earned him the sobriquet of "Wolf" Thompson. Through his relationship with Henry M. Steele and H. I. Kimball of the Scribner's publishing firm, Seton was one of several important guests invited to a dinner at the New York Players' Club on November 14, 1896. Kimball hosted this formal gathering in honor of Scottish novelist and playwright James M. Barrie, who was living in New York at the time. Among the luminaries in attendance were Frederic Remington, Hamlin Garland, and Theodore Roosevelt. During the course of the banquet, Steele called on Seton to relate some of his wolf stories; Seton happily obliged and became an instant celebrity among the company present. Garland and Roosevelt were added to his lifelong circle of friends.[9]

Seton especially craved Roosevelt's acceptance of him as a fellow naturalist. In the 1880s, when he began sending specimens to the Smithsonian, Seton had been brought into correspondence with other upcoming young naturalists with whom he frequently exchanged animal skins. Among them was Roosevelt, from whom he received bird specimens the former had collected at Oyster Bay, Long Island.[10] Not until the Players' Club banquet, however, did they meet personally. Roose-

velt, serving at the time as the city's police commissioner, was immediately impressed with Seton's wolf hunts and wildlife studies and invited him to speak at the Boone and Crockett Club's annual luncheon at
the Metropolitan Club.[11]

The Boone and Crockett Club was an elite association of amateur
riflemen dedicated to the scientific study and preservation of America's
big game, though not at the expense of "manly sport," and the promotion of further exploration of the West. Roosevelt had founded it in December, 1887, with several of his fellow outdoorsmen, including Owen
Wister, Gifford Pinchot, Madison Grant, Elihu Root, and Caspar Whitney. George Bird Grinnell, a crusader against wanton destruction of
parks and wildlife ever since his experience as a young scientist in the
Ludlow expedition to Yellowstone National Park in 1875, was also a
charter member.[12] As owner-editor of *Forest and Stream*, Grinnell propa-
gated the ideas of the club, which received its formal charter in January,
1888, with Roosevelt as president, a position he held until 1894. From
1889 on, the club wielded considerable influence in Congress. Its members lobbied for the Committee on Parks, which helped create the National Zoological Park, and also worked for passage of the Forest
Reserve Act (1891) and the Park Protection Act (1894), which saved Yellowstone from ecological destruction. In addition, the club was instrumental in the creation of the New York Zoological Society in 1895.[13]

Seton's wolf stories scored a hit with the club members and led to
further speaking invitations and commissions to illustrate their publications.[14] Because of his tendency to play down politics and hunting exploits, however, Seton was never recruited into their ranks; nevertheless,
they liked his contributions to *Forest and Stream* and his stories, often
colored by his uncanny imitations of bird calls and mammal cries. Over
the next few years, Seton supported their efforts to improve the conditions of captive animals in zoos.[15]

Seton soon found a social club in which he could more freely promote his ideas. In 1896, Madison Grant offered the directorship of the
New York Zoological Park to William T. Hornaday. Like Seton, Hornaday was a staunch preservationist who refused to compromise his principles on wildlife issues, even while supporting the measures for which
the Boone and Crockett men lobbied. Displaying democratic initiative,
Hornaday, early in 1897, set about founding a rival association, the
Camp Fire Club of America. Its membership consisted largely of men
who had been excluded from the more cliquish group. Seton was a

charter member of the Camp Fire Club, along with A. A. Anderson, Dan Beard, and G. O. Shields. Several noted businessmen and artists also joined, as well as such authors as Hamlin Garland, Dillon Wallace, and later, Zane Grey.[16]

The Camp Fire Club operated under the strict conviction that animals, especially those in settled areas, had a right to live regardless of their usefulness to man. Their official news organ was *Recreation* magazine, founded and edited by George O. Shields, a Civil War veteran and another wildlife activist. *Recreation* was for a time an effective competitor to Grinnell's *Forest and Stream*, and through it Seton and his colleagues preached their purist conservation doctrines. While it, too, effected social airs, Hornaday's association was definitely less political and more intellectual than the Boone and Crockett Club.[17]

It was through Shields and the Camp Fire Club that the Setons made a memorable outing to Yellowstone Park in the summer of 1897. Seton had been appointed "special correspondent" for *Recreation* with the express purpose of examining the condition of the park's large animal population. Even Grace looked forward to the venture with mounting anticipation as she and her husband purchased camping gear and other necessities for "roughing it" in the wilderness.[18]

The couple took the train from New York to Chicago, where they stayed two days, then made a half-day stopover in West Salem, Wisconsin, to meet with Hamlin Garland. Garland, who was planning a sojourn among the Sioux at the Standing Rock Reservation in North Dakota, accompanied the Setons on the Northern Pacific line to the western plains. Indeed, both Seton and Garland had many common interests in Indian culture and the West in general. Garland especially admired Seton's skill as an illustrator and wildlife authority: "He knew certain phases of the West better than I," Garland later wrote. Not only were they the same age, but both had experienced firsthand the frontier of the homesteaders. Seton had hoped that Garland could rearrange his schedule to accompany them to Yellowstone, but as the latter stated, "I had already arranged for a study of the Sioux, and as his own plans were equally definite, we reluctantly gave up all idea of camping together, but agreed to meet in New York City in October to compare notes."[19] At Miles City, Montana, the two men parted company.

The Setons reached Livingston on June 9 and breakfasted at the Albermarle Hotel. In a journal entry, Seton expressed disappointment at having seen "no game of any kind, large or small, excepting a prairie chicken." From Livingston, the couple rode the Northern Pacific's park branch line to the depot at Cinnabar, where they boarded one of the famous Tallyho stagecoaches for the five-mile journey to the hotel at Mammoth Hot Springs. Undoubtedly, they soon familiarized themselves with the peculiar jargon often used by the park employees.[20]

Yellowstone Park was then under the supervision of the U.S. Army, a move made in 1886 for better law enforcement. The administrative headquarters was located at Fort Yellowstone, established as a one-troop post in 1891 near Mammoth Hot Springs. At the time of Seton's visit, the fort was being enlarged to accommodate two troops of the Sixth Cavalry, whose detachments of two to fifteen men at various "soldier stations" throughout the park were vigilant in the constant fight against poachers and highwaymen. The superintendent was Capt. George Smith Anderson, commander of Troop I, Sixth Cavalry, a West Pointer and a veteran of the southwestern Indian wars. Anderson was faced with several problems, including the attempt to segregate park lands in order to build a railroad line to Cooke City, Montana; the illegal hunting of buffalo by poachers seeking to take advantage of the high prices offered for bison "scalps" by taxidermists; and the poor conditions of the park's roads. However, he tackled them with a zeal characteristic of his Scots-Irish background, becoming known locally as the "Czar of the Yellowstone," and by 1897 he had the park's administration in good order.[21]

Of course, Anderson was more than happy to play host to the *Recreation* magazine correspondent and his wife who alighted from the stagecoach and trooped into the lobby of the National Hotel with the other passengers in their linen dusters and Shaker bonnets. The Setons spent the following day refreshing themselves and taking in the wonders of the hot spring terraces. Certainly, they fit in perfectly with the tourist set of the "gay nineties," for Eastern formality was considerably lessened in this thermal resort. In addition to the natural features, there were the nearby store where one could buy a souvenir spoon to "convince the friends at home that no wonder has been missed" and the photography studio of Frank Jay Haynes, with its elkhorn fence, which had available stereopticon views or postcard prints handsomely produced in Germany.[22] Seton, however, was anxious to get away from the bustle of the resort and into the wilderness where he could find animal subjects for his sketch pad and camera.

Accordingly, the Setons left Mammoth Hot Springs on June 11 in a military wagon provided by Captain Anderson. Accompanying them were Elwood T. Hofer, a noted park scout and guide, and Col. Samuel Baldwin Marks Young of the Fourth Cavalry, who in a few days would succeed Anderson as acting park superintendent. An effective law enforcer, Young was able to continue the smooth operation established by his predecessor.[23] The party followed the old Miners' Road, which ran south and east from Livingston to Cooke City and John F. Yancey's Pleasant Valley Hotel near Tower Junction.

Of all the old Western characters Seton encountered, "Uncle John" Yancey clearly made one of the most lasting impressions. An unreconstructed rebel from Kentucky, Yancey had traveled the West since he was sixteen and numbered among his friends the famous mountain man and Crow chief, Jim Beckworth.[24] In 1882, after a checkered career as a scout and prospector, Yancey had arrived in Pleasant Valley near the junction of the Lamar and Yellowstone rivers and built a hostelry to accommodate teamsters and miners traveling between Cinnabar and Cooke City. By 1897, he had leased ten acres of land and expanded his operations to include a two-story log hotel with a kitchen addition, a saloon and stage station, and a large barn and cowshed. Admittedly, Yancey's Pleasant Valley Hotel was primitive; even Captain Anderson thought it poorly suited for Eastern guests. Nevertheless, Uncle John had enjoyed the patronage of several notables, including Owen Wister and senators George Vest and Boies Penrose. Indeed, he gladly accommodated anyone brave enough to stay and stomach the swill he served for food, especially his homemade "Kentucky tea."[25]

Arrangements had been made through Elwood Hofer for the Setons to occupy a tumbledown log shanty near the main hotel building. This abandoned cabin had fallen into disrepair, and with the proprietor's permission, Seton began at once to make it habitable, using materials from a nearby scrap lumber pile. The price agreed upon for room and board (including meals) was five dollars a week, plus extra for horses and laundry. In all, the Setons stayed there nearly two months.[26] Even Grace took the crude "pioneer" lifestyle in stride, especially whenever there were other tourists—many simply camping out in tents—for company.

Seton wasted no time in beginning his explorations of the area, traveling on horseback to seek out wildlife and enlisting the services of Elwood Hofer and another old-timer, Dave Roberts, as guides.[27] He was especially interested in checking the numbers of elk, buffalo, and other large game in the park. While there were some of these animals in corrals for the tourist's pleasure, nothing equaled the thrill of seeing a herd in the wild. Around Junction Butte, Seton had his first encounter with pronghorn antelope and their white rump "heliographs," which flashed in the distance as tiny white specks. Once he sketched a baby antelope hiding motionless in the grass atop the butte,[28] and also attempted to photograph animals with his "cameo," as Roberts, in his Western slang, called the Kodak. They once came upon some elk grazing near Tower Falls, but the wind was blowing from the wrong direction, and the skittish herd "fled clattering, reeling and crashing" at the men's approach. Occasionally noticing buffalo skulls strewn across the meadows, Seton's guides recalled the time not long gone when buffalo had been abundant in every valley.[29]

While most visitors to Yancey's lodgings emphasized the crude conditions, Seton concentrated on the animal life around the place. He studied the string of beaver ponds and dams on nearby Lost Creek, marveling at the work of "nature's engineers." Behind the hotel was a ridge of broken rocks inhabited by marmots, where Seton and his wife secured what were among the first photographs of "whistlers" in the wild. Always the experimenter, Seton once caught a skunk in a box tap and, without exciting his quarry, carried it to his makeshift "studio" enclosure to photograph it. No one but Grace was willing or daring enough to help, but the experiment was successful, and Seton released the animal the next morning. From that time on, the skunk and its mate were regular night visitors to the shanty. Seton often left them food scraps and later pointed out how their scavenging habits helped to clean up the garbage.[30] Perhaps his most memorable story from the sojourn at Yancey's concerned a mongrel pup named Chink, whose owner was a park employee. Chink often proved a source of amusement to the campers in his vain attempts to catch the picket-pin ground squirrels whose mounds dotted the area and in his humiliating encounters with a sly coyote that often lurked about the garbage pile.[31]

Seton kept a detailed list of all the birds and mammals he found in that vicinity, compiling them for articles he was preparing for *Recreation* magazine. At the same time, he had his first real experience with oral history, for it was here that he interviewed several notable old-timers. He became acquainted with, in addition to Yancey, J. H. "Old Pike" Moore and Adam "Horn" Miller, prospectors, guides, and buffalo hunters who had been in Montana since the gold rush days of the 1860s;

Tazewell Woody, former "forty-niner" and long a favorite scout in the Yellowstone region; and Tom Duffy, a stagecoach driver later hired by Buffalo Bill's Wild West show. During his Deadwood Stage days, Duffy had made a harrowing solo run through a blinding blizzard in March, 1882, the very same storm in which Seton had been snowbound on the train to Winnipeg.[32] Seton lovingly drew all these representatives of times past in his sketchbook. He also met "Calamity Jane" Canary, the legendary heroine of the dime novels he had read as a boy, who had recently obtained permission to sell postcard pictures of herself in the park. Seton wanted to sketch her as well, but "Jane wouldn't pose."[33]

Intermittently, Seton enjoyed the company of A. A. Anderson, his old friend from Paris days. A few years earlier, Anderson had come to the Rockies for a change of pace and had purchased choice acreage on the Graybull River, southeast of Yellowstone Park. Here he built up a substantial herd of cattle and started breeding horses as well.[34] As a fellow Camp Fire Club member, Anderson was well aware of Seton's mission; he made it a point to call on him and even furnished the artist-naturalist's party with extra horses. Seton and Anderson spent many relaxing hours fishing and camping in the wild. On this outing, the tycoon-portraitist had with him his little daughter Lizzie, who amused Seton when she called cowbirds "cowboy birds." On July 6, Anderson and the Setons attended, by invitation, the farewell banquet for the retiring superintendent at Mammoth Hot Springs.[35]

Having completed his observations in the northern areas of the park, Seton and his party left Yancey's on August 1. Although he had a few disagreements with Uncle John concerning prices for meals, since their stay had been lengthy, Seton thereafter held the crusty proprietor in high regard.[36] After following the Yellowstone River and its spectacular canyon, the travelers passed by the Mud Volcano, a natural wonder that Seton considered abominable: "They talk of the mouth of hell; this is the mouth with a severe fit of vomiting," he later wrote. Indeed, he took little interest in geysers and "any of the abominable cavities of the earth that nature so plainly meant to keep hidden from our eyes." At Yellowstone Lake, with its unfinished hotel, the Seton party met Sen. J. N. Sallinger and his wife, with whom they fished and picnicked.[37]

So far, Seton was disappointed at not having seen any of the bears for which the park was famous. Colonel Young, however, assured him that plenty were to be found at their next stop, the Fountain Hotel. Built in 1891 to accommodate 350 guests, the Fountain was noted for its hot springs, baths, and formal balls. Its most famous attraction, however, was its daily bear-feeding. At about six o'clock each evening, the hotel employees dumped the kitchen garbage some hundred yards behind the building, and in a few minutes ten to sixteen bears would appear for their supper. Like many observers, Seton realized that such "entertainment" ultimately could be detrimental to both bears and people;[38] nevertheless, he had a wonderful time sketching and photographing the ponderous creatures. Although most of the species he recorded were black bears, a few grizzlies also ventured by; Seton even noted one female black bear that did battle with an old male grizzly to protect her young. Since many of the bears were "regulars," the hotel staff had given them names. It was here that Seton became acquainted with Old Grumpy and her sickly, lame cub Little Johnny, whose story he later told.[39]

While her husband spent his hours at the garbage heap, Grace "did the conventional thing and saw the sights." After a week at the Fountain, the Setons took the long day's ride north back to Fort Yellowstone and Mammoth Hot Springs. On the way, at Golden Gate Canyon, the naturalist made his initial acquaintance with the small creatures known as conies, or "rock rabbits," which built their nests in the jumbled piles of boulders. Summing up his experiences in Yellowstone, Seton admitted that "it was solely the joy of being among animals that led me to spend all one summer . . . in the Wonderland of the West."[40]

The trip was far from over for the couple, however. At Billings, they took the Burlington and Missouri River line to the Crow Reservation in southeastern Montana. Like Garland, Seton harbored a special fascination for the Plains Indians and wanted to spend some time among them, although by mid-August his schedule did not allow for a lengthy stay. The entire visit lasted less than two weeks, but that memorable fortnight had a significant impact on Seton's life.

At the Crow Agency headquarters, the Setons were greeted by the acting agent, Lt. J. W. Watson, and noted artist Elbridge Ayar Burbank. Trained at the Chicago Art Institute and in Munich, Burbank had been commissioned by his uncle, Edward E. Ayar, first president of the Field Columbian Museum of Chicago, to do a series of portraits of prominent Indian chiefs.[41] He proved an accommodating host to the Setons and showed them the rise above the Little Bighorn, dotted with white markers, where Custer and his men had fallen in 1876. Watson furnished horses for the three-mile ride to the site, and despite her lifelong experience in riding, Grace's mount proved exceedingly difficult to handle. On the return trip from the battlefield, her rawboned bay suddenly bolted nearly all the way back to the stables. Grace managed to stay on and was unhurt save for her dignity. The next day, Burbank took the Setons on a five-mile bicycle ride to a grove of "dead-trees," cottonwoods in which the Crows interred their dead. Coming upon one wrapped mummy that had fallen and been partially "exhumed" by coyotes, Burbank extracted from it some brass rings and a wooden armlet, which he presented to Grace. While Seton searched the grove for wildlife, Burbank climbed a tree to examine other corpses. Minutes later, two Indians rode up and warned the trio not to "touch 'em." Realizing the Crows' sensitivity, the party bicycled back to the agency "like spanked children."[42]

During the next few days, Seton interviewed some of the old Crow scouts who had participated in the ill-fated Custer campaign. One outstanding individual was White Swan, a brave who had been maimed as a result of wounds suffered while on a scouting mission for Custer. Being deaf and dumb, White Swan communicated in the sign language known by all Plains tribes. Never pensioned by the federal government for his services, he managed to eke out a living selling pictographs of himself and animals. Seton not only bought many of his art pieces, but became his willing student in the art of sign language.[43]

Seton collected other Indian artifacts as well. After purchasing some buckskin from a local trader, he commissioned Lottie Shoestring, an adept seamstress, to make him a beaded war shirt. Lottie had earlier made a similar shirt for Gen. Nelson A. Miles, then U.S. Army chief of staff, who, despite his service record, had long been in sympathy with the Indians. In Burbank's studio, Seton painted a portrait of Lottie's husband, a prominent Crow named Sharpnose. He also examined the Indians' tepee lodges and the various designs that decorated them.[44]

Seton was outraged at the injustices that the government's white employees were imposing on their Indian charges. While he was there, a company of troops from nearby Fort Custer surrounded the tepee of Gray Wolf (or Hairy Wolf), a Crow subchief, and forcibly took two of his children away to the agency boarding school "according to law." During the next few days, tension filled the Crow camp as Gray Wolf and his friends staged a protest meeting to denounce this outright kidnapping.

Seton became further incensed at the attitudes and actions of the local missionary, the Reverend Mr. Burgess. A young Episcopalian minister recently graduated from seminary, Burgess was appalled at the Indians' dances and other "pagan orgies." Friction erupted after Clifford White-Shirt and Lottie Jack-Knife, a young Crow couple, asked him to marry them in a Christian ceremony. Halfway through the service, Burgess suddenly noticed the groom's long plaits of hair and refused to go on until White-Shirt had shorn them. When Seton, who witnessed the proceedings, boldly intervened on the Indian's behalf, the ceremony broke up, and the couple subsequently was married "after the manner of their own people in the way of the long ago."[45]

One outstanding personality on the Crow Reservation was the colorful chief Plenty-Coups, named for his warbonnet of eagle feathers, one for each valor, or coup, that he had earned during his earlier years as a young brave.[46] A gifted speaker, Plenty-Coups calmed the tempers of Gray Wolf and his friends, dispelling any thoughts of open rebellion they might have been harboring; he urged them instead to have patience and fight their battles through legal channels. Perhaps witnessing this dramatic display of Indian oratory inspired Seton all the more to join the growing roster of Indian sympathizers. Later, he and Burbank paid a visit to the country store that Plenty-Coups managed. Seton became intrigued with the chief's crude but ingenious bookkeeping system: under a totem for each customer, a pencil stroke indicated each dollar that customer owed.[47]

Word of Seton's kindness to the Little Bighorn veterans, as well as his stand against the missionary's legalism, had spread rapidly throughout the Crow camp; before their departure, the Setons were invited by Plenty-Coups to be guests of honor at a Grand Council in his tepee. At the ceremonial, Seton was welcomed as the distinguished stranger who loved and understood the wild things. In sign language, he expressed his acceptance, declaring that he and his wife had traveled "for three sleeps" to make the chief's acquaintance. A squaw then handed Plenty-Coups an elaborately decorated soapstone pipe lit with a coal, with which he blew four smokes to the Four Winds (representing the four directions). He then handed it to Gray Wolf on his right, who repeated the process, then to White Swan on his left, and so on down the line in a zigzag fashion. Despite the pipe's foul smell, Seton did his part dutifully. Finally, it was passed to Grace, who was seated near the tent door. She remembered it as "the nastiest tasting and smelling thing that ever got into an unwilling mouth," but even she performed the ceremony in a diplomatic manner. After all, it was an honor to have the

Great Spirit "accept greeting from the paleface squaw." When their train left the agency on September 3, the Setons felt a new appreciation for Plenty-Coups and his race. As Grace said later, "Long may he couch on sage brush, talk in sign language, and write in pictograph: Civilization has nothing to teach him."[48]

The Setons' last stop on their tour was at Medora, North Dakota, in the heart of the Badlands. Practically a ghost town by 1897, Medora was the product of the Marquis de Mores, an ambitious French nobleman whose ranching and meatpacking empire had petered out as a result of falling prices and the terrible blizzard of 1886–87. Consequently, he had departed, leaving behind his slaughterhouse and spacious "chateau."[49] His most famous neighbor had been Theodore Roosevelt, who came in 1883 to improve his health, hunt game, and try his hand in the "beef bonanza." With several partners and characteristic tenacity, Roosevelt had established two ranches, the Maltese Cross (or Chimney Butte) and the Elkhorn, on the Little Missouri River some twenty miles apart from each other. Like de Mores, Roosevelt found his ranching efforts curtailed by the economic recession and the "Winter of the Blue Snow."[50] Yet his influence remained strong: he had helped organize the Little Missouri Stockmen's Association, and he continued to use his Elkhorn cabin for annual fall hunts before selling out entirely in 1898.[51]

It was into this world of dudes and cattlemen that the Setons set foot on September 5, 1897. They were greeted at the Medora depot by another Badlands pioneer, Howard Eaton. Eaton had first come to the Badlands from his native Pennsylvania in the fall of 1880 to hunt along the Little Missouri, already advertised as a sportsman's paradise. The following year, Howard and his brothers Alden and Willis returned, and with his old hunting guides established the Custer Trail Ranch at the confluence of the Little Missouri and Davis Creek, about five miles southwest of Medora, naming the ranch for its position on the trail of the fatal 1876 Little Bighorn expedition.[52] Friends and associates of de Mores and Roosevelt, the Eatons had also suffered heavy losses in the hard winter and therefore turned the Custer Trail into the West's first dude ranch enterprise, playing host to numerous Eastern sportsmen and tourists.[53]

The Setons were soon added to the Eatons' guest roster after they made the five-mile ride to the ranch. Grace described the main house as "a large two storey affair of logs, with a long tail of one storey log outbuildings like a train of boxcars." Several other eastern guests were staying at the Custer Trail, but as Grace pointed out, the cowboys "were better mannered than the two New York millionaires' sons who had been sent there to spend their college vacation and get toughened." That evening in the ranch house's dining hall, some of the Easterners reportedly made Seton "apologize for keeping his coat on during dinner."[54]

Seton was delighted to accept the Eatons' invitation to join them on a wolf hunt. The main target was Mountain Billy, a cunning wolf whose notoriety among the Badlands ranchers equaled that of Old Lobo in New Mexico. A known cattle raider since 1894, Billy's monstrous tracks had been found many times along the river bottoms and about the ranch buildings early in the mornings. Even the Eaton children claimed they had seen Billy while riding to school, but no one had had a chance to get a shot at him. Dogs were afraid to follow him, and like Lobo he was too clever for traps and poisons. The center of Billy's range was Sentinel Butte, and it was toward that rugged formation that the twelve-member troupe headed on the morning of September 6 with a chuck-wagon and nine dogs. Among these mixed canines were a few sleek thoroughbred greyhounds that the Eatons kept for running coyotes, and a white bull terrier that was a real scrapper whenever a quarry was brought to bay. That terrier further showed its mettle on the first night out when it killed a long-tailed weasel, thus preventing serious injury to a cowboy who had accidentally bedded down too near its lair. Seton skinned this prime specimen and took the hide back with him.[55]

During the next two days, the Setons and their hosts observed antelope and mule deer, which often distracted the fleet greyhounds. In his heart, the naturalist was glad that the rough terrain was advantageous to the bounding hoofed mammals, enabling them to escape the hounds.[56] Overall, Seton was impressed with the rugged beauty of the Badlands, deeming them "the most bewildering . . . fantastic formations I ever saw." Grace, on the other hand, called them "arid horrid miles of impish whimsical nature." Her main recollection of that hunt was the intense summer heat. Indeed, midafternoon temperatures topped one hundred degrees; the dogs could not run, and one reportedly died from heatstroke. Even the muddy waters of the Little Missouri looked like an inviting drink. Grace's only animal trophy was a rattlesnake, which she killed with a frying pan. Mountain Billy easily eluded the weary party, and Seton simply recorded in his journal, "wolf hunt unsuccessful."[57]

The disappointment of the hunt was superseded the following day by the semiannual roundup of cowboys from the Custer Trail and neighboring outfits. Grace, in an adventurous mood, got her first experience as a "cowgirl" when she insisted on accompanying the hands to the roundup early in the morning. Upon tasting firsthand the dust and drudgeries of herding cattle, however, she afterward declared that she was never again tempted by the "rough riding and adventures of the Calamity Jane order." Seton, meanwhile, spent most of the morning compiling notes and observations. Later in the day, he and several other guests arrived on the scene, two miles from the ranch house, in time for the noon meal, followed by the cutting out and branding of the calves.[58]

On September 10 the Setons left Medora for Chicago, where the naturalist went to the Field Museum to view its extensive collections and deliver his weasel specimen.[59] Back in New York, he finished compiling his reports and submitted them to G. O. Shields. His six-part series, "Elkland," appeared in *Recreation* from September through the following February. These articles reveal that while Seton longed for a more simple past, he also planned for the future, expressing ideas on how best to preserve the few remaining wilderness areas. He was especially interested in new proposals concerning the creation of more national parks to serve as wildlife sanctuaries.[60]

At the same time, he recognized the historical significance of events as remembered by the old-timers he had encountered. He considered their oral history an "endangered species" and felt that historians should record their stories of the frontier as they lived them. He criticized the magazines for concerning themselves mainly with "trifling diplomatic and political events overseas" at the expense of what was occurring in this nation's development. In a burst of Turnerian rhetoric, Seton remarked: "This westward march of the white race has at last been completed, and a vast empire finally wrested from a weaker race. Thus, though the fate of a continent of land, untold treasures of gold and millions of human beings decided within two generations—after thousands of battles and thousands of deeds of incredible heroism on both sides, it has not yet occurred to the average historian that here is any event worth writing about."[61]

Certainly others shared Seton's feelings. Theodore Roosevelt was especially anxious to hear more of the artist-naturalist's visit to his old Badlands haunts. Much of what Seton expressed in his "Old Timers" article was inspired by Roosevelt's multivolume history, *The Winning of the West.*[62]

Seton especially wanted public awareness of the Indian, his importance in history and his current plight. Having earned the confidence of the Crows, Seton declared that he would one day publish their version of the Indian wars. His antipathy toward the federal government's reservation policy having been fueled, he began collecting quantities of information to support his admiration of Indian customs. At this point, however, his interest in Indians did not translate as easily to the printed page as did his knowledge of animals. Reservations could never do for Indians what sanctuaries did for wildlife.[63]

Seton's blending of nostalgia with his pleasure in the present and future of the American West is best stated in the following extract from a journal entry:

> Here by the campfire we sit . . . amid the historical scenes in this ancient land of the Crows. . . . Here I am gathering the fragments of their past history . . . and while hearkening to wild tales of the mountains and of the past there comes over me a strange feeling of sadness that almost shapes itself into question, 'Why was I born too late?' Then common sense reminds me that the glamor of memory and romance is over it all; that twenty years from now the present will wear the same charm for the younger men, and that after all, the best, the very best of all times is the living present.[64]

CHAPTER 8

A Traveling Storyteller

Soon after his return from his paid vacation, Seton received word of the death of his mother in Toronto. As a result, the controversy surrounding the family name came to a head once more. In 1877, while Ernest was still in high school, his father's widowed sister had immigrated to Toronto and joined the Thompson household. She allegedly tried to persuade Joseph to assume his titular rights, but his "constitutional dislike of effort" curtailed any action on his part. Two of the older brothers subsequently adopted the hyphenated surname "Seton-Thompson" and in February, 1883, Ernest completed legal steps in assuming the full name of Ernest Evan Thompson Seton. It was under that name that he produced his first articles and illustrations. However, several of the brothers did not like the idea of the family divided by different surnames and reportedly expressed their disapproval to their mother, who coaxed Ernest into using the name Thompson for as long as she lived. Although reluctant to do so, Ernest complied and later compromised by adopting Seton-Thompson as a nom de plume. After Mrs. Thompson's death, however, her son felt himself released from his promise.[1]

The issue was further complicated by Msgr. Robert Seton, then rector of St. Joseph's Catholic Church and School in Jersey City and later archbishop of New Jersey. An amateur genealogist, Robert was allegedly a distant relative and was regarded as "the historian of the family." In February, 1898, Seton attended the annual banquet of the New York Genealogical Society by invitation of the Scribner firm's new art manager, Samuel W. Marvin. There he had the opportunity to become acquainted with his clerical kinsman, who at the time was preparing a history of the Seton family in Scotland and America. Certainly, the monsignor was interested in the artist-naturalist's possible connection. During the course of their conversation and in subsequent correspondence, Robert claimed that all the Setons were sportsmen and had literary gifts; therefore, Ernest was "a true scion of the line and impelled by its best tradition and interests."[2]

Although his mother's passing enabled Seton to use what he deemed his rightful name, he had already taken out several copyrights in the earlier form. Nevertheless, he personally considered the Thompson surname defunct. In an interview, he remarked, "Certainly never with my approval am I addressed as Thompson; that is like calling a man Gregor when his name is MacGregor."[3] He prudently decided to have the matter cleared in the courts, which meant a long, slow process. Finally, in November, 1901, the New York Supreme Court ruled in his favor—but as Seton later quipped, "I've been kept explaining the confounded thing ever since."[4]

Despite such controversy, Seton was well on his way to the top as a popular writer. Seton had found, in addition to *St. Nicholas* magazine, another outlet for his animal narratives in a new juvenile publication called *Our Animal Friends*. He also continued turning out articles for *Forest and Stream* and *Recreation*.[5] His first publication for *Scribner's* magazine, "The Birds That We See," had secured for him still another major outlet, and the subsequent success of "The King of Currumpaw" caused that publisher to encourage him to produce more. The February, 1898, issue of *Scribner's* carried the story of Silverspot, based on Seton's observations of crows in Canada.[6]

Seton's next step was the publication of several magazine stories in book form, a common practice among popular authors. After gathering and revising eight of these stories, he sent them to Scribner's; in July, 1898, the contract was signed and the copyright secured in October. *Wild Animals I Have Known* was a best-seller. The two thousand copies of the first edition sold within three weeks and by the end of the year three more printings had been sold out. Such instant success was due mainly to growing public awareness of the danger of wildlife extermination. Seton's confession of guilt in Lobo's death, in particular, received an overwhelmingly sympathetic response. C. Hart Merriam thought all the stories quite entertaining: "That rabbit kick [in the story of Raggylug] will surely go down to posterity as a masterpiece," he wrote. Other authors agreed. Mabel Osgood Wright, whose book on mammals Seton illustrated, was awed by his love for the primitive. The power of his tales, she declared, came from the fact that he had *lived* the wild life. And Joel Chandler Harris, author of the Uncle Remus tales, said of *Wild Animals*: "I was afraid to read it owing to the fact that I am engaged on some animal autobiographies to be embodied in a successor to the Thimblefinger books; but the pictures were so alluring in the first place and the text in the second, that I could not help myself—and now I am afraid folks will find traces of Thompson [Seton] in my stories. Well, if the traces are read, 'twill be all the better for me." The book's success led to a permanent contract between Seton and Arthur H. Scribner, the head of the publishing firm.[7]

To advertise his book, Seton started his tours on the lecture circuit in the spring of 1898. From its humble beginnings, the Chautauqua movement had expanded to become the most significant venture in American popular education. Through its International Lyceum and Chautauqua Association, thousands of culture-starved communities were reached as local associations sprang up nationwide,[8] and Seton took full advantage of the movement in promoting himself and his works. Private clubs in New York paid as much as a hundred dollars to have him speak at their functions. Never merely reading his stories, Seton instead talked freely and acted them out, and he soon discovered that his powerful voice and "stage presence" could hold an audience for an hour or more. During 1898 his lectures took him to Washington, D.C., where war fever was rising over the crisis with Spain, and to the Chicago Art Institute, where he captivated his audiences with the story of Lobo. William M. R. French, director of the Institute, told Seton afterward that he could "repeat that lecture as often as you please" and, prophetically, that it would be popular for generations to come. Later, French wrote that Seton's "Picturesque Side of Wild Animals" was the most popular of that year's lecture series. J. A. Allen also commended Seton's performance as unique, "as good as it was novel," and a credit to the Linnean course.[9]

Before long, swamped with requests for lectures nationwide, Seton began arranging engagements through professional managers and regional lyceum bureaus. One interested person was James B. Pond, who numbered Mark Twain and Henry Ward Beecher among the luminaries whose speaking tours he managed. Having attended one of Seton's lectures incognito, Pond eagerly obtained for Seton a contract stipulating that all Seton's expenses would be paid, plus six hundred dollars a week. Pond booked Seton's engagements the remainder of his life. Over the next several years Seton booked his tours through various American and Canadian agencies; in England, he already had a reliable manager in the person of Gerald Christy, whom he commended for his honesty.[10]

Certainly, the engagements meant being away from home, sometimes for weeks at a time, but they greatly boosted the sale of his books and

ensured his financial independence. For the rest of his life, Seton was
monetarily in "easy circumstances." Although life on the road was often
hectic, his body and voice "grew stronger," and his renditions were
noted for their clarity, even in large auditoriums. George Seton Thompson proved a valuable aid in his brother's endeavors. From his Chicago
printing shop, George produced ads and circulars for distribution
through the Chautauqua Bureau.[11] Thus, while Theodore Roosevelt
was galloping to glory as leader of the Rough Riders, Seton was enjoying his own rise to fame as an eloquent storyteller.

The pressures of arranging and keeping speaking dates heightened
the naturalist's desire to escape into the western wilderness from time to
time and reap "a harvest of observations." On August 17, 1898, the Setons succumbed to his "mountain madness" and left New York; ten days
later, they met Howard and Alden Eaton at Medora, where they passed
the night and learned that Mountain Billy was still at large. Continuing
west through Montana, the Setons found lodging at the "hotel" on
the shore of Grays Lake, Idaho.[12] There they made final preparations for
a wilderness pack trip through Wyoming's Wind River country. Grace
came fully prepared for this journey, even to a riding skirt of her own
design, and in anticipation of wet weather, the whole party had not only
slickers but also saddle covers designed by A. A. Anderson. As Grace
later remarked, "I do not rough it; I go for enjoyment and leave out all
possible discomforts."[13]

On the morning of August 29, the Setons left Grays Lake in a celerity
wagon, which contained their supplies and equipment. The two-day
ride to the Jackson Hole country was delayed by several hours when the
driver lost his bearings. Grace never forgot one night at a log hostelry
run by a Mormon family. "The history of our brief stay there belongs
properly to the old torture days of the Inquisition," she wrote, "for the
Mormon's possessions of living creatures were many, and his wives and
children were the least of them." The next day, they crossed the rugged
Teton Pass and dropped down into the lush valley beyond, fording the
winding Snake River four times in the process. During the last cross-
ing, the wagon became stuck momentarily, and the Setons almost lost
part of their gear to the raging current. Finally, about midnight on August 31, the weary travelers reached the Leeks Ranch near Jackson, Wyoming, and received a hasty supper.[14]

The ranch was one of several in the Jackson Hole area. Some had earlier played host to Owen Wister and other notables. After observing

area game and fishing the streams and lakes for a few days, the Setons moved on to the ranch homestead of J. Pierce Cunningham, a few miles south of Jackson Lake and in the shadow of the magnificent Grand Tetons. Mrs. Cunningham, who "had been imported from the East by her husband," was an excellent cook and a gracious hostess. Twice a week she served as a vicinity's postmistress by handling the mail to and from Jackson, thirty miles to the south. While at the Cunningham Ranch, Grace, with the help of her husband, successfully trailed and shot two bull elk with her Winchester. Subsequent feelings of remorse were dissipated when Mrs. Cunningham, who was impressed by her shooting ability, treated her guests to a meal of elk steak, "the most delicious of meat when properly cooked."[15]

Late in September, A. A. Anderson arrived from his ranch with two men and a pack train of sixteen horses. The Setons were amazed at this "westernized" Eastern tycoon who felt "equally at home in a New York drawing-room or on a Wyoming bear hunt" and who "had made mountain traveling a fine art." Starting from Jackson Lake, the party left the Teton Valley and crossed the Continental Divide over the often trackless Wind River Mountains. More than once, Seton strayed away from the group while stalking elk and other hoofed mammals and, finding himself lost, had to "regulate" his fears and rely on his own tracking ability to find his way back to camp. This area was a haven for grizzly bears, the bane and challenge of all men who lived and hunted in the northern Rockies. Seton was especially fascinated by the "sign posts" these bears made with their claws in establishing their territory. Battling treacherous cliffs, bone-chilling winds, and early mountain snows, the party continued over the Shoshone Range into the Bighorn Basin, a favorite hunting area of Theodore Roosevelt and William Hornaday. Here Grace added a pronghorn antelope to her list of animal trophies.[16] Here, too, Anderson and the Setons witnessed a rare drama of nature when a young pronghorn buck suddenly dashed in among the horses to escape a larger male rival. Seeing the human intruders, the victor ran off toward its harem of does, while the loser, after regaining its wind, fled in the opposite direction. The only other witness to this scene was a golden eagle perched on the rocks nearby. Seton afterward felt himself a fellow creature with the vanquished antelope.[17]

Seton encountred more colorful Western types in the persons of Anderson's two hired packers. He described the horse wrangler as "a typical old-timer mountaineer . . . content to live his life and do his bit without talking about it." In contrast, the trail cook, whom Seton later dubbed Hank Fry, was a former cowboy with a questionable past. In his heyday as a mustanger, he had ridden the ranges from New Mexico to North Dakota, often one step ahead of the law.[18] Once, when Grace was alone in camp, Fry gave her a shock when he boasted of his wild exploits, which included a prison record and at least three killings to his credit. Later, when she scolded her husband for leaving her alone with the "multi-murderous cook," he was said to have replied, "Humph! Do you think I don't know those wild mountaineers? They are perfectly chivalrous, and I could feel a great deal safer in leaving my wife in the care of that desperado than with one of your Eastern dudes."[19]

On October 8, after recrossing the Divide and spending three days and two nights in a raging snowstorm, the exhausted party arrived at Anderson's Palette Ranch. Located on Piney Creek, a tributary of the Graybull River near the Meeteetse Rim, the ranch was situated "150 miles from the railroad, 40 miles from the stage route, and surrounded on the three sides by a wilderness of mountains." The nearest town was Meeteetse, whose saloon won considerable notoriety in Anderson's eyes. The ranch's dominant feature was the main house, built of logs. Its interior, however, was more reminiscent of European hunting lodges. The living room had a stone fireplace and was decorated with tapestries, fur rugs, and hunting trophies; the guest room featured silk-sheeted beds, softly glowing lanterns, and a crystal mantelpiece from Japan. Even the bathroom was tiled. Grace was particularly impressed with someone "who can thus blend harmoniously the human luxuries of the East and the natural glories of the West."[20]

In addition to his horses and cattle, Andrson raised wolfhounds and other hunting dogs. He also kept tame animals, including some buffalo given to him by his friend "Buffalo Bill" Cody, and he allowed no hunting within a twelve-mile radius of the ranch. The Setons agreed with their host that this place was one of the "most delightful in the world," and one of the most healthful.[21]

Anderson's next-door neighbor was another noted Wyoming pioneer, Col. William D. Pickett. A cousin to Gen. George Pickett of Gettysburg fame, he too had served the Confederacy as a private secretary to Jefferson Davis. At the close of the Civil War, Pickett moved west to recover from the "camp fever." Over the years, he had built up substantial cattle holdings on the rich grasslands of the Graybull. When the U.S. government established a post office in the vicinity, Pickett became its postmaster. He named it Four-Bears after lying in ambush one night and killing four grizzlies on that spot. It was Pickett who had helped Anderson establish his claim and build up the Palette Ranch. Although the two men had had occasional disputes over game laws and grazing rights, these were resolved after barbed wire was introduced to the area. From the colonel, Anderson learned many techniques of hunting and trapping the ferocious "silvertips," as the grizzlies were sometimes called.

Noting Seton's interest in bears, Anderson and Pickett told him stories about Wahb, a huge grizzly that had been menacing their livestock off and on for several years. Indeed, the Setons had noticed certain signs in the woods along the Graybull that betrayed the great bear's presence, most notably his track, which "looked big enough for a baby's bath tub." More than once, Anderson had attempted to trap Wahb—so named by the Shoshones because of his light color—but without success. Wahb's exploits became legendary among the valley residents. One of his favorite haunts not far from the Palette was a sulfur spring, which he reportedly used as a "bath." Yet not even Colonel Pickett, considered one of the West's most successful bear hunters, had been able to bring down the Meeteetse giant.[23]

The Setons spent several days at the Palette, enjoying the mountain air and scenery (as well as their host's French wines) and attempting to extract more "priceless secrets" from the wilderness. With signs of an early winter becoming evident, however, the couple boarded the train at Billings on October 20 for the return trip to New York.[24] Weary of unpredictable mountain weather and riding over treacherous trails, Grace was especially glad to be back in her element again.

For her husband, their travel experiences had supplied more ideas for short stories and books. Later, he expressed his admiration for the old mountaineers, giving a few pointers on how to best approach these oral sources of history and folklore:

It is always worth while to cultivate the old guides. Young guides are often fresh and shallow, but the quiet old fellows, that have spent their lives in the mountains, must be good or they could not stay in the business; and they have seen so much and been so far that they are like rare old manuscript volumes, difficult to read, but unique and full of value. It is not easy to get them to talk, but there is a combination that often does it. First, show yourself worthy of their respect by holding up your end, be it an all-day climb or breakneck ride; then at night, after the others have gone to bed, you sit while the old guide smokes, and by a few brief questions and full attention, show that you value any observations he may choose to make. Many happy hours and much important information have been my reward for just such cautious play.[25]

Even then, Seton admitted, not all old-timers could be persuaded to talk about themselves. "The life of solitude and the lack of social intercourse have decivilized and repressed their natures," he explained in an interview. "It is the tendency of living too much with Nature to become silent and to remain dumb concerning all that one learns from her."[26] In light of that statement, Seton perhaps saw himself more clearly as a "middleman" between the wilderness and the city and thus felt all the more compelled to reveal what contemporary man could, like the Indians and white frontiersmen, learn from the natural world.

CHAPTER 9

To the West Coast

Back in New York, Seton resumed his busy lecture and writing schedule. He completed the manuscript of a second book, *The Trail of the Sandhill Stag*, for Scribner's in the summer of 1899. At the same time, he began preparing a third manuscript on the exploits of Wahb, the Meeteetse grizzly, and contacted Frank H. Scott, president of the Century Company, to discuss its publication. *The Biography of a Grizzly* first appeared as a three-part serial in *Century* magazine and later in book form.[1]

Through the Camp Fire Club, Seton's ideas on improving conditions in zoos made significant headway in the New York Zoological Society. His advice was sought not only by William Hornaday and Madison Grant, but also by Samuel P. Langley, secretary of the Smithsonian, who supervised the completion of the National Zoological Park in Washington. Impressed with Seton's reports and recommendations, Langley eventually published them in the Institution's annual report. In addition, Seton and fellow club member Dan Beard proposed the establishment of an American school of animal artists, for whom the New York Zoological Park would provide a nucleus of models. Such a move would not only augment the existing knowledge of native American species but also help to displace the traditional emphasis on "exotic" species from Africa and Asia. Although the heyday of the animalier had passed, Hornaday acted on Seton's suggestions and pushed for artistic facilities. As part of that move, Seton graciously lent the society many of his original drawings, including those from his *Art Anatomy*. One member praised them as "the best ever issued."[2]

By the summer of 1899, Seton was ready to go west again, this time on the first of his transcontinental lecture tours. Leaving New York on August 1, the Setons caught the Canadian Pacific line at Winnipeg. (Grace later recalled their amusing experiences with ten pounds of blackberries and two large bouquets of sweet peas delivered to their Pullman sleeper by well-meaning friends.) Stopping over in Carberry, Seton looked up old friends and visited old haunts. While he undoubt-

edly noted further depredations of "progress" in his beloved prairie
province, his wife had a rather different reaction:

Everything even yet looks so immodest on those vast stretches. The clumps of
trees stand out in such a bold brazen fashion. The houses appear as though
stuck on to the landscape. Even an honest brown cow cannot manage to melt
herself into the endless stretch of prairies. In fact, the little scenic accidents of
trees and hollows, which mean fruit and flowers, are mainly due to man.

From Carberry, the Setons continued across the plains of Saskatchewan
and Alberta to the mountain resort of Banff. Here they spent four days
exploring and observing wildlife among the towering pinnacles, woods,
and glaciers of the Canadian Rockies. Among other things, they attempted to track bighorn sheep but soon discovered that horses were
not as surefooted on glacial rockslides as their intended quarry. Arriving
at Vancouver on August 21, they took the steamer across the Inside Passage to Victoria, British Columbia's capital, on Vancouver Island.[3] At
each stop along the Canadian Pacific route, Seton talked with hunters
and taxidermists, making notes and sketches of their specimens and trophies. In Victoria he visited the natural history museum and made special arrangements to observe the caribou herds on the Queen Charlotte
Islands.[4]

Moving down the Pacific Coast, Seton gave talks at Seattle, Tacoma,
and Portland. In California, he spoke on the Berkeley campus of the
University of California and crossed the bay to see the sights of San
Francisco. One place of interest was Union Coursing Park, where he observed greyhound racing, with jackrabbits as their quarry. He was also
invited to lecture at some of the city's private business clubs. There he
became acquainted with members of California's literary echelon.[5]

The zoos in San Francisco were of particular interest to Seton. He
was appalled at the prisonlike cages used for bears and other large animals at the zoo in Golden Gate Park and became particularly sympathetic with Monarch, a huge California grizzly from the Tehachapi
Range south of Bakersfield. A known killer of cattle and sheep, Monarch had been the zoo's primary attraction ever since his well-publicized
capture by Allen Kelly, features editor of the *San Francisco Examiner*, in
1889.[6]

One unusual personality whom Seton met was Louis Ohnimus, a veteran mountaineer and former superintendent of the defunct Woodward
Zoological Gardens, who had helped Kelly snare Monarch with inge-

nious pit traps baited with meat. A humane individual, Ohnimus declared that he was able to keep his animals healthy and happy for the sixteen years the zoo was in existence by emphasizing animal companionships and dividing their daily meals "to give them something to think about," thus breaking the day's monotony. Unfortunately, when the zoo closed down, all the animals were ordered shot in their cages. Seton incorporated many of Ohnimus's ideas into his own recommendations for zoos.[7]

From the Bay Area, the Setons went to Grace's hometown of Sacramento to visit her father, Albert Gallatin. A business associate of Collis P. Huntington and Mark Hopkins, Gallatin had, among other things, numerous mining interests. His circle of friends included Joseph Steffens, a partner in a local paint and oil firm and the father of the muckraking journalist Lincoln Steffens. The Setons undoubtedly saw the Victorian mansion where Grace had spent her childhood before her father sold it to the elder Steffens in 1888. Steffens sold the house in 1903 to the state of California, which made it the governor's mansion.[8]

On September 2, the Setons took the train to the gold mining town of Placerville, accompanied by Louis Ohnimus and Frank Powers, a San Francisco attorney and rancher, who with his wife had met the Setons at the Berkeley depot. On the way, the combination freight and passenger train stopped at a peach orchard long enough for Seton and his companions to harvest choice fruit from "California's cornucopia." At Placerville, the party outfitted for a pack trip into the rugged Sierra Nevada. Seton hoped to see grizzlies, but the local sheriff's report that these bears were "very rare" was discouraging. A buckboard and horses for the trek were furnished by the Powers Ranch just outside of town.[9]

The road into the Sierra Nevada was dry, and soon everyone was caked with blinding, choking dust. Powers and Ohnimus explained that this trail was used by area sheepmen and their flocks, and the Setons soon realized why so many cattle ranchers came to despise sheep as the "lowest level of brute creation."[10] For the moment, the naturalist agreed that sheep drives should be regulated "so many to the square mile." His guides went on to say that the herders were "an ornery lot, mostly Mexican trash." Such statements proved more factual than prejudiced, for shortly thereafter the party came upon a large flock of sheep. As they passed the bleating mass, a small mongrel dog, which looked as though it had been mistreated, joined up with the travelers. Seeing the animal's condition, the Setons had no heart to drive it away. That evening, while the men were off scouring the woods, the swarthy Mexican sheepherder suddenly confronted Grace and demanded the dog's immediate return. In response to his threatening gestures, Grace unsheathed her rifle and ordered him off. Uttering a barrage of "hog Spanish," the sheepherder retreated. Ohnimus stood guard that night to make sure he did not return.[11]

The pack trip lasted nearly three weeks and took them to the Mount Tallac area southwest of Lake Tahoe. It was on this excursion that the Setons awoke one morning to discover the tracks of a mountain lion that had sneaked past the sleeping group and stampeded the horses the night before. Another evening, when encamped near a herd of cattle, the men tried milking a cow but discovered that the milk was tainted with blood and threw it out. After everyone had retired for the night, the silence was suddenly broken by the bellow of a bull working itself into a frenzy over the spilt milk. Here the mongrel proved itself a real cow dog by helping to drive off the enraged animal. Powers and Ohnimus followed, brandishing their weapons, and returned to assure the Setons that the bull would not come back. The party camped one night at the Calaveras "Big Trees" (giant sequoias) and another in the Nassau Valley.[12]

At the conclusion of this wilderness sojourn, the travelers returned to the San Francisco Bay Area. Seton, in addition to speaking at Stanford University and other places, found time to observe the seals from the Golden Gate. On October 2, under arrangements made by his sponsors, he visited the "grand old man of the Sierras," John Muir, at the latter's home in Martinez. "I found the old gentleman coldly aloof and little disposed to converse," Seton recalled, "choosing to talk of his own discoveries among the glaciers." However, when Seton correctly identified some tracks in Muir's garden as those of coyotes, the old nature philosopher "was most genial and accepted me as one of the real brotherhood." The two men discussed Muir's books before the Setons left to continue their tour.[13]

Stopping over in Fresno, Seton interviewed several old pioneers from the gold rush era. At Bakersfield, where he gave a lecture, Seton met James M. McKenzie, a former Texas Ranger who had ridden from Eagle Pass south to Durango in 1852, taking note of the wildlife in that vicinity. Seton was especially enthralled with tales of McKenzie's bear-hunting exploits in California during the 1860s. His techniques had been passed on to his son, James, Jr., who with a friend had successfully hunted down Old Clubfoot, a notorious killer grizzly, in the mountains of Kern County during the previous summer. At a nearby ranch, Seton was shown Clubfoot's skin, and he made observations of game animals before going on to Los Angeles and Pasadena for more lecture engagements.[14]

From California, the couple rode the Santa Fe line across the desert to the booming hamlet of Flagstaff, Arizona. Since they wanted to see the Grand Canyon, they put up at the rambling, two-story Palace Hotel, which was "far from being a palace." Grace later described their impressions of Flagstaff's false front architecture: "Then does man erect a structure of his on [nature's] surface, as a fleck of soot mars a beautiful woman, putting up a false front, painting its pine boards to look like brick and its pine furniture to look like mahogany, papering its walls to look like marble, curtains that imitate lace, a melodian that imitates a piano, tissue paper that is cut and twisted into shameless shapes of flowers in an imitation Worchester vase—nothing honest but the fly-paper and the spittoon." Seton had hoped to explore the San Francisco Peaks area above Flagstaff, but his efforts were hampered by mixed snow and rain that turned the town's streets into "rivers of slush."

The wild, seventy-mile stage ride to the Grand Canyon was one that the couple never forgot. Seton had hired a private carryall, or mud-wagon, that was pulled by a team of "four half-broken mustangs whose principal endeavour seemed to be to stay off the ground as much as possible." At each of the two stage stations along the way, the horse were changed—not without struggle, for they "represented many bloods but principally cayuse." The driver explained that these fresh steeds were being broken to harness for the next year's tourist season. It was with great relief that the Setons arrived at the log hotel on the Grand Canyon's South Rim.

The next morning dawned cloudy and misty, but the Setons stepped out in their rain gear and waited. At midmorning the fog lifted, revealing the grandeur of the canyon. Overwhelmed, Seton composed his impressions in poetry before he and Grace set out for a horseback ride along the rim. They had wanted to ride down into the canyon, but Bright Angel Trail was "out of repair and dangerous" because of the recent rains. As they were saddling up, a small group of Apaches came by, selling badger skins, baskets, and beadwork. "It is good to be here," wrote Grace prophetically, "before the railroad and the funicular to the bottom and the modern hotel and all the tiresome civilization that is sure to come, and before the Indians gave us Greek beadwork . . . the savages out-savaged.[15]

Leaving the canyon on October 15, the Setons endured the jolting stage ride once more. The following day, they set out for the next lecture date, in Denver; then, after a few days observing wildlife on the eastern slope of the Rockies, they left for home. In all, the roundabout trip had covered more than ten thousand miles and lasted slightly over two months.[16]

The 1899 journey was significant to Seton in that it set a precedent for future cross-country tours; field trips into the wild were usually made in conjunction with his schedule of speaking engagements. More important, the journey enabled him to establish influential contacts on the West Coast and to generate new ideas for stories. From his Fifth Avenue apartment, Seton continued turning out manuscripts, negotiating contracts with publishers, and planning more lectures. By 1900 he was so widely in demand as a speaker that he reluctantly had to decline a few invitations.[17] His popularity was further boosted by the publication of his wife's first book, *A Woman Tenderfoot*, which recounted many of their travel experiences from her perspective. The book ranked high on the popularity list and helped establish Grace as a writer in her own right.[18]

Although Seton deemphasized his studies in ornithology during this time, he maintained his contacts with the AOU. In 1899 Frank Chapman launched *Bird-Lore* as the official voice of the National Audubon Society. As the number of local Audubon chapters grew, their reports became too numerous for inclusion in the *Auk*, a strictly scientific journal, so *Bird-Lore* became the magazine of popular ornithology. Seton occasionally contributed humorous bits of poetry concerning the mythical origins of various species.[19]

In the summer of 1900, the Setons made an overseas tour to Norway to observe reindeer herds and study the Laplanders' methods of domesticating them. While examining these Old World relatives of the caribou, Seton undoubtedly recalled his first encounter with a "tame" caribou bull he had attempted to sketch at Madison Square Garden in 1889, courtesy of the Barnum and Bailey Circus. He had decided from that amusing experience that this antlered creature was "a strange mixture of wariness, erraticness and stupidity." What perhaps prompted him to make the Norway trip (in addition to his wife's wishes to go back to Europe) was the successful effort of Sen. Henry C. Teller and others in introducing Lapland reindeer to Alaska as part of a domesticating program in 1896.[20] Believing that such a program would succeed in establishing the caribou as a range animal, Seton probably wanted to study the animals and their behavior patterns himself. In addition, while touring the land of the fjords, he picked up many old Scandinavian folktales that he incorporated into some of his animal stories, most notably "The Legend of the White Reindeer."[21]

In the course of his travels, Seton had seen the West being transformed by the influx of railroads and big business. He had seen the cities of the Pacific slope become urban cultural oases. He had seen wealthy, affluent migrants displacing the earlier pioneers and promoting civic growth from their elegant hotels and Victorian homes.[22] He had likewise seen the domination of the cattle kingdom by Eastern capitalists and the resulting changes, open ranges and unspoiled wilderness areas fast disappearing as farmers came by the drove to turn the West into the nation's food basket. He had seen living relics of the passing frontier and heard their tales of days when wild game abounded. Now game animals were being either killed off or forced to retreat to public parks and private preserves. And while the animals themselves were falling victim to sportsmen's guns, their forest homes were falling victim to the axes and sawmills of lumber companies. Seton had seen it all. While he was one of the many affluent tourists visiting the wonders of the West, and while his wife came from the family of civilization's boosters, Seton was determined, through his writings, to preserve that vanishing past for posterity.

CHAPTER 10

Animal Outlaws

While Seton was attaining popularity as a public figure, trends in American thought seemed to move in his favor. At that time the United States, particularly the urban areas, contained a highly stratified society, both economically and socially. Although interclass conflicts temporarily subsided during the Spanish-American War, they again emerged after 1900 and once more threatened the nation's unity.

The predominant assumption in Western thought at the turn of the century was that all life, whether human or animal, was more or less predetermined. Many upper-class Americans embraced the theories of Herbert Spencer, who argued that free competition and the survival of the fittest were just as basic for society as they were for nature. However, there were others who envisioned a universe in which almost everything could be challenged and changed by human reason. Pragmatists like William James and John Dewey argued that though there were natural laws for animals and plants that could not be broken, man, on the other hand, could shape his society and environment to suit his interests.[1]

These clashing streams of thought were reflected in the authors of the so-called "new literature." Compared with previous literary trends, the works of authors like William Dean Howells, Frank Norris, Jack London, and Theodore Dreiser tended to be more urban-centered, less limited to middle-class characters and themes, and more consciously environmental. Their characters were early "anti-heroes" rather than prime movers, and their determinism veered away from that of the nineteenth century. Quantitatively, the new literary movement showed an attitude of indignation as its authors delved into such touchy themes as politics, religion, and science. Few of the great writers readily accepted Hamlin Garland's notion that fiction should reflect life and show its unpleasant sides in order to transform society; however, a host of lesser talents eagerly plunged in and added their voices and pens to the spirit of reform. Thus Alfred Kazin could call this spurt of literary realism "a history of grievances."[2]

Ernest Thompson Seton was a bright star among these "lesser talents." He had attracted a large enough reading audience to become a best-selling author, and his lectures helped all the more in that respect. Indeed, Seton's writings contained elements of the two underlying Progressive streams of thought, enabling him to attract both mainstream and outlying regionalist (sometimes radical) authors. He was a great believer in Dewey's "perpetual open frontier," with its emphasis on creativity. He embraced the new "social gospel," which preached that men were basically more alike than different and were by nature inherently good. He was anti-Spencerian in his belief that unmitigated competition, rather than rewarding the best, might select the least ethical. Overall, Seton supported the popular belief that science itself was the ultimate in self-government and that the scientific spirit, in the words of Walter Lippmann, was "the discipline of democracy, the escape from drift, the outlook of a free man."[3] Yet throughout his animal stories, Seton's retention of traditional determinist-environmentalist thought clearly shows. Man's presumed dominion over nature was, in his eyes, clearly illusory.[4]

The publication of *Wild Animals I Have Known* helped establish the realistic animal story as a new literary form. Ever since his first nature essays for *St. Nicholas* in 1887, Seton had gradually shifted his style from mere fable and folklore to a biological, deterministic stance. In so doing, he adopted the standard Canadian approach of attempting to view life from the animal's perspective. While he considered his stories scientifically accurate, he did mix fact and fiction in order to give his reading audience dramatic introductions to particular animals. Essentially, his main message was that man had a special kinship with the beasts; therefore, the latter should be enjoyed and respected, not destroyed. On his wilderness field trips, Seton recorded precise details of animal appearance and behavior. Previously, however, the naturalist had found it difficult to restrain the artist, who wanted to dramatize an animal's "heroism," or the moralist, who sought to interpret wildlife behavior. His quasi-factual stories proved to be the perfect vehicle for all three concerns. In developing his style, Seton frequently tended to push beyond the limits of scientific accuracy and embellish details for the sake of his art. While the scientist uses a word to mean only one thing, the artist uses a word as a symbol with many meanings. In this use of language, both artistically and scientifically, Seton may be seen as a sort of historian, recording accurate details about animals but placing his facts in a pattern to suggest interpretation. Yet he denied writing fiction or moral parables, insisting in his prefaces that his stories were "literally true." Seton was soon to discover that certain of his scientific colleagues were unprepared to grant such poetic license.[5]

The question of how much Seton "humanized" his animal heroes has been a subject of debate among literary analysts in recent years. Critics have either praised or belittled his works, with no apparent middle ground.[6] The secret to his hybrid of literature and natural history, however, lies in the simple fact that Seton was well aware of the contemporary literary trends. In several instances he simply borrowed the styles of his peers and applied them to his own.

Seton's dog stories, for example, emphasize the standard themes of the dog's faithfulness to its master and its role as a "middleman" between the wild and tame aspects of nature. In the story of "Bingo," the dog hero seems to be degenerating into a wolfish lifestyle when he joins a pack. Yet he remains true to his master and keeps the wolves away when the narrator (who is Seton himself) is caught in the traps. The dog-master relationship is further exploited in the story of "Chink." Here, the master's first love is his "pard," despite the dog's foibles, but the price of that loyalty is Old Aubrey's job in Yellowstone Park, for in helping Chink he breaks a man-made law. Seton's experience with the Eaton brothers' bull terrier inspired in part at least two well-known tales. "Snap" represents animal nature harnessed by man to help him subdue his environment. Although the ferocious Snap seems unmanageable at first, he proves useful when given a wolf-hunting job for which his breed was meant, and he loyally follows that job to his death. In the tale of "Billy, the Dog That Made Good," Seton plays with the Tolstoyan theme of destiny and circumstance producing the hero. At the most critical moment, Billy shows "the stuff that a good bear dog is made of," while the Terrible Turk, a pit bulldog, proves "a bully, a coward, a thing not fit to live." Both Snap and Billy have proved themselves good bull terriers, earning love and respect from their masters. Unlike Jack London, Seton neither evades tragedy nor slips into "a celebration of the hunter's world." "Wully" is the exact opposite of London's "White Fang": because of human neglect after his separation from old

Robin, Wully degenerates into a Jekyll-Hyde sheep killer and dies violently after his last owners uncover his double life.[7]

Although not all of Seton's animal tales are set in the West, much of his style is strongly influenced by the literary images of the West prevalent during that time. Occasionally, he uses wild animals as villains: the "Mephistophelian" coyote of "Chink"; Old Reelfoot of "Billy, the Dog"; and the Kogar Bear of "Foam." More often, however in attempting to illustrate man's conflicts with nature, he characterizes such carnivores like formula western outlaw heroes. For instance, while carrying a personal admiration for Lobo, whom he lauds as a "grand old reprobate," Seton realizes that the wolf's destructive habits are detrimental to the ranchers' means of livelihood and thus seeks to end his marauding ways. Such conflicting viewpoints reflect, to some extent, his own persecution complex. These animals are outlaws because man, by his paradoxical mixture of cruelty and kindness, made them that way; thus, conflict is inevitable. Some of these outlaw heroes, like Tito, Domino, and Badlands Billy, ultimately win their battle against man and his dogs. Others, like Lobo and Garou, the Winnipeg Wolf, die fighting for their freedom. Monarch, because of his weakness for honey, ends up a caged prisoner.[8] Vixen, the devoted mother of "The Springfield Fox," gives her captive pup poisoned bait to save it from a "fate worse than death" before departing for parts unknown. Wahb, plagued most of his life by unfriendly animals, hard winters, and man's traps and rifles, becomes a sullen loner "with neither friendship nor love." Afflicted in his old age by rheumatism and tricked by a lesser bear into giving up his territory, he chooses a classical "Roman" death by asphyxiation when he walks into Yellowstone Park's Death Gulch.[9] Whatever their end, Seton is clearly in sympathy with his animal outlaws, who are seen as victims of circumstance and their very natures. They, like their "West," die out.

The familiar Western themes of the chase, confrontation, and retribution are also frequently used by Seton. Examples include the "barbarous" fox hunt, in which the heroic Domino makes his escape, while the sheep-killing mastiff, Hekla, floats off to a well-deserved end. King Ryder, the wolfer in "Badlands Billy," gets his just deserts when the wolf he had orphaned sends his pack of hounds over the cliff to their doom. The most graphic example of a Western-type "showdown" is the last stand of Garou, the Winnipeg Wolf, at the slaughterhouse; the telephone, representing civilized man's technology, proves the key factor in enabling the "posse" of men to locate the outlaw and turn the dogs on him. Surrounded at last, Garou heroically battles his howling adversaries before falling to the hunters' guns.[10]

Not all of Seton's dramatic confrontations end so violently. This is particularly true of his treatment of certain herbivorous mammals, some of which are almost redemptive "cosmic beasts." In *The Trail of the Sandhill Stag*, when Yan finally confronts his intended quarry face to face, he realizes that he cannot kill this harmless, glorious creature. Love and respect for nature triumph over the hunting instinct; his inner conflict is resolved, and he accepts the limitations of his intimate knowledge fatalistically. Unlike Yan, Scotty MacDougall in "Krag, the Kootenay Ram" is crazed by his lust for the hunt and its trophies as he stalks the bighorn. But after he succeeds in killing his prey, Scotty's overwhelming guilt leads to his destruction at the hands of the "Mother White Wind" in the form of an avalanche. Such stories contain a spiritual and mystical quality. Like Herman Melville's *Moby Dick*, they are effective in driving home the theme of nature's uncompromising aspects, something Seton earlier expressed in his painting, *Awaited in Vain*.[11]

Most of Seton's human characters are undesirable types, and their world is anathema to animals. Wolfer Jake, the tipsy cowboy of "Tito," is a far cry from Wister's or Remington's noble knights of the Western ranges; so is "Wild Jo" Calone, who sets the story of the Pacing Mustang in motion with his cowboy dialogue. Both Jake and Jo have a weakness for whiskey and thus squander their pay on a good time with the boys.[12] Certain ethnic stereotypes also appear throughout Seton's works. Fiddler Paul in "The Winnipeg Wolf" is representative of the brutal, villainous Métis so common in Canadian literature, while Pedro and Faco Tampico in *Monarch* reflect the cowardly, shiftless "greaser" image of Mexican-Americans. The cockney Jap Malee and his cohort Negro Sam, in "The Slum Cat," are urban versions of the Duke and the Dauphin, Mark Twain's conniving river rascals in *The Adventures of Huckleberry Finn*.

Through such degenerate folk, Seton expresses his contempt for the prevalent attitudes of his time. These personifications of materialism and industrialism seek to devour the pristine wilderness and the natural order of things that his animal heroes represent. The cattle and the sheep of the Western range are seen merely as "four-legged cash," and the men who herd them as vanguards of the urban-industrial society, with all its ills, soon to follow. Because of his high connections, Seton often found it better to express his opinions through "conventional" attitudes, such as the traditional Westerner's view of sheep, animals which he once called "grumbling hoofy locusts." Yet his underlying motives are evident; he once stated: "I am not a sheep owner and I do not love sheep. My sympathies are all with the forest."[13] Sometimes he purposely assumed the role of the civilizer: the first-person narrator of "Snap" is a barbed-wire salesman. Whatever position he took, however, Seton always emphasized the Westerner's homespun philosophy. He never failed to express the outdoorsman's appreciation for his domestic animals and their importance to his occupation. At the burial of Snap, who is fatally wounded by the wolf he has slain, the dog's rancher owner remarks: "By jingo that was grit—c'lar grit! Ye can't raise cattle without grit."[14]

Double meanings and symbolism are evident. The horns of Krag, the Kootenay Ram, are not merely a prized hunting trophy; they may also represent the vast wealth and innumerable secrets of the natural world which humanity so greedily attempts to exploit. "The Slum Cat" is not just the tale of an ordinary stray cat (the conglomeration of Seton's cat observations in Toronto and New York) who makes it by sheer pluck and luck; it is a lighthearted commentary on American society, particularly on the gullibility and shallowness of the rich and their failure to understand the masses. Outwardly, the cat becomes a pedigreed "Royal Analostan" and is thus admitted to the elite rank of "patrician" cats that get the first pickings from the liver man. But at heart, she is still a slum cat, and nothing can ever change that.[15]

The truly outstanding human characters in Seton's tales are the children and young people, whose impressionable minds and love for mystery allow them to enter part of the natural world. Little Jimmy Hogan, the abused son of the saloon owner, is the only friend of the Winnipeg Wolf. Likewise, Lizette Prunty is the only human who can touch the usually ferocious razorback boar, Foam. Sometimes such youngsters are instrumental in winning certain of their adult peers over to their side. Bob Yancey's little daughter prevents her frustrated father from getting rid of Silly Billy, thus enabling the pup to prove his mettle later. An extreme example of child-animal unity is the story of a seven-year-old boy who becomes lost on the prairie and survives for three weeks by sharing a den with a badger.[16] In the tale of Domino, young Abner Jukes is at first overcome by his desire for the chase, but after he witnesses the fox's dramatic escape and begins courting the gentle Garden-girl (who has earlier saved Domino from the horde of hounds and hunters), the "shadow" is removed; no longer does he see the silver fox merely as a valuable pelt.[17]

Occasionally, Seton plays with the Progressive-Turnerian themes of patriotism and free individualism. In one scene, the Garden-girl lovingly prevents Domino from raiding a wild turkey's nest by surrounding it with metal objects, which the fox associates with traps. The objects she uses are chain links, a broken plowshare, and a horseshoe—symbolizing friendship, labor, and luck, all essential ingredients of the American dream. The clearest reference to these themes appears in the story of "Little Warhorse." After the jackrabbit hero is captured in a rabbit drive and sent to a coursing park, he gains the admiration of Mickey Doo, an Irish-born jack trainer. With the boss's consent, Mickey vows to set Warhorse free after he outshines the greyhounds thirteen times. To show this, the Irishman uses a gatekeeper's punch to stamp the rabbit's long ears with stars, one for each achievement. "He is won his freedom loike every Amerikin done," he quips. However, the boss reneges for monetary reasons and persuades Mickey to run Warhorse once more against two new hounds. Just as the exhausted rabbit is about to be done in, Mickey intercedes and turns Warhorse loose on the prairie. The trainer's closing remark, "Shure an its ould Oireland that's proud to set the thirteen stars at liberty wance more," reflects the fierce patriotism of both Irish and Americans.[18]

Seton makes widespread use of local color, and many of his characters are based on real people whom he met during his travels. Colonel Pickett, for example, is instrumental in setting the story of Wahb in motion and remains a prime mover throughout the action. Frequently, Seton changes or plays around with names: the Penroof brothers in the narratives of Snap and Badlands Billy are the Eatons; the Chimney-pot Ranch, which figures prominently in "Tito," is Roosevelt's Chimney Butte; Lan Kellyan and Lou Bonamy, the captors of Monarch, are Allen Kelly and Louis Ohnimus.

Seton was always interested in what finally became of the heroes of his tales. In 1902, he learned that Mountain Billy's pelt was finally taken near Sentinel Butte by Montana cattleman G. W. Myers. Three years later, on a return visit to the zoo at Golden Gate Park, Seton was pleased to find that Old Monarch, whose frustrated desires for freedom he had compared to a dammed-up river's flow, had mated and sired two healthy cubs.[19] Admittedly, Seton was not always historically accurate as to the

real fate of some of his animal outlaws; old Wahb, for instance, was finally shot by A. A. Anderson, who displayed the carcass in his studio.[20]

While Seton borrowed heavily from European classical and romantic
genres, one outstanding feature of conventional western lore was popularized in his story, "The Pacing Mustang." The hero is a wild black stallion who makes himself a nuisance by running off several mares belonging to area ranches in eastern New Mexico. The conflicts between man
and nature come into play as "Wild Jo" Calone and his fellow cowboys,
stimulated by a five-thousand-dollar reward offer in Clayton, seek to either kill or capture the Pacer and stop him from adding to his "harem."
They finally manage to retrieve the mares by "walking" them to exhaus-
tion, but the Pacer, like so many outlaw stallions of lore, seems possessed of supernatural stamina.[21] The honor of capturing the mustang
falls to an unlikely old saddle tramp, Tom "Turkeytrack" Bates, who in-
geniously snares his quarry at a water hole by using his brown mare as
bait. But the Pacer, like Lobo, will not give up his freedom and chooses
a suicidal death by leaping off the wall of Piñabetitos Canyon. In a later
version of the tale, the stallion takes his captor with him. As Seton explained: "At this, the close of the great heroic age of the West, it seemed
the proper ringdown for the last great scene—the magnificent horse,
the peerless old horseman, the symbols of their kind, meeting in heroic
and final stance, in tragic double sacrifice."[22] While Seton was certainly
not the originator of wild mustang lore, his "Pacing Mustang" probably
influenced Zane Grey and other writers to use the theme.[23]

Although his animal tales are not true "formula" westerns, Seton in
his own way sought to preserve for his readers one aspect of the West
that by 1900 was rapidly dying. He knew that technological changes
were inevitable, but because of them, his beloved natural world was in
danger of vanishing for good. Along with the lone mountaineers and
gunmen of other western authors, Seton's animal outlaws have emerged
as larger-than-life heroes of a bygone era.

Nearly all Seton's books featured his unique marginal drawings, done
like cartoons in a comic strip. He experimented with various artistic
styles, sometimes departing from realism for more dramatic effect. His
full-page illustrations, on the other hand—featuring dramatic action scenes and portraits of the animal heroes—stuck closely to detailed
realism.

Grace proved a valuable aide in her husband's literary endeavors. A staunch believer in his works, she was often busy with pencil and ruler, arranging the marginal drawings and doing artistic decorations for his latest publication. She not only was his chief critic but also managed the finances and helped widen his market by treating publishers and lecture managers to dinner or tea.[24] Seton dedicated *Wild Animals I Have Known* to her, giving her the rather masculine pet name of "Jim" and featuring a caricature of her riding a fiery steed. What inspired such a nickname is uncertain, but judging from some of his writings and correspondence, it must have been a term of endearment.[25] In the main, Seton also supported her views on women's rights and her rise in feminist circles. He encouraged her writing talents and, on occasion, attended some of her women's organization meetings, particularly those of the Pen and Brush Club, an exclusive group of women artists and authors of which she once served as president.[26]

In Grace's accounts of their travels, *A Woman Tenderfoot* (1900) and its sequel *Nimrod's Wife* (1907), the reader is presented a more conventional "Eastern city" view of the West and its wilderness, with only passing mention of Seton's wildlife interests. Grace gave her husband the name "Nimrod" after the ancient Biblical king who was "a mighty hunter before the Lord"—appropriate for one who was always hunting the innumerable secrets of wilderness. Like him, she assumed literary license in playing around with names and combining episodes from several trips into one. Despite certain differences of opinion, the Setons enjoyed traveling, and throughout their earlier years together their marriage seemed secure—although one literary critic remarked: "It is only Mr. Ernest Seton-Thompson's own remarkable personality and talent that keep him from being known as 'Mrs. Seton-Thompson's husband.'"[27]

Seton's animal stories made a significant impact among his reading public, particularly the youth toward whom they were directed. Many authors and editors, as well as young readers, considered them far superior to Rudyard Kipling's *Jungle Book*. One twelve-year-old boy who had read both authors was asked which one he liked better. He replied, "Well, I like the Jungle stories; I think the animals are fine, but the animals in the other book [*Wild Animals I Have Known*], you know, are *real!*"[28] Even Kipling himself, who read some of Seton's earlier works and became acquainted with the author in 1898, could not deny that statement.[29]

The secret to the overwhelming success of Seton's tales lay in the fact that they showed an undying faith in both the young and the aged. Child instinct, he reasoned, is closest to that of animals, thus allowing for a mystical unity; the elderly, such as old Indians and frontiersmen, have realized their limitations and are thus able to find their way back into the land and culture from which they grew.[30] Moreover, traditional family values are evident in these stories; children and their elders could easily identify with loving, devoted mothers like Molly Cottontail and Vixen. For these reasons, Seton's lectures as well drew widespread response, and when he spoke, auditoriums were filled, sometimes to capacity, with adoring children and their parents. One boy in Colorado Springs sent the artist-naturalist a photograph of himself and an accompanying note "as a token of gratitude for the many pleasant and instructive hours spent with you." Even Theodore Roosevelt's children absorbed Seton's books. At Sagamore Hill his sons named "one brown cock and hen" among the chickens "Lobo" and "Blanca."[31]

Seton's success quickly led to additional outlets for his work. Frank N. Doubleday, a promoter of the arcadian myth, viewed Seton's progress with mounting interest; before long, Seton considered Doubleday a friend and potential publisher. Edward Bok, editor of the *Ladies' Home Journal* and vice-president of the Curtis Publishing Company, was also aware of Seton's popularity with children. A sharp businessman with an eye for quality and a sense of family tastes, Bok had published works by such leading authors as Mark Twain, Kipling, and Garland. By 1900 he had increased his magazine's monthly circulation to 800,000, eclipsing that of any other American periodical, and in time Seton was included on Bok's list of contributors.[32]

It was for Bok that Seton first published his "Wild Animal Play" in 1900. This charming piece of creative drama was reportedly suggested by some children who asked for help in playing the characters in *Wild Animals I Have Known* and *Biography of a Grizzly*. Seton designed the animal costumes, and composer Daniel Gregory Mason wrote an original score for this skit, which was meant strictly as an amateur production. Climaxed by the fall of the evil Sportsman at the hands of the fairylike "Angel of the Wild Things," the message of this poetic presentation was clearly the same as that of the stories that inspired it. Kipling, not to be outdone, completed an animal play a year later, which allegedly reflected Seton's formula.[33]

Five years later, Seton's famous Wild Animal Quilt design appeared in the *Ladies' Home Journal*. He and Grace had supposedly obtained the idea for this pattern in 1897 from a woman in Montana "who was raising the idea of a whole quilting sisterhood by introducing forms of flowers as decorations." The Indian-style patterns of plants and animals were blended into a color scheme whose general effect was soft and pale like the Yellowstone landscape. Seton agreed with Bok that such a design, which required expensive silk, would be difficult to manufacture but have considerable market value.[34]

The most noted "fad" in which Seton's stories had a hand came about after the publication of "Johnny Bear." This tale, which appeared first in *Scribner's* magazine and then in his second short story collection, *Lives of the Hunted*, concerns a sickly Yellowstone bear cub who is literally "spoiled" to death by the well-meaning Fountain Hotel employees.[35] In December, 1901, when Seton told this story to the students of Bryn Mawr College as part of a lecture on the animals of Yellowstone Park, Little Johnny made such a hit that the graduating class adopted him as their mascot. Then one of the students, it is said, went to a toy shop in New York and asked manufacturer Morris Michton whether he could make a score of little woolly bears. The toymaker gladly accepted the proposition and soon found a ready market for the new products. The following summer, Teddy Roosevelt, by then president, went on his famous bear hunt in Mississippi after settling the anthracite coal miners' strike. His refusal to shoot a lame brown bear his party had caught was well publicized, especially by *Washington Post* cartoonist Clifford Berryman. This new publicity prompted Michton to name his toys "teddy bears"—and the rest is history.[36]

CHAPTER 11

Wyndygoul

Seton's fame had its price, as he admitted in a letter to Elbert Hubbard, the noted New York wit. In attempting to meet the demands of his busy schedule, he was nearly always swamped with work. "I undertook one or two things under the impression that there were thirty days to the month and twenty-four hours to the day," he wrote, "but that, I find, is a thing of the past."[1] Nevertheless, he enjoyed his laurels, which enabled him—among other things—to improve and expand his living conditions.

In 1900 the Setons moved to a spacious apartment and studio in A. A. Anderson's Beaux-Arts building on the corner of West Fortieth Street and Sixth Avenue in New York.[2] The walls of their airy abode, which overlooked Bryant Park, were decorated with Seton's artwork. On his shelves, carefully arranged under various headings, were his voluminous collections of scientific works, journals, and photographs; in one corner was the head of a bighorn ram that could easily have been a model for Krag. There Seton labored for as much as sixteen hours a day. "It is not the kind of home I would have chosen for myself," he remarked, "but with my desk and drawing board before me, I ignore the rumble of the elevated train."[3]

At the same time, Seton's newly acquired wealth enabled him to find suitable acreage in the country on which he could build his kind of home. The tiny community of Cos Cob, facing the harbor at Greenwich, Connecticut, was an old colonial fishing village "strung along one side of one long street." A short commuter trip on the New York, New Haven and Hartford Railway out of the city, Cos Cob became a favorite colony for aspiring artists and writers at the turn of the century. These young hopefuls had only contempt for the established rich who were mainly concerned with business and politics, preferring the townspeople and fishermen who "fitted into the land- and seascapes." As Lincoln Steffens observed, the village with its surrounding woods was a good place to "think it out and put it down."

Since 1898, Seton had looked at several possible sites in the Cos Cob woodlands, where some property sold for as little as ten dollars an acre. His search for the right spot sometimes led him on long walks and more wildlife observations. Lincoln Steffens, who was seeking a tract of his own, often accompanied Seton on these "real estating" jaunts, and the journalist later recalled:

> I suppose "childlike" is the word most people would use to describe the animal sense he had for springs, water courses, trees, plants and shady nooks that we saw. Real estate men and the natives could not understand what he saw in tangled swamps and hopeless woods. They preferred land that had at least been cleared. . . .
> Seton saw in land, not only what a painter looked for, but for the animals. "How deer would love that," or squirrels or owls.

Steffens found pleasure in taking walks and buggy rides with the artist-naturalist. From Seton, he gained "a new interest in nature."[4]

In 1900, Seton finally purchased portions of three abandoned farms on a 120-acre tract less than an hour's commute from New York. He named the place Wyndygoul, after a legendary ancestral estate in Scotland, and proceeded to construct his own little wilderness sanctuary. The idea was a symbolic reversal of Turner's frontier hypothesis: instead of imposing himself on nature, Seton would attempt to show how man could help restore the land to a wild state by practicing sound conservation and reintroducing vanished species. By allowing the primeval wilderness to reclaim the pastoral, he hoped to return the West to the East.[5]

The tract's most conspicuous feature was a brook-fed alder swamp, which Seton transformed into a lake, stocking it with trout, bass, and various species of ducks and geese. An island in the center of the lake provided ample nesting grounds for the waterfowl and other birds. While he wisely decided against bringing in deer and potentially dangerous mammals, he did import smaller herbivores such as rabbits, opossums, and muskrats, and his game birds included pheasants, guineas, and even peacocks. Although peacocks traditionally designated affluence, Seton probably saw them as representative of nature tamed by man and also of his Victorian heritage.[6]

Seton's Wyndygoul estate was patterned to some degree after that of William Brewster, his fellow ornithologist in Concord, Massachusetts. Brewster helped supply the cultivated birch and pine seedlings that Seton planted in the old pastures. Along with the lake and local rock formations, many of which were coated with lichens, mosses, and vines, these trees served to create an environment resembling that of Ontario's Laurentian Shield, in which both indigenous and imported species could live in freedom.[7] Wherever possible, Seton simply allowed nature to be the architect, but his creative genius was evident in a few artificial habitats, most notably his hollow tree. A subject of several articles, this realistic structure was fashioned in such a way that the naturalist could investigate whatever species inhabited it: near the largest of the tree's branches, Seton installed a casement that enabled him to photograph "any bird which chose this perch."[8]

In the midst of this zoological wonderland, on the heights overlooking a wooded ravine, Seton planned his house and various outbuildings. He carefully selected this site so that nothing would obstruct his view of both the lake and nearby Long Island Sound. "I regard the mountains as highly impertinent," he once said. The house, whose style was most accurately described as "Tudor-Indian," was two stories high. The basement and lower story were constructed of rough-hewn, green-tipped stones quarried near the site, while the upper story was half-timbered rose terra-cotta stucco, with hand-hewn beams cropping out here and there. The low, irregular slate roof, brownstone chimneys, wide verandas, low entrance door, and quaint arrangement of windows all served to create "a very natural and pleasing picture." The story is told of the time when Seton instructed his hired painters to do the window frames in light blue. He and the chief painter were mulling over which shade to use when a bluejay suddenly screamed past. Seton looked up and laughed, "Did you hear the bluejay? As I hit the right shade he said, 'Bl-loo, Bl-loo.' That's it! That's it!"[9]

Like Frank Lloyd Wright, who at the time was developing his theories from John Ruskin and others, Seton believed that buildings should grow from, blend into, and be a part of the natural environment. There should be no sham or imitation construction and no artifice; instead, one should build "in the nature of materials." That is, each element was to be exploited to disclose its inherent color, texture, function, and shape.[10] Seton's emphasis, however, was on the practical and the picturesque rather than on organic growth and function. In the planning and building of Wyndygoul, whose specifications he drew up himself, Seton followed seven basic principles and spared no expense to achieve them. First of all, the purpose had to dictate the plan, no matter where it led. Second, the building had to be of sound construction and, third, it had to be honest and unashamed, with no pretenses whatever. Fourth, there should be soft pastel colors—among the easiest features to incorporate into a house, but too often ignored by builders. Fifth, the human touch was necessary for quality and charm; to Seton, the machine was "death to art." Sixth, a building ought to emphasize curvature; after all, nature had no mathematically correct, long straight lines, so these were necessary only in floors, doors, and windows. Finally, the house would reflect simplicity with no fancy trappings.[11] Throughout his life, Seton often expressed his scorn for the "cheap ugliness" of American cities and chided the mansions of New York millionaires for their cheap and fake construction.[12] He liked to imagine New York with the colorful, decorative motifs of Venice and other European showplaces. Wyndygoul was a compromise of Seton's and his wife's loves: in the wilderness, yet not too far from the city. Seton certainly enjoyed the advantages of his country estate, especially since it was away from zoning ordinances and other city "rules, regulations, precedents and customs." There he felt free to express his individuality, and his central buildings reflected the Victorian-wilderness tensions that so characterized him. He allowed some modern conveniences—electricity, a pressure tank, a central boiler in the kitchen—but the house as a whole emphasized the primitive environment. At the same time, the thick walls, massive wood cornices, and heavy beams of the studio ceiling definitely showed the English nobleman's love of solidity. Seton's baronial inclinations were further revealed by the bay-windowed studio overlooking the lake, and from the front door the view over the tops of the hemlocks and across the sound to Oyster Bay. On clear days there was even a glimpse of Theodore Roosevelt's Sagamore Hill estate.[13]

The grounds of Wyndygoul were crisscrossed with miles of walkways and nature trails. At certain points, framed bridges and arches were erected so as to allow natural growth to encase them. One bridge across the rocky stream was entwined with dogwood, which became a mass of bloom in May. At the entrance to the estate on Orchard Street were two wrought-iron gates held by imposing stone pillars, each topped with an iron bulldog. With his characteristic humor, Seton wrote Elbert Hubbard: "If you should be in the neighborhood, ring us up and we will chain up the iron bulldogs so that nothing will harm you or make you afraid."[14] In the center of each gate was a bronze shield sporting a brass "S." The quarter-mile driveway to the house was flanked by "an aisle of greenery whose Gothic arches recall Bryant's famous line: 'The groves were God's first temples.'"[15] Behind the main house was a hay barn and a stable for four horses and two cows; over the stable a room lighted by a gabled window was used interchangeably for a groom's quarters and storage space, and next to it was a spacious pigeon loft. Seton dubbed this structure his "Nativity Barn," after Albrecht Dürer's engraving, and boasted that despite its crude looks and green tarpaper roof, it would outlast three ordinary frame barns. Around the perimeter of his "manor," Seton erected a ten-foot wire mesh fence topped with barbed-wire entanglements. His intention here was to allow trees and vines to conceal these artificial barriers and make them look natural.[16]

The Setons spent the greater portion of the warmer months at Wyndygoul, returning to their downtown apartment only "when the snow flies." After the main house was completed, he moved most of his fifty-odd volumes of animal photography, all alphabetically arranged and appropriately labeled, to his country studio. In addition, there were his shelves of pencil sketches, notes, and letter files, as well as numerous plant and animal specimens that he exchanged with fellow scientists. The collection of animal track prints that he and Grace obtained at the Bronx Zoo were also stored there. Admittedly, Seton found it difficult to write or paint at Wyndygoul, so great was his passion to be outdoors. A skilled carpenter, he would sometimes steal away from his easel or desk, get out his tools, and engage in some kind of repair work—whether real or imagined.[17]

Seton especially treasured his journals, his "mine of facts for his stories and memories." He once joked that "Messrs. Gould, Morgan, Vanderbilt, and Rockefeller once made a bid for them, but the trust had not enough money to buy them." There was nothing he liked better than hiking through his woods or rowing on the lake, recording in his latest volume every animal activity that he happened to see. Seton compared his compilation of "untooled" facts to the pieces of a mosaic: "When enough are brought together, no matter how ragged, they will fit each other—the right ones always fit, the wrong ones never do—and when they are put together they will surely spell TRUTH." When asked what was the most difficult thing he faced in creating a magazine story or book from his mounds of information, he replied, "To put what I want to say in 4,000 words, then cut it down to 2,000, still preserving what I would not leave unsaid."[18]

Besides writing, sketching, and observing wildlife, Seton engaged in another sort of activity at Cos Cob. Having joined the American Breeders' Association in 1898, he began experimenting in commercial fur farming, raising minks, martens, otters, foxes, and even bobcats. Although he enjoyed only limited success, Seton advocated fur farming as a practical means of preserving fur-bearing animals and used his own experience to support several authoritative magazine articles.[19] The most successful of these ventures was his skunk farm. Although skunk pelts were cheaper than most furs, Seton found that he could make good profits by raising and selling live breeders. While the farm was never very large, Seton kept his skunks until after World War I, when falling prices and an increasingly busy schedule prompted him to sell them to a friend in England, who subsequently did well with them.[20]

Although Seton often tended to look down on the established wealthy families as snobbish, he enjoyed moving in New York's big business circles. This was especially true in his friendship with A. A. Anderson, who more than once invited him to speak in the private clubs at Cape Charles and other seaside resorts.[21] Nevertheless, he did manage to release himself from society's artificial trappings in a number of ways. His personal untidiness, manifested in wild, shaggy locks and slouchy hat, made a lasting impression on the visitors he invited to "take the census of the woods" at Wyndygoul. Since he was seldom known to shave or bathe, his bodily presence was frequently preceded by his smell. While touring the grounds, visitors never knew quite what to expect from their uncanny host. Once, when Grace hallooed him from across the lake, her husband answered back with a moose's mating call. Another time, after commenting that he was as hungry as a wolf, Seton let loose with a perfect wolf howl. While he had "a gleeful way of wrecking conventionality," his guests, for the most part, loved it. And with all his relaxed informality, he still possessed an "unassailable dignity." Even though he was not a musician, Seton's "tall, swinging form" and unkempt hair caused some to style him a "dark-haired Paderewski."[22]

Seton particularly relished the company of prominent personalities. Lincoln Steffens, who erected his own house near Greenwich Harbor, dropped by on several occasions. A friend of the Gallatin family since childhood, Steffens came to be fond of Seton and attempted to get more mutual acquaintances to purchase property nearby. Other neighbors included painters John Henry Twachtman and Childe Hassam—both friends of Robert Henri—and authors Bert Leston Taylor, Wallace Irwin, and Irving Bacheller. Controversial editors and publishers like Gilman Hall of *Ainslee's* and *Everybody's* and Don Sietz of the *New*

York World, also had their homes at Cos Cob.[23] In addition Wyndygoul's guest list included Juliet Wilbor Tompkins, Richard LeGallienne, Lloyd Osbourne, Carl Lumholz, Emery Pottle, Mark Twain, Gertrude Lynch, Cecelia Beaux, William Hornaday, and C. Hart Merriam. Theodore Roosevelt took time from his hectic schedule to come around on occasion, as did the pioneer psychologist Havelock Ellis and his freethinking wife, Edith Lees. Seton once introduced Edith as "a prophetess from the wilderness, neither wholly woman nor wholly man, but wholly human."[24]

Another liberal thinker always welcome at Wyndygoul was Elbert Hubbard, whose witty periodical, the *Philistine,* was noted for its stinging commentaries. Hubbard's socialistic Roycroft community at East Aurora, New York, was known nationally for its quality furniture and tooled, leather-bound books. Notorious as a bigamist, Hubbard preached a humanistic, "health-and-salvation" gospel that featured fresh air, honest toil, individualism, and positive thinking. His attacks on conventional social and religious mores and his emphasis on man's mystical relationship with the universe were shared to a great extent by Seton and probably had a marked influence on the latter's liberal views. On occasion, Seton looked forward to a "bully time" with Hubbard at the annual Roycroft convention in July.[25]

Of course, Seton did not hesitate to extend his welcome to other literary figures. When James Whitcomb Riley, the "Hoosier Poet," commented favorably on a Seton lecture given in Dayton, Ohio, the artist-naturalist sent him a personal invitation to come to "the restfullest spot on earth."[26] Even when he was busy at his studio desk, Seton gladly welcomed callers, expected or otherwise. Apparently, having visitors around helped rather than hindered his drawing—a source of puzzlement to writers like Hamlin Garland, who could work "only in a solitude and silence."[27]

In New York, Seton attended many formal dinners and informal gatherings with his literary cronies, with whom he freely exchanged philosophies. Once, at the home of Juliet Wilbor Tompkins in January, 1900, Seton became involved in a heated discussion with novelist-journalist Frank Norris, who had recently returned from covering the Boer War in South Africa. When Norris questioned the justice of England's position in that conflict, Seton's "British blood" was stirred: "Filled with English imperialism," reported Garland, who observed the incident, Seton "defended the war in Africa with fiery eloquence. His black eyes glowed with a menacing light, but Norris held his own with entire good humor. He knew what he was talking about."[28]

Seton, who especially admired Mark Twain and his works, was one of several dignitaries invited to a formal banquet at the Metropolitan Club on November 28, 1902. The occasion was Mark Twain's sixty-seventh birthday, and the copper plate at Seton's place featured a caricatured self-portrait etched by the beloved author. The signed card accompanying it read, "Ernest Thompson Seton: with best regards of the tamed animal." On the back of a menu, Seton drew a bear cub, which Twain added to his treasured mementos of the occasion.[29]

Among all the men of letters, Hamlin Garland was one of the few who really understood Seton. Along with his wife Zulime and his brother-in-law, sculptor Lorado Taft, Garland spent many enjoyable hours at Wyndygoul and Bryant Park. Culturally attached to a unique brand of provincialism, he had emerged as a Populist crusader on behalf of decentralism in politics and impressionism in literature and the arts. Like Seton, Garland kept voluminous diaries from which he extracted material for his autobiographical works, his essays, and his fiction.[30]

Almost from the time of their first meeting, Seton had toyed with Garland's idea of Western localism and began promoting the formation of "a guild or brotherhood of the West," to be composed of artistic and literary people who "found their inspiration" in that region. Convinced that Eastern authors were "wholly European in thought," Seton championed the works of men like Bret Harte, Joaquin Miller, Edward Kemeys, and E. W. Deming. To him, they performed their craft "because they have a story that they burned to tell, not because they are enamoured of their art." In effect, Seton had a story that he himself longed to tell, only part of which could find expression in his animal tales and essays.[31]

Such aspirations were reinforced by Seton's initial contacts, beginning in 1899, with members of the new literary circles on the West Coast. It was in California that he first met such magazine writers as Juliet Wilbor Tompkins, who wrote for the *San Francisco Wave*, as well as the poet Edwin Markham and his wife Anna Catharine, with whom he maintained lifelong contact.[32] Seton also became acquainted with David Starr Jordan, the liberal president of Stanford University, whose anti-imperialist views were temporarily overshadowed in the years following the Spanish-American War. Jordan's biological determinist opposition to war and power, along with his ichthyological studies and protests against wanton seal hunting in the Pacific, undoubtedly made a strong impression on Seton's own philosophy.[33] Always striving to build up his university, Jordan was happy to have Seton and other Eastern guests lecture on his campus. Having read Seton's works, Jordan lauded his use of local color and considered animal characters like Lobo far above Kipling's Akela because of "absolute truthfulness" to details.[34]

The friendship of two leading regionalists, Charles F. Lummis and Mary Austin, further stimulated Seton's interest in the West. Charles Fletcher Lummis, a New Englander of impeccable background and a college classmate of Theodore Roosevelt, gained notice in 1885 with his 3,507-mile walk across the continent to Los Angeles, where he was hired by the *Los Angeles Times*.[35] After covering the Geronimo campaign in Arizona, Lummis delved into America's pre-Columbian and Hispanic past, walking in the company of the pioneer archaeologist Adolph Bandelier. Thereafter, despite three unhappy marriages and occasional conflicts with certain colleagues, Lummis became an eloquent booster of California and the Southwest through books, essays, and poems. Among other things, he emphasized the celebration of nature in the West as well as its ethnic heritage.[36] In 1894, he became editor of *Land of Sunshine* (later *Out West*) and transformed it into a high-quality journal that advertised the region's virtues. Around it, Lummis began a literary circle that attracted Jordan, Markham, and other upcoming writers. Like Seton, he kept private journals and freely blended fact and fiction in his published work. As he achieved material success, he began constructing his "home-made house," El Alisal, following architectural principles similar to those applied to Seton's Wyndygoul.[37]

After 1899, Seton was a welcome guest at El Alisal. He and Lummis spent many hours exchanging stories and ideas. An authority on borderlands history, "Don Carlos" Lummis was able to supply Seton with early Spanish accounts of native fauna, as well as oral accounts obtained during his travels. Fascinated with his host's Indian artifacts, Seton later lauded the "fait accompli" of his Southwest Museum. Grace patterned some caricatured animal illustrations for her books after those on Lummis's petroglyphs. In his editorials and reviews, Lummis never tried to hide his biases, and Seton was among those who received unfailingly sympathetic treatment from him.[38]

Seton, in turn, took a great interest in the Lummis family. He was especially fond of the daughter, Turbese, whom he labeled a "sweet and wonderful child." A few years later, when Turbese went to the National Cathedral School in Washington, D.C., Don Carlos asked the Setons to look in on her, as she needed "a particular touch with the Right People."[39] In 1911, when Lummis suffered temporary blindness from "jungle fever" while on an archaeological expedition in Guatemala, Seton offered him and his son Jordan words of encouragement: "The poor body may go blind, but the spirit sight grows keener."[40]

Mary Hunter Austin likewise shared Seton's views of the relationship between science and the environment. College-educated in her home state of Illinois, Mary had moved with her family to California's San Joaquin Valley in 1888. From her unhappy childhood on, she had thought of herself as part of the "ongoing stream of life" in the natural world. Every rock, plant, and animal, even in barren deserts, thus appealed to her. Like Seton, she was a charismatic storyteller and earned a reputation as a feminist and spokesperson for minority groups.[41]

Seton had first met Mrs. Austin at Bakersfield in October, 1899. He was among the authors whose works she found delight in reading in the midst of a cultural and physical desert. At that time, she was beginning her own career as an author, her first stories and poems having appeared in periodicals like *Land of Sunshine*.[42] After divorcing her husband, Stafford Wallace Austin, and moving to New York, Mary frequently visited the Setons and exchanged books with them. Grace was especially glad to have her speak at luncheons and women's group meetings.[43]

Such contacts became more frequent as Seton traveled more and more. Although he no longer had to go north or west to find wilderness, he still worked occasional field trips into his schedule in the interest of science and recreation. During 1901–1902, Seton made several nationwide lecture tours. At every stop, he took note of the scenery and sketched any signs of wildlife he happened to spot; several observations of jackrabbits in Kansas formed the basis for his story of Little Warhorse. He could not help noticing the changes the plains wheat farmers had imposed on the prairies. Seton described the box and strip farmhouses and false-fronted town buildings as "the ugliest things ever used as human dwellings," the only structures with a "touch of picturesqueness" being the grain elevators. He noted that the reason "Kansas jacks" were so destructive to agriculture was that the farmers foolishly killed off such "feathered policemen" as hawks and owls; consequently, community rabbit drives were held to check the rapidly multiplying populations. Seton later added this species to his Wyndygoul menagerie.[44]

It was in Topeka, Kansas, that Seton met Charles J. "Buffalo" Jones, another larger-than-life figure of the Old West, noted for his efforts at preserving buffalo and crossbreeding them with cows to produce the "cattalo." Although the panic of 1893 had forced Jones to curb these activities, Seton lauded his experiments and became fascinated with his adventures, especially his 1897 voyage to the Canadian arctic tundra.[45] Later, through the Camp Fire Club, Seton helped secure several speaking engagements for Jones. While the colorful plainsman tended to exaggerate certain episodes, Seton and Roosevelt, in particular, had faith in the essential truth of his tales. Furthermore, the success of Jones's experiments figured in William Hornaday's formation of the American Bison Society, which Seton and others were invited to join.[46]

Colorado was another favorite field "laboratory" for Seton. In the spring of 1901, he visited the home of W. R. McFadden, a fellow naturalist, in Denver. Seton took note of McFadden's trophy collection and was particularly intrigued with his freak animals. Before going on to California, with a stopover in Salt Lake City to observe the buffalo on John H. White's Antelope Island in the middle of the lake, Seton made plans for a field trip in the Colorado mountains later in the year.[47]

One of the best-known legends among western sportsmen concerned the mysterious "fantail" or "gazelle deer," supposedly a dwarflike version of the common whitetail. These deer, which were quite rare, were said to jump zigzag, making them difficult to hit. Hoping to find evidence to substantiate such tales, the Setons and their party set out from Rifle on August 26 and spent several weeks studying mule deer and their behavior patterns in the area around Pagoda Peak.[48] The expedition's only sour note was a game warden's arrest of Seton and company for "running deer" on September 30. According to Grace, the source of contention was a half-grown fawn that she and the guide had reportedly mistaken for a "fantail." Lacking clear evidence, the game warden apprehended Seton as the leader of the group, although he had never once used his gun. Bond was set at a hundred dollars for the naturalist's appearance in court on or before October 4. Grace later described in detail the amusing Western courtroom scene at the Meeker Town Hall. Whatever misunderstandings there were, the incident was shrugged off on October 5 when the warden, allegedly a man with a shady past, withdrew the charges. The Setons subsequently "scuttled out of town" and returned to New York.[49]

The following year, the Setons and another New York couple made a

pack trip into the Bitterroot Range on the Montana-Idaho border. This
excursion was arranged with W. J. Leeds, a rancher in Hamilton, Montana. The guide was W. J.'s brother, Abe Leeds, a noted bear hunter
whose traps and snares Seton sketched. Seton later declared that the Bit-
terroots were "the roughest of all mountains." Twenty-eight horses
were required to haul the camping gear over the crooked trails, and the
whole trip was characterized by near mishaps. In Lost Horse Canyon,
the party rode over a mile through a forest fire that was being contained
by rangers. Once, Grace had a solo encounter with a grizzly bear, which
fortunately proved docile and ambled on. Another time, Seton sprained
his wrist in attempting to retrieve his wife's frisky mount. While traveling through a heavily wooded area one day in late September, the party
almost met disaster when they ran into a nest of yellowjackets. It was
while hiding from the wasps that Seton found the baby snowshoe rabbit
that he carried for twenty miles in his hat and kept overnight under a
leather case. That night, the little prisoner's thumping on the leather
"sounding board" attracted others of its kind, and by the light of an
acetylene lantern, the party witnessed the "rabbit dance." The next
morning, Seton photographed his captive and released it.[50]

Such events provided the Setons with more ideas for stories. Grace,
in her city-girl manner, compared the chirping noises of the conies to
those of "a lot of Chicagoans on their doorsteps on a summer evening."[51] But the most famous Seton tale derived from the Bitterroot
Mountains experience concerned a particularly ornery horse. After
leaving Hamilton, the party had ridden over the border to the Leeds
Ranch in Idaho, where Abe picked up a bay horse with a black mane
and tail for the hunters to use as bear bait. This stallion had a mean
streak and a habit of fooling people by pretending lameness. In the
story, Coaly-Bay, as Seton named him, is portrayed like any other Western outlaw horse. He has an independent spirit and refuses to submit to
the saddle and bridle. After going through a succession of frustrated
owners, he is bought by Abe Leeds for five dollars. In his journal Seton
recorded that the guide killed the bear bait a few days later, but in the
tale Coaly-Bay escapes from his would-be executioners, dodging the fatal bullet and becoming symbolic of "the eternal Spirit of Revolt against
the Spur of Oppression."[52] When he first published the story in 1909,
things were happening in Seton's life that probably inspired him to
show his feelings through the character of Coaly-Bay. Having broken

loose earlier from his father's tyranny, the legalism of Scottish Calvin-
ism, and the bridled limitations of the art world, he was equally determined not to be saddled by the things certain critics were saying about
his animal stories.

CHAPTER 12

Nature Fakers

The success of Seton's works encouraged other aspiring authors to pursue the nature genre that he had popularized. Several minor Canadian writers such as Arthur Heming, W. A. Fraser, and Archie McKishnie tried their hand at it, but it was Charles G. D. Roberts who equaled Seton in demonstrating the animal story's best features. Although he had developed his style independently, Roberts always claimed that it was the success of *Wild Animals I Have Known* that encouraged him to continue pursuing the genre. In fact, he sent a copy of his *Kindred of the Wild* to Seton, acknowledging him as the "King of the craft," and later dedicated his *Watchers of the Trails* to his "fellow of the wild."[1] While Roberts was more poetic and much less a scientist than Seton, the two men became close friends after 1899. When he visited New York, Roberts spent many an afternoon at Seton's apartment studio and, with his brother and sister-in-law, Will and Mary Fanton Roberts, was often in attendance at Wyndygoul.[2]

At first, most critics reacted mildly, if not always favorably, to Seton's stories. Often, the literary critics tended to confuse Seton's overt sympathy for animals with sentimentality, despite evidence that such an approach was not necessarily premeditated.[3] Moreover, they argued that man was attracted to the beasts by the human qualities that established his kinship with them. In the *Atlantic Monthly*, George S. Hellman wrote that while a nature writer may successfully appeal to the public for a time in recreating an animal's life, "unless he has something of the poet in him; unless he appreciates and causes his readers to appreciate the human significance of animal action, not explicitly, but by suggestion, not in the technical language of scientific research, but in the more appealing, more imaginative manner of creative writing, his work will not endure as literature." Therefore, Seton's animals were immortal not for the little-known scientific facts on behavior that they revealed but for their undying devotion toward their mates and young.[4] Seton, on the other hand, was interested primarily in promoting his works' scientific value; he once stated that writing fiction was "entirely out of my line." But his reading and listening audiences were clearly more sympathetic with the views expressed by Hellman and other critics. When criticized for ending his stories so tragically, Seton explained:

For the wild animal there is no such thing as a gentle decline in peaceful old age. Its life is spent at the front, in line of battle, and as soon as its powers begin to wane in the least, its enemies become too strong for it; it falls.

There is only one way to make an animal's history untragic, and that is to stop before the last chapter.[5]

Nevertheless, he did succumb by degrees to the wishes of his readers, and many of his later stories ended on a happier note.

The much-touted controversy surrounding the validity of the realistic animal story has its roots in the fact that critics from the scientific world did not entirely understand Seton's generalizations. Sometimes, he adopted an autobiographical "devil's advocate" stance, hoping to influence his readers into questioning traditional values toward animals and wilderness. Difficulties arose, however, when he tried to draw psychological deductions from his recorded facts; these made him vulnerable to widespread criticism. Moreover, the success of both Seton and Roberts spawned a host of imitators. Foremost among these was William J. Long, a Congregationalist clergyman in Stamford, Connecticut, whose nature writings revealed a complete abandonment of science in favor of sympathy. In obviously anthropomorphic works like *School of the Woods* (1902), Long naively accepted as divine truth "any rare old hunter's tale or farmer's recollection." And in several instances, Long attributed reason to his animal subjects, whereas Seton was careful to point out instinct as the key to an animal's survival. At the time, Seton knew nothing about Long or his writings; otherwise, he might have sought to correct the latter's scientific errors.[6]

The opening shots of the so-called "nature faker" controversy were fired by the venerable "Seer of Slabsides," John Burroughs. Schooled in the transcendentalist thinking of Henry David Thoreau and having walked through the Civil War years in the company of the poet Walt Whitman, Burroughs had in 1895 built his own secluded retreat and wildlife sanctuary near his West Park, New York, home. With his flowing white beard, "Oom John" had an uncanny ability to charm young and old alike with his highly moralistic nature philosophy.[7] Like most of his colleagues, Burroughs believed that a nature story without scientific backbone was unsuitable for publication. However, his concepts of animal behavior were severely limited, and up to that time the majority of his observations had been made only in the Hudson River Valley and the Catskill Mountains. Nevertheless, in March, 1903, Burroughs published a scathing attack on Roberts, Seton, and Long in the *Atlantic Monthly*. In particular, he equated Seton's works with Long's and denounced both authors as "sham" naturalists. Afterward, Burroughs admitted that he might have "overdone it and showed too much temper"; certainly, he knew nothing of Seton's background, nor had he read any of the latter's scientific articles.[8]

Meanwhile, William Brewster and other friends of Seton became highly indignant at Oom John's "singularly unjust and ill-tempered article." Seton, too, was shocked by the tone of the attack, deeming it "so bitter, so unfair, and so untrue that it began to be amusing." For years he had held the Seer of Slabsides in high esteem and had even published a poem in *Century* magazine as a tribute to the old nature philosopher. Of course, the newspapers hoped that Seton would issue a public reply to Burroughs's denunciation, but he prudently followed the advice of his friends to maintain a "dignified silence" and make no comments whatsoever. Instead, he resolved to win over Oom John at the first opportunity.[9]

The opportunity soon came in the form of a dinner party given for "the fifty outstanding New York writers" by Andrew Carnegie at his Fifth Avenue mansion. Supposedly acting on Seton's suggestion, the steel magnate arranged to have him seated next to Burroughs. While their dramatic first meeting was likely not the "ultimate chastening experience" for the old man that Seton later presented in his autobiography, Burroughs apparently enjoyed the "trap" that Carnegie had set, and Seton was able to relate to Burroughs the extent of his wilderness travels. They left the banquet on amiable terms and subsequently began to visit and correspond regularly. After examining Seton's scientific library, journals, photographs, drawings, and specimen collection at Wyndygoul, Burroughs was won over completely.[10] Soon after the Carnegie banquet, Oom John accompanied President Roosevelt on his trip to Yellowstone Park and the Sierra Nevada, where they camped out with John Muir. That experience, along with the visits to Wyndygoul, expanded Oom John's horizons.[11]

By 1905, Burroughs had devoted more of his attention to the study of animal behavior. Although he never embraced the theory that learning had a significant function in the animal world, he did recognize the multidimensional aspects of instinct and admitted that Seton "easily throws all other animal story writers in the shade." For the rest of his life, Burroughs maintained an interest in Seton's scientific studies and apparently called on him often for advice. Although impressed with the picturesque environment of Wyndygoul, he confessed that he "did not like quite so much rich man's style." Still, Oom John concluded that Seton's "way of loving nature is not mine, but doubtless just as genuine."[12]

The reconciliation between Burroughs and Seton did little to lessen the furor over nature faking, however. Theodore Roosevelt, a longtime friend and defender of Burroughs, joined in the fracas by labeling all nature writers as "yellow journalists of the woods" and criticizing them for misleading youngsters with false information about animals. Roosevelt believed in the accuracy of Seton's observations but felt that he was going overboard in stressing his stories' scientific merits. Since Seton tended to "mix romance with his facts," T. R. did not deem him as great an authority on the big game of the West as the old-timers who had spent most of their lives hunting them.[13] Herein lay the essential difference in their thinking: Roosevelt had gained most of his wilderness experience by hunting game and reliving the Turnerian frontiersman's mythical existence. He was especially leery of accounts related to writers by Indians because of their mystical approach in attributing supernatural traits to beasts. Actually, authors like Long and Jack London were far more deserving of Roosevelt's criticisms than was Seton. Roosevelt never seemed to realize that Seton's wilderness sojourns far outdistanced his own, or that the artist-naturalist was equally concerned with teaching children the truth. In essence, the truth as expressed by the two men differed in terms of morality.[14]

As the controversy gained momentum, others were drawn into it and began to take sides. In 1909, Clarence Hawkes dedicated his book *Shovelhorns* "to my brother naturalist and friend, Ernest Thompson Seton, who blazed the trail for the new school of American nature writers, and whose classical animal stories have caused tens of thousands of people who never cared for nature before, to become interested in out-of-door life." Zane Grey, on the other hand, linked Seton with London, calling them "pure fakes as far as animals go. What they write is . . . a closet product."[15]

In the meantime, Roosevelt and most of his colleagues had focused their attacks directly on Long, who—unlike Seton—chose to strike back publicly. In the *New York World*, he branded T. R. a "bloodthirsty hunter." Seton and Roberts were almost forgotten as Roosevelt, backed by such scientists as William Morton Wheeler and Frank M. Chapman, hammered away at Long's arguments. Soon Lyman T. Abbott, editor of the *Outlook*, voiced the opinion of many by chiding Roosevelt for exerting too much energy in controversies not affecting his political leadership: "the *Outlook* hopes that Dr. Long and Mr. Thompson Seton will continue to write about animal life and that children will continue to read their books."[16] Finally, E. W. Nelson of the Biological Survey, aided by Edward B. Clark of *Everybody's* magazine, conducted a symposium in which they solicited the opinions of Hornaday, Merriam, and others concerning nature faking. In their replies, they all zeroed in on Long, with no allusion to Seton.[17]

Although the issue was never entirely resolved, Seton came through, for all practical purposes, in the clear; as he continued writing and lecturing, his popularity among natural scientists, as well as the general public, increased. Robert Yerkes, the Harvard psychobiologist, sought him out for advice and referred graduate students to him. If nothing else, the nature faker controversy spurred further research in the area of ethology.[18]

The dispute instilled in Seton a greater determination to prove himself as a natural scientist. He had apparently learned that sometime before the Burroughs article, Long had made cutting remarks about his bird paintings at a meeting of the Connecticut Audubon Society. Eventually, Seton came to detest him.[19] Furthermore, Seton liked to think that Roosevelt was always on his side. And even though they did not necessarily have a common view with respect to animals, they did value their friendship in other ways. For one thing, Roosevelt appreciated Seton's inventive genius. Early in 1909, Seton devised and patented a scale with a beam for weighing killed game. Roosevelt found it useful during his African safari later that year; *Scribner's* magazine featured a picture of him weighing a lioness on it. Differences of opinion certainly did not deter them from exchanging specimens and stories of their adventures in the wild.[20] Roosevelt knew it was foolish to classify Seton with "his would-be emulators"; for all the zeal he displayed during the heat of the fray, Roosevelt never singled out or attacked Seton individually. And even though he had been delighted with the Burroughs article, he, too, had questioned the old man's repudiation of the theory that animals teach their young. At the same time, he was in agreement with Frank Chapman in questioning the desirability of humanizing animals or of attributing to one individual the traits of many. Since Seton was straddling a fine line between art and science, his colleagues felt that he could best prove his credibility by leaning more toward science. Roosevelt supposedly once told him, "Burroughs and the people at large don't know how many facts you have back of your stories. You must publish your facts."[21]

Seton agreed that it was time to erase any doubts that might have been implanted in the public mind. Accordingly, he deemphasized his quasi-factual tales and began to defend his interpretations by way of the popular essays. His most notable example was "The Natural History of the Ten Commandments," in which he argued that morality is an extension of instinct. Here he shared the views of the German scientist Ernst Haeckel, one of the pioneers of modern ecology, who preached man's limitations within nature. While not denying the existence of competition in the biological order, Seton concentrated on the mutual aid demonstrated by wolves and other social creatures. Such behavior, he stated, was also innate in man, but because of man's overemphasis on reason, it had been denied expression. Therefore, man had alienated himself from both his environment and his ancestors.[22] Seton also occasionally delved into the realm of children's fantasy to drive home his points. In his *Woodmyth and Fable*, many of the simple stories—derived from Aesop, Kipling, and Indian folklore, as well as his animal observations, are actually social commentaries in thin disguise. "The Cure of the Gulper" encourages the application of the free enterprise system to curb the abuses of the railroads, while "The Fate of Little Mucky" attacks muckrakers who complain about social ills but do little to correct the situation. Even in these tales, Seton implied that the key to the solution was innate morality operating by instinct.[23]

His primary efforts, however, were much less philosophical. To gain more notice from the scientific world and restore the confidence of critics, Seton knew he would have to demonstrate a compatible comprehension of biology. Therefore, he developed a twofold plan: first, he would compile all available published data on the mammal species known to occur in Manitoba, into which he would incorporate his own field observations and revise obsolete conclusions; next, he would restate his animal behavior theories in a context that he hoped the skeptics would accept. With these goals in mind, Seton began work on his two-volume study, *Life-Histories of Northern Animals*. As a preview, he published in *Scribner's* magazine and others some fragments of early findings for the forthcoming work. Such a move, Seton figured, would evoke public response to his research and help him gain new insights.[24]

Synonymous with the preparation of his mammalogical synthesis was Seton's role in the mounting conservation efforts of both Canada and the United States. In many of his lectures, the artist-naturalist stressed the urgent need for more wildlife sanctuaries and better conservation laws. Already he had firm political connections in Ottawa, including his charter as official naturalist to Manitoba. After the assassination of President William McKinley propelled Theodore Roosevelt into the White House in 1901, Seton had connections in high places in Washington as well. More than once, the Setons were dinner guests of the president, and one of Roosevelt's favorite art pieces in the White House was Seton's painting of a grizzly.[25] Seton was thus frequently used as a go-between by the two governments in their negotiations, especially where parks and wildlife were concerned. Many naturalists in the higher echelons of the Canadian government asked his advice and sent him specimens and reports of their findings. Seton's position in the Camp Fire Club also heightened his influence in the United States. Working through the media and various sportsmen's clubs, Seton became a powerful force in America's domestic conservation movement. Businessmen and state legislators consulted his opinions. Even conservation groups in Germany and other parts of Europe became interested in his work with animals.[26]

Seton geared many of his travels toward conservation activities. Over the years his desire to pursue and kill big game for mere sport had diminished; instead of a gun, he preferred "hunting" with his sketchpad and camera. Grace, too, who was a dead shot with a rifle, gradually came to share her husband's distaste for trophy-hunting. The last animal she ever brought down was a bull moose near Lake Kipawa, on the Quebec-Ontario border, during a canoe and fishing trip in the fall of 1905. The moose head was subsequently hung on the living room wall at Wyndygoul.[27]

The highlight of Seton's scientific research was his memorable seven-month expedition to the barren subarctic tundra of Canada's Northwest

Territories in 1907. Accompanying him was Edward A. Preble, an associate of C. Hart Merriam in the Biological Survey, who had previously explored the far north and the Hudson Bay areas. Along with Merriam, Preble had become one of Seton's chief consultants in the area of wildlife studies.[28] Their adventures in the northern Canadian wilds were later documented by Seton in *The Arctic Prairies*. He was as fascinated with the tundra as he had been earlier with the prairies and plains of Manitoba and New Mexico. Once more he was in his element with little danger of generalizing; throughout the journey, Seton's love for the wide open spaces was combined with the excitement of his study of minute detail as he and Preble gathered natural history data. Specimens of flora and fauna different from those previously obtained in Ontario and Manitoba were added to Seton's collection. Among the large game animals of the far north, he and Preble observed herds of caribou and musk oxen, and they studied the endangered wood buffalo in the restricted Mackenzie grounds.

In addition, Seton noted the frontier atmosphere of the Canadian north country. He recorded such unforgettable characters as Maj. A. W. Jarvis, commander of the Mounted Police escort that accompanied the travelers part of the way; "Madame X," the half-blood "social queen" of Smith's Landing; and the Indian and half-blood employees of the Hudson's Bay Company who hauled trade goods up and down the lakes and rivers and over the portages in their scows and canoes. These employees, like the accommodating Billy Loutit, the elderly Weeso, and the crafty Beaulieus, had helped guide previous scientific expeditions; now they did the same for Seton and Preble. One memorable campsite was the abandoned shack erected by Buffalo Jones and his companions on the south shore of Great Slave Lake ten years before. The bleached skeletons of wolves Jones had killed at close range still lay scattered about the place, verifying the plainsman's tales of being surrounded by a hungry pack.[29] With his romantic sense of history, Seton compared the overall scenes of this last remote frontier to the unspoiled reaches of the Missouri a century earlier:

For the uncivilized Indian still roams the far reaches of absolutely unchanged, unbroken forest and prairie leagues and his knowledge of white men only in bartering furs at the scattered trading posts, where locomotive and telegraph are unknown; still the wild Buffalo elude the hunters, fight the Wolves, wallow, wander and breed; and still there is hoofed game by the million to be found where the Saxon is as seldom seen as on the Missouri in the times of Lewis and Clark. *Only* we must seek it all, not in the West, but in the far North-west; and for "Missouri and Mississippi" read "Peace and Mackenzie Rivers," those noble streams that northward roll their mile-wide floods a thousand leagues to the silent Arctic Sea.

There were times, however, when Seton and his companions did not consider this primeval country a paradise, particularly when they encountered hordes of mosquitoes and biting flies.[30]

Seton's arctic adventure had several important results. For one thing, he had explored and made the first accurate maps of Aylmer and Clinton-Colden Lakes for Canada's Royal Geographic Society. Furthermore, he and Preble had discovered and named the Laurier and Earl Grey rivers—after the Canadian prime minister, Sir Wilfred Laurier, and Lord Grey, governor-general of Canada, who helped sponsor the expedition. At Seton's urging, the Canadian government passed a law prohibiting any unauthorized person to enter the newly established Wood Buffalo Park in the Mackenzie District (in present-day Alberta) in order to keep poachers out.[31]

The journey to the far north was only part of the extensive research Seton undertook for the synthesis of his *Life-Histories*. His studies drew him back to the British Museum during his lecture tours in England, as well as to the Smithsonian, the Library of Congress, and the American Museum of Natural History. But by 1909 the project was complete and ready to go to print. Each chapter of the *Life-Histories* contains a painstaking compilation of all known facts and literature, plus original observations and interpretations, on each species discussed. In addition, it is the first work of natural history to include accurate maps showing the distribution of a multiplicity of species. In preparing the volumes, Seton was careful not to criticize harshly any viewpoints with which he disagreed; he allowed the facts to speak for themselves.[32]

Life-Histories was overwhelmingly applauded by the American scientific community, which recognized its value to zoology. Gifford Pinchot, Madison Grant, William Brewster, J. A. Allen, and Henry Fairfield Osborn all sent glowing tributes. Frank Chapman declared that "Seton has done for mammals what Audubon did for birds but he has done it better." Merriam and Hornaday also lauded the work's merits. Even Theodore Roosevelt deemed it "one of the most valuable contributions" to the study of natural history and predicted that it would be a standard text for the outdoorsman's library "a century hence." Gloating in the midst of this positive response, Seton confided to Roosevelt that he one day hoped to add two more volumes to "make it complete for Canada."[33]

Seton received additional encouragement as his involvement in the conservation movement deepened. Like Hornaday and other colleagues, he felt that the annual conservation congresses did little good in achieving actual wildlife preservation. During the next few years he pushed to change that, even to the extent of personal political lobbying. For some time the Biological Survey, backed by the Audubon Society and other groups, had worked to push through Congress a bill essential to the protection of migratory birds. Finally, in January, 1913, the bill passed the House but then became stalled in the Senate. Hearing of this, Henry Ford, who was himself interested in bird preservation, sent a private secretary to enlist the aid of Seton and John Burroughs as lobbyists. The two naturalists promptly went to Washington and conferred with the recalcitrant senators; as a result, the Bird Protection Bill was soon passed into law. Later Seton boasted that it was he who did most of the persuading.[34]

Such triumphs heightened Seton's popularity. With the success of Life-Histories, his critics were mollified, and public confidence in his animal stories built up. Books like Monarch, the Big Bear of Tallac (1904), Animal Heroes (1905), and Biography of a Silver Fox (1909), most of which had come out during the nature faker controversy, increased in popularity and demonstrated that his scientific work stimulated the writing of his tales. Edward Bok and other publishers encouraged Seton to do more scientific essays. Edward F. Bigelow, managing editor of the Guide to Nature, considered him a "real naturalist," not merely a writer of animal fiction. In 1909, the Camp Fire Club awarded Seton its gold medal "for the most valuable contribution to popular natural history of the year" and elected him its president. In that position, he invited such celebrities as explorer Robert L. Peary to speak at the club's special functions.[35]

Admittedly, Life-Histories can be seen as a sentimental journey back to the land of Seton's "golden years." Even while praising it, Merriam and other scientists pointed out such "twaddle" as talk of suicide and similar generalizations about animal behavior. Nevertheless, these minor flaws were generally overlooked, and Seton's credibility as a naturalist was never again seriously challenged. Later developments have proved the majority of Seton's theories valid; only in a few areas—notably animal suicide—did he err.[36]

Although he perpetually sought to curry favor with other big names, Seton at the same time saw himself as the people's translator, the popularizer of natural science. What many Progressives objected to was Seton's inability, in his attempt to link art with science, to separate fact from morality. Having studied Darwin, he concluded that human morality could be derived from what became the science of ethology. As technology threatened to destroy the wilderness, so did it also threaten to destroy morality. The wilderness inhabitants, both animal and human, were united with it and thus were gradually evolving toward an absolute moral state of grace. To discover moral peace within himself, civilized man needed merely to look to his wilderness roots. Seton's basic definition of morality has been summed up as "a balanced combination and learning premised on the survival, not of the individual, but of the individual within the community of all living things"; anything contrary to such a communal concept was not considered moral, nor did it have a chance for survival. Modern scientists might be more sympathetic to Seton's views, but his Progressive contemporaries, during the height of technological advancement in America, were not ready to swallow the doctrine that man with all his reason was merely a small part of the vast natural world and not vastly superior to beasts.[37]

Regardless of what Progressive leaders thought about Seton, families across the United States, Canada, and Great Britain clamored for his books and flocked to hear him speak. His popularity among children was exemplified in Winona, Minnesota, where he lectured in December, 1902. "Certainly never was a lecturer more happily advertised or more loyally supported than Ernest Thompson Seton has been by the school children of this city," reported the *Winona Morning Independent*. In part, Seton's talks had been advertised by posters made by some of the children, two of whom were handicapped; afterward these posters were auctioned off, with the money going to the children.[38] Of course Seton, like reform-minded Progressives, was concerned with the moral development of America's youth. While writing his animal stories and enduring the venom of the nature faker controversy, he was also busy seeking to apply his scientific principles to current social reform movements for young people. For his model, he chose that aboriginal group of American heroes who, in his eyes, best lived up to his idea of morality.

CHAPTER 13

The Genesis of Woodcraft

In the first decade of the new century, Seton was at the height of his productive life. He seemed to possess limitless energy, even while royalties from second editions and reprints of his works continued to supply his income. Increasing markets for his books developed, not only throughout the United States and Canada but also in Britain and other parts of Europe.[1] Through his pen and voice, Seton had given audiences a new appreciation for the world of nature. Even his own brothers could not help taking notice. One reportedly asked him, "How is it, you and I have been in the same parts of America for twenty years, yet I never see any of the curious sides of animal life that you are continually discovering?" The artist-naturalist replied, "Largely because you do not study tracks." J. Enoch Thompson, who served in the Spanish consulate in Toronto, was enthusiastic about *Life-Histories*, deeming it Ernest's "magnum opus." Seton was especially pleased to learn that his nephew, Stuart Logan Thompson, was pursuing biology and natural history. He later referred to Stuart as "the only nephew who spoke his language."[2]

Like Theodore Roosevelt, Seton was a firm believer in "the strenuous life," which his own lifestyle certainly reflected. This major cultural impulse was characterized by a new general emphasis on youth, adventure, and the great outdoors. In place of the materialism and conformity of the "Gilded Age," there arose the ideal of physical fitness based on sports and rigorous exercise to revitalize the American character. This fascination with the outdoor life accounted for, in part, not only proliferation of nature stories by Seton and others but also an increase in literature on America's pioneer past. Historical figures such as the frontiersman and the Indian that exemplified the "strenuous life" became favorite subjects.[3]

In turn, these ideals led to the rise of youth organizations, all with basically the same goal of reinvigorating the American character through its children. Like other Progressive reformers, Seton had a heartfelt desire to instill traditional American values of honor, physical courage, and independence of mind and spirit through outdoor activity. His ideas regarding youth were similar to the Darwinian, biological developmentalist theories expressed by G. Stanley Hall, with whose controversial study on adolescence Seton became familiar. According to Hall, the child's life stages paralleled the history of the human race, culminating in civilized adulthood.[4] Seton shared his colleagues' concerns that most inner city children had little or no chance to see the world of nature, and that juvenile crime was on the upswing as a result of urban conditions. Acting on the assumption that sport was the great incentive for outdoor life, he reasoned that nature study showed the intellectual side of sport. City youth, in order to enjoy the outdoors, must be taught to enjoy it. What set him apart from other reformers was his selection of the pre-colonial "Noble Red Man" as his ideal human. In so doing, Seton became a major interpreter of Indian culture and history at a time when interest in that field was increasing among white Americans.[5]

Seton's own boyhood experiences provided the basis for his theories on youth training. Remembering his father's abuses, he came to admire the loving manner with which most Indians reared their children. Thus he rejected harsh discipline in favor of fairness, gentle guidance, and peer group pressure as means of correction. In his own unhappy, restrictive home, Seton's escape had been the "make-believe" world of play, where he had felt free to set his own lifestyle bounded only by the imagination; that had been the "ideal life . . . with all that is bad and cruel left out." Recalling his summertime campouts with his friends in the woods near Lindsay, Seton incorporated them into his ideas on "woodcraft," which he defined as the "oldest of all the sciences."[6]

Seton's attitudes toward religion figured strongly in his philosophy of education. In rebelling against his father's strict authoritarianism, he had rejected his Presbyterian upbringing with its emphasis on original sin and the general depravity of mankind. He looked upon Calvinist doctrine as a religion of child sacrifice, comparing it to "the worship of Moloch," and he blamed it for depriving him of many boyhood joys. Although he sometimes lectured in church auditoriums and befriended certain men of the cloth, Seton refused to participate in any form of organized religion and carried a general antipathy for ministers of all faiths. Besides that, he vehemently disliked Saint Paul: he felt that the apostle's conservative teachings had stifled the original spirit of Christianity that Christ preached; furthermore, Paul's view of women seemed

contrary to Grace's feminist view and Seton's own romantic images of
the ideal woman. While he never acknowledged God as a personal Being
"by reason in logic, biology, or dynamics," Seton concluded that "all
children come here direct from God and are pure as God can make
them." Therefore, instead of functioning as a reform institution, education should function to keep children from being corrupted by the
world around them.[7]

Combining these intuitions with the theories of Hall and William
James on the power of instincts (fear, love, curiosity, pride, pugnacity,
ownership, ambition, constructiveness), Seton reasoned that if men
were created in God's image, they should rely on their instincts and the
basic wisdom of past generations, rather than on the artificially imposed
moral codes of contemporary society. One favorite proverb that he often
quoted was Ralph Waldo Emerson's statement: "If ye be of good ancestry, cast aside your judgment, and trust yourself indomitably to your
instincts, and you won't go far astray." But since the building of good
character was imperative to the viability of American society, Seton concluded that "the highest aim of education is not scholarship but manhood." He felt that American education, with its emphasis on con-
trolled classrooms and a textbook curriculum, had so far failed in that
endeavor. Moreover, Seton argued, since basic instincts were not appre-
ciably altered after childhood, prisons and reformatories only produced
hardened criminals. Therefore, the essential activity during childhood
was "not learning to work, not learning to be a scholar, not learning to
be a citizen, not learning to be a soldier,—but to play." Knowing that a
boy's natural inclination was toward gang loyalty, he made it his objective to channel the play instinct into guided peer group activities. While
his emphasis on the primitive set him apart from John Dewey and other
liberal educators, Seton did embrace portions of their progressive
doctrines.[8]

As he saw traditional moral values deteriorate under the influence of
urban growth, industrial technology, and the demise of the family farm,
Seton deplored the loss of the skills and practical knowledge that were
products of that simpler era. He also opposed the new emphasis on
team athletics, fearing that such an interest would serve to divide the
nation into a majority of spectators and a small group of paid gladiators.
Above all, Seton was convinced that America was quickly losing the virtues that had made her great in the first place. He stated that "money
grubbing, machine politics, degrading sports, cigarettes, town life of

the worst kind, false ideals, moral laxity, and lessening church power, in a word 'city rot' has worked evil in this nation." The answer was not an urban reform mission but the return of America's young to the outdoors by teaching them simple woodcraft skills and restoring through nature in the wild the old personal independence of the frontier era. In Seton's words, his main goal was to "combat the system that has turned such a large proportion of our robust, manly, self-reliant boyhood into a lot of flat-chested cigarette smokers, with shaky nerves and doubtful vitality."[9]

Seton's decision to use as a model the Indian, with his mystic relationship to the environment and decentralized tribal form of government, stemmed from his early contacts with the red race. As early as 1890, he had mastered the intricate distinctions among several linguistic groups in Canada. Furthermore, Seton wanted to pass on to others the skills of tracking, stalking, and survival that he had learned from people like Chaska. From the Indian's "childlike faith" in the supernatural traits of animals, he had attained a pantheistic reverence for nature. In addition, he had found a means through which he could restate the history of Indian-white relations from the perspective of the former. Ever since his visit to the Crow Agency in 1897, Seton had been determined in his heart to set things straight. For one thing, he came to despise George A. Custer; contrary to the belief of many Western-hero worshippers, he thought Custer had gotten what he deserved. As a matter of fact, Seton ranked Custer alongside his father and Saint Paul as the three most undesirable men in history. However, because he later had occasion to meet the Indian fighter's widow, Elizabeth Bacon Custer, and grew to admire her, Seton never published anything to debunk "Yellow Hair" for as long as she lived.[10]

More important, Seton gained a greater realization of the struggle for identity that the Indians were enduring in the white man's world. During his 1901 summer lecture tour, when he visited the Pine Ridge Reservation in South Dakota for several days as the guest of the local agent, Dr. James R. Walker, Seton talked with Sioux and Cheyenne Indians, some of whom were veterans of the 1866 and 1876 wars. As he made their acquaintance, he closely studied their lifestyles and folklore. Among other things, he observed smoke signals and from them worked out a standard code. He also investigated the education system of the schools operated on the reservation by the Bureau of Indian Affairs. (And, of course, there was time to tour the rugged Black Hills and observe buffalo in nearby Custer State Park.) Impressed with Seton's work, Walker later wrote that his visit was "like finding a shady spring of sweet water, and I am again thirsty." Subsequently, Walker passed on to Seton his own studies of Sioux religion long before formally publishing them.[11]

On that same tour, Seton visited several Indian curio dealers on the West Coast and bought some of their wares. In Montana he made his first visit to the Blackfoot reservation and sketched their tepees and ceremonial relics. On the train to Montreal, while returning to New York, Seton encountered Jean Louis Legare, the colorful Canadian frontier Indian trader who had arranged the surrender of Sitting Bull and his Hunkpapa Sioux followers to American authorities in 1881. At the time, Legare was on his way to Buffalo to participate in the Pan-American Exposition (where President McKinley was assassinated on September 6).[12]

Such contacts further prompted Seton to champion the red man's cause, and in December, 1901, he was one of several delegates in Washington attending the organizational meeting of the Sequoya League, named for the inventor of the Cherokee alphabet. Spearheaded by Charles F. Lummis, the league set out "to make better Indians by treating them better."[13] With the backing of President Roosevelt, who stressed a policy of "real mercy, justice and common sense," the Sequoya League launched its crusade to improve the lot of several West Coast and desert tribal groups.[14]

It was during this time that Seton cemented his friendship with the "dean" of American Indian Progressives, Charles A. Eastman (Ohiyesa). A Santee Sioux from Minnesota, Eastman already had a distinguished record as a government physician and YMCA youth worker. In his writings and speeches, Ohiyesa criticized many aspects of white society, declaring that well-meaning white reformers, political and clerical, did not always practice what they preached.[15] In Seton, he found another sensitive voice to help express his own convictions in defense of his people. It was Eastman who helped arrange the artist-naturalist's visit to Pine Ridge in July, 1901. Seton also found out that Ohiyesa was the nephew of John Hunter, the Sioux brave who had tried to coerce him out of his moose that wintry day near Carberry years before.[16]

Seton's sympathy toward the aboriginal American was heightened even more by his knowledge of the tragic history of Indian-white conflicts in the area of his Wyndygoul estate during the early colonial period. Cos Cob, in fact, was named for a seventeenth-century Indian chief, whose Wecquaesgeek, or Sinawa, tribe once occupied this area.

The Sinawas belonged to the loose Wappinger Confederacy, an Algonquin group consisting of nine tribes closely related to the Mahicans and Delawares. When the Dutch and English first settled the vicinity, the Wappingers rendered valuable assistance and established peaceful trade relations with them. But as was all too often the case, intertribal hostilities, into which the whites were inevitably drawn, exploded into bloody frontier warfare. In 1640 the settlers became involved in a five-year war against the western bands of Wappingers, including the Sinawas. Seton often told the story of how colonial troops came stealthily on the night of December 24, 1643, to Cos Cob's stockaded village of Petuquapaen near present Greenwich, built bonfires at each of the entrance gates, and shot down every man, woman, and child who tried to escape the flames. Only eight survived. The following spring, the Wappingers sued for peace, and their power quickly waned. By the 1750s, their confederacy had largely dispersed.[17]

Located to the right of Wyndygoul's driveway was a prominent boulder reached by a dim trail through tangled undergrowth. This huge, moss-covered rock was said to have been the home of an old Indian named Ab, reputedly descended from Chief Cos Cob. Ab had built a shack on the south side of the cliff facing the ocean; the holes he had made in the rock for the timbers of his dwelling were still evident. "What more fitting than that the happy hunting ground of a vanished Red Man should fall to one in such sympathetic touch with his life and his traditions," remarked one observer.[18]

Certainly, its having been the scene of such dramatic events, along with its wildwood setting, was an important factor in prompting Seton to build his country estate there. In addition, it may be remembered that he had aspirations of creating an intellectual community of Western artists and authors to duplicate those he had seen on the West Coast. As an organizational symbol, Seton chose the thunderbird, labeling it "the central ganglion of the Western world" because of its mystical unifying qualities among all North American tribes. "It would symbolize all that such a guild could ever hope to be and would unite us with the learned past of this wonderful West we inherit," he wrote. When he visited Charles F. Lummis at El Alisal in May, 1901, Seton sketched in his host's guest book a Mexican-style thunderbird logo and penned below it a poem stating that the idea for such a guild was as old as the days of Montezuma. Although the Aztec empire had long since "turned to dust," the thunderbird had prevailed over the centuries, and with it the spirit of comradeship similar to that which Wyndygoul afforded him and his friends. By using that ancient creation motif, Seton in a sense hoped to revive Montezuma's guild with "all his men of brains." While it is unclear how well he really understood the thunderbird's creation symbolism, Seton's interest in the mythical creature probably stemmed from his familiarity with Smithsonian Institution reports he had received in exchange for bird specimens.[19]

Unlike some writers of the West, Seton was far removed from any charges of nativism. He was able to carry Hamlin Garland's ideas beyond "geographically determined cultism" in identifying the Indian with a noble past. His distinctions between East and West were strictly in cultural terms, with little or no reference to the evils of urban immigration as opposed to the virtues of the Western pioneer lifestyle. To him, the East was merely Europe reconstituted; the West, because of its aboriginal tradition, was the true America.[20] Like Garland, Seton became absorbed in Indian lore and agreed with George Catlin's views of the native American as one who was totally "adapted to a certain environment." Both authors likewise applauded the passing of the lone frontiersman and urged understanding between the white and red races. Seton, however, considered all white men perpetual immigrants and saw them as the red man's burden. He believed that the "true" American should do away with the pioneer model, "adopt the best things of the best Indians," and come to the realization that "those live longest who live nearest to the ground . . . the simple life of primitive times."[21] Seton's obvious break from the Turnerian frontiersmen was expressed in the following contemptuous statement:

> I found them almost without exception treacherous, murderous, worthless, without the shadow of a claim on our respect but this: at best a measure of dull, brute grit that came in some sort from consciousness of their better weapons, of guns to match the arrow and the bow, and knowledge that, backing them, though far away, was an army of their kind, in overwhelming numbers coming on.

Certainly he continued to applaud those whites who swallowed their prejudices and learned from the Indians. But as far as a model for youth was concerned, not even the pioneers who preceded civilization had the same degree of reverence for the wilderness and its creatures as did the Indians in precolonial times.[22]

From the days when he and Robert Henri had discussed Edward

Bellamy's leftist preachments in Paris, Seton maintained considerable interest in the complex facets of utopian socialism. His spirited exchanges with Garland and others at Wyndygoul on such topics as the single tax deepened his research on the subject. Perhaps influenced to some extent by the teachings of the Russian scientist Peter Kropotkin, whose Darwinist concepts of nature's morality and mutual aid paralleled his own, Seton began to equate *socialism* with *sociability*. He applied the latter term to Indian tribal structure, comparing it to that of the first-century Christians and seeing it as a practical solution for America's social ills. Earlier the Indian concept of tribal land ownership had been expounded by Henry George in his monumental *Progress and Poverty* (1880). Like George, Seton condemned private property as the root of "all misery and poverty among the Whiteman." Tribal ownership, he reasoned, automatically led to wise use of the land and eliminated "over-drain" of natural resources.[23] Furthermore, Seton was familiar with the works of pioneer anthropologist Lewis Henry Morgan, noted for both his pathbreaking studies in animal behavior and his works on Iroquois ethnology. Many of Seton's organizational schemes were patterned after Morgan's Grand Order of the Iroquois, a secret society founded in 1843 and dedicated through careful research to improving the situation of Indians. Centered in Aurora, New York, this exclusively white organization's members dressed in authentic Iroquois costumes and observed religious rites of the once powerful Five Nation Confederacy. In drawing from Morgan, George, and possibly Kropotkin, Seton continually reiterated his belief that nationalization of the land and its resources would call a halt "to abject poverty and to monstrous wealth."[24]

Clearly, Seton borrowed freely from various schools of thought and was never exclusively in any one camp. In constructing his ideal model, he was heavily influenced by the standard romantic conventions as set forth by Rousseau and subsequently popularized by Cooper, Longfellow, and Thoreau. His eclectic interests were brought together by his overwhelming concern for the environment itself. As the physical embodiment of a spiritual union between man and his environment, the Indian had a special place in Seton's value system. Acquainted with Cooper's "noble savage" from his boyhood, he later became familiar with the muckraking tradition expounded by Helen Hunt Jackson's *Century of Dishonor* (1881). Thus, in developing his concept of the ideal Indian Seton recognized the theme of persecution and oppression and at the same time weighed the advantages of red societies over those of the whites. Indeed, the whole woodcraft scheme has been summed up as a culmination of Rousseau's child-centered education theory, incorporating G. Stanley Hall's theory of recapitulation.[25]

By 1902, Seton had come to know personally many North American Indians, including several prominent chiefs. Soon the Bureau of Indian Affairs took notice of his work and acknowledged him as an authority on Indian culture. Certainly Seton was upset by the methods federal officials used to induce Indians to adopt the garb and customs of white civilization, especially "returned students" from Carlisle and other Eastern schools. Such inducements seemed to him little more than outright coercion, the results of which were more ruinous than constructive.[26] In his woodcraft scheme, Seton found a nationwide vehicle through which he could crusade for Indian rights, instill a new appreciation for their culture and contributions, and push for better conditions on their squalid reservations throughout the West. The impressionable youth of America, he hoped, would learn from him and carry on his cause.

CHAPTER 14

Black Wolf and the
Woodcraft Indians

As early as 1898, Seton had considered the publication of a dictionary of woodcraft, with emphasis on Indian folk tradition, for Frank Doubleday. Doubleday did not follow up on the proposition, but word of Seton's scheme soon reached the ears of Edward Bok through their mutual friend, Rudyard Kipling. Subsequently, Bok invited Seton to begin a regular "boys' department" section for the *Ladies' Home Journal*, which would "appeal in all its contents to boys in their relation to outdoor subjects." Seton accepted Bok's proposal and in the summer of 1901 signed a formal contract with the *Journal*. The following year, under the title "Ernest Thompson Seton's Boys," he began a series of short articles launching his proposed youth organization.[1]

Even before the appearance of the first article in May, 1902, the lord of Wyndygoul had an opportunity to try out his ideas in his neighborhood. The story relates that certain neighborhood boys were incensed at Seton for fencing in the farmland where they had previously hunted, picnicked, and roamed freely. Seeking to regain lost privileges, they began a campaign of harassment by tearing down his fences, shooting his animals, and painting choice graffiti on his gateposts. Seton, with characteristic understanding, refused to instigate punitive action. Instead, he marched into the one-room Cos Cob schoolhouse one morning in April, 1902, and invited the young vandals "to come up to the Indian Village on my place" to camp during the coming Easter break.[2]

Seton had indeed fashioned on the estate grounds a makeshift village. Included among the diverse artifacts were northern Plains tepees, "gorgeous with pictures of warriors and buffaloes," and two Algonquin canoes of Malecite birchbark.[3] The dominant feature of this modular Indian camp was a large council ring, around which were several rock paintings. The council fire in the center of the ring was encircled by a stone necklace representing the Great Spirit. Four arms extending from

138

its circumference symbolized spirit, mind, body, and service; at the end of each arm was fastened a lamp with three rays, which stood for the laws of woodcraft. Obviously, this fire-centered circle, patterned after a Navajo sand painting, was a symbolic picture of nature's cycle. But as Seton explained, it also "led men to think about the Great Mystery over all." Even the broad veranda of the main house was decorated for the occasion, with Indian blankets and rugs hanging among the animal trophies.[4] Having instructed each of the boys to bring two blankets, Seton furnished crude beds with straw ticks for the sleeping area. For a camp cook, he secured the services of John Hansen, a local contractor who was also the estate's groundskeeper.[5]

Everything was thus in order by the appointed Good Friday. At around five o'clock that afternoon, forty-two neighborhood boys between the ages of ten and sixteen, each carrying two blankets, gathered at the gate on Orchard Street to see how well the unorthodox landlord followed up on his invitation. Although Seton was momentarily overwhelmed by the size of the group, he bade them come in and gather around the council ring. Next, he allowed them to swim in the lake to work off their "animal energy." At sunset, the boys were treated to a hearty meal. Then came the highlight of the evening when the campers gathered around the council fire to hear Seton talk about the ideals that the Indians upheld and the healthy life they lived, bidding his young listeners to follow their example. "I told them of Indians and Plains life," Seton later wrote, "gauging my stories in a steady crescendo till I had renewed the Fenimore Cooper glamour of romance, and heightened it to a blaze of glory." This combination of reason and theatrics served to create the desired atmosphere; in a matter of minutes, he said, he could "feel the thrill of intense interest [and] their regret that the noble red men were gone before their day."

The following day, Seton declared a democratic election in which his boys maneuvered their gang leader to the position of Head Chief, or Sagamore. Other officials similarly elected were the Second and Third Chiefs, to fill in for the Head Chief in the event of the absence; the Wampum Chief, to serve as the camp treasurer and handle tribal property; the Chief of the Painted Robe, to keep the minutes and records; and the Chief of the Council Fire, to have not only the "exclusive privilege" of making fire but also the duty of seeing that the grounds were policed. As the adult advisor, Seton bestowed upon himself the title of Medicine Man. These officers, along with five others to be elected, would constitute the Council of Twelve. Headed by the Sagamore, the Council would make the laws, settle disputes, and fix the dues. Nearly all of the laws were aimed at the protection of and respect for the wilderness and its inhabitants, with little reference to conventional social mores other than prohibitions against smoking, drinking, and swearing. Rebellion against the Council would be punishable by expulsion from the tribe. Whenever the Head Chief called for order, he held up the two-fingered "Buffalo Horn" salute, and everyone in the camp became quiet.[6]

The boys were taught to "think Indian." They learned plant and animal identification, trail-marking, and stalking, as well as various Indian arts, crafts, and rituals. These educational aspects were incorporated into their games, like the "dummy deer" hunt. Leonard C. Clark, ten years old at the time and later a local attorney, recalled this challenging game in which one boy was selected to hide the burlap "deer." Attached to the bottoms of his footwear were protruding iron stencils that left noticeable "tracks" on soft ground. If a group of trackers successfully spotted and "shot" their quarry with homemade bows and arrows, the boy who had concealed the animal would be the camp "janitor" until he was excused or voted to be "brought back to life."

While Seton never endorsed team sports, in which one party won glory at another's expense, the boys did vie for individual honors, or coups, represented by feathers. Anyone who could demonstrate skill in athletics like canoeing, swimming, and running; in nature studies; or in "woodlore" activities such as archery, tracking, and handicrafts was awarded a coup for that activity. One who particularly excelled in such things earned a grand coup, a feather with a red or white thread at the top. After the first camp, the Sagamore was usually the one with the most coups (twenty-five or more). With their earned feathers, the boys made Indian headdresses and decorated their blankets. For "scalps," they frequently used horsehair.

The campers also took on Indian names, based usually on a personal trait, ability, or physical characteristic. As a brave achieved greater status among his fellows, he often would be assigned a new name. Only Indian names were allowed at camp. A violator had to "run the gauntlet" between his fellow tribesmen's legs and get slapped on the rump.[7] As Medicine Man, Seton picked for himself the name Black Wolf, not merely because he was an authority on wolves, but also because the Wappinger Confederacy reportedly used the wolf as its totem.[8]

The success of that trial campout inspired Seton to hold more gatherings for his "Sinaway" tribe during the summer. Certainly he welcomed new prospective "braves," and promised as a further incentive that those who left the most orderly campsite would get first choice of campground the next time. Gradually Seton put greater emphasis on authentic Indian implements. Moccasins were preferred over shoes, and headbands and warbonnets over hats. Siouan tepees, complete with wooden poles, were standard shelters. Seton had nothing to do with military tents and even scorned the Sibley tent because of its "ugliness" and cumbersome iron pole. Matches were considered inferior to rubbing sticks and bow drills in lighting fires. Lessons in identification of edible wild plants, knowledge of herbal remedies, and survival in the wild became standard fare.[9] Seton's most fundamental teaching was honesty with one's fellow man. That key virtue was essential for membership of good standing in a tribe. In addition, great emphasis was placed on the care and development of the body. A strong body meant a strong soul. Here Seton stressed the importance of personal faith and often dealt with the Indians' spiritual concept of nature. Soon the boys came to idolize Black Wolf, and some considered him a second father.[10]

Word about the camps quickly spread, and the "Seton Indians" expanded from one tribe into several. Each tribe had different leadership, but all adhered to the flexible set of guidelines laid down by the Sagamore. As more neighborhood chapters organized outside his own, Seton went personally to check up on them. In New Jersey, at the campground of the first tribe in that state, Black Wolf received a rousing welcome from boys who had hidden "in ambush" to await his arrival.

The *Ladies' Home Journal's* publication of Seton's articles, which outlined the themes and demonstrations of camp activities, further stimulated the phenomenal growth of the Seton, or Woodcraft, Indians. In fact, Seton considered the six-part series to be the first edition of his woodcraft manual, or "Birch Bark Roll." During the first few years, however, he toyed with different names for the handbook. The second edition was entitled *How to Play Indian*, and the following three, privately printed by Douglas Paige in New York, were called *The Red Book*. But when *Red Book* magazine threatened to file suit against the author and the printer, Seton then changed it to its best-known name, *The Birch Bark Roll of the Woodcraft Indians*.[12]

Having launched his movement, Seton proceeded to start publicizing it, and toward that end he planned to write his woodcraft dictionary.

However, Rudyard Kipling allegedly persuaded him to publish his ideas in the form of a novel, arguing that such an approach would hold more public appeal. Heeding that suggestion, Seton presented a serial entitled *Two Little Savages* in his *Ladies' Home Journal* column during 1903.[13] He then published it in book form in time for the Christmas season that year.

In recent years, critics have considered *Two Little Savages* Seton's most endearing piece of work. The story is an autobiographical account of his own boyhood ventures into the Don Valley and his summers on the Blackwell farm. As usual, many names are fictionalized; Lindsay becomes the town of Sanger, while the Blackwells are the Raften family. Indeed, the story is a Canadian version of Mark Twain's *Tom Sawyer*, complete with an array of local characters, all based on people that Seton and his young friends had encountered. To himself, Seton assigns the name "Yan," an egocentric gesture he first employed in *The Trail of the Sandhill Stag*. This name, derived from his cabin hideout in the isolated glen near the Don River, is said to be an expression of his hermit self, reflecting his desire to commune with nature alone. Bill Raften, the father of Sam, Yan's fellow "savage," is superficially a tough, conservative farmer. But underneath, he is a kindly, understanding father figure, far better than Yan's own father. Mrs. Raften is a fountain of motherly sympathy as well as a fine farm wife.

The overall plot is thin but solid enough to hold the reading audience. Some elements of the standard western are evident in the bitter quarrel between Raften and Caleb Clark, the old trapper who befriends the boys and passes on to them his knowledge of woodcraft. Once the two men hunted and trapped together as partners, but enmity grew between them because of a horse trade and some payments that Caleb owes Raften, who is the local magistrate. Even worse, Caleb is about to be thrown off his homestead by the unsavory Dick Pogue, who has married the trapper's sole next-of-kin, Saryann, just so he can get the property. Since Caleb does not like farm work, Pogue uses that as an excuse to try to expel him from the community. As young students of the woods, Yan and Sam gradually help ease the bitterness between their "teacher" and Raften. The breakthrough occurs when Bill Hennard, the vicious three-fingered tramp, threatens the little "savages." Both Caleb and Raften come to the rescue, and in their fight against a common enemy, effect a reconciliation. In the end, Raften helps turn the tables on Pogue and restore the poor but dignified backwoodsman to his rightful place in the community—Seton's hidden plea for Americans to restore the Indian to his rightful place in society.[14] While his impressions of the Canadian rural landscape are much more optimistic, his images of the yeoman farmers and their often mortgaged homesteads were derived to some extent from Hamlin Garland's stories as well as his own experiences.[15]

In promoting his woodcraft scheme, Seton effectively used Victorian piety in reuniting the man-child with his environment. Recently, there has been speculation on how the mothers of America must have reacted to the implications of the "pantheistic heresy" prevalent throughout the narrative. Yan and Sam go to great lengths to understand various tribal rituals. Through diagrams and detailed directions, the reader is shown how to fashion objects like tepees, bows and arrows, and a council fire. Both craftsmanship and diversity of origin are stressed, acquainting the reader with the cultures of different tribes—Crows, Sioux, Piegan, and Blackfoot—even though the story is set in Ojibwa country. Throughout the narrative, Seton freely allows himself to teach and philosophize. In one scene, when Caleb shows the boys how to make an Indian drum, the reader is also taken through the process step by step. Caleb then commences beating the instrument and chanting; so mesmerized are the boys by the sound that their "savage instincts" are aroused, and they begin dancing to its beat. Overall, the Indian and nature study themes are interwoven and serve to unite Indian, animal, child, and wilderness in "purest innocence." In the end, Yan achieves high status through his woodcraft activities. Similarly, the experience has a positive effect on other local boys, particularly young Guy Burns, who is transformed from a sniveling, "dirty little cuss" into a brave of high standing. Seton's propaganda purpose is obviously achieved.[16]

By the time of the book's publication, about sixty tribes of Woodcraft Indians had formed throughout the nation. Journalists who observed Seton's camps at Wyndygoul sent back favorable reports. A reporter for the *New York Herald* found it hard to believe that "so wild a scene could be found within forty-odd minutes of New York," while Charles G. D. Roberts commented that "here at Wyndygoul, the East and West meet amicably."[17]

To provide a forum for other leaders who chose to use his methods, Seton added the concept of the Confederation, or Nation, to his program. This "League of Seton Indians" would meet once a year in a Grand Council, presided over by a Grand Head Chief to be elected by the Grand Council every three years. Each of the tribal Councils of Twelve would elect one delegate from its ranks to attend the meeting. All of the positions in the Grand Council, like Keeper of the Wampum, Keeper of the Birch Bark Roll, and Keeper of the Talley, were larger-scale versions of the tribal council officers. As the movement spread and achieved more sophistication, it took on new titles and rituals reflecting various linguistic cultures native to the geographical regions represented on the Grand Council. Everyone in the League, as in the individual tribes, adopted Indian names of their own choosing.[18] The pan-Indian ideal was thus brought forth in the structural framework for both the separate tribes and the League as the unifying organization, but not at the expense of decentralization and a considerable degree of local autonomy. Although adults were there to offer guidance, they were not meant to be in charge. Seton had carefully remained in the background in the formation of his Sinaway Tribe; adult leaders within the Grand Council would likewise relinquish absolute control to the youth.

Seton felt that such a decentralized government would create an atmosphere that allowed for simultaneous development of rights and responsibilities, both of which he perceived as social instincts. Democratic operations would make the League more inclusive to youngsters born into the American tradition. Above all, it would help "bring together young people from various so-called stations, break down the barriers that society has foolishly placed between them, and establish in their minds while they are young a finer kind of humanity, a real understanding that the important thing is the association of the human spirit." As a forum for debate on principles, the League was the movement's only semblance of a national organization.[19]

By 1904, Seton's Indian camps were the talk of New York social circles, and Black Wolf was quick to take advantage. That year, he invited his fellow Camp Fire Club members to spend their summer outing at his Standing Rock Village on Lake Wyndygoul. Scientists were especially drawn to his emphasis on nature study, both botanical and zoological, as well as to his preachments against the wasteful use of natural resources, even in building fires—bonfires were out of the question.[20] In addition, Seton's rules prohibited killing any animal except for scientific purposes, and he felt that a solid background in preparing specimens would help restrict even that form of killing; notebooks were preferable to specimens in accumulating knowledge of the natural world. The lessons in natural science that he developed for the boys found publication in magazines like *Country Life in America*, and Black Wolf was always glad to have his colleagues contribute tidbits of their expertise to his young braves.[21]

Soon, observers became aware of the overall positive effects the camps had on the boys. In July, 1906, John Burroughs heartily endorsed Seton's doings in a letter to President Roosevelt:

Seton has got hold of a big thing in his boys' Indian camp. . . . I have been there once and much impressed with it all, and with good results to the boys that are sure to follow from this scheme. All the boy's wild energy and love of deviltry are turned to new channels, and he is taught woodcraft and natural history and Indian lore in a most fascinating way. I really think it well worthy of your attention and encouragement.

The president readily agreed, casting aside the trials of the nature faker controversy to put his seal of approval on the program. Later Burroughs helped Seton revise the *Birch Bark Roll* and served for many years on the League's advisory board.[22]

Seton's emphasis on Indian history and folklore also held strong public appeal. In that respect, he had a firm supporter in Pauline Johnson, who since their first meeting in 1893 had looked upon him as a "Medicine Brother." Although born of mixed parentage, Tekahionwake proudly claimed the blood of her father, a Mohawk chief, and became noted for her lectures and recitations performed in ornate native costume. She often consulted Seton for advice and compared his movement to the history of the Iroquois League. After Pauline died of cancer in the spring of 1913, Seton was asked to write the preface of her posthumously published book, *The Shagganappi*, which she dedicated to boys' organizations throughout America. As time went on, Black Wolf frequently sought to emulate her manner of presentation whenever his topic concerned Indian lore.[23]

Seton's main debt to Pauline Johnson was for her influence in his characterization of Tecumseh. In 1886, Charles Mair, a founder of the Canada First movement and a noted author, presented a drama—in the rhetorical style of Shakespeare—on the life of the great Shawnee chief, portraying him as a Canadian national hero and a noble "example of true manhood and patriotism." Tekahionwake subsequently applauded Mair's sensitivity to Tecumseh and all red men.[24] To Seton, Mair's

Tecumseh seemed a true-life example of his own heroic Indian model; he called the Shawnee statesman "the most Christlike character" in America's past. In fact, Seton saw in Tecumseh's theory of aboriginal rights a biological extension of the animal instinct of territoriality.[25]

To remain clear of any charges of simplistic romanticism, Seton also delved into the works of contemporary ethnologists and historians. Among them were Frances Densmore and James O. Dorsey, both of whom he had met at the Smithsonian.[26] His closest colleague there was Frederick Webb Hodge, whose *Handbook of American Indians* became Seton's standard reference. A longtime proponent of Indian reform, Hodge was one of the key men in the Sequoya League. Seton frequently sought information from him on coups, warbonnets, and archery techniques, and enlisted his support for the Woodcraft program. In 1907, when Hodge discovered that the rank of Sachem equaled and sometimes superseded that of Sagamore in many Algonquin societies, Seton decided to make the Head Chief the Sachem and the Second Chief the Sagamore (originally, the order had been the reverse). He likewise consulted Charles F. Lummis in his attempts to ensure historical accuracy.[27] In addition, he subscribed to Edward S. Curtis's North American Indian project and regularly referred to the multivolume study that developed from it. He also corresponded with Natalie Curtis, whose classic work on Indian music and folklore is still considered outstanding. Through her, Seton became acquainted with the ethnomusicologist Alice Fletcher, whose translation of the "Omaha Tribal Prayer" was incorporated into the Woodcraft campfire ritual. This prayer and the accompanying vigil, meant to create a Spartan imagery, served to reinforce Seton's idea of history.[28] He also became interested in the music research of Frederick R. Burton. In 1901, Seton and Garland had attended a performance of Burton's cantata, *Hiawatha*, at the Sportsmen's Show in Madison Square Garden. Impressed, they later sent financial contributions to aid his pathbreaking study of Ojibwa songs. Burton, in turn, expressed considerable interest in Seton's work with boys. By giving credit for his ideas to well-known scholars, Seton hoped to verify further his argument "that to forget primitive man is to court race ruin."[29]

Alongside his historical research, Seton took full advantage of his lecture schedule. After one session in Santa Barbara, California, a strange, mystic woman who had studied Oriental religion in India allegedly told him that he was an American Indian chief reincarnated "to give the message of the Red Man to the white race so much in need of it."[30] And spread the message he did. During the summers, Seton lectured on Indian topics at youth camps and used the local Chautauquas to introduce his program in other areas across the country. His woodcraft talks were especially popular among the students of Bureau of Indian Affairs schools such as Haskell Institute at Lawrence, Kansas.[31] If nothing else, Seton's efforts did stimulate a degree of public sympathy for Indians. In this, he was supported by Hamlin Garland, who in 1902 wrote a sympathetic portrayal of Plains reservation life in his novel *The Captain of the Gray Horse Troop*. Garland penned much of that manuscript in a Cheyenne tepee he had bought at Pine Ridge and erected, complete with authentic trappings, on the grounds of his summer cottage in Wisconsin. In the summer of 1902, Seton came by to help dedicate the firehole, and inside Garland's portable retreat, the two men smoked "a symbolic pipe of meditation."[32]

While Seton was enjoying the rapid growth of his "family" of Woodcraft Indians, his own family had a new addition. Despite her busy schedule as a feminist leader, Grace had taken an active interest in her husband's youth work; many former Woodcrafters remembered her as the "first aid lady" at their campouts. In the summer of 1903, the Setons discovered that they were about to become parents, and the morning of January 23, 1904, saw the arrival of baby Ann, named for Seton's great-grandmother. Leonard Clark recalled the time when Grace came out carrying her infant daughter and introduced the new "papoose" to the wide-eyed boys.[33]

Certainly, Ann's birth served to increase Seton's interest in children. His intense, fatherly devotion to his daughter was clearly evident, not only in journal entries and letters but in his activities and published writing. On his arctic voyage in 1907, he named his birchbark canoe the *Ann Seton* after her. Later, he dedicated his *Biography of a Silver Fox* "to the one for whom it first was told." Certain human characters in his animal tales were developed with Ann definitely in mind.[34] Nothing brought greater joy to Seton than to watch his dark-haired child grow up among the wildlife on his wilderness estate. Many birds and mammals, including chipmunks and baby skunks, were just as fascinating to her as they had been to the boy in Lindsay forty years previously. As one commentator stated: "Nature is a rediscovery for a parent, and the world of the spotted salamander, the tiny red newt, the leopard frog,

the painted turtle, and the bluejay becomes a reawakening. Stories told
to one child make easy telling to others, and words for children's books
are not difficult to find."[35]

Indeed, Ann was an uncommonly bright, imaginative little girl who
was acting out her own plays by the time she was six. She always managed to "find something interesting in everything," especially her father's stories and lectures. When Ann reached school age, the Setons,
instead of sending her to public school, hired an accomplished young
governess who taught her French and the other "usual accomplishments
of a well-educated young lady." With her occasional bright remarks, she
became an instant favorite among many friends and relatives. William
Hornaday often looked forward to seeing "Little Miss Seton" and her
parents. George S. Thompson, Seton's brother from Chicago who took
time off from his printing business for a memorable visit to Wyndygoul
in the spring of 1911, was impressed with his niece's knowledge and the
quality of her education. As he did with the Woodcraft Indians, Black
Wolf also sought to apply his principles in bringing up his own child.[36]

Alongside his parental responsibilites, Seton continued to work feverishly at promoting his Woodcraft program. Because of his strict emphasis on the outdoors, many tribes were automatically allied with summer
camps. This, plus the fact that the basic structure outlined in the *Birch
Bark Roll* left the actual organizing to local bodies, worked to the program's disadvantage by making it seasonal and thus reducing its potential range. Nevertheless, by 1910 it was estimated that about 200,000
boys in the United States had joined the Woodcraft Indians.[37] Support
from other youth workers and from Seton's circle of fellow naturalists
seemed to indicate the direction he hoped his movement would take.

Seton's cause was further boosted by the zeal with which his "graduates" spread the word. One of these was Miller Jordan (Silver Fox) of
Rutherford, New Jersey, who had achieved the rank of Sagamore within
the League. In the fall of 1908, Jordan began his own campaign among
the boys' clubs and playgrounds in the New York slums. Backed by the
city's Parks and Playgrounds Association, he demonstrated Indian dances
and tepee construction to scores of underprivileged youth and, with the
active support of association directors Jacob Riis and Luther Gulick,
was instrumental in the formation of several inner-city tribes. His detailed reports to Seton prompted the Medicine Man to come and see
firsthand the problems that Jordan encountered in the slums. After lecturing at the Henry Street Settlement and the Christ Church House,

Seton revised certain aspects of the *Birch Bark Roll* to fit the needs of urban youngsters. His most noted innovation was "roof camping," in which modular Indian villages could be set up on the tops of buildings; flowers, vines, fruits, and vegetables could be cultivated there in the open air and sunlight; and bird colonies could be encouraged by providing rooftop nesting boxes. In this way, an underprivileged city boy would have a small bit of the West and wilderness brought to him. The experiences of Jordan and other senior woodcrafters seemed to validate Seton's dictum that "when the right kind of teacher comes along, a little child shall lead him."[38]

These efforts to modify the Woodcraft scheme for downtown youth attracted the attention of Howard Bradstreet, chairman of the Neighborhood Workers' Association and a colleague of Jordan's. Early in January, 1910, Bradstreet called a public meeting to consider proposals. Among those present besides Seton were Luther H. Gulick and his wife Charlotte. As president of the Playground Association of America and chairman of the Russell Sage Foundation's Playground Extension Committee, Gulick already had a distinguished record of YMCA youth work. The meeting ended with the endorsement of Seton's recommendations but under a different name: Woodcraft tribes in the metropolitan area would thenceforth be "Indian Scouts." The principles of woodcraft would not be disrupted by this step; Gulick and others expressed a firm desire to retain continuity with both the country's unique cultural features and existing youth groups. Seton spent much of the following month lecturing at Christ Church House to the adult leaders who would put his revised program into operation. By approving this move, Seton disclosed his own uncertainties as to the effectiveness of woodcraft in the inner city. Nevertheless, in New York and other urban centers, tribes sprang up among playground and church groups, YMCAs, and even some independent private academies.[39]

The Gulicks' New York home was one informal meeting place where Seton came to work out ideas on modifying his plan. Halsey Gulick, Luther's son, recalled that Black Wolf once gave a firemaking demonstration on the living room hearth with a pair of rubbing sticks. After he laid them aside and resumed talking, ten-year-old Halsey sneaked the apparatus into the next room, where he and two of his friends spent an uninterrupted hour trying to duplicate Seton's fire-lighting method. Fortunately, they could get only smoke, and Halsey—unnoticed—restored the sticks to their place by Seton's chair.[40]

The main reason for adopting the name "Indian Scouts" was the desire of Bradstreet and others to take advantage of the Boy Scouts, a new youth movement that had already taken Europe by storm and was beginning to attract attention on this side of the Atlantic. Begun in England, this new boys' organization was more centralized than Seton's but seemed to possess certain advantages in its character-building program. Even as he was launching his urban woodcraft experiment, Seton was seeking to incorporate his principles into the new movement.

CHAPTER 15

From Medicine Man
to Chief Scout

The Woodcraft Indians was the first of several youth organizations to appear in the United States during the Progressive Era, and, until 1910, it was the largest. Through it, many Americans found an effective way to not only keep their sons out of mischief but also retain the influence of the wilderness in contemporary civilization. In 1905, Seton's fellow Camp Fire Club member Daniel Carter Beard began an alternative organization called initially the "Sons of Daniel Boone." Beard's model was the buckskinned frontiersman, the antithesis of Seton's noble Indian hero. Despite such differences, the two men maintained a steady, if somewhat tempestuous, friendship through their mutual interest in art, conservation, and the outdoors. Indeed, at the time Seton launched his boys' movement, Beard was serving as editor of *Recreation* magazine.[1]

It is adequate to say that in a sense both organizations were merely forerunners of the Boy Scouts of America (BSA). When the Boy Scout concept crossed the Atlantic, Seton and Beard sought to weave their programs into it. The movement's overnight success is a significant reflection of American thinking during that time: in the public eye, Scouting offered a practical solution to the innate fears that American society was tearing itself away from its pioneer roots. Joseph Knowles, an eccentric Boston journalist and nature lover, enthusiastically endorsed the movement. "Simply because we are a civilized people," he said, "does not mean that the days of wilderness colonization are over."[2]

Most historians agree that the Boy Scout founder, Sir Robert S. S. Baden-Powell, did "Anglicize" many of Seton's woodcraft principles to fit his own scheme's patriotic slant.[3] Although Baden-Powell's program was less centralized than such English youth groups as the Boys' Brigades and the Church Lads, the key to its popularity in the United States lay in the fact that it allowed more adult supervision and more closely reflected middle-class progressive values than did Woodcraft.[4] In

addition, Seton's passionate dedication to his Woodcraft gospel resulted
in a lack of flexibility on his part. But although he tended to be over-
zealous and sometimes allowed his ego to get the best of him, his genuine concern for the wilderness, young people, and especially Indians,
spurred him on.[5]

As early as 1902, Seton had made plans to tour England for the express purpose of spreading his movement abroad. On October 13, 1904,
at the Stoke Newington Congregational Church in London, he began a
series of analytical talks on the topic "The Red Indian as I Know Him."
At various schools throughout England, Seton enchanted audiences
with his Indian lore, during which he distributed copies of the *Birch
Bark Roll*, then in its third edition. The response was almost overwhelming. At Eccles in November, a man named William Knight established
the "Seton Nature and Athletic Association," which adopted Black
Wolf's guidelines without alteration.[6]

It was probably during this tour that Robert S. S. Baden-Powell first
heard of Seton's scheme. A man with a distinguished military career,
Baden-Powell had been knighted for meritorious service during the
Boer War: after holding the town of Mafeking for 215 days before the
arrival of reinforcements in the spring of 1900, he was hailed by his
countrymen as a "hero among heroes." The success of that campaign
was due in part to a corps of local boy messengers mounted on bicycles.
Organized by Baden-Powell's chief staff officer, Lord Edward Cecil,
these youngsters dutifully carried dispatches to and from the front.
Even before that episode, Baden-Powell had written a book entitled
Aids to Scouting for NCO's and Men (1899), which had its roots in an 1884
army manual he had published and which emphasized character development in addition to "field efficiency." After establishing the South African Constabulary in 1903, Baden-Powell returned to England and
found that his book had been adopted for use in the schools.[7] The seeds
for the Boy Scouts were thus planted.

Baden-Powell immediately became interested in Seton's work, and
during the summer of 1905, he reportedly attended one of Black Wolf's
summer camps at Wyndygoul as a guest of the Camp Fire Club. Former
Woodcraft Indians who claimed to remember Baden-Powell at that
camp have argued that this marked the real beginning of the Boy Scouts
of America. Since the British general took Seton's ideas to his homeland, the Boy Scouts thus came from England back to the United States,
as the Medicine Man always claimed. At any rate, Seton made another

speaking tour of England in March, 1906.[8] Among those attending his lectures were the duke and duchess of Bedford, who afterward introduced him to Lord Roberts. Along with Baden-Powell, Roberts had served with distinction in South Africa before retiring from the army in 1904 and subsequently pushing for the formation of a citizen army. The Woodcraft program stirred the interest of His Lordship, who then discussed it with Baden-Powell.

Whether Baden-Powell actually visited Wyndygoul in 1905 or first met Seton through Lord Roberts the following year is uncertain. What is certain is the fact that the general first sent his plan for "training boys in scouting" to Roberts on May 6, 1906. Soon after that, possibly at the earl's suggestion, Seton forwarded a copy of his manual's sixth edition to Baden-Powell. On August 1, Baden-Powell wrote to Seton expressing gratitude for the book and hoping, upon its completion, to send him a copy of his own scheme "which curiously runs much on the lines of yours." In formulating his own theories, the hero of Mafeking had not seriously considered the woodcraft approach prior to reading the *Birch Bark Roll*. Therefore, judging from his background and earlier consultations with leaders of the Boys' Brigades, Church Lads, and YMCA groups, the resemblance of his original scheme to Seton's is questionable.[9]

Not until October 30, 1906, did Seton personally meet with Baden-Powell to compare ideas over lunch. The general, noting the Woodcraft program's democratic nature, noncompetitive activities, and "high quality scouting practice," decided that his own scheme was almost identical to Seton's in several respects. Hoping that they could "work together in the same direction," Baden-Powell forwarded a copy of his *Aids to Scouting*. In a burst of enthusiasm, Seton initially gave it a favorable response but later regretted his hasty endorsement of a program that was "all soldiering, by a soldier, and for soldiers."[10]

Whereas Seton's scheme called for the formation of its own organization, Baden-Powell's plan was flexible enough to be adopted as a supplement to existing groups. In essence, the general's main goal was to develop qualities of strength, courage, self-reliance, and reliability—traits basic to the making of a good citizen. While woodcraft was an important part of that process, Baden-Powell saw it merely as an ingredient to maintaining the Empire and achieving a patriotic end. Although he and Seton kept up a regular correspondence, they did not see each other again for over a year; meanwhile, each continued promoting his respec-

tive philosophy, yet not once did Baden-Powell play down Seton's "phenomenal success" with the Woodcraft movement.[11]

Like Seton, the general secured the services of a publisher, C. Arthur
Pearson, to help advertise his scheme. In the summer of 1907 he held an
experimental camp at Brownsea Island off the Dorset coast. The success
of that camp ensured public interest in the Boy Scout program, and
Baden-Powell proceeded to compile his handbook, *Scouting for Boys*. All
the while, he kept Seton informed of his doings and promised him
credit for anything extracted from the *Birch Bark Roll*.[12]

Apparently, Baden-Powell and Pearson were careless in living up to
that promise. When Seton returned to England for a third round of lectures in 1908, the general presented him with the first few installments
of his manual. Leafing through them, Seton was "astounded to find my
ideas taken, all my games appropriated, disguised with new names, the
essentials of my plan utilized, and not a word of acknowledgement to
me, or explanation why I should be left out of a movement that I began." Further evidences of outright plagiarism surfaced when Seton
stopped by the Boy Scout headquarters in London and bought a pair of
"B. P. tracking irons" which were exact replicas of those used in his own
"deer hunt." The general apologized for his oversights and assured
Seton that the situation would be remedied.[13]

The truth of the matter was that each man considered himself the
founder of a new youth program and, up to that time, considered the
other his collaborator. In his self-delusion, Seton unwittingly allowed
his own campfire to fade away, at least in England. He had convinced
himself that the Boy Scouts were simply Woodcraft Indians in uniform,
but Baden-Powell saw no reason to limit his program to a model rele-
vant only to North America. Certainly, Baden-Powell had no firsthand
knowledge of the American and Canadian frontiers or any experience as
a naturalist. Possessed with considerable imagination, he nevertheless
lacked Seton's originality, and considering his military background, it is
little wonder that his model was patterned after Kipling's soldier heroes
instead of Cooper's noble red men.[14] Nevertheless, their attempts at col-
laboration continued, and in the summer of 1908, a New York publisher
accepted Pearson's offer to reprint *Scouting for Boys* in the States on condition that the "Briticisms" be removed. Baden-Powell had specifically
stated that he had no desire to interfere with Seton's Woodcraft plan and
even contributed a chapter on scouting, at the latter's request, for the
seventh and eighth editions of the *Birch Bark Roll*. However, Black Wolf

became increasingly suspicious of having his Woodcraft Indian sent back to America with the education of a British soldier and in the garb of the South African constabulary. It was clear to him that there were two separate schemes evolving from what he had hoped would be a shared enterprise. "My aim," he declared, "was to make a man; Baden-Powell's to make a soldier."[15]

Desperately attempting to stave off what he saw as a potential threat, Seton sought to discredit the Baden-Powell manual. For one thing, he regarded prescribed uniforms as an imposition of homogeneity. After all, individual diversity was one of the main themes he had promoted in allowing his boys to make their own Indian outfits. He also singled out those points of the Scout law commanding unquestioning obedience to parents, patrol leaders, and scoutmasters, and patriotic loyalty to church and state as being autocratic. These aspects of Scouting tended to rob youngsters of childhood freedom and spontaneity, and through such militant teachings "you run the risk of making a lot of little prigs now and of disrupting their steady development into citizens of high and independent character. . . . It is like forcing an orchid to flower two seasons ahead, by using chemicals. . . . Yet it blooms, but dies early, and . . . never seeds.[16]

Seton also attacked the Scout motto ("Be Prepared"), suggesting that it actually meant "be prepared (for war, understood)." Overlooking the beam in his own eye, he noted the motto's egotistical play on Baden-Powell's initials. What was worse, by deemphasizing native lore Baden-Powell had practically eradicated Woodcraft's spiritual qualities, and with them the sense of biological continuity between child and environment expressed in *Two Little Savages*. Supposedly, the Scouts could draw spiritual sustenance from hikes in the woods, where they would learn the ways of pioneers who best reflected the traits of manliness and efficiency.[17] Furthermore, Black Wolf's articles on such activities as tracking, estimating measurements, and signal fires had been copied almost verbatim in the Baden-Powell handbook. The titles and functions of his Bands, Tribes, and Medicine Men had been revised as Patrols, Troops, and Scoutmasters; Tenderfoot, Second, and First Class Scout ranks had superseded his Braves, Sagamores, and Sachems. Even the ideas for merit badges, which later became an integral part of the Scouting program, had been taken straight from Seton's coups.[18]

In the second edition of *Scouting for Boys*, Baden-Powell sought to mend the situation by citing specific references to Seton's work, but by

1909, Seton was ready to take the offensive and demand nothing less than credit for planting the seed in the first place. Clearly, he was overstating his case, and even though Baden-Powell consented to publish a statement of "indebtedness . . . for several details," the general was obviously becoming impatient with Black Wolf's petulance.[19]

As Seton feared, Baden-Powell's Boy Scouts attracted a growing amount of attention in the United States as early as 1908. What appealed to many Americans was the more universal soldier model and the fact that Scouting offered a more flexible, year-round program for *all* members. Indeed, the Doubleday, Page firm urged Seton to discard his Indian model on the basis that there were "too many Americans who think of Indians either as dirty and loafing degenerates, or as savages, to make the idea popular when they think of educating their children." But Seton stuck by his guns, firmly convinced that his increased following meant a corresponding decline in widespread racism.[20] His modified urban program showed the extent of his unwillingness to forsake the Woodcraft Indians. When the Boy Scouts did come ashore in America, Seton was braced and ready to work toward allying his braves with them.

The entrance of Dan Beard into the fray was to prove another barrier to Seton's efforts. He, too, had observed Seton's Woodcraft camps at Wyndygoul, where he had been known as "Dan Cider Beard" since he brought his own keg of cider. However, Beard was no scientist and cared little for the American Indian. His Sons of Daniel Boone, later called Boy Pioneers, were organized in groups called "stockades" and dressed in buckskins and coonskin caps. Beard's pompous nationalism and Leatherstocking model proved a more obvious synthesis of Seton's and Baden-Powell's schemes, and like Baden-Powell, he agreed that Scouting's main objective was to strengthen character and "turn out useful, self-reliant, alert, honest citizens."[21] Although he considered himself the real father of the Scouting idea, with Seton and Baden-Powell as mere junior partners, Beard's Turnerian concept of democracy allied him more closely with the British general. Indeed, Baden-Powell deemed the intrepid explorers of America's frontier prime representatives of peacetime scouts. "Character is to be found among those men who still have to fight their way with nature," he argued.[22] Seton scorned such rhetorical bombast from his two patriotic associates. Despite their disclaimers to the contrary, he saw only the threat of militarism in their boys' uniforms. Nevertheless, he still strove to shape the Boy Scout program and make it an international vehicle for his dreams of a Woodcraft Indian confederacy on the lines of Tecumseh's ideals.[23]

In the spring of 1910, regimented Boy Scout groups began sprouting throughout the country. William Randolph Hearst's American Boy Scouts, whose members drilled with arms in public, was the most dubious example. Two U.S. Army officers, Col. Peter S. Bomus and Brig. Gen. William Verbeck, also announced plans to begin militant Scout organizations. Baden-Powell's approach thus seemed the least of all evils, even for Seton. While working through the New York YMCA to launch his inner-city program, Seton had made the acquaintance of Edgar M. Robinson, chairman of the Boys' Work Subcommittee of the YMCA International Committee, and William D. Murray, another subcommittee member. A native of New Brunswick, Robinson had endorsed Seton's woodcraft principles and shared the latter's hopes of incorporating them into the Boy Scouts. On May 9, 1910, the three men met with two representatives of the British Boy Scouts and YMCA, W. B. Wakefield and Charles E. Heald, at the city's Union League Club. Here they discussed plans for formally introducing Scouting to the United States. After the meeting, they took the night train to Washington, where they joined Chicago publisher William D. Boyce.

Boyce is generally credited with ushering in the Boy Scouts of America (BSA) despite the fact that Beard's and Seton's groups were already in existence. The story of how Boyce was aided in a London fog by an English Scout who would not accept a tip for his "good turn" remains an endearing account to all associated with the organization. Inspired, Boyce had returned to his home country and on February 8, 1910, incorporated the BSA in the District of Columbia. On May 10, Seton and company joined him in applying for a charter from the Congressional Committee on Education. This first attempt ended in failure, however. Boyce subsequently turned the reins over to Robinson and bowed out of active participation.[24]

Despite this temporary setback, Seton continued to push for his brand of Scouting. With Robinson's support, he published the eighth edition of his *Birch Bark Roll*, entitled *The American Boy Scout*, in which he presented intact his Indian motif. In the meantime, Seton and his colleagues plotted their strategy to launch the BSA in opposition to Hearst's American Boy Scouts. On June 5, a conference of representatives from thirty-seven youth work agencies was held at the YMCA building in New York. The chairman was another New Brunswick native, Colin H. Livingstone, vice-president of the American National Bank in Washington, D.C., who had been named in Boyce's proposed charter. The primary concern of the meeting was that funds be made available to help reach the poor. The Boy Scouts of America was thus officially begun on June 21, 1910. A temporary Executive Committee was elected with Seton as chairman; Lee Hanmer of the Russell Sage Foundation as secretary; and George D. Pratt, a prominent New York Republican leader and Camp Fire Club member, as treasurer. In turn, they formed an Organization Committee comprising Robinson (who was given a year's leave of absence from his YMCA work), Livingstone, Luther Gulick, and Jacob Riis. Later in the summer, Frank Presbrey, a leading New York advertising executive, and Dan Beard joined the ranks. John L. Alexander, another YMCA boys' work secretary, was selected as the subcommittee's managing secretary.[25]

In his new position Seton recommended the preparation of a new manual. Since Baden-Powell's revised edition of *Scouting for Boys* contained a better structural framework and method of presentation, combining it with the *Birch Bark Roll* would make the BSA's chances of gaining a national charter more favorable. Accordingly, the Organization Committee gave Seton the task of preparing the book, and at one point during the agonizing process, he became so frustrated that he wrote Baden-Powell: *"There is not an important idea in "Scouting for Boys" that I did not publish years ago in "Two Little Savages"* (Seton's italics). On that note, the first official BSA *Handbook* came out under Seton's name.[26]

The Executive Committee also made plans to conduct a camping experiment—along the lines of the Brownsea Island project—at Silver Bay, New York. As chairman, Seton agreed to absorb the expenses and handle the administrative details. After lecturing on his own interpretation of scouting to various YMCAs, Chautauquas, and charities, he arrived at Silver Bay on August 16, 1910. Although Robinson, Murray, and Alexander were titular leaders along with Seton, it was Black Wolf who actually ran the whole enterprise, ably assisted by his inner-city disciple, Miller Jordan. Approximately 150 people from urban centers like New York, Boston, Newark, Pittsburgh, and Jacksonville attended this first BSA "jamboree." Even Canada was represented by a delegation from Toronto. The boys were divided into groups of six, each under an adult leader. They erected tepee shelters, cooked their own meals, and in the evenings sat around the council fire learning the standard Woodcraft Indian ceremonials. Yet while the young campers absorbed Black Wolf's preachments, their supervisors were instructed in the fine points of Scoutmastership by W. B. Wakefield, who sought to curb the heresies of the "red tory," as his British colleagues called Seton. On August 28, "Uncle Dan" Beard arrived on the scene in time to have his picture taken with the leaders. The next day, to Seton's dismay, he disfigured "every big tree in camp" by giving the eager boys hatchet-throwing demonstrations. "I got the blame," Seton lamented. Overall, it was clear to most of the leaders that the Silver Bay camp was not an overwhelming success. With the exception of Robinson, none had committed himself openly to Seton's idea of Scouting. At their next meeting in New York on September 5, they decided that Baden-Powell's approach was superior to Seton's Indian mode.[27]

Even before the Silver Bay camp, factionalism had already become evident within the hierarchy. Livingstone, Pratt, and Hanmer, in particular, never shared Seton's enthusiasm for Indian values and considered the inclusion of Baden-Powell's material in the handbook a definite triumph. Well aware of their animosity, Seton initially had the firm backing of Robinson, Gulick, Riis, and Alexander. He was especially wary of Dan Beard hovering in the wings, knowing full well that the latter's reactionary views would be a welcome boost to the Baden-Powell camp. As it was, Seton's reputation in New York circles, coupled with his charisma and stage manner, obviously made him the moving force behind the Boy Scout program.[28] Thus an uneasy truce and an outward show of camaraderie existed between the factions throughout the summer and early fall of 1910.

Baden-Powell, who was lecturing in Canada, did not attend the Silver Bay camp. On the eve of his return to England, however, he was guest speaker at the organizational dinner hosted by Seton at the Waldorf-Astoria on September 23. In a convivial gesture, Baden-Powell declared to his audience that Seton and Beard were the real fathers of Scouting while he was "only one of the uncles." Nevertheless the concealed attempts of the Livingstone faction to have him bring out a more complete edition of *Scouting for Boys*—because it contained a more "progressive course of instruction"—reflected its burgeoning power.[29] Despite his chairmanship, Seton soon found his cause in serious jeopardy. Even Theodore Roosevelt, who had been made honorary vice-president of the BSA, suddenly came out in favor of the Baden-Powell plan: "Your especial aim is to make the boys good citizens in time of peace, and incidentally to fit them to become good soldiers in time of war, although the latter inevitably follows, being what might be called a by-product of the former."[30]

By mid-October, Seton was confronted with the fact that his program, while it looked good in print, was proving ambiguous and inefficient in practice. Sporadic financial contributions from people like Boyce were far from adequate in meeting the growing demands placed on headquarters from inquisitive boys and aspiring scoutmasters. The addition of William Verbeck and Peter Bomus to the hierarchy gave added strength to the Baden-Powell forces. Soon, W. D. Murray and other fence-sitters drifted into their ranks. Even Robinson, Gulick, and Riis were compelled to admit that functionally Seton's plan was too loosely coordinated to win national approval. The top priority was to obtain the elusive federal charter, and that required evidence of greater cohesion.[31]

Acting on the provisions of Boyce's original incorporation articles, the organizers elected a new permanent Executive Board, which in turn created a National Council, both dominated by conservative bankers, businessmen, educators, social workers, military personnel, and Republican politicians. Because of Seton's personal appeal, they dared not risk public disapproval by eliminating him from the ranks entirely. Instead, they bestowed on him the title of "Chief Scout," and even that was largely ex officio. Dan Beard, along with Verbeck and Bomus, was neutralized as a "National Scout Commissioner." In effect, all existing boys' organizations, including the Woodcraft Indians, were merged under the BSA banner. While Seton and Beard had little actual power, both men were colorful advertisements and helped give the BSA a more Western-American flavor. Ultimately, Uncle Dan proved the more valued supporter, especially after the BSA's purposes and bylaws were drawn up. Few of these objectives set well with Seton, and his relationship with Beard was at times sorely tested.[32]

The Executive Board began its operations at the end of October, 1910. Under its direction, the main office was moved from the YMCA building to new quarters on Fifth Avenue. At the first annual meeting in January, 1911, the National Council elected Colin Livingstone as president, Lee Hanmer as secretary, and George Pratt as treasurer. But the most significant move occurred when Edgar Robinson resigned as executive secretary to resume his YMCA duties. His replacement was James E. West, a young Washington attorney whose concern for youth led him to a long association with the YMCA and who, as a confidant of

Theodore Roosevelt, had served the president's administration in various positions. Although West had observed one of Seton's camps in 1908, his preference for Baden-Powell's approach was obvious from the start. His full-time appointment, made possible with funds from the Russell Sage Foundation, ensured the BSA's bureaucratic centralization.[33] While he was considered "an efficiency expert of the highest order," West soon became the Chief Scout's chief nemesis.

Although Seton had become a mere figurehead, his name lent prestige and, for some, credibility to the Boy Scout package. His presence also proved a hedge against potential competition by allowing him little time to manage the Woodcraft Indians. But even as he basked in his new title, the Chief Scout knew that he had been sidestepped. Not wanting to drop the woodcraft ideal yet realizing that a sounder structure was needed, Seton continually sought to achieve a synthesis. This effort was evident in the compilation of his revised manual early in 1911. In England, he conferred with Baden-Powell on incorporating more organization material before piecing together several old magazine articles and adding new and more interesting detail. Seton then submitted this lot to the BSA Editorial Board, from which he had also been excluded. The board's directors, Murray, Pratt, and A. A. Jameson, felt that the new handbook "reflected too much the adult piont of view"; they proceeded, behind the author's back, to make extensive deletions and add essays by different authors.[34] The informational summary that resulted set the precedent for all subsequent BSA handbooks during the next fifteen years. Seton was furious; rescuing the extracted items, he further embellished them and included them in his *Book of Woodcraft*, which was published as the eleventh edition of the *Birch Bark Roll* the following year. The BSA Editorial Board attacked this book, declaring that it came straight out of the Boy Scout handbook. Seton immediately reminded his colleagues that his work was the basis for the handbook in the first place.[35]

Down but not out, the Chief Scout thus engaged the BSA Executive Board in a bitter political struggle. He accused West and Livingstone of being "Philistines" for removing "spirituality, the power of ceremony, the charm of romance and the importance of the beautiful" from the Scouting program. This dissension soon spread to England, where Scout leaders eyed West's ascendancy with mounting distrust. In turn, West began to raise suspicious eyebrows at Seton's frequent transatlantic tours.[36]

Still, the Chief Scout continued to raise funds and promote the movement as its official spokesman. Writing to Elbert Hubbard in January,
1912, Seton invited him to come down in July and see "a hundred boys
in camp. I think you would realize that it is an important thing in all its
phases." But in his lectures, his primary emphasis was on preaching the
gospel of woodcraft "to the heathens at the west end of the Gitchie
Gumie." He claimed that any public opposition to the BSA was "based
on these totally unnecessary military methods," and charged that many
aspiring scoutmasters were little more than drill sergeants whose "entire
notion of Scout activity is military evolution."[37]

While Seton's actions were bordering on the paranoid, the frustration
he was experiencing is understandable. After all, he had devoted much
time, energy, and money to construct an organization he hoped would
meet the needs of boys as boys perceived them. He felt that since the
Executive Board was apparently more concerned with administration
than with methods and types of program activities, those needs were
misunderstood. It was easy for him to imagine that many parents actually sent their sons to the local Scout troop for disciplinary or utilitarian
reasons.[38]

As he dug in to save his program, Seton made wide use of not only
his voice but also his pen. Remembering Kipling's advice on publishing
his ideas in novel form, the Chief Scout set to work preparing a sequel
to *Two Little Savages*; the result was *Rolf in the Woods*, which he dedicated
to the BSA. In essence, the novel reflects Seton's own brand of Scouting,
which involved the whole demanding art of life in the wilderness. His
ideal Scout is developed in the character of the young hero, Rolf Kitter-
ing. As Seton stated in the preface, "the influences that surrounded the
youth of America a hundred years ago [i.e., those of the wilderness] . . .
made of them, first, good citizens, and, later, in the day of peril, heroes
that won the battles of Lake Erie, Plattsburg, and New Orleans."[39] Essentially, that was the goal toward which the BSA was working with
American youth a century later.

Set in Connecticut and upstate New York during the War of 1812, *Rolf
in the Woods* is unique among Seton's works. For one thing, it is a historical novel written partially to commemorate the approaching centennial anniversary of that conflict; the Battle of Lake Champlain and the
accompanying border skirmishes figure prominently in the story's climax. For his background information, Seton consulted not only Roose-

velt's *Naval War of 1812* and other published sources but also several un-published manuscripts and oral histories by the descendants of those who lived through the war. In this endeavor, he was assisted by his friend and fellow youth worker, Edmund Seymour, who spent his early years in the Lake Champlain area. From the Navy Department's library and war records, Seton extracted information on Adam and Noah Brown, the shipbuilding firm that constructed and launched Thomas MacDonough's flagship, the U.S.S. *Saratoga*, in forty days.[40]

The moral superiority of Seton's ideal pre-Columbian Indian is par-tially developed in the character of Quonab, whose true-life counterpart was the legendary namesake of Ab's Rock. Being the "last of the Myanos Sinawa," Quonab is by nature friendly, profoundly religious, and highly moral. It is he who teaches young Rolf, orphaned nephew of an abusive former soldier, the "true way" of life through woodcraft. The Indian's moralisms blend in nicely with the action of the story itself. Since Seton abhorred militarism, the war—with its causes, and its horrors—is largely confined to the background. Instead, he concentrates on Rolf's peaceful thrills in learning the secrets of the wilderness. The antics of the dog Skookum, probably a play on Jack London's dog heroes, pro-vide not only comic relief but also a further symbolic link between man and nature. Secondary characters such as the wealthy, college-educated greenhorn Van Cortlandt, the two-faced Canuck François la Colle, and the affable fur trader Si Sylvanne with his grassroots philosophy, all help move the story along. The reader is thus provided with a good back-woods yarn hearkening back to the era of the "vanishing American" that Quonab represents. Only toward the end does Seton allow combat to creep in when Rolf puts his woodcraft training to practical use as a scout and courier for the American forces. His valor is proved when he risks his life to thwart a British ambush. At the end, with peace restored, Rolf is ready to take his place as a citizen of the growing young nation. His success in the mercantile business and marriage to Annette Van Trumper, his "lady-in-waiting," completes his transformation to the role of civi-lizer. Yet Rolf never forgets the kindness of Quonab and the principles he taught. This moving drama of America's past closes when Rolf, twenty years later, comes upon the aged Quonab's lifeless body on top of Ab's Rock. His last living link with the past is broken.[41]

Seton's feelings of nostalgia and the inevitability of change, drawn di-rectly from Cooper, could not have been better expressed. Here, indeed, is the oxymoronic synthesis of his own woodcraft ideas and those of Baden-Powell. The unique role of the Indian in the shaping of American character remains a primary focal point.

The Chief Scout also did not hesitate to use magazines to promote his Scouting ideas. In 1910, the novelist Theodore Dreiser requested that Seton compile a series on Scouting for his periodical, the *Delineator*; as things worked out, however, the articles appeared instead in another popular magazine, the *American Boy*. These ten essays, similar in nature to those he had written for Edward Bok, contained some orthodox subjects—"How to Begin as a Scout," "Courtesy and Scouting in the Street," "What Is a Gentleman?"—but the greater portion was given over to such Indian topics as making a willow bed, lighting a fire with a bow drill, and performing native American dances (complete with music). As always, the articles were accompanied by detailed diagrams, and most by a short story to hold the young reader's attention.[42] When BSA headquarters purchased its new magazine, *Boys' Life*, in 1912, Seton's pen was quickly enlisted for its pages. His first article for the new periodical, "Smoke Signals, Sign Talk and Totems," appeared in the December, 1912, issue and was continued in February, 1913. Here Seton emphasized the universal value of sign language in contributing to intertribal understanding. Sandwiched between the two parts of the article—in the January, 1913, issue—was a New Year's message that focused on the War of 1812 centennial. The century of peace between Canada and the United States, represented by a common, unguarded border, clearly showed the "spirit of brotherhood" hovering over the two nations. Likewise, Seton argued, the Boy Scout movement should seek to foster the brotherhood of man as its main goal; instilling such an innate desire in contemporary youth would leave its impression on tomorrow's adult leaders and voters. The story of "The Badger Who Was Brother to a Boy" carried these thoughts a step further and brought attention once more to the bonds between man and beast.[43]

By October, 1913, Seton had been awarded a monthly column, which he entitled "Around the Camp Fire." Perhaps some Editorial Board members saw this move as a means of making amends for the harsh treatment they had accorded his *Book of Woodcraft*. Frank Presbrey, who was on the board, may also have seen the opportunity to use Seton's name as an advertising gimmick to increase circulation. At any rate, Seton used these brief columns to his advantage, continuing to acquaint Boy Scouts with nature study, Indian ways, and other aspects of woodcraft. In one issue he featured the sweat lodge and its cultural and religious significance to many tribes. In another he gave instructions for building a Council Ring, pointing out that "the foundations of our civilization and religion . . . found in the Campfire the focus at the beginning." Seton also suggested that all patrols adopt a totem, preferably an animal indigenous to their area. The gray wolf, he said, was "the peerless Scout," symbolizing perfection, and any patrol choosing that name could consider itself "in the very first rank in all things." [44]

Assuredly, Seton did increase readership of *Boys' Life* among the swelling Boy Scout ranks. *Rolf in the Woods* became a best-seller, equaling if not surpassing *Two Little Savages* in popularity. [45] Seton's writings for boys also continued to enhance his popularity among members of the growing "wilderness cult." Often he attended luncheons and was a guest speaker in the company of such wildwood enthusiasts as Robert Underwood Johnson, associate editor of *Century*. Although the bookish, dapper Johnson cared little about camping out, his interest in wilderness preservation led to many "spiritual lobbying" efforts before Congress. In the Boy Scout movement, especially Seton's version, he undoubtedly saw the opportunities for boys to get close to nature, and he eagerly gave his support. [46]

It began to look as though Seton could work within the bounds of the BSA, despite his differences with other leaders. Things seemed to look his way even more favorably when new girls' organizations started using his methods. But the winds of war, coupled with his uncompromising will, served to change public attitudes and make him a "lone wolf" once more.

CHAPTER 16

DeWinton and the Fall of
the Chief Scout

Along with his involvement in the Boy Scout program, Seton had a significant influence on girls' organizations. Around 1905, Lina Beard, Dan Beard's sister, began thinking seriously of starting a girls' recreation program modeled on her brother's Sons of Daniel Boone and Seton's Indians. Undoubtedly, Grace and other like-minded feminists had expressed similar wishes to include girls in outdoor activities. Once, presumably at her suggestion, Seton's Sinaway tribesmen invited the local schoolgirls to a supper at Standing Rock Village. For the occasion, the young braves provided six bags of rice, each of which was poured into a pot of boiling water. Soon they discovered how much rice expands when boiled; what began as one potful grew into enough for four. The former Woodcraft Indians who recalled that amusing episode claimed that both the Girl Scouts and the Camp Fire Girls had their "unofficial beginning" among the Woodcrafters. Elizabeth Hoisington, a local tomboy, sometimes joined in their activities. Indeed, as early as 1908, girls began getting involved in the Woodcraft programs, although the organization did not officially become "coed" at that time.[1]

Luther and Charlotte Gulick are generally credited as the founders of the Camp Fire Girl program, which had its genesis soon after the organization of the BSA. During the summer of 1909, the Gulicks held an experimental camp for their three daughters and some of their friends at their country home on Sebago Lake near South Casco, Maine. It proved to be a success. After consulting with Seton, Mrs. Gulick decided on using Indian lore as a camp theme for 1910. The name and motto for the camp (which became the organization motto) was "Wo-He-Lo," an Indian-sounding word coined from the first two letters each of "Work, Health, and Love." Using methods she had learned from Seton, Mrs. Gulick taught her charges natural science and outdoor recreation in the Indian manner. The girls made fringed ceremonial gowns embellished with colored patches symbolizing their individual interests. These, too, were copied from designs Black Wolf had given their leader. Although they fashioned headbands, the girls never wore feathers, as did braves. Like the Woodcrafters, they adopted Indian names patterned after physical or personality traits. Their achievements were rewarded with special honors, represented originally by strings of shells and later by colored beads. While the Sebago Lake camp was in progress, William Chauncey Langford, poet, social worker, and friend of the Gulicks, organized another girls' camp in the woods near his Thetford, Vermont, home. Langford also used Woodcraft Indian motifs, and it was he who first coined the name "Camp Fire Girls." However, the Sebago camp set the precedent for the movement.

On March 20, 1911, Luther Gulick chaired a meeting at the Horace Mann Teachers' College "to consider ways and means of doing for the girls (nationally) what the Boy Scout movement was designed to do for boys." Among those present was Grace Gallatin Seton, who was elected to the new committee on organization. A second meeting, held on April 7, was addressed by her husband. Tall and spare, with his unkempt hair and handlebar mustache, Seton stood as "straight as the Indians whose cause he espoused." He reiterated the aims stated by Gulick, stressing that the work should be undertaken to develop womanhood and that beauty should be brought out in every point. Seton was later elected to a men's advisory committee, as was Dan Beard. Uncle Dan endorsed the Camp Fire Girls with the same zeal as he did the Boy Scouts, and for the rest of his life he remained a friend of the organization. On April 10, James West issued a press release from BSA headquarters announcing a "National Society for Girls Like the Boy Scouts."[2]

The problems of consolidating the new movement were compounded when Gulick, for health reasons, was forced to retire temporarily from the leadership. Questions arose over how much difference there should be between boys' and girls' achievement requirements and whether or not certain boys' activities would be suitable or interesting for the opposite sex. (Grace Seton was said to have been too slavish in her use of the *Birch Bark Roll*, much more than her husband would have been.) In Baltimore during a lecture tour, Seton reported that he had found a group of girls waving a "Camp Fire Girls" banner. Chapters soon sprang up in other places, awaiting word from the organizers. Furthermore, two rival, and more militant, groups clamored for attention: the Girl Scouts of Clara A. Lisetor, a journalist in Des Moines, Iowa; and the Girl Guides of Rev. David Ferry in Spokane, Washington. Accordingly, in early June, the organizers decided to pursue a program of amalgamation. An executive board was elected with Charlotte Gulick as president, Jane Addams of Hull House fame as vice-president, and Grace Seton as treasurer. They originally called the organization the "Girl Pioneers of America," a name proposed by Lina Beard, who was given the title "Chief Pioneer." Funds were provided by the Russell Sage Foundation, and headquarters were set up in New York with branch offices in the Midwest and far West. However, that first summer program proved unsuccessful, mainly because there was no real merging of ideas or personalities. Fortunately, the scheme was saved from complete dissolution in September by the return of Luther Gulick, who put the Camp Fire Girls of America, as it was renamed, on a solid footing. Gradually, other girls' programs, except for Juliet Low's Girl Guides in Savannah, Georgia, either died out or merged with the Camp Fire Girls. Mrs. Low's group, founded in 1912 and derived from Lady Agnes Baden-Powell's English Girl Guides, later became the American Girl Scouts.[3]

Of all the American youth organizations, the Camp Fire Girls came closest to adopting Seton's original Woodcraft scheme. While their program structure was more centralized, their Council Fire meetings were taken directly from *Birch Bark Roll*. The Indian's pictorial symbolisms and his love of beauty, purity, and the outdoors remained unique features of the movement. The girls chose not only individual Indian names, but also group names derived from historic tribes. The Camp Fire ranks, like Wood Bearers, Fire Makers, and Torch Bearers, were likewise patterned after the Woodcraft concept. Seton also helped write and categorize the requirements for various honors. To the Health Craft requirements of abstaining from candy and sodas between meals for three months, he once proposed adding: "To abstain forever from the damnable and swinish, filthy, ruinous habit of chewing gum." Those exact terms were not incorporated, but for a short time the early manuals kept another of his additions: "I will prove that my constancy will stand the test of fire, not fire that can harm the body, but the fire that burns the soul. For this, I will do any tasks set up for me by the Council and prove my fortitude, even when it means the wounding of my vanity and humbling of my pride."[4]

Certainly the Camp Fire Girls could not have had a better public relations man than Seton. Their membership grew rapidly as more and more inquisitive girls heard his lectures and became interested. He may have had a hand in the inception of the Blue Birds, the branch of the Camp Fire program for younger girls (ages six to ten). The first group of Blue Birds, whose name was allegedly inspired by the Maurice Mae-terlinck operetta, met at Greenwich in the summer of 1913. On special occasions, the area Camp Fire Girls (and Blue Birds) were invited to the Woodcraft Indians' powwows at Standing Rock Village. One memor-able outing occurred in the fall of 1914 as part of the finale for a confer-ence of adult Camp Fire Girl leaders, or Guardians, held at the Ameri-can Museum of Natural History. On the last evening, a Friday, Seton entertained the Guardians with his stories and animal calls. The next day, forty Guardians took the train to Greenwich and made the three-mile hike to the Seton estate. Local Boy Scouts served as honor guards for the visitors, who were treated to an outdoor barbecue and demon-strations of camping activities by the youngsters. Of course, the real highlight of the evening began with a rousing cheer at Black Wolf's ap-pearance; he lit the Council Fire with his rubbing sticks and proceeded with his repertoire of stories "acquired through his intimate contact with the life of the wilderness and the red man."[5]

During his promotion campaigns, Seton found himself on the road more frequently than ever before. "Life is just one darn hop after an-other," he wrote to Charles Lummis. His personal charisma proved an important factor in the organization of local Scout troops and Camp Fire Girl chapters across the nation. One tour in the fall of 1911 took him to Tulsa, Oklahoma, where he observed the oil fields with their wooden "forests" of derricks and pumphouses. In his mind's eye, here was an-other example of technology's blight scarring the once pristine western wilderness. Among the college campuses on his agenda was Southwest-ern University at Georgetown, Texas, where he met Professor C. A. Nicols, an authority on Indian life. Responding to Seton's lecture on the destruction of the primitive Indian, Nicols said, "I am afraid we have stamped out a system that was producing men who, taken all round, were better than ourselves."[6]

Seton also lectured widely in Canada and continued his overseas travels in a vain attempt to reestablish his Indian model in England. Al-though he continued to meet with Baden-Powell on occasion, Gerald Christy and other friends of Seton were increasingly concerned about the widening breach between the two Boy Scout leaders.[7] As part of his strategy, Seton often resorted to the moralisms he derived from the animal world. In May, 1913, when the Setons visited Chillingham Castle in Northumberland, the Chief Scout made it a point to observe and photograph its famous herd of wild cattle. These were the sole remnants of the Roman Uri, from which many domestic breeds were descended. When he and a groundskeeper came to the aid of a bull in trouble, the ferocious animal showed its gratitude by charging its rescuers. Seton narrowly escaped injury, while the groundskeeper was butted and bruised several times before the bull rejoined the herd. Capitalizing on the episode, Seton made a play on the Boy Scout motto: the ill-prepared groundskeeper had learned the hard way that the Chillingham bulls were just as "ornery as old Texan wild cattle." Even after that close scrape, Seton could later say: "A gun may be needed for my own species, but I have never yet been in serious danger from a native wild animal." To his young audiences, Seton closed by stating: "Be prepared and the danger will pass you by."[8]

Despite Seton's personal charm, his Indian hero never had the same initial appeal in England as it did in North America. The Baden-Powell family's Boy Scouts and Girls Guides, with their Kiplingesque "Tommy Atkins" model, proved the best cultural expression of British youth. Frank Atherton of West Kirby in Cheshire wrote that he had once tried to start a tribe, but failed because most of the "chaps" were Boy Scouts (whom he scorned as "all show") and "the remainder a hopeless crowd." One small group, which called itself the Legion of Frontiersmen, did adopt a woodcraft format, but—as its name implied—its model was the Leatherstocking figure of Dan Beard's Boy Pioneers.[9] Clearly the Woodcraft Indian was out of place in a society increasingly concerned with the impending crisis in the Balkans, Kaiser Wilhelm's troop movements in Germany, and the security of Britain's overseas possessions.

Meanwhile, Seton's works continued to garner a sizable income. Inspired by the success of Wyndygoul and remembering his earlier real estate ventures with his brothers in Canada, Seton decided to invest in a new choice piece of property around Greenwich. There were several underlying motives for this move. The "horseless carriage" was replacing the horse and buggy, and more people were retreating from the city to build suburban homes. Orchard Street was probably becoming quite noisy to a man who liked the quiet solitude of a wildwood environment. Also, the lord of Wyndygoul was interested in expanding his fur farming operations and providing a more remote "wilderness" area for his young campers. Like the Indians of old, he was perhaps ready for a change of scenery. Although he put the house up for sale or lease in 1912, he apparently continued to use the grounds for camps at least through 1915. When Frank H. Powers, his old lawyer friend in San Francisco, heard of the proposed move, he attempted to persuade Seton of the advantages of California real estate. But while he was retreating before the onslaught of progress, Black Wolf, in consideration of his family and position with the Boy Scouts, was not ready to forsake the East Coast entirely.[10]

DeWinton, as Seton named the new tract (after Carberry's original name), was located just east of downtown Greenwich and near the community of Riverside. Generally its landscape was like that at Wyndygoul. As before, Seton brought in native trees and constructed an artificial pond, which he named Lake Peequo, perhaps a corruption of the term "Pequot." One unique feature on this place was a rocky "Indian" cave in which his Woodcrafters could hold their rites. The new "cottage" was built in the same "Tudor-Indian" style as his first house and allowed to "grow naturally" along lines befitting the site. The plaster in the walls contained Indian petroglyph decorations. Over the next few years, the Setons made several additions and improvements to the new house. Hamlin Garland recalled the spring of 1915 when he helped his friends out by painting "some big vases on the gateposts and a part of the garden fence, greatly enjoying the warm spring air." All about the grounds were "blossoming cherry trees, lighted with exquisite sunshine." One addition which Garland helped with was built for Ann (then eleven years old) and jokingly referred to as the "Ann-ex." Another quaint wing, later featured in a magazine article, was for the kitchen. Like the rest of the house, its vine-covered walls and overhanging story were supported by rough beams. Niches in the rock chimney were said to be reserved for the busts of those hired cooks who stayed in the employ of the Seton household for more than a year.[11]

Seton's nearest neighbor was the novelist and journalist Irving Bacheller, whose Thrushwood estate was next door to DeWinton. Lincoln Steffens had his country home, Little Point, near the harbor at Riverside. Both newspapermen strongly supported Seton's youth work and they, along with Garland, were occasional guests at his Indian camps and council meetings. Garland recalled one night in October, 1915, when Seton, dressed in a new buckskin Indian outfit, led the way to the council rock where nearly a hundred boys and girls had assembled. "Their adoration of 'Black Wolf,'" he stated, "is something like that of which the young Sioux feel toward their chieftains and medicine men." Indeed, he "appeared very picturesque and poetic under that clear sky and in the light of the campfire." More than once, Garland and other distinguished visitors were treated to one of Seton's "glorious" lobster dinners.[12]

Such blissful respites did not lessen Seton's mounting conflicts with the Boy Scout executives. The furor over the 1911 handbook's revision continued to plague him. Early in 1914, he filed a complaint with head-quarters, charging that the Editorial Board had altered the material under his name in such a way that it did not represent his ideas. Certainly he felt that the board should have at least obtained his permission to make the changes. Furthermore, he had submitted the draft with the understanding that he would be chairman of the board itself, but he had been excluded from its meetings, and hence, from its policymaking. Seeing this, James West sought to disarm his antagonist in the hope of avoiding a public showdown. It was at his urging that the Editorial Board appointed Seton associate editor of *Boys' Life*. Even this diplomatic gesture could not be achieved gracefully, as Seton had to share the position with Dan Beard.[13] In the meantime, Frank Doubleday, who had produced the 1911 handbook, was upset over the board's decision to give a rival firm, Grosset and Dunlap, the publishing rights to the 1914 edition. Knowing that his personal friendship with Seton was a factor behind that move, Doubleday negotiated with BSA representatives. In August, 1914, he tried to persuade the Chief Scout to resign and have the controversial material omitted as a formal gesture of protest.[14]

Although Seton had already considered resigning, he refused to go quietly; there were matters of principle at stake. Instead, he continued to demand a larger voice in policy decisions. For the moment, West was in a bind. He was determined not to allow the twofold impression that Seton had a legitimate grievance and that the BSA had been unfair to the man who had been instrumental in getting the movement going and attracting so many boys to its ranks. At the same time, West was clearly seeking to steer the organization away from the Woodcraft Indian theme's continued dominance. The question was how to make Seton's exit as painless as possible without tarnishing the hierarchy's reputation. To solve that problem, West played his last trump card.

It was brought to the executives' attention that Seton had never become an American citizen. More than once, Theodore Roosevelt and others had tried to persuade him to take out his naturalization papers, but apparently Black Wolf did nothing about it. Although he used the excuse that his numerous commitments, travels, and government red tape prevented his papers from being completed, Seton probably had little desire to change his citizenship. Obviously, West was aware of that fact and thus felt safe in using it as a pretext for ousting Seton. John L. Alexander criticized this ploy as "flimsy" and felt that Seton should relinquish his position to avoid such coercion.[15] Nevertheless, Seton decided to pursue the issue to its close after perceiving West's petty intrigue. Before sailing for England late in January, 1915, he reportedly expressed his "intention to take out my papers as soon as the European situation is cleared."[16] However, the BSA bylaws required that the Chief Scout stand for annual reelection, and the annual meeting was slated for February 11. With Seton absent and no one else nominated for the position, the office was left vacant. After his return in April, Seton conferred with Livingstone, Pratt, West, and other board members, who presumably informed him that unless he was then, at that very moment, a U.S. citizen, he would no longer be eligible to hold any BSA office. Outfoxed at last, Seton tendered a formal letter of resignation to the board in May. Never once did he acknowledge that "the question of my British birth had [any] bearing on the case whatever."[17]

Ironically, world events played an indirect role in hastening Seton's departure from the Boy Scout leadership. Soon after the outbreak of World War I in Europe, Seton is said to have written to the British government, the minister of Militia and Defence in Ottawa, and the War Department in Washington to offer his services. But on the grounds of his age—he turned fifty-four in 1914—he was politely turned down. On that basis alone, one could say that the charges of pacifism hurled at him by his critics were largely fabricated.[18] However, circumstances in the spring of the following year may have caused him to have more pacifistic leanings. The ship on which Seton departed for England on January 30 was the ill-fated *Lusitania*. In his journal, Seton recorded how the British liner approached its destination flying the American flag because "we were in great danger of German submarines," and upon its arrival at Liverpool, he noted that "ten German spies [were] arrested as they landed." Fortunately, no submarines menaced that particular trip, or his return voyage on the *St. Louis* in April.[19]

In early May, after facing the music with the BSA executives, Seton retreated with his family and Hamlin Garland to work on his still unfinished house at DeWinton. There, on May 8, they received the news of the sinking of the *Lusitania* by a German U-boat torpedo; among the 1,198 fatalities was their friend, Elbert Hubbard. Appalled by the tragedy, they "gave up all . . . plans for recreation, and sat on the lawn, or strolled about the garden striving to counteract the horror of it." Perhaps Seton came to believe more strongly that had his woodcraft principles been applied to the current situation, such an episode would likely not have occurred. Whether or not he aligned himself with the left-wing philosophies of David Starr Jordan and other anti-imperialists is uncertain. At any rate, Seton was disturbed at the militant fervor the *Lusitania* disaster generated in America, which served to push his ideals farther into the background. "I try to find some ray of comfort in this black abyss of horror," he wrote after the United States entered the war in the spring of 1917. "I hope I am right in believing that we are paying for a great recent epoch of material prosperity and will emerge from this agony on a spiritual plane so high that war will no longer be a possibility among men."[20] Yet even before the American doughboys marched to the tune of George M. Cohan's "Over There," rumors began to circulate that Seton was in league with pacifists and anarchists.

Once again, Black Wolf's own petulance proved detrimental to his cause. His defeat at the hands of the BSA executives continued to rankle, and neither side was willing to drop the issue. It was another blow to Seton when Theodore Roosevelt notified West that the BSA had within its ranks "certain leaders . . . [who] have used the Boy Scouts organization as a medium for the dissemination of pacifist literature and . . . as a propaganda for interfering with the training of our boys to a standard of military efficiency."[21]

But Seton added fuel to the fire when he told a *New York Times* reporter that his resignation resulted from personal conflicts with West, who he felt was "a man of great executive ability but without knowledge of the activities of boys, and who, I might almost say, has never seen the blue sky in his life." West promptly shot back, accusing Seton of being "in harmony with the views of anarchists and radical socialists on the question as to whether the Boy Scouts of America should stand for patriotism and good citizenship." The primary reason Seton had been expelled as Chief Scout, West claimed, was his persistent opposition to the chapter on patriotism in the handbook, especially the pledge of allegiance, and his argument that boys should be left "free to support our country when they thought our country was right and to damn it when they thought it wrong."[22] Priding himself as being the object of such an attack, Seton made it clear that he was not in sympathy with the BSA's current trends. In addition to his feud with West, his relationship with Dan Beard had by this time completely disintegrated. Loyal to the Executive Board in most matters of principle, Uncle Dan could be counted on to assume the role of the organization's spiritual guide. As for Seton, he vowed publicly to devote the remainder of his life to the Woodcraft Indians.[23]

As a postscript to the controversy, the January, 1916, issue of *Boys' Life* published a vindictive statement saying that Seton had been "dropped" by the National Council at its February, 1915, meeting and "did not resign from the position as alleged." The anonymous author reassured young readers that the movement was "in no wise affected" by his removal, that the pages in the manual written by Seton added "nothing essential" to the Scouting program, and that they could be "easily replaced in future editions by eminent American citizens." Undoubtedly, the notice was slanted to leave the impression that Seton's work had been of little value to the BSA.[24]

Seton's ouster, indeed, had more to do with his chronic objection to Scouting's military aspects than with his citizenship. In that sense, he could perhaps be labeled a pacifist. Of all the Boy Scout founders, Seton alone saw and questioned what was evidently a militaristic threat. By refusing to resign, he had ensured that the issues at stake were given a more public definition. Be that as it may, the long-awaited federal charter—which limits membership to American citizens—was finally granted to the Boy Scouts of America by Congress on June 15, 1916.[25]

CHAPTER 17

The Spartans of the West

Even while promoting the Boy Scouts and trying to match wits with the executives, Seton still found time to escape into the western wilderness, studying wildlife, and maintain contacts with the Indians. Late in August, 1912, the Setons made a return visit to Yellowstone Park; his mission was to make an updated list of species in the park for the U.S. Biological Survey.

Certainly the Setons could not help noticing the changes that had occurred in the previous fifteen years. A general hospital had been added to the array of buildings at Mammoth Hot Springs. The Gallatin Road connecting Bozeman, Montana, with the West Entrance had been opened, and for the first time, rail passengers could come into the park via the East Entrance from Cody, Wyoming. Crusty old John Yancey had died of pneumonia in 1903, just days after he had attended President Roosevelt's dedication of the famous North Entrance arch. Subsequently, his nephew had sold the family's lease to the Pleasant Valley Hotel after the main building had burned. Elsewhere in the park, the Lake Hotel had been enlarged, and the Fountain now had a rival in the form of the rustic Old Faithful Inn.

The park superintendent was Col. Lloyd Melton Brett of the First Cavalry. As the last army officer to run the park, Brett helped prepare it for two far-reaching changes: automobiles instead of horsedrawn vehicles and civilian rather than military administration.[1] The colonel took an immediate interest in Seton's work and proved an accommodating host.

Seton secured Thomas E. Newcomb as their trail guide, and he was another colorful western character who had been on both sides of the law. Raised on a farm in Missouri, he had ridden for a short time with Frank and Jesse James before becoming a hunter and scout for the army. After suffering a broken leg, he had been befriended by the Sioux and had known Crazy Horse personally. But when the Sioux went on the warpath in 1876, Newcomb scouted for Gen. George Crook and fought in the battle of the Rosebud. He won considerable notoriety when he murdered the famous scout "California Joe" Milner during the Black Hills gold rush and also when he was fined for poaching elk in Yellowstone Park. Yet he had served the park authorities well as an extra scout and detective on at least two occasions. The son of a steamboat captain, Newcomb claimed Israel Putnam and Daniel Webster among his distinguished ancestry. In his company, Seton camped out in the wild areas of the park and made several photographs of the fauna. Whereas veteran Westerners usually told tall tales and played harmless tricks on their Eastern guests, Seton once turned the tables on Newcomb with his "hoodoo elk" joke. After encountering several skittish elk near the south shore of Yellowstone Lake, the naturalist singled out a dozing cow elk, crept up close enough to pet it, and in effect "talked" it into making various poses for his camera. When the baffled guide asked how he did it, Seton replied that he had merely "made medicine" on his subject.[2]

Among other things, Seton tried stalking the bighorn sheep on the slopes of Mount Washburn and Mount Evarts. At Mammoth Hot Springs, he observed bats in the noxious Devil's Kitchen and, with Colonel Brett's permission, secured a specimen for the Biological Survey. The Setons also spent one night at the Fountain Hotel. When a bear cub was heard whining below their window the next morning, the hotel employees declared that "it was Little Johnny calling on his creator." Before leaving, Seton compiled his list of species and made arrangements with Colonel Brett to return in the winter for more photographs. Subsequently, he incorporated many stories, observations, and snapshots of the trip into his book *Wild Animals at Home* (1913).[3]

After leaving Yellowstone Park in September, the Setons visited their old friends at the Crow Agency. Although White Swan had died in 1910, many Little Bighorn veterans were still living. Hearing that one of them, Curley, was sick with a boil over his kidneys, Seton went to his lodge and performed a crude feat of surgery on the sore spot with his sterilized hunting knife. Curley was up and out riding his horse the next day, and the Crows afterward claimed that Seton was the only man who stuck a knife into the old scout and got away with it.[4] Seton also encountered the Reverend Mr. Burgess, the resident missionary with whom he had locked horns over the Indian wedding fifteen years before. Since then, the clergyman's legalistic attitudes had mellowed to the point where he considered Indian dances a clean, healthy form of exercise; he even thought that they should be introduced into the public schools.

Upon leaving the Crow Agency, Grace continued on to New York, while her husband made a side trip by stagecoach to the Standing Rock Reservation in North Dakota. Riding with him was Father A. M. Beede, a Jesuit priest on his way to begin duties as a missionary at the agency. Like Seton, Beede was interested in Indian culture and concerned about the government's treatment of its "wards." The Chief Scout ended up staying three weeks at the padre's new mission post.[5]

Seton's devotion to the Indian was thus heightened all the more. While most of the nation primed itself, and its youth, for the approaching world conflict, his "overwhelming, and empirically based, social passion" was the cultural freedom and human dignity of the red man.[6] He was not alone in this crusade; for example, his old friend George Bird Grinnell was likewise appalled by the poverty, disease, and accelerating death rates on the reservations. From 1889 on, Grinnell wrote numerous books and articles in which he sought to promote public sentiment on behalf of the Indians and remind white Americans of their constructive role in the nation's development. Seton could always count on him for advice and support in his own endeavors.[7]

Seton could likewise depend on the unfailing friendship of Charles Eastman. He, too, had been instrumental in the founding of the BSA and Camp Fire Girls, having served on the former's National Council. Married to a white schoolteacher, Elaine Goodale, Eastman made his home in Massachusetts and became the father of five. Hamlin Garland later recalled many instances when the Eastman family stopped by DeWinton to visit. Seton often enjoyed boating with them on Lake Pecquo.[8] When Eastman applied for the BIA Indian Commission, based on his previous seven-year experience as a special agent for the Sioux family allotments, Seton used his own political connections and wrote to President William H. Taft on Ohiyesa's behalf.[9]

With the backing of such friends, Seton turned more of his attention to Indian rights. Before his Yellowstone trip in 1912, he had prepared a manuscript on "The Spartans of the West" for inclusion in his *Book of Woodcraft*. Remembering the terrible conditions of the Chipewyans he had seen during his 1907 arctic voyage, Seton felt that the primitive Indian was "without degrading vice until the White-man introduced whiskey, horrible diseases and the love of money." This was not to imply that Indians possessed no faults whatsoever but, by stressing that which was laudable in Indian society, to effectively counteract the prevailing image of a "dirty, filthy, squalid wretch, a demon of cruelty and cowardice, incapable of a human emotion and never good till dead." The Indian would thus be cleared of all charges except that of cruelty to his enemies.[10]

After scrutinizing the accounts of frontier army officers who had conducted what he deemed a genocidal mission, Seton brought out apparent confessions of their own guilt. These he reprinted, along with analytical commentary endorsing the Indian interpretation, to edify his young readers. From James Mooney, another Smithsonian ethnologist who embraced the Indian cause, Seton extracted details concerning the Wounded Knee Massacre, declaring that it had no parallel in the history of human cruelty: "As sure as there is a God in Heaven, this thing has to be met again, and for every drop of righteous blood spilled that day . . . a fearful vengeance is being stored and will certainly break on us."[11]

In conjunction with tragic historical events, Seton described the primitive religion of the First Americans as having grown out of the land itself. Their songs, stories, dances, and craftsmanship merely reflected the general belief "that the Great Spirit is in everything, everywhere, all the time." Seton thus readily agreed with Eastman that the Indian saw no need of setting apart one day of the week as holy, "since to him all days were God's." In restating the white man's conquest and settlement of the West, Seton argued that the early pioneers survived only because they adopted Indian ways. But as time went on, they forgot the kindnesses shown by their red benefactors and allowed their own self-made laws, culture, and religion to justify their prejudice.[12]

Seton was especially intrigued with the dramatic flight of Dull Knife and his Northern Cheyennes from the Indian Territory to their old Wyoming homeland in 1879: "I was taught to glorify the names of Xenophon, Leonidas, Spartacus, the Founders of the Dutch Republic or the Noble Six Hundred at Balaclava, as the ideals of human courage and self-sacrifice, and yet I know of nothing in all history that will compare with the story of Dull Knife as a narrative of magnificent heroism and human fortitude." His major source for details of that episode was the eyewitness account of Edgar Beecher Bronson, a Nebraska rancher, from whom he freely quoted by permission. It proved a fitting climax for Seton's historical examples of Indian character.[13]

Upon completing his manuscript, Seton asked Mooney, Grinnell,

Hodge, and others to critique it for historical accuracy. All responded positively except Mooney, who apparently disagreed with some of Seton's romantic interpretations. Another interested individual was Robert G. Valentine, whom Seton considered "the best Indian Commissioner we have ever had." Valentine's own sympathy toward the red man proved a feather in Seton's hat. When *The Book of Woodcraft* came out in the fall of 1912, "The Spartans of the West" received an overwhelmingly favorable response from these colleagues.[14] After the *New York Herald* published a scathing exposé on national Indian policy, Seton wrote a supportive letter to the editor in which he further protested the government's expedient justifications for breaking treaties and asserted that "the record of our official dealings with the Indians is far worse than anything we can find in Russia or Spain's colonies during modern times. It is . . . 'an unbroken narrative of injustice, fraud and robbery.'"[15]

With his credibility as an authority on Indian culture firmly rooted, Seton visited more reservations throughout the West. In December, 1914, he made his first tour of the pueblos in New Mexico. Following a stopover in Albuquerque on December 10, he spent two days photographing and sketching details of Laguna pueblo's adobe architecture. His guide was John Saracino, an Apache whom he dubbed "the merriest Indian I ever met." Although the local agent had told Seton that it was inappropriate for his entourage to visit Acoma because of the religious celebration going on there at the time, the Chief Scout was determined to do so. Meeting with Acoma's governor, José Antonio, Seton bribed his way through by saying that he was from Washington and a friend of Charles F. Lummis and even offering a dollar. While not allowed to see the dances, he did manage to sketch and photograph the old Spanish mission and the surrounding houses. He also purchased several clay pots from the women. Afterwards, he considered the Sky City much less picturesque than Laguna. In both villages, he noted the changes the outside world was beginning to effect: stovepipe chimneys in place of the old-style hole in the roof, and the modern garb of the young people contrasting with the traditional costumes of their elders. Traveling to Santa Fe, Seton toured the sights and lunched with several prominent citizens, including the noted archaeologist Sylvanus Griswold Morley. In Albuquerque, he stayed at the Alvarado Hotel and became impressed with its Pueblo House. Part of Seton's interest in New Mexico's adobe buildings stemmed from his fascination with Spain's ba-

Self-portrait (pen-and-ink, 1879). (Courtesy Seton Memorial Library, Philmont Scout Ranch)

The Elms, the farmhouse built by Seton's father near Lindsay, Ontario (watercolor, 1877). (Courtesy Seton Memorial Library, Philmont Scout Ranch)

The Thompson homestead near Carberry, Manitoba (watercolor, 1882). (Courtesy Seton Memorial Library, Philmont Scout Ranch)

Barnyard at DeWinton (1892). (Courtesy Seton Memorial Library, Philmont Scout Ranch)

Old Homestead (1892). (Courtesy Seton Memorial Library, Philmont Scout Ranch)

Cowshed at DeWinton (1892). (Courtesy Seton Memorial Library, Philmont Scout Ranch)

Marsh Hawk (watercolor, 1890).
(Courtesy Seton Memorial Library,
Philmont Scout Ranch)

Triumph of the Wolves, or *Awaited in Vain* (oil, 1892). (Courtesy Seton Memorial Library, Philmont Scout Ranch)

Wolves at Night. (Courtesy Panhandle-Plains Historical Museum, Canyon, Texas)

Calf (1892). (Courtesy Seton Memorial Library, Philmont Scout Ranch)

Antelope Sighting Danger (1900). (Courtesy Panhandle-Plains Historical Museum, Canyon, Texas)

Evensong (1901). (Courtesy Seton Memorial Library, Philmont Scout Ranch)

The Skunk and the Unwise Bobcat (*Then Take That*) (1905). (Courtesy Seton Memorial Library, Philmont Scout Ranch)

The Tenderfoot and His Caller (1910). (Courtesy Seton Memorial Library, Philmont Scout Ranch)

Silly Billy to the Rescue (1915). (Courtesy Seton Memorial Library, Philmont Scout Ranch)

Tracks of the Common and Spotted Skunk (1902). (Courtesy Seton Memorial Library, Philmont Scout Ranch)

Within the illustration:
rt hind   rt fore
Am Mus 1919
by E T S
Jan 16 1923
E T Seton
11 in   12 in   12½
Peccary Tracks, Catalina Mts   Ari

Plate CIX. — Details of Collared Peccary

Details of the Collared Peccary (1923). (Courtesy Seton Memorial Library, Philmont Scout Ranch)

Old montezuma made a Guild of all his men of brains
Who got their inspiration on the mountains or the plains
And some were Rulers, some were Priests, & some were Craftsmen skilled
But all had given the world _ideas_ that entered in this Guild.
The Thunder-bird, their emblem dwelt, where clouds & peaks confused
And the only Test of membership was, _What has he produced._

Now Royal montezuma's gone, his Empire turned to dust
But who shall say the Bird has flown or that the Guild is lost
No, no, the inspiration of the Great West never flags
The Spirit in the Thunder-bird still haunts its ancient Crags
The Guild still lives, its tribute gives, refined by memories
And when the Brethren meet [as now] They know it and are glad

alisal
Los Angeles
5 may 1901

Ernest Thompson Seton

Poem written by Seton in the Charles F. Lummis housebook (1901). (Courtesy Southwest Museum, Los Angeles)

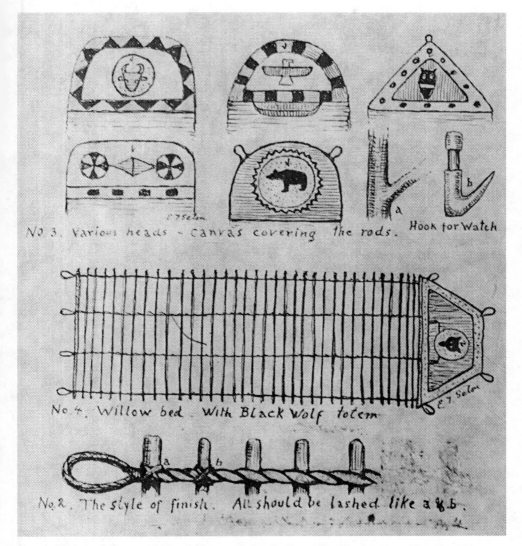

No. 3. Various heads – canvas covering the rods.   Hook for Watch

No. 4. Willow bed – with Black Wolf totem

No. 2. The style of finish. All should be lashed like a & b.

Seton's illustrated instructions on how to make an Indian willow bed (1902). (Courtesy Seton Memorial Library, Philmont Scout Ranch)

Blackfoot Man and Woman (watercolor, 1937). (Courtesy Seton Memorial Library, Philmont Scout Ranch)

How the Bluebird Came (1941). (Courtesy Seton Memorial Library, Philmont Scout Ranch)

Nanaboujou and the Rabbit's Fire Dance (1941). (Courtesy Seton Memorial Library, Philmont Scout Ranch)

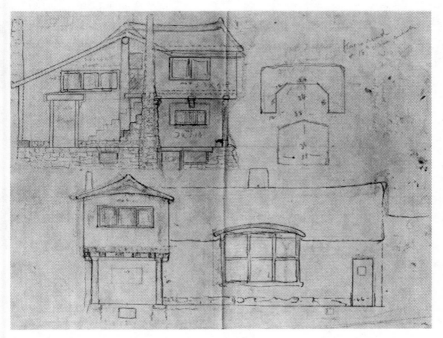

Architectural drawings for Little Peequo (1928). (Courtesy Seton Memorial Library, Philmont Scout Ranch)

Architectural drawings for Seton Village (1933). (Courtesy Seton Memorial Library, Philmont Scout Ranch)

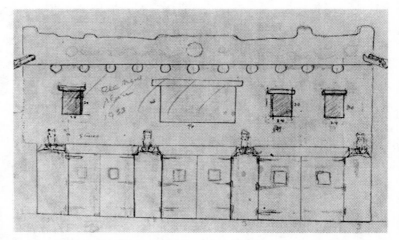

Architectural design for Seton Village (1933). (Courtesy Seton Memorial Library, Philmont Scout Ranch)

roque architecture, which he had sketched during a tour of that country the previous year.[16]

After his ouster from the BSA, Seton took his family on another southwestern tour in August, 1915. In Oklahoma, as guests of former Indian agent John Homer Seger, they visited several churches, schools, and other white men's "follies" in the Indian communities around Weatherford and Anadarko. When Seton asked one Indian if he had ever known an honest, sincere white missionary, the answer was a definite "no." From Seger and George Bent, who joined them later, he recorded little-known facts concerning Custer's 1868 campaign on the Washita. Certainly, Seton was in complete agreement with Seger when the latter remarked that "Custer was everything a man didn't oughter be."[17]

From Oklahoma, the Setons went on to Santa Fe, where they met with Sheldon Parsons and other local artists. At the Santa Fe Club in the DeVargas Hotel, they met the Wyoming rancher-politician John A. Kendrick, who was serving at the time as a special attorney for the federal government. With him, they took the train to Taos, where they visited the studios and galleries of several noted artists, and there Seton ran into his old bunkmate from wolf hunting days, Jack Brooks. The two men spent a couple of days reminiscing and collecting specimens. Seton also met leading residents of Taos pueblo and sketched its architecture. After seeing his wife and daughter off to visit friends and relatives in California, Seton and Sheldon Parsons toured the ruins of the cliff dwellings in Frijoles Canyon. Former governor L. Bradford Prince then treated them to a sumptuous dinner at his Santa Fe home, where Seton admired Prince's collection of Spanish colonial relics.[18]

Seton's travel plans also included a tour of the Navajo and Hopi reservations in northeastern Arizona. Arrangements were made through the Hubbell family, whose vast trading empire encompassed the whole of the Navajo country. In a borrowed, broken-down automobile, Seton and his hosts braved the blistering desert, with its occasional sandstorms, cloudbursts, and flash floods, to reach remote villages and isolated hogans. At the ancient Hopi town of Oraibi, he met and established a lasting friendship with Gerald and Ina Sizer Cassidy, both noted for their paintings and articles dealing with Pueblo Indian life. He was particularly impressed by Gerald's talent with frescoes.[19] With the Cassidys, Seton visited the major Hopi pueblos and took careful note of their customs and beliefs. At Walpi, where they witnessed the annual Corn Dance and Snake Dance, Seton was awed by the dancers' ability to control the poisonous rattlesnakes. "The only scoffers in the crowd who were very disrespectful," he wrote, "were seven young Indians from Carlisle. I think they were Navajos." He also noted, with some concern, the division among the tribe over the changes the white man's government had imposed; some Hopi families had moved away rather than allow their children to "turn into whites."

In the Navajo country, Charlie and Ramon Hubbell pointed out the windmills and other technological improvements made on the reservation, which Seton, of course, viewed with mixed emotions. He also called on several resident traders, artists, and anthropologists, including John and Louisa Wetherill of Kayenta and his old friend, E. A. Burbank. From them, he gathered various artifacts and recorded examples of Navajo folklore. Before returning to Gallup to catch the westbound train, Seton spent a memorable night at Don Lorenzo Hubbell's adobe home and trading post at Ganado. Here he observed the Navajo rug weavers and bought several of their products, for which the place was famous.[20]

In Los Angeles, Seton had a grand time with Charles F. Lummis. He had a standing invitation to Don Carlos's famous "noises"—informal evenings of "music, poetry, good fellowship and Latin dance"—held on special occasions at El Alisal. After rejoining his family, Seton went north for a two-day lecture stint at San Francisco's Bohemian Club. While there, he and Ann took in the Panama-Pacific Exposition, and Seton commented prophetically in his journal that the fair's California-mission architecture "sets a new face for the whole world of building."[21]

Early in the fall of 1916, as war fever increased throughout the nation, the Seton family took a three-week vacation to Glacier National Park in Montana. At Many Glaciers, St. Mary's Lake, and other famous sites, the former Chief Scout recorded in detail the numerous kinds of animal life he saw. They also called at the Blackfoot Indian Agency in Browning, where Seton had several prominent contacts. His reputation as a friend of the Indians was just as great among the Blackfoot as elsewhere. In a special ceremony, they gave him the name of *Ah´-pas-to* or "Sign Talker"; Grace was called *Ni-se-ta-pi-ak* or "Good Squaw"; and twelve-year-old Ann became *Ne-ché-poi-é* or "Indian Talker."[22]

These various western ventures determined the subsequent direction of Seton's career and perhaps held the key to his unrepentant opposition to the BSA's military aspects. After all, it was the superiority of the U.S. Army and its weapons that had helped the whites triumph over their red adversaries in the first place; in addition, blind duty to flag and government, plus the love of money, had caused men like Tom Newcomb to fight against their Indian friends. This argument, so effectively expressed in his "Spartans of the West," was reinforced in Seton's mind on December 15, 1915, when he dined in Washington with the prince of Wild West showmen, "Buffalo Bill" Cody. When their conversation turned to Indians, Cody allegedly remarked: "I never led an expedition against the Indians but that I was ashamed of myself, ashamed of my government and ashamed of my flag; for they were always in the right and we were always in the wrong. They never broke a treaty and we never kept one."[23]

The contemporary plight of a minority group, however, was not the primary concern of the mighty Republican elite at that moment. As the war clouds in Europe drifted closer to America's shores, Roosevelt and his colleagues abandoned Seton's eccentricities in favor of Baden-Powell's concept of Scouting for boys, and the majority of the American public, at least in the East, seemed to follow suit. In their eyes, integrity came more and more to be synonymous with technology, homogenization, and efficiency; Seton's realism was more and more out of line.[24]

Initially, after 1915, Seton could rely on support for his program only from his small circle of literary companions and certain friends at the American Museum and the Smithsonian. As his travels in the West continued, however, many friends and contacts there extended to him their heartfelt blessings, if not their outright support. After Mary Austin's move to New York, Seton eagerly sought to enlist her active participation in his brand of Scouting.[25] His visits to the pueblos and communities of the southwest perhaps stimulated him to consider making the Land of Enchantment his home, for although he continued making improvements on his DeWinton estate, Seton seemed to sense that his "Camelot" was beginning to crumble in the East. While America's fighting men (including former Woodcraft Indians) turned their faces toward France and the war against Kaiser Bill's "Huns," Black Wolf turned his weary countenance more longingly toward the setting sun. Before deciding on that move, however, he made one last concerted effort to bring his West back to the East.

CHAPTER 18

The Woodcraft League
of America

While Seton focused on his Indian crusade, the rest of the nation, led by the scholarly idealist Woodrow Wilson, turned its attention toward winning the Great War and "making the world safe for democracy." Even though Seton's middle age had ruled out active military service for him, his family rendered its share of service to the cause in other ways. Grace "raised the money to buy, equip and operate six Ford trucks for camp and transport service between Paris and the front." For this and other wartime fund-raising, she was "decorated and highly honored" by the French. Soon afterward, in 1919, her husband for his wildlife conservation efforts and youth work was awarded the silver medal of the Société l'Acclamation de France, the first official French peace decoration received by an American.[1]

For the time being, the utopian socialists were divided over the issue of the war. Many who had heretofore championed peace and the New Freedom program lost their zeal in the distraction of the crusade for justice in Europe.[2] Nowhere was this martial air more prevalent than among the youth organizations Seton had helped found. The Boy Scouts flexed their patriotic muscles by holding Liberty Bond drives, aiding the Red Cross, cultivating war gardens, and serving as government "dispatch bearers." The Camp Fire Girls followed suit and formally adopted their famous "Minute Girl" uniforms, consisting of the red tie, white blouse, and blue skirt.[3]

As the war progressed, Seton cast an attentive eye toward the pan-Indian reform efforts in America. Ever since the Roosevelt administration, various individuals, pressure groups, and congressional committees had worked to turn public opinion against attempts by the BIA and groups like the Indian Rights Association to "Americanize" the Indians at the expense of tribal traditions.[4] The Society of American Indians (SAI), formed in 1911 by Fayette A. McKenzie, further emphasized the importance of native Americans as a distinct race and encouraged self-reliance and initiative on their part. After permanent SAI headquarters were established in Washington, J. N. B. Hewitt of the Bureau of Ethnology emerged for a time as the SAI's dominant figure. Unlike Seton, Hewitt placed greater emphasis on heredity than on environmental and spiritual aspects. Believing that Indian improvement would be predicated on a strictly scientific knowledge of the red man's past, he scorned the "noble savage" myth. For that reason, Charles Eastman, who felt that the organization should be concerned more with the moral and social welfare of the Indians and less with government, took little hand in its affairs for the next few years. Such conflicting viewpoints weakened the SAI's attempts to bring about desired changes. But by 1918, with Eastman as its president, SAI had adopted a platform calling for the immediate abolition of the BIA and a modified version of Wilson's self-determination ideal. Moreover, there was a growing belief in rugged American "groupism," which ran contrary to the Turnerian idea of rugged individualism.[5]

Although Seton was never directly involved with the SAI, he undoubtedly kept up with its activities through Eastman and his contacts at the Smithsonian. Indeed, many of his ideas paralleled those of the SAI. His close association with ethnologists gradually instilled in him a belief that the Indian, like the wolf and the grizzly bear, was victimized by persecution based on ignorance. While martyrdom always held special appeal for Seton, his ecological mind could immediately correlate the sufferings of an entire race alongside those values opposed to the survival of other species.

After 1915, Seton's continued efforts to apply Hall's recapitulation theory resulted in a "dreadful inconsistency" that was to hamper his youth work. By then, he no longer saw pre-Columbian Indian life as a mere stage in the growth of civilization. Having questioned contemporary American values, he began to rationalize the woodcraft "game" into the reality of life, "where the 'savage' state became the truly civilized state [and] where that which was to act merely as a preparatory stage itself became the end of moral striving." Not surprisingly, Seton came to believe that the Indian was not only attuned to nature but that he *was* nature. "Woodcraft originally constructed man out of brutish material, and woodcraft may well save him from decay," he wrote in the fourteenth edition of the *Birch Bark Roll*.[6] Remembering his early success with his Sinaway tribe, Seton was determined more than ever to prove

that the Indian lifestyle "was a better system, a better thought." Those
who shared his concepts were expected to "deal chiefly with the natural
instincts of the growing child, offering a vast range of developmental
activities, spiritual as well as physical, the choice of which is left to the
child's free will."[7] Seton thus maintained his abiding faith in democratic
principles, deeming them nature's own instigation. More than ever, he
was determined that no young brave would be able to "scoff at the public opinion of playmates" or impose his own views upon others.[8]

   Accordingly, in 1916, Seton reorganized his movement and gave it a
more sophisticated air as the Woodcraft League of America, adopting as
its logo the buffalo horn symbol of the Plains tribes. With Seton himself as Chief, the organization was set up with Mark Sullivan (author of
Our Times) as secretary, Elon Huntington Hooker as treasurer, and
Philip D. Fagens as executive secretary. Its Council of Guidance included such notables as John L. Alexander and Hamlin Garland, who
served as the council's historian. Grace chaired the business committee.
Those who actively participated in the Woodcraft League's functions
were automatically members of its National Council. Among those
listed at one time or another on the Council's rolls were John Burroughs, Irving Bacheller, Frank M. Chapman, Natalie Curtis, Frank N.
Doubleday, Madison Grant, Ida M. Tarbell, Lorado Taft, and Henry Van
Dyke. The League's headquarters in New York City were located originally on West Twenty-ninth Street and later West Forty-eighth Street.[9]

   In revamping his program's content, Seton classified by color three
areas of individual achievement: "Red honors" were the athletic coups,
"white" the woodlore section, and "blue" the nature study category. In
these, he stressed the importance of group participation as a biological
law. More elaborate decorations for honor were awarded by an eagle
feather for the warbonnet or a wampum bead (or medal) for the coat, or
both. Red tufts or tassels decorated the awards for grand coups. Each
brave not only designed his own regalia but also had to be prepared to
explain its significance. In this way, an individual could better himself
without drawing comparison with his fellow braves. One who earned
forty or more coups was automatically made a Sachem and entitled to
sit on the Grand Council without election. Badges indicated various
tribal positions, and woodcraft degrees became the counterpart of the
BSA's merit badges.[10] Moreover, woodcraft activities and achievement
requirements varied according to age groups: the Little Lodge program
was set up for younger boys, the Big Lodge for those age thirteen and

over. Upon attaining puberty, Little Lodge members were initiated into the Big Lodge by a sweat lodge ceremony adopted from the Delaware tribe.[11]

Gradually, the role of formal athletics declined in importance, while the woodlore and nature study categories became more significant. Seton's emphasis on the symbolic importance of the chase thus gave way to skills such as animal photography, which called for considerable adroitness and endurance.[12] Here the Chief retained his belief in the "implied respectability" of natural science, comparing it to motherhood and linking it to sport "without the brutalities."[13]

Following the success of *The Book of Woodcraft*, Seton further supplemented the skill demonstrations in subsequent manuals with more explanatory material. In this way, young readers were introduced to recently discovered aspects of Indian history. He also gleaned new Indian songs and dances from works by various scholars. While most of these were related to animals (the Shoshone Dog Dance, the Ojibwa Snake Dance, and so on), Seton selected them on the basis of their spiritual tenor. They served to illustrate his unswerving belief that "pagan" Indians, like the animals, observed most of the Ten Commandments: namely, those traced to biological roots. Often Seton explained how the Indian mode of worship, with its emphasis on stoic self-denial, moderation, and humility before all living things, became his own religion. It was this "reverence for life" that he hoped to pass on to his following. Seton's inclusion of the Ghost Dance Song was a clear reflection of that mode of thinking.[14]

Later on, Seton adopted several new Indian "exploits," particularly nightly vigils, that would allow older adolescents to "win a name." His innovation of "Dog Soldiers," whose job it was to maintain discipline, was added to parties going on overland hikes and canoe trips. These "soldiers" were carefully chosen by the Sachem and bound to an oath of strict obedience. The Chief's pan-Indianism was clearly evident in his directions for constructing all the material necessities for a mobile wilderness campsite—everything from Algonquin birchbark canoes to Arapaho beds to a Navajo mat loom.[15]

In addition, Seton launched an official program for girls within the movement. Their camping activities and requirements for ranks and honors were similar to those of the boys, with some modifications; indeed, many ideas that the Gulicks had obtained from Seton for the Camp Fire Girls appeared once again among the Woodcraft Girls. The girls could make their ceremonial gowns to fit their individual tastes, for example. Grace's feminist influence was particularly strong; for example, there was a degree for "woman's power in history," which stressed the role of women in the nation's affairs.[16] Above all, in both the boys' and girls' programs, the chief stressed his three rules for having fun: that it "be made, not bought with money," that it "be enjoyed with decorum and decency," and that the best fun was "in the realm of the imagination."[17]

Seton thus formed what he hoped would be a viable alternative to the militant Boy Scouts and Girl Scouts. In the spring of 1917, he launched the *Totem Board* as the Woodcraft League's official news organ, a monthly publication filled with such diverse material as articles on wildlife conservation, animal tales, instructions for different handicrafts, book reviews, and Indian folklore.[18] Through this periodical, as well as his lectures and correspondence, Seton emphasized his scheme's primitive basis. As he said in a letter to Mary Austin: "I know of no way to help the American boys and girls better than through giving them the Woodcraft League program, and this is the feeling of every leader who has carefully tried it."[19]

During this time, Seton's animal tales remained immensely popular, and in 1916 he published another short story collection, *Wild Animal Ways*. The inclusion of "Coaly-Bay," which had earlier appeared in *Collier's*, is particularly significant. Since he had recently been ejected as Chief Scout, it is easy to link the outlaw horse's rebellious spirit with Seton's stubborn refusal to be bridled by the BSA executives. As Chief of the Woodcraft League, he probably felt free at last to reform America's youth in his own way.[20] Yet as the specter of war hung over the land, Seton felt an increasing restlessness. Hurt by his treatment at the hands of the BSA, he more than ever felt the need to be accepted by society as he was. That thought, coupled with his wish to reach a wider reading audience, prompted Seton to pen the least typical of all his works.

The Preacher of Cedar Mountain is Seton's only conventional "Progressive" novel. Although elements of his primitivist doctrines appear, the book contains no side illustrations or animal heroes. Laced with social commentary, the story is set for the most part in the Black Hills around Deadwood, South Dakota. But it is not the Deadwood of Wild Bill Hickok, Jack McCall, and Calamity Jane. Instead, the reader sees the West in transition as the gold strikes level off and farmers begin to come in. Only a small rowdy element, like Pat Bylow's crowd, is left of the earlier pioneers.

Seton's own dilemma is shown in the person of the main character, Jim Hartigan. Born in the Ontario backwoods of Seton's youth, Jim is a mixture of Celtic and Saxon blood and has both a gentle and a wild side to his nature. His boyhood environment is the frontier atmosphere of the Canadian logging camps. The boys' number-one tutor is "Fighting Bill" Kenna, whose personal religion is to feed the hungry and honor his "wurd as a mahn." These principles, in addition to a knowledge of boxing and a love for horses, are passed on to Jim. However, Jim's widowed mother proves a restraining influence, and her dying wish is for him to become a minister of the Gospel. For a time, it seems he will become anything but that as his reputation as a prankster and pugilist grows. But during a Methodist revival, when a small child is injured by one of his pranks, his heart melts, and Jim mounts the mourner's bench in genuine repentance. Therefore, "a child or a little girl could bully him into absolute submission."[21]

In developing his story, Seton injects several moralistic commentaries. He describes the Saint Patrick's Day and Orange Day festivals as having as "evil spell" about them, since normally amiable Catholic and Protestant neighbors often wind up harassing each other. The mayor of Links (Lindsay) owns the sawmills and is the community's "Rockefeller." His big brick house and his wife's diamonds symbolically cut them off from the rest of society, especially during times of recession. Seton reveals the effects of industrial capitalism when he writes: "Many a man has been ruined by a high, unbroken level of success. Intellectually, it makes for despotism and a conviction of infallibility. In the world of muscle, it creates a bully."[22]

True to his mother's prayers, Jim begins his ministerial training at a conservative college in the East. However, he loathes the books, preferring to spend his time in athletics and contact with nature. He is a romantic, as reflected in his Irish chanteys and choice of poets like Scott and Browning. Seeing this, yet realizing his potential, the college directors send Jim west to the fictional Black Hills community of Cedar Mountain for a trial period as a pastor's assistant. There he discovers that the townspeople are generally cold to the pharisaical doctrines in which he was trained. His inner conflict—whether to withdraw completely from the world or live the best life possible in it—heightens as he tries to adjust to his new environment. Not always can he overcome the world's temptations. Confronted in essence with three religions—his own legalistic background, the democratic pragmatism of the towns-folk, and the nature worship of the Indians—he must choose which one to follow in order to be the best Christian example to his congregation.

Although *The Preacher of Cedar Mountain* is merely a standard American Progressive novel set in the West, wide use of the western formula is evident. Seton's familiarity with Owen Wister is reflected in Jim's love for horses. Like the Virginian, the preacher treats his horses humanely and fights those who mistreat them. When he buys Midnight, a black steed with a temper that "isn't spoiled," for his circuit riding work, he declares: "If your bronco-busters take him in hand, they'll ride him in a week, but they'll make a divil of him. I'll take him in hand and in three months I'll have him following me 'round with tears in his eyes, just begging me to get on his back and go for a run."[23]

But while Cattleman Kyle of the Circle K Ranch appears as a minor character, the story has no gun-toting cowboy hero. True to his mounting antipathy toward "bronco-busters," Seton expresses preference for the graduates of Europe's riding schools who know "how to get the best out of the horse." As a western hero, Hartigan more closely fits the "strong, clean, God-conquered manhood" image promoted by the Canadian mythmaker Ralph Connor.[24] Blazing Star, whom the preacher transforms from a mangy wagon horse into a champion "speeder," is a symbol of Jim's own potential.

Seton's treatment of women in the novel likewise reflects the Westerner's reverence of womanhood. The heroine, Belle, like Wister's Molly Wood, is the educated woman-on-the-pedestal who "tames" Jim by steering his worldly loves into beneficial channels. With her loyalty and encouragement, Jim emerges as a successful preacher and missionary to Chicago's urban youth. Another side of Western womanhood is presented in the character of Hannah, the strong-willed wife of a fast-talking Yankee insurance agent, John Higgenbotham. While Seton probably developed her with Grace in mind, Hannah's equal partnership in John's business is symbolic of the West's rapid utilization of new ideas, like equality for women. More important, she is a prophetic picture of what Belle will become to Jim.

Seton's treatment of Indians is equally significant. On the train going to his new assignment, Jim meets a Jesuit priest (patterned undoubtedly after Father Beede) and four of his Sioux charges. Here Seton explicitly states the need for missionaries to respect the Indians' nature worship and approach the story of redemption at their level of understanding. Soon, Jim unwittingly finds himself more tolerant of the Indians, as well as of the "papist" Jesuit. Later, the preacher ascends the lofty peak for which the town of Cedar Mountain is named and comes upon a young Sioux making his manhood fast and seeking a vision. Seeing that he has intruded on someone's holy place, Jim immediately goes back down. Later on, the mountain becomes his own "holy ground."

The Indians' craftiness, mixed with their religion, is shown in the outcome of the horse races at Fort Ryan. Deprived of their land and freedom to roam, Red Cloud and his Oglala braves peacefully fight back by depriving the horse soldiers of their bets. Chaska, the young visionary from Jim's initial mountain climb, reappears as the Indians' jockey. Since Chaska personifies Seton's ideal "child of nature," he is assigned the name of the author's Cree friend in Manitoba.

Other stereotypes appear throughut the story, each playing a key role in Jim's fulfillment. Charlie Bylow, Pat's brother and Jim's first convert, proves a true friend to the preacher during the latter's weak moments. Philosophical Peter Carson, the town doctor, is a source of homespun wisdom based on human instinct. Rev. Josiah Jebb, under whom Jim initially works, "has no more knowledge of the world than a novice in a convent."[25] Colonel Waller is a patriotic Southern gentleman who stands by his duty as a soldier and refuses to admit defeat, especially when the Indians outwit him. There are villains, too. The shady schoolmaster, Jack Lowe, and the red-haired seductress, Lou Jane Hoomer, try to discredit Jim by playing on his weaknesses and attempt to prevent his union with Belle. In Chicago, the "ferret-eyed" Squeaks attempts to ruin Jim's inner-city ministry by framing the local political boss, who is the preacher's biggest supporter.

The most outstanding supporting actor in the drama is Jack Shives, whose blacksmith shop is Cedar Mountain's "neutral territory of free speech." As the town's pragmatic theologian of American Progressivism, Shives voices the community's (and Seton's) attitudes toward preachers and churches. He urges Jim to pursue "a religion of common sense and kindness of which, as near as I can make out, is what the man Jesus did preach." In the Gospel according to Jack Shives, Jesus and his disciples were, in a sense, socialists, while Paul was "that little lawyer feller that succeeded in twisting things around to the old basis of 'get all you can.'" The apostle's rules regarding women may stem from one "that had a

dressing down from some woman and probably deserved all he got."
Through the voice of Shives, Seton accuses Paul of instigating the ideas
of big-time capitalism that subsequently corrupted the church and
showed favoritism to the "privileged few." Thus the man who steals
bread for his starving family is excused. In his eyes, Eastern industrialism
poses a real threat to the democratic ideals that Cedar Mountain represents. After Jim and Belle return from their elopement in Deadwood,
they are received in triumph by the townspeople, particularly by Shives,
who quips, "Now I know you are human in spite of your job! You've
gone up about ten pegs in my scale."[26]

The Preacher of Cedar Mountain is a highly moralistic tale, and it is one
of Seton's least-known works. Apparently, the majority of his readers
wanted Seton to remain the animal storyteller and Indian folklorist, and
many pious souls were ill prepared for his attacks on Saint Paul and the
established church. Nevertheless, Jim Hartigan emerges as a true Progressive in the Theodore Roosevelt tradition and spreads his Westernized
social gospel from his Cedar Mountain House (containing elements of
the YMCA and Jane Addams' Hull House) in Chicago. Upon receiving
his seminary degree from a more liberal institution than he had originally attended, he answers a call to succeed the Reverend Jebb as pastor
of the Cedar Mountain congregation. The townsfolk fear that he will
soon be called to the big city, but "the city came to the man and might-
ily grew about him."[27] Thus we have an oxymoronic blending of East
and West, with primary emphasis on collective values as the key to civilization. Traces of Seton's woodcraft principles can be seen in his stress
on the western wilderness as a source of revitalization. Coming as it did
during America's entry into World War I, the novel seemed to picture
the rise of a virtual utopia built on the harmonic blending of the three
religions that Jim has resolved within himself. If nothing else, the book
showed Seton's own innate desire to found such an ideal community in
the West.

Alongside such fiction, Seton turned out more scholarly works on Indian culture. Ever since his meeting with White Swan in 1897, he had
wanted to publish a study of sign language. Throughout the next
twenty years, as time permitted, he had conducted extensive research on
the topic among various tribes, particularly the Yanktonnai Sioux and
the Piegans. Using sign language, he was able to converse at length with
several linguistic groups; much of his historical information on the Indian wars was obtained in this manner. He also drew on Garrick Mallery

and other early authorities.[28] However, a real breakthrough occurred with the discovery of the "Hadley Indian Sign Prints," a pictographic representation of hand signs devised by Lewis F. Hadley, a missionary at Anadarko, Oklahoma. Indeed, Seton was personally responsible for unearthing and preserving the now-famous prints. By 1914, he had compiled a preliminary syntax of Indian sign language, which he asked F. W. Hodge and others at the Smithsonian to proofread and supplement.[29] Two years later, he sent to Hodge a sign language dictionary based on the Hadley prints. In the meantime, Francis La Flesche, another ethnologist, suggested that Seton focus on the Cheyenne code, which he considered the best because it was done almost entirely by one hand. Seton readily agreed with La Flesche and subsequently hired Cleaver Warden, a full-blood from the Cheyenne Agency in Oklahoma, to help him edit his work. Of course, Seton did not hesitate to make personal contacts with Warden's Cheyenne neighbors. Writing to Hodge from the Indian School at Concho, Oklahoma, in the spring of 1917, Seton stated that he had visited with some of "the best sign talkers I ever came across."[30] Upon completion of the project in 1918, Seton offered to give to the Smithsonian the approximately eight hundred drawings of signs that he used as illustrations. To this day, his *Sign Talk* remains an important work on the subject, especially in the light of recent studies in semiotics.[31]

While conducting his sign language research, Seton came across Henry Rowe Schoolcraft's six-volume *Historical and Statistical Information* on the American Indian tribes. Seeing that the valuable "Archives of Aboriginal Research" had no index, he expressed an interest in compiling one himself. After learning that Hodge and others in the Bureau of Ethnology were in the process of starting that very project, Seton offered his help and eagerly maintained a personal interest in their efforts, which eventually came to fruition.[32]

The close of the war saw the passing of certain of Seton's friends and colleagues. On August 13, 1918, Luther Gulick, the Camp Fire Girls' beloved "guiding spirit," succumbed suddenly to a heart attack during the summer camp at his Sebago Lake estate. Later that year, the deadly Spanish flu epidemic took the life of Charles Eastman's daughter Irene, whose singing voice and Indian recitations had been an inspiration to Seton and other youth workers.[33] What touched Seton even more deeply was the death of Theodore Roosevelt on January 6, 1919. Summing up his friendship with the former president, Seton stated:

It is very difficult to appraise fairly the gifts of a man in the highest possible place of power; but we whose business it is to learn, and gather up the learning of the world of the outdoors, do not hesitate to give to Roosevelt a position in the front rank of naturalists.

He and I have several times differed in matters of detail, but in all large issues of my interests we have been at one; and I treasure today among the best of things I own, an autographed letter of praise that he wrote in 1909, when my most ambitious book was published (*Life-Histories of Northern Animals*); just as I treasure the memory of those early days when he was the first man of position in New York to give me the hand of good fellowship as a naturalist.

We can but sadly recall and paraphrase the words of the prophet on another occasion of national bereavement: "Know ye there is a great man, and a Prince, fallen this day in our nation!"

For the remainder of his life, Seton kept in touch with the Roosevelt family. Kermit Roosevelt, who had inherited his father's spirit of adventure and love for the outdoors, later served on the Woodcraft League's Council of Guidance.[34]

As the "war to end all wars" cooled into a period of uneasy peace, Seton momentarily turned back to his zoological studies. When E. W. Nelson did his series on North American mammals for the *National Geographic*, it was Seton who provided him with illustrations.[35] In the spring of 1919, he became a charter member of the American Society of Mammalogists (ASM), founded on April 3 of that year by C. Hart Merriam, who was its first president. Naturally, the ASM officers were glad to have Seton contribute information from his animal observations to their *Journal of Mammalogy*. Through this organ, he published some of his recent findings on squirrels, mice, and other rodents, emphasizing their importance in the biological order; from his fur farming experiences, he wrote about the behavior and anatomy of fur-bearing animals. In one article he outlined his orderly method of recording pertinent data, and the cover of the *Journal's* early issues featured Seton's drawing of a pronghorn antelope buck surveying its badlands domain.[36]

Having likewise kept up with advances in ornithology, Seton resumed contributing to the *Auk* and *Bird-Lore*. Yet behind their scientific façades, these articles revealed a distinct longing for his "golden years" in Manitoba. Certain bird species were becoming increasingly rare; the passenger pigeon, of which he had specimens in his collection, had become extinct.[37]

During this time Seton served on the advisory council of *Bird-Lore*. In that capacity late in 1920, he penned a short article entitled "Why Do

Birds Bathe?" and asked for responses, which he compiled and published in the following spring issue. Seton also endorsed the newly developed practice of bird banding as a practical method of preservation,
recalling his experiences in Manitoba during the 1880s when he tagged
and marked birds with printer's ink and microscopic lockets. In the *Auk*
he took a scornful look at how developments in the English language
had complicated the nomenclature of various bird species.[38]

In relation to his latest scientific and literary accomplishments, Seton
continued to be a favorite speaker. He was especially popular among the
"Roycrofters," Elbert Hubbard's disciples in East Aurora. Following in
his father's footsteps, Elbert (Bert) Hubbard II had taken over the reins
and continued promoting his school of "genial iconoclasm" through the
lecture circuit and a new, equally witty magazine, the *Roycroft*. At the
1918 Roycroft Convention, the Chief was such an overwhelming success
that he was invited to speak again at the next two annual meetings.
However, a bit of unpleasantness developed in the fall of 1920 when the
Roycroft editors sought to publish one of Seton's stories without his
consent. Seton claimed having "other plans to publish it serially."[39]

That fall, the Chief and his wife made what he labeled their "Great
Vaudeville Trip," since it was arranged through the Orpheum Circuit.
Following a lecture in Saint Louis, the Setons arrived at Fort Worth,
Texas, on October 8 and spent several days meeting with Boy Scout
leaders and performing at the Majestic Theater. At Fort Worth's City
Park, where he held a Grand Council, Seton observed squirrels in the
pecan trees. On October 21, local cattleman Schuyler Marshall took
the Setons to his ranch near Dallas. There the Chief took note of the
shrikes, or butcher birds, and their practice of impaling prey on barbed-
wire fences.[40]

After holding another Grand Council at Hermann Park in Houston,
Seton met with several prominent zoologists at the University of Texas
in Austin. With them, he arranged to make observations of the local
fauna along the Colorado River and in the surrounding Hill Country.
Among other things, he studied the anatomy of squirrel specimens, especially their digestive systems. Always the commentator with the restless pen, Seton wrote in his journal a humorous piece of prose called
"Sweet Music of the Gasoline Torch" about the Texas ranchers' practice
of burning off prickly-pear spines so that their cattle could eat the
plants.

From Austin, Seton and his party drove a borrowed "motor car" to

San Antonio. On the road, he spotted "four cottontails, two dogs, two rats, one possum and one very large skunk," all killed by cars (Seton later commented that "the cottontail suffers more than any other from cars").[41] Over a thousand children and their parents in San Antonio attended the Grand Council meeting to hear Black Wolf speak. Afterward, boys from the San Antonio Military School formed the Alamo Tribe of Woodcraft.[42]

Probably the most interesting naturalist Seton encountered on that tour was Dr. Charles A. R. Campbell, an enthusiastic expert on bats. Several years earlier, Campbell, who taught at the San Antonio Academy of Medicine, had recognized the value of bats, not only as an effective predator of mosquitoes and other pests but also as a source of high-grade guano fertilizer. Therefore, he had constructed several artificial bat roosts on the shore of Mitchell Lake, about twelve miles southwest of San Antonio. From these, as well as from natural caves in the area, Campbell harvested several thousand pounds of guano and found a ready market among area greenhouses, florists, and farmers. His successful efforts were soon noticed and practiced worldwide.[43]

Seton's own interest in bats stemmed from early observations made in Toronto and Manitoba. He recalled one evening at Wyndygoul in July, 1912, when eight-year-old Ann reported strange animals on the roof of the porch. On closer examination, Seton discovered a row of more than thirty bats, and that night he observed the little mammals flying about the place. But the next morning all had gone and were never seen again. Seton therefore theorized that bats sometimes roam around in bands during the summer.[44]

From that time on, his research on the habits of bats increased, and in the spring of 1916, he published one of his most unusual animal stories, "Atalapha, a Winged Brownie," in *Scribner's* magazine. (It was also one of the tales included in *Wild Animal Ways*.) By comparing bats to the brownies of European folklore, Seton condemns the traditional attitude toward them as plague carriers and denizens of death; he contends that they are actually plague preventers because they control insect pests. Atalapha is a Great Northern, or hoary, bat in the Mount Marcy area of the Adirondacks south of Lake Placid. The young son of Haskins, the millwright, wounds the bat slightly with a shotgun pellet and captures it. Later, when the bat escapes, Seton reveals that the boy had died from some type of pestilence because people in that area have thoughtlessly decimated the flying mammals. Before narrating Atalapha's escape, however, Seton treats his readers to an experiment carried out by the family doctor on the "winged brownie." When the doc "blindfolds" the bat with candle wax and releases it in the house, the animal demonstrates its built-in "sonar" (long before the term was invented), which enables it to catch flies and avoid colliding with walls and other objects. People of that time thought that a bat could "see with its wings." The reader is also acquainted with the hoary bat's mating habits and winter migrations to Bermuda, the "land of eternal summers and palm trees."[45]

Like Seton, Campbell fought the traditional evil image of bats and stressed their beneficence in the control of malaria and similar diseases. His efforts were recognized not only by Seton but also by William Crawford Gorgas, surgeon general of the army and a pioneer in the battle against yellow fever. Furthermore, Campbell was instrumental in getting legislation passed in Texas for the protection of bats, the first such law in any state.[46]

Seton was thus anxious to see Campbell's artificial habitats firsthand, and the doctor was happy to accommodate him. At Mitchell Lake, Seton studied the roosts closely, but because of the cold November weather, he had little success in taking live specimens. The naturalist also noted other forms of wildlife at the lake, including that strange armored creature known by its Spanish name, armadillo.[47] He kept in close touch with Campbell after the tour, and when the latter published a book on his bat experiments a few years later, Seton wrote the introduction.

Even as Seton was promoting his program on the vaudeville stage, things were happening to change the face of his America. The aftermath of the war brought about a change of attitudes and lifestyles, particularly on the East Coast. Within the following decade, the Chief would seek out a new site for his "Camelot" retreat, only this time, it would be located somewhere out West.

CHAPTER 19

Little Peequo:
Looking Westward

While Seton was busy with his travels and pen, the "Roaring Twenties" were ushered in on a somewhat negative note. Although Grace and her feminist colleagues had a field day with the passage of the Nineteenth Amendment, controversy raged in Washington over the Senate's rejection of the Versailles Treaty. The nation's economy toppled briefly into the abyss of postwar recession. Moreover, the Red Scare erupted through leftist elements in America's labor force and journalists, among them Lincoln Steffens, who declared he had "seen the future" in Lenin's Russia.[1] It was the era of bootleggers and "speakeasies," flappers and daring fashions, silent movies and radio broadcasting. The sins of Hollywood's screen idols, along with the popularity of Freudian principles, began to disturb the more morally minded public, who with the conservative *Literary Digest* wondered if the younger generation really was in peril. F. Scott Fitzgerald emerged as the literary spokesman of the "Jazz Age," while the works of other young skeptics like Sinclair Lewis quickly became best-sellers.

It was clear to Seton and other observers that the nation was becoming spiritually weary. Tired of President Wilson's preachments of America's duty to mankind, people sought to concentrate on their private lives and shove public affairs out of their minds altogether. Their chief means of escape, along with movies, radio, and spectator sports, was the automobile. Although the new administration in Washington proved mediocre and scandal-ridden, Americans as a whole were glad to return to "normalcy."[2]

The 1920s also saw the growth of new fraternities among city-dwelling Indians who sought to retain their identity. These clubs included whites in their membership, sometimes even in leadership posts. Their primary purposes were fraternal and social rather than reformist and political. Seton was especially interested in the Tepee Order of America, which had appeared in New York around 1915. Founded by Rev. Red Fox St. James, a Disciples of Christ minister of mixed Welsh and Blackfoot ancestry, the Tepee Order was intended as a way for native American Protestant youth to study Indian history, languages, customs, and outdoor activities. Its office titles and general format followed the pattern of the Woodcraft League; the major differences were the Tepee Order's secrecy and emphasis on exclusiveness. In fact, St. James envisioned it as an Indian-led alternative to Scouting, which catered largely to white youngsters. By 1920, an adult phase had grown out of the fraternity. Its rituals and degrees were drawn from the practices of Masonic lodges and those of the Improved Order of Red Men, a white fraternity dating back to the early nineteenth century and dedicated to preserving Indian virtues.

Other pan-Indian fraternities, of which Seton was probably aware, were the Grand Council Fire of the American Indians (later the Indian Council Fire), begun in Chicago in 1923, and several similar clubs in Los Angeles. Despite their "national" titles, most of these were strictly local or regional and reflected the characteristic outlooks of area tribes. Such fraternities helped set a pattern for an urban Indian subculture and played an important role in the development of the Native American Church (which used peyote in its rituals). Certainly it was no mere accident that modern pan-Indianism coincided with the rise of conservation movements, emphasis on wilderness camping, and nature-oriented youth groups such as the Woodcraft League.[3]

As Seton watched these trends with mounting interest, he knew that he was not getting any younger. In August, 1920, he reached his sixtieth birthday. His dark, shaggy locks had begun to show traces of gray. In addition, his eyes had troubled him intermittently for twenty years as a result of excessive easel and desk work, and he was fitted with special bifocals, courtesy of Steese and Weeks, New York's leading oculists.[4] Nevertheless, Seton still possessed his youthful vitality, and his spiritual vision was far from dimmed.

With characteristic zeal, Seton continued to promote his woodcraft guidelines as practical solutions to the problems of the new decade. In a scathing article entitled "Why Wear Clothes?" he attacked social hypocrisy as seen in the fashion industry. His thesis was that the societies where the most clothing was worn, like seventeenth-century France or contemporary Turkey, had the lowest moral standards, whereas primitive Indian and African cultures were found to have higher standards. Clothing, therefore, did not make people any more virtuous. He also argued that some articles of clothing helped bring on such disorders as lupus and psoriasis. From his own experience, Seton claimed that certain skin problems disappeared when he relieved himself of wool flannel underwear and made other modifications in his wardrobe. Clothing, he argued, should be chosen primarily on the basis of protection from the elements and personal comfort, particularly in outdoor activities. As always, he cited the Indians as historical examples of this mode of thinking. While ornamentation was still a consideration, Seton felt that it should be last, not first, in the list of priorities, contrary to the attitudes of most fashion designers. He urged men to "get rid of hard-boiled shirts, collars on the half-shell and tight boots." In athletic exercises, both men and women should wear those things that "give absolute freedom of the body and a measure of sun and air on the skin that would go a long way towards the ideal."[5]

Alongside his pragmatism, Seton put new emphasis on woodcraft's spiritual aspects. In 1921 he published *Woodland Tales*, a collection of romanticized woodlore where the influences of Thoreau's transcendentalism, European fairy tales, and Greek mythology blend with his Indian lore. The religious theme is clearly reflected in his personification of nature as "Mother Carey" or the demigod Nanaboujou, as well as in the appearance of the Great Spirit and several lesser Indian deities. Seton also personifies wild flowers, birds, and insects even while adhering to scientific fact. Like his earlier *Woodmyth and Fable*, many of these folk tales contain hidden barbs aimed at society, politics, and current events. For example, it is easy to imagine the "singing" contest between the songbirds and the cicadas as a pun on the clash between classical and popular music, and the continual "bickering" among the katydids as a slap at Congress or the judicial system. Toward the end of the book, Seton explains the Woodcraft League's various symbols, comparing them with the common "totems" used by businesses and society in general.[6]

The Chief's pantheistic reverence is also shown in his story of "Bannertail, the Gray Squirrel." Early in 1922, Seton published this tale of a squirrel that grows up in captivity on a New Jersey farm and later uses its "wisdom" (instinct) to survive in the wild. Here he drew heavily from his mound of squirrel data, including those gathered in Texas in 1920.[7] As in previous animal stories, the author is scientifically accurate in relating the squirrel's life and behavior patterns, but hidden social commentaries are also evident. In one scene, Bannertail drives off a red squirrel and eats its mushroom dinner. However, this particular mushroom is a "madcap" that causes the squirrel hero to "go loco" and suffer a "hangover" the next morning. It is a clear reference to the harmful effects of alcohol and Seton's support of Prohibition: the mushroom is to the gray squirrel what booze is to man. Bannertail comes to loathe the "madcap" and "teaches his young to do likewise." Seton closes the tale by preaching that the squirrels' habit of burying hickory nuts is "Mother Carey's" way of ensuring a continuous supply of trees. By "unwritten law," the squirrels leave 5 percent of the nuts to reproduce. Man is therefore foolish and wanton in killing off Bannertail's kind, for in so doing, he also diminishes the hickory, a major source of timber.[8]

Bannertail marked a revival of public interest in Seton's animal stories. His earlier works enjoyed continued popularity among young readers, and publishers were eager to turn out new editions. Doubleday, Page offered a limited edition of six of Seton's most popular works as the "Library of Pioneering and Woodcraft," advertising in the *National Geographic* and other widely read magazines. Subsequently, a new generation of youngsters came to idolize Seton as the "wizard of woodcraft and animal lore." Frank Crane, a fellow naturalist, declared: "I have turned to the livest man I know. He has lived much outdoors, knows the birds, beasts, and, as Saint Francis of Assisi would say, 'Our brother the sun and our sisters the wind and woods.' He is Ernest Thompson Seton."[9]

Never hesitating to promote himself, Seton reviewed his literary accomplishments in an essay addressed to an authors' benefit meeting in January, 1921. In a letter, he stated: "As I look over these various productions, I realize that the 'fool editors' rejected those in which I was trying to be 'literary' and accepted those in which I tried to tell in the simplest way a story that came from my heart." He spoke his mind with equal freedom on current issues like the Bonus Bill: "If the young strong men should receive a bonus," he wrote, "so should all of us who gave our time and effort freely for the cause when at home. Crippled and maimed soldiers should, of course, be cared for."[10]

In a new effort to secure more memberships and support for the Woodcraft League, Seton made two cross-country lecture tours through the desert Southwest to California. On the first, in early 1922, Seton stopped over in New Orleans, which—although usually advertised as a "city of romance"—Seton labeled "the most sordid, dirty, ugly town I ever was in." Indeed, he looked down on all of what he called "the sad south." Traveling the "Sunset Route" of the Southern Pacific line along the Rio Grande in western Texas and the Gila River in Arizona, Seton recorded his observations of wild creatures. In Los Angeles, he called on Charles Lummis, who gladly accepted the Chief's invitation to speak at the "Grand Council of the Woodcraft Folk" on February 13. Lummis also helped organize the city's first annual Woodcraft Potlatch on February 27. This event featured a three-course Indian-style dinner, with "buffalo off the hoof" as part of the menu.[11]

One of the area's League officers, John Barry, owned a ranch in the Mojave Desert near Victorville, California. In March, Seton and other Woodcrafters, including a Paiute Indian handyman, helped Barry construct a new desert house to be used for council meetings and campouts. On its completion late in the month, Seton lauded the simplicity of the structure and the way it blended with the environment. Built of native stone, the cabin contained one large living room, an open fireplace, bunks, and a bathroom with running water, all for less than five hundred dollars. The builders also made good use of old telephone poles and other available materials.[12]

During the construction, Seton observed and collected specimens of numerous small desert creatures. Like Mary Austin, he did not consider this arid setting a real "desert" since it did contain life—especially during the season that he was there, right after the early spring rains. He described the distant San Bernardino Mountains as "peaks that rise up, up, abruptly up, to bear, each high above his noble shoulders in the gentle blue, a crown of white—the crown without which no mountain ever can be in the noblest rank, a cap of shining snow, a blazoned promise to mankind that this year the blessedness of water will not fail." As always, Seton gathered pieces of folklore from the local residents for use later in magazine stories. His studies on kangaroo rats and other desert species also became sources for stories.[13]

After New Year's Day in 1923, Seton made a second tour, this time accompanied by his daughter Ann, by then a young lady of nineteen. At Tucson, they met Dr. Charles Vorhees, a naturalist and professor of biology at the University of Arizona. With him, Seton made a field trip across the Mexican border to study the wildlife of the Sonoran Desert before going on to California. In Los Angeles, Seton was stricken with an inflamed bladder that laid him flat on his back for a few days. However, he and Ann were able to stop by the Barry Ranch and the house he had helped build before they returned to their home in the Connecticut woods.[14]

It was during this tour that Seton met Upton Sinclair, the erstwhile muckraker of the Progressive Era, at the latter's home in Pasadena. Having moved to California during the Great War, Sinclair hoped to provide a socialistic alternative to the corruption-ridden American democratic system. Apparently, their conversation turned to the election of judges, for in subsequent correspondence Seton defended the English judiciary system as the best in Western man's history. Although both men had socialistic leanings, Seton was not in agreement with Sinclair's vision of a "social revolution" as a solution to the world's evils; the Chief had never entirely shed his Victorian British background. Moreover, he argued that the "democracy" of ancient Athens was, in reality, oligarchy.[15]

Politics notwithstanding, Seton did succeed in forming new Woodcraft tribes and attracting potential adult leadership. In addition, his popularity among the Boy Scouts and Camp Fire Girls remained strong. As they began to develop local councils which, in turn, set up permanent camps, he was often requested to come and help direct summer training courses for adult leaders.[16] Part of the secret of his success was the dedication of a young woman recently added to Seton's staff at the Woodcraft League's national headquarters. Her name was Julia Moss Buttree.

Julia Moss, the oldest of seven children, was born in New York City on May 15, 1889, to Episcopalian and Jewish parents. From an early age she possessed a love for music, singing, and dancing. Realizing this, Julia's parents made many sacrifices so that she might obtain the necessary training. "I was always a skinny, scrawny youngster with red eyes and straight hair," she later quipped, "but I've been fortunate to have good friends who think I'm great." After her graduation from Hunter College with a bachelor's degree in classical languages and a master's in drama, Julia taught at a local elementary school, where she developed a serious interest in youth work, and later was part of the drama faculty at Hunter. In 1913 she married E. B. "Ted" Buttree, a contractor and realtor.

Julia always liked to tell the story of her first meeting with the Chief in 1918, when she had gone at the invitation of friends to hear one of his lectures. As he mounted the platform, she was not overly impressed with Seton's unusual appearance and aggressive personality. But then, as she related:

When the first words came from his lips, an electric thrill went through me. The depth of tone, the roundness of enunciation, the clarity of diction, the sheer magic of speech gripped the whole assembly. The children, who had been fussing and fidgeting in their seats, sat still and enthralled, even long before the sense of the story could have had any message for them.

He told a simple tale which lasted for perhaps ten minutes. At the beginning, I was engrossed in his technic, but soon I fell under the spell of the narrative. Yet, when the speaker ceased, I realized that I had not taken in the end of the story—I had been wholly lost in the cadence of his voice.[17]

From that moment on, Julia Buttree was a lifelong associate of the Chief and his cause. At the conclusion of the program, she was introduced to Seton, who reportedly took her hands in his and said, "My, we could have a lot of fun together!"[18]

Indeed, Julia proved a valuable asset as Seton's secretary. She assisted him in his research and editing, and sometimes lectured with him. While his topic frequently concerned wildlife, hers was always music or drama, especially as the Indians knew them. Her ability as a storyteller matched his own. An effective organizer, Julia was instrumental in forming several new tribes.[19] In Seton's words, she was "a woman of rare excellence, of unusual gifts, college bred, talented, a scholar, a writer, an artist, a joyful comrade, an indefatigable worker; and above all gifted with that most uncommon gift called common sense."[20]

It was also during this time that Seton constructed "Little Peequo" Cottage, on the grounds of his Connecticut estate, as the Woodcraft League's new headquarters. (This move was due, in part, to a fire that did about six hundred dollars in damage to the main house on November 22, 1922.) The two-story, "Tudor-Indian" cottage was furnished not only with Indian artifacts but also with English antiques; as part of his interior decorating scheme, Seton was interested in obtaining valuable fire irons from the collection of a wealthy antique dealer in England.[21] He also remodeled the dam that formed the artificial pond and made other alterations on the grounds. One notable addition was an artificial bank with which he hoped to attract swallows. But although a family of kingfishers and another of phoebe birds raised several broods there, no swallow was ever seen nesting in the clay and masonry embankment.[22]

On its completion, Seton declared that Little Peequo would become "one of the little wonderlands of the world." He conducted his first camp from the new "Ranch House" in the summer of 1924. At that memorable outing, Seton reportedly "tamed" about four hundred boys from the slums of New York's Lower East Side. He accomplished this by forming the roughest of the group into "Dog Soldiers" and having them take a solemn oath, sealed with blood, at the "haunted cave." By asserting peer pressure, these "Dog Soldiers" helped keep order in the camp. The Chief's methods made a favorable impression on members of the New York Rotary Club, who helped sponsor the boys. Grand Councils were also held at Little Peequo on appointed days and "moons," as the months were termed.[23]

Changes were occurring in Seton's family as well as on his property. Ann, his only child, was approaching twenty and, in her father's words, "developing into quite a kid we can be proud of." In her teens, Ann had received the finest secondary schooling and exposure to things cultural available to anyone in her social status.[24] Well traveled, she also was of great help to her father in formulating his Woodcraft programs and did the notation to some of the Indian songs that he used. Also, her writing talents were already becoming evident.[25]

Early in the spring of 1923, Ann announced her engagement to a local man, Charles Cottier. As Seton recuperated from his bladder inflammation, his household bustled with preparations for the wedding, which was set for June 30. When the day came, the father of the bride noted in his journal: "The end of a big chapter in our lives."[26]

Through all these hectic events, Seton devoted the greater portion of his time and energies to his last major scientific project. For some time he had wanted to revise his *Life-Histories* and expand it to include the wealth of information he had obtained since his 1907 arctic voyage. Between 1919 and 1927, Seton cut down on his lecture tours, wrote fewer stories, took no holidays, and turned down all but a few social engagements. (One scheduled appearance for which he failed to show up proved particularly disappointing to a young bird enthusiast named Roger Tory Peterson.)[27] During that eight-year period, Seton worked feverishly at running down references, examining letters, and looking up newspaper accounts. Julia Buttree and others from his secretarial staff assisted the Chief in this endeavor.

Seton's like-minded friends, of course, awaited this latest "crowning achievement" with high anticipation. He welcomed any information on and illustrations of various mammal species that they could supply.

Many agreed with Charles Lummis that Seton's new study, with its emphasis on wildlife conservation, would be "the first serious attempt to give wild animals a fair hearing."[28]

The resulting four-volume work, *Lives of Game Animals*, immediately created a stir in natural history circles. No one could help noticing the way Seton expressed his sense of humor by giving animals personality. In preparing the manuscript for each volume, Seton had made a separate table of contents for each animal treated; on this contents page he also put a "synoptic drawing," that is, an unrealistic "summation of the life and character of the animal." W. L. Finley at Scribner was at first horrified by the idea of including these caricatures in "an otherwise erudite book." But Seton's persistence won out. Subsequently, many mammalogists reacted favorably to the drawings as unique expressions of animal character.[29]

The first volume, which appeared in 1925, introduced the original deluxe edition of 177 sets; the succeeding three volumes came out during the following three years. The complete set contained a total of three thousand pages, fifteen hundred illustrations, and one hundred maps, all magnificently done by Seton's own pen and brush. This edition sold for twenty-five dollars per volume, a high price for that day.[30] Doubleday, Page later printed a less expensive edition.

As Seton hoped, *Lives of Game Animals* was enthusiastically received by the scientific community. In 1926, after the second volume appeared, he received the John Burroughs Medal for his service in wildlife conservation. This award was an amusing twist of irony because it was Burroughs who had really initiated the work's creation by attacking the authenticity of Seton's animal stories twenty-three years before. The following year, after the publication of the third volume, the National Academy of Sciences awarded Seton the Daniel Giraud Elliott Medal, the highest honor a naturalist could receive. In addition, the Academy of Foreign Relations Board of Governors made him an honorary member, and the Canadian Wild Life Department at Ottawa gave him its undying support for any recognition he might receive.[31]

Of course, *Lives of Game Animals* was not without its critics. The California naturalist Donald Culross Peattie felt that even in this work, Seton had a "lamentable tendency toward a false humanizing of animals." But most scientists agreed with William Vogt, editor of *Bird-Lore*, who defended Seton's masterpiece as "undoubtedly one of the greatest natural history works ever produced in this country."[32] Written at a time when many large species were threatened with extinction, *Lives of Game Animals* has remained a leading work on the subject.

Along with his scientific achievement awards, Seton was also rewarded, although somewhat ignobly, for his work with the Boy Scouts. On April 9, 1926, after reading the latest edition of the *Handbook for Scoutmasters*, Seton wrote to Colin Livingstone, arguing that Baden-Powell's interpretation of the BSA's genesis was "so flatly contradicted in many particulars by documents, and so wholly unfair to everybody but himself, that I feel bound to write the facts." Seeking to cool his wrath, Livingstone and James West sent a notice stating that Seton was to be among the first twenty-six recipients of the BSA's Silver Buffalo Award "for distinguished service to boyhood." The medals were to be distributed at the sixteenth annual BSA meeting in Washington during the first weekend in May. Baden-Powell and President Calvin Coolidge were to be the guests of honor.[33] As a follow-up, Livingstone cautioned Seton not to say or do anything that would stir up controversy "until we have an opportunity of sitting down quietly and discussing the whole question as it appears to you and to ourselves." Obviously, the executives were hoping to stave off potential embarrassment, at least during Baden-Powell's visit. Not until April 27 did West actually invite Seton to attend the meeting itself, and by then Seton had scheduled a lecture tour for that weekend. Thereafter, West occasionally resorted to this delay tactic for subsequent important events where Seton's presence might provoke disharmony.[34]

Although Seton considered it an honor to be awarded the Silver Buffalo, it apparently did little to dampen his smoldering feud with the BSA National Council. In August a letter asking for correspondence concerning the movement's origins was circulated, and Seton was quick to respond.[35] From 1926 on, he produced numerous letters reflecting his bitter opposition to Scouting's militaristic trends. At one point, West and Mortimer Schiff, vice-president of the BSA, tried to buy him off by contributing funds to the Woodcraft League. But Seton saw through that and in 1927 sent West a manuscript outlining his own version of the BSA's founding and expressed his intent to publish it. West curtly replied that Seton's facts were erroneous and that to let them appear in print would be a grave mistake.[36]

Throughout the struggle, Seton had one firm supporter in Edgar M. Robinson. Although Robinson was no longer on the board, the BSA could usually count on his aid in developing and expanding various

facets of the program.[37] It was to him that Seton sent drafts of his historical critiques for approval before mailing them to West and his colleagues. Although Robinson occasionally reprimanded the Chief for
overstating his case, he invariably agreed that Seton had "just cause for
his dissatisfaction with the lack of expressed appreciation of his contributions both to Baden-Powell and to the Boy Scout movement in his
country."[38] Nevertheless, the controversy continued to seethe.

Still vainly seeking to counteract America's materialistic trends, Seton
put new emphasis on conservation in his promotion scheme. This was
one goal he hoped to accomplish in the publication of *Lives of Game
Animals*. Even as he was working on it, he also wrote a few scientific
articles on nature for popular magazines, recalling the days when wild
game abounded and Indians freely roamed the land.[39]

This nostalgic attitude was even more obvious in his lectures. In the
fall of 1924, Seton made a speaking tour through Canada and was appalled at the changes that the twentieth century had brought to his beloved Manitoba. Addressing the Canadian Club at Chateau Laurier in
Ottawa on November 15, he gave an impassioned speech on the desperate need for better conservation measures. Seton told his audience of
how he had just traveled by car over the prairies he had known in his
youth and had not seen "*one wild living creature*." "We cannot afford to
rob our children of their futurity in natural history," he warned. While
in Ottawa, Seton conferred with the Wild Life Branch of the Canadian
Interior Department and suggested the establishment of small sanctuaries, like his own at Wyndygoul and DeWinton, as a means of preserving wildlife.[40]

Seton's preachments succeeded in attracting a few new adult leaders
to the Woodcraft League. Charles Lathrop Pack and his son Arthur
Newton Pack, who edited *Nature* magazine, became eager boosters; the
elder Pack served on the League's advisory council.[41] Another man join-
ing the organization's Council of Guidance was Clyde Fisher. Since 1913,
Fisher had served on the curatorial staff of the American Museum
of Natural History in its education branch.[42] His education degrees,
coupled with his interest in natural history and ethnology, made him a
welcome addition to the Woodcraft fold, especially during Seton's summer training courses. As always, Seton encouraged those who chose careers in natural history and Indian studies and gave their publications
favorable reviews.[43]

Despite the dedication of Seton and his colleagues, the Woodcraft League as a whole no longer enjoyed the popularity it had once had on the East Coast. Funds were more difficult to raise, and at one point the editors of the *Totem Board* had to suspend its publication temporarily.[44] Ironically, it was Seton's unique "scheme of education in outdoor life" that ultimately proved the movement's weakness. Although the League's membership increased, it was small in proportion to the growth expressed by the Boy Scouts, Girl Scouts, and Camp Fire Girls. Clearly their more flexible programs were better suited to the needs of children growing up in the postwar urban and technological boom. Few city youngsters really cared to camp out in primitive Indian fashion, and although other groups borrowed heavily from Seton's ideas, none adopted his decentralized "Red Indianism" in its entirety. In postwar England several small, socialistic organizations were begun by young dissenters who had broken away from the Boy Scouts on pacifistic grounds and subsequently adopted Seton's woodcraft principles; one of these, the Order of Woodcraft Chivalry, made Seton its Honorary Grand Chieftain. Even though these groups flourished for a time, all but one eventually faded away.[45]

Along with his organization's financial woes, the Chief was confronted with marital problems. Although the Setons celebrated their thirtieth wedding anniversary in June, 1926, their individual lives had been drifting apart ever since the Great War. Seton's annual lecture tours, which usually occurred during the winter and early spring, consumed three or four months at a time; these, plus his summer training courses, caused him to be away from home for as much as six months out of the year. Grace usually remained in New York or Greenwich. While her husband was on the "gypsy trail," she kept him informed of the latest happenings at DeWinton. She was not excited about having to look after the animals on the grounds, however, and she once complained of the chipmunks eating the buds off her lilies. "I don't know how to stop them short of murder," she wrote in frustration.[46]

As an author and feminist leader, Grace did a considerable amount of traveling on her own. During the 1920s, she made trips to China, India, Egypt, and other exotic places. On these sojourns, she accompanied safaris and met with notable world leaders, including Mahatma Gandhi and Mrs. Sun Yat-Sen. In Europe, Grace participated in international women's group conferences on feminist and other reforms. These tours resulted in several travel books to her credit, but as Seton bluntly stated, "They set us ever farther apart."[47]

Throughout this time, the lively Julia Buttree continued to serve as the Chief's faithful assistant. As his marriage grew colder, Seton became increasingly attached to her. While Grace's primary concern was women's rights, Julia was wholeheartedly supportive of Seton's most passionate concerns and remained loyal to him throughout his various conflicts.[48] Obviously, Grace was aware of their deepening friendship; as time went on, her suspicion must have become evident, for a few years later Seton was admonishing his wife to "receive Mrs. Buttree in a spirit of kindness" at the Woodcraft meetings.[49]

Such difficulties revived the restlessness in his sensitive soul. Seton's work, whether literary, scientific, or in the realm of social reform, had become an obsessive thing. His publications had won him great recognition and many awards, including membership in the prestigious National Institute of Arts and Letters. Yet as the decade wore on and age crept up on him, Seton began to question the worth and validity of his achievements. In his introspective moments he seemed to sense a void, "the uneasy feeling . . . that something is left undone—in another time and another place." More than ever, he began to notice the general aloofness of New York society.[50] Out West, where Indians still made up a significant portion of the population, people seemed more receptive to Seton's preachments. He thought perhaps that was where he needed to go to find fulfillment and experience a new beginning.

Seton was not alone in that mode of thinking. In the West, as in other developing regions, many of the prevalent cultural currents moved away from colonialist attitudes. This quest for a distinct identity often found a positive outlet in the development of literature, architecture, and the fine arts. At the same time, relatively low population densities attracted Eastern intellectuals who shunned the materialistic values of an industrialized America.[51]

Many of Seton's old cronies had succumbed to this regionalist migration since the close of World War I. Irving Bacheller, having lost his Thrushwood mansion to a fire and seen the war firsthand as a frontline correspondent in France, had moved to Winter Park, Florida, to become a distinguished faculty member of Rollins College. Charles Eastman, his marriage having failed along with his summer camps for boys and girls, had retreated to Stone Lake, Wisconsin, where he disappeared from the public eye for a time.[52] Mary Austin, dissatisfied with the New York atmosphere and longing for her beloved "Dry West," had built her "Casa Querida" adobe on Santa Fe's Camino del Monte Sol. Even Hamlin Garland was ready to exchange the smoke and cold of New York and Chicago for the warm climate of Southern California.[53]

What made the Western regionalists distinct was their emphasis on the relation of folklore to literature and historical retrospection. Their mission was not merely to provide local color but to bring America's art and literature back to their beginnings in the heartland.[54] Seton found himself increasingly sympathetic with their views and goals. In the eyes of many of his Eastern neighbors, he was an eccentric rebel seeking to escape American society. His Woodcraft movement was seen as little more than "an unwanted, illegitimate child of industrialism and a reaction against spreading urbanism."[55] In order to save his program, Seton needed to move it, in essence, back to the land of its roots. The Spanish Southwest, where much of his support lay, seemed a logical choice for the League's new national headquarters.

Seton's move to accomplish that aim began in the early summer of 1927. While the rest of the nation idolized Charles A. Lindbergh and enjoyed the "ballyhoo" of Coolidge prosperity, the Chief announced plans to make a special visit to several Plains Indian reservations and spend the latter part of the summer among the New Mexico Pueblos studying Indian music and dancing. Writing to Charles F. Lummis in early June, Seton hoped that the ailing Don Carlos would be able to join him in New Mexico. He knew that the editor's presence would better enable him to enlist the trust and cooperation of Pueblo leaders.[56]

The tour, sponsored jointly by the Woodcraft League, American Museum of Natural History, and Staten Island Museum, commenced early in July. Armed with letters of introduction from the commissioner of Indian Affairs, Seton and his party—which included Julia Buttree and Clyde Fisher—visited the Sioux reservations in the Dakotas. At Standing Rock, where they joined in the Sioux ceremonials, they were shocked at the local agent's ruling that no Indians under age forty could perform their people's "pagan" dances. They were pleasantly surprised to discover that "Father" A. M. Beede had exchanged his clerical garb for a law degree and was now working at the agency courthouse on the Indians' behalf. After interviewing elderly chiefs and warriors who reminisced about "better" days, they made it a point to visit Sitting Bull's grave and the Slim Buttes battleground.[57]

On July 30, Seton and his colleagues were the guests of Senator J. J.

Hall, who entertained them with a garden party at his Denver, Colorado, estate. Here the Chief had everyone sit Indian style in a circle and participate in an amusing and instructive program of woodcraft stunts, including "cloud sweeping" contests. The Denver socialites seemed to enjoy it. Seton also paid Hall a high compliment for putting through federal measures for the protection of migratory birds.[58]

After arriving in Santa Fe on August 3, the party continued south to Santo Domingo pueblo to witness the Corn Dance, a ritual little changed over the centuries. In his journal, Seton noted that at one end of the village was a temporary dancehall, where Indian couples danced the Charleston to the music of a jazz band. In this setting of ancient and modern contrasts, Seton met with Lummis and other acquaintances, including Amos Pinchot and the Gerald Cassidys.[59]

Also present was Dr. Edgar Lee Hewett, chairman of the Department of Anthropology at the University of New Mexico. Before assuming that position, Hewett had served as director of American research for the Archaeological Institute of America and the Museum of New Mexico in Santa Fe. Renowned for his studies on pre-Columbian Indian sites, Hewett was instrumental in encouraging the Indians of the Southwest to produce drawings and watercolor paintings of their ceremonial dances.[60] Seton was more than glad to have Hewett as a friend and supporter of the Woodcraft League.

From Santo Domingo, the Seton party launched a tour of all the Rio Grande pueblos from Taos to Isleta. At each, Seton and Lummis contacted the chiefs and other leading residents. Through them, Black Wolf was able to make detailed studies of their various rituals. True to their outdoor gospel, Seton and his fellow Woodcrafters camped out around Taos and Santa Fe. At the capital city, they attended teas and receptions hosted by Sheldon Parsons and other artists. Gerald and Ina Cassidy, whose combination home and studio was located on Canyon Road, showed them through that art colony. There was also time to call on Mary Austin and her niece Mary Hunter at Casa Querida.

After attending the Intertribal Indian Ceremonial in Gallup, Seton hosted a formal dinner for his supporters at Santa Fe's La Fonda Hotel on August 28. The following night, he held a Grand Council in the patio of the art museum. About two hundred persons attended, including Richard C. Dillon, governor of New Mexico. The occasion was given an international flavor by the presence of two Dutch high school girls, who represented their country's Woodcraft organization. During the next few days, Seton had occasion to address the Santa Fe County school-teachers and visit the Los Alamos School. With Professor Hewett, he conferred with other university faculty members, including Ralph Emerson Twitchell, the New Mexico historian. Departing from Lamy on September 4, the Woodcraft leaders spent a few days in Chicago organizing leadership training courses and rested briefly at Winona Lake before returning to New York.[61]

By and large, Seton's "Indian trip" was a success. He had found the people of New Mexico open to his woodcraft gospel, and during his stay several new tribes had been organized. Although his schedule did not allow him to stay over for the annual Santa Fe Fiesta, which commenced during the first week of September, Seton deemed his visit "like the opening of a new epoch."[62] And indeed it was, for Black Wolf soon felt again the old urge to go west. In his later years, he referred to this urge as the "Buffalo Wind," his mystical, poetic version of the "call of the wild." Seton had obtained that term years before from an old half-blood in Manitoba who referred to the warm Chinook winds that blew in from the south in April. To hunters like him, that meant the return of the buffalo on their annual spring migrations. At any rate, there was a new insistence in this siren call.[63] The Land of Enchantment would soon see and feel the Chief's presence.

CHAPTER 20

The College of
Indian Wisdom

To restless souls seeking a change of pace and scenery, New Mexico was truly a "Land of Enchantment." Here, from the heavily forested Taos Mountains down the Rio Grande and Pecos valleys to the sun-baked pinnacles of the Guadalupe Range, stretched a land of startling contrasts, clear sky, and fresh air. It was a land of antiquity where man's recorded history was "no more than a line the thickness of writing paper" compared with the eons of geologic time represented in the colorful sandstone and shale cliff formations.[1]

Historically, New Mexico was steeped in legends and archaeological finds of prehistoric Indian settlements. The civilization of the sedentary Pueblos had gradually been mixed with the Hispanic culture brought in by conquistadores, settlers, and clergymen during the seventeenth and eighteenth centuries. This unique blend of cultures had proved resistant to the culture of the Anglo-American soldiers and frontiersmen pushing their way over the Santa Fe and Chihuahua trails into the heart of the desert Southwest. And even though railroads and other technological advances had ensured the triumph of American democratic rule, New Mexico's liberal environment and sparse population made it attractive to disillusioned artists and authors. Here was a new "frontier" where they could perhaps find themselves.

The literary and artistic salons at Taos and Santa Fe had therefore experienced a phenomenal growth during the 1920s as resident painters like Bert Phillips and Ernest Blumenschein gained national prominence through exhibitions at major galleries in the East. In Santa Fe, Mary Austin considered herself the undisputed queen of the town's literati, which included such muses as Alice Corbin Henderson, Willa Cather, Spud Johnson, Witter Bynner, and Oliver La Farge. In addition to Sheldon Parsons and the Cassidys, the Santa Fe art colony on Canyon

Road included Kenneth Chapman, Russell Cheney, John Sloan, and Seton's old chum from Paris days, Robert Henri. Basically, these people all dealt with the conflict between industrialism and primitivism. In condemning America's materialistic attitudes, they often focused on the dilemma of the Indians in a changing world. Moreover, the artists sought in their paintings to blend art with the natural environment, something that American society had not yet achieved. To them, the Indian was a perfect representation of this merger. Their primitivist vogue thus encouraged Indian painters to exhibit their talents, thus introducing many white Americans to native art.[2]

In addition, the New Mexico regionalists vigorously aided many of the red men's reform movements. This was especially true in their support of the American Indian Defense Association (AIDA), formed in 1923 to combat the passage of the Bursum Bill and the attempts of Interior Secretary Albert B. Fall to open reservation lands to oil and gas interests under the General Leasing Act of 1920. While these two measures were defeated, another circular issued by the commissioner of Indian Affairs in 1923, the Dance Order, tried to discourage any dance or ceremonial deemed "pagan and immoral" by the predominantly white Indian Reform Association and the missionaries. It was the enforcement of this ruling that Seton and his fellow Woodcrafters encountered at Standing Rock in July, 1927. He, along with regional authors and AIDA members, opposed the measure on the grounds of violation of religious freedom.[3]

Things took a turn for the better when Fall's successor, Herbert W. Work, formed the famous Committee of One-Hundred to review and advise the government on Indian policy. Several of Seton's old friends and acquaintances, including David Starr Jordan, F. W. Hodge, and Charles Eastman, were among the distinguished members of this committee, which proved instrumental in the eventual defeat of the Dance Order, the passage of the Indian Citizenship Act, and similar measures. By 1924, the betterment of America's Indian populace was a growing national concern.[4]

These developments probably influenced Seton's decision to move to New Mexico. Although he feared that Indian citizenship would diminish tribal identity, Seton was pleased that more white Americans were beginning to appreciate the red man's culture, particularly their arts and crafts. He perhaps figured that if he aligned himself with the regionalists in New Mexico and in California, his Woodcraft program would soon be back on a solid footing and once more be used as an effective tool in the crusade for Indian justice.

What was more, Seton decided that Santa Fe was best suited to be the "primitive spiritual capital of nature in America." A small, self-contained hinterland city devoid of large industries, Santa Fe was attractive to those who sought its special environmental qualities. It was a visible symbol of historic continuity and social integration, whose emphasis was on regional heritage and whose architectural variety and complexity showed the diversity of its intermingled populace. Somewhere among the furrowed, evergreen-studded foothills near the route of the old Santa Fe Trail, the Chief resolved to build a new center of "spiritual refreshment for millions between the ages of four and ninety-four" and a training center for leaders of the outdoors cult movement. Here, too, he would be close to Indians whose old way of life had not been destroyed and whose maintenance of communal integrity was guaranteed by the federal government's recognition of Pueblo title to most of their cultivated ancestral lands.[5]

With that vision planted in his mind, Seton began formulating plans for the move. After his return to Greenwich in the fall of 1927, Seton completed his *Lives of Game Animals* and other writing projects. In many lectures, the Chief placed new emphasis on the "Message of the Redman" and eagerly endorsed the regional spokesmen for Indian reforms. He especially complimented Mary Austin as an "original" thinker and considered her works on Indians "worthwhile contribution[s] to the riches of our child-life." He was in complete agreement with her preference for "the real Pueblo songs and methods to the dilutes and hybrids of literature in the past generation."[6]

As part of his plan, Seton began a family membership program. Concerned that many parents were not communicating with their children, he used his emphasis on play as a means of bringing families together. Seton considered Theodore Roosevelt, who always liked to play with his children and grandchildren, the ideal example of this approach, which would add a new dimension to his movement's emphasis on character development.[7]

Seton and his colleagues next decided on Los Angeles as the new location for the Woodcraft League's executive office. Not only was the "City of Angels" a growing commercial and cultural center, but many of Seton's friends and supporters lived in the area. Moreover, it was a center for Indian reform movements and ethnological studies in the West. Certainly Charles Lummis's Southwest Museum stood out as a visible reminder of that fact. To the end of his life, Lummis remained a firm believer in Seton's woodcraft gospel. When Don Carlos "crossed the Great Divide" on November 25, 1928, the Chief sent the Lummis family a letter of condolence lauding the man's accomplishments.[8]

To raise needed funds, Seton launched a series of annual winter lectures in the Los Angeles area. Despite the advent of movies and radio as top entertainment, Seton was still in great demand as a speaker, even in churches. At Los Angeles's Temple Baptist Church on February 15, 1929, Seton talked on "Woodcraft, a Way to Manhood." The pastor followed up with a rather appropriate sermon entitled "What a Boy Is Worth." The Chief also spoke and advertised on radio. The response was overwhelming, and by the fall of 1929, the Woodcraft League's executive offices had moved into new quarters at 405 South Hill Street.[9]

Accompanied by his secretary, Julia Buttree, Seton made annual summer trips to Santa Fe to "spy out the land" and select the best location for his "city on the hill." During these exploratory excursions, they made more visits to the Pueblos and gained the confidence of the local Indian community. With the help of the Dorman and Galt real estate firm, Seton carefully investigated several available tracts of land in Santa Fe County. One primary consideration was the availability of water wells. Finally, late in 1929, the Chief and secretary selected a twenty-five-hundred-acre plot about seven miles southeast of downtown Santa Fe. This land, located in the hills along the Arroyo Hondo, was originally part of the grant made by the king of Spain to Sebastian de Vargas after the "Reconquest" of New Mexico in 1692.[10] In an area laced with local legends, the site had often been used by Mexican shepherds bivouacking with their flocks. Evidence of their campsites abounded. The high places, dotted with piñons and junipers, commanded a view of the Sangre de Cristo Mountains to the north and the Jemez, Cerrillos, and Sandias toward the south and west. For Seton, the place had a mystical quality. In February, 1930, he officially took title to the land, previously owned by "a German who apparently lives in California."[11]

The duo next looked for a site on which to construct the new Woodcraft League facilities. Sometimes they spent hours, even days, hiking and camping in the rough terrain while searching for just the right spot. One glorious evening, while standing on a hill viewing a New Mexico sunset, the couple decided that this site was the one on which to build a

permanent home, with the village surrounding it. Seton then returned
briefly to Greenwich to settle his affairs, and in June, 1930, he and Julia
were back in Santa Fe, this time to stay.[12]

By that time, Seton and his wife had gone their separate ways. Although Grace always spoke highly of her husband's vital contributions
"to the literature and youth of the world," their differences in interests
and choice of living environments had gradually caused them to part
company. Not even the fact that Seton was now a grandfather could
convince him to return to the East permanently. He had found his new
"wilderness," and that was where he was content to spend the remainder
of his days. Only once did Grace visit his new creation; she stayed only
three days. In the meantime, her world travels took her to Japan, Indo-
China, and the East Indies and sometimes proved detrimental to her
health. Still, she did keep Seton informed of her activities and family
matters.

Certainly, the Chief was concerned about the welfare of his family,
particularly his daughter Ann and her two children, Seton (named for
his grandfather) and Pamela. Ann's marriage had ended in divorce,
however, and none of the family escaped the effects of the worldwide
depression brought on by the crash of the stock market in 1929. Even
Grace admitted that "affluence is not the word to describe my financial
condition, either." Yet she and Seton generously doled money out of
their savings to help Ann pay the bills and put the children through
school.[13] Ultimately, the situation proved something like a blessing in
disguise, for it was during this time that Ann turned to writing as a
profession. Although she later remarried, "Anya" Seton thus began her
rise in the literary world as the author of historical romances. Her first
book, *My Theodosia*, appeared in 1941.[14]

Seton was always willing to help other less fortunate family members.
Remembering the generosity of his brothers toward him during his
"starving times," Seton sought ways to repay them. One Christmas, he
returned a $1,000 check to his brother George in Chicago as a gift, "re-
ceipted in full." He also sent money to help pay debts and educate the
younger children and grandchildren of his brothers in Toronto. When
his brother Enoch died in the summer of 1928, Ernest sent $149.50 to
help pay the funeral expenses.[15]

As the Great Depression settled over the country, Seton and his colleagues set to work erecting camping facilities and temporary living

quarters on his new "Rancho." Seton Village, as it was named, had its beginning on a broad, level spot on the western slope of a tier of hills. Starting with Seton's first house, a row of adobe buildings designed to resemble ranch huts were erected along a dirt lane that branched to form an oval plaza at its western end. After completing his first house on the southeastern corner of the plaza, the Chief began erecting another long, one-story adobe called Lagunita (Little Lake), on the southwestern end. It contained vigas, stone chimneys, and a small walled patio. Other buildings included an office, a print shop, and a crafts shop known as Foothill Lodge. This structure also served as the original museum, for it was here that the Chief displayed his vast collection of Indian artifacts. Seton also had most of his art pieces, his specimen collection, and library volumes freighted from Greenwich to the village.

Several guest houses, built in the adobe style, were also constructed around the plaza. These were given such names as the Zoo Lodge, the Submarine, and the 'Dobie House. Two of them, the Pullman Car House and the Red Barn, were built around old railroad cars laboriously hauled up from Lamy, six miles away. Their conversion into houses was achieved by plastering the exteriors of the cars with adobe, allowing them to retain their rectangular shapes.[16]

Seton hired native Hispanic and Indian laborers to construct the buildings and landscape the grounds. In his journal for 1931–32, he kept a detailed list of expenses, the hired men's wages, their names, and the times that they came in. He also made note of the temperature and other weather conditions, problems with the elements, and what was built that day. Of course, Seton meticulously made sure that everything was constructed according to his specifications; if he found something badly done, he simply had the builder tear it down and start over. For running water, Seton hired an expert, J. D. Sheets of Albuquerque, to dig wells, install plumbing, and erect a windmill.

During construction of the village, Seton and Julia Buttree made several trips by car throughout the state, giving lectures and establishing contacts. His journal entries about rough gravel roads, occasional muddy stretches, flat tires, and other automotive problems present an accurate picture of New Mexico as it was before paved highways. Seton had a poor opinion of Roswell, declaring that "the town seems to have no historical values," and that it knew nothing of Billy the Kid. However, he was impressed with the fertility and pastoral scenes of the Hondo and

Ruidoso valleys, especially the numerous apple orchards. They often went along with Ted Buttree on his business trips to El Paso where he had several real estate investments.[17]

Seton also had another goal besides his village. Although he was still technically a government official of Manitoba, the Chief finally decided to go all the way in taking out naturalization papers. Using Mary Austin and other friends as "vouchers," he momentarily put aside all other considerations in order to complete the entire naturalization process. On November 6, 1931, Seton became an American citizen.[18]

Having accomplished that, he and his colleagues worked to complete the Village facilities for his first summer college, which was similar to the training courses he had held for youth organization leaders back East. To complete the buildings around the plaza, they were painted with grotesque Indian symbols. Carved wooden Indian figures and animal totems adorned the grounds near the building entrances. Indeed, the Village was not only a reflection of Seton's desire for the picturesque but also, in a sense, his own version of the concept of culture translating environment into landscape.[19] Near the museum—craft shop, the dirt lane from the plaza intersected a graded road that ran from the main highway through the Village and north to the Arroyo Hondo. Another outstanding feature was a small zoo in which Seton kept a few live specimens of native fauna in wire cages.[20]

The facilities were finally ready, and Seton's "College of Indian Wisdom" was officially opened in the summer of 1932, with twenty-five camp leaders from all over the nation attending. They were housed in the Indian village that had been constructed just north of the main plaza, with tepees, wickiups, a few log cabins, a dining hall, a Pueblo kiva, and a Navajo hogan that was the main auditorium. While Seton Village was equipped simply that first summer, it was adequate to house, feed, and teach students the primitive elements of outdoor life that Seton praised.[21]

Using the media to advertise his new institute, Seton reiterated his aim of regenerating society by a return to the open-air life.[22] He once told a psychologist that he had experienced spiritual rejuvenation in New Mexico after a long struggle to shake off the early influence of his "originally-correct-Calvinist-Scotch-Hell-Fire-family." The *Santa Fe New Mexican* referred to Seton as "a prophet of the real four-square gospel—body, heart, mind, mankind." A *Los Angeles Times* reporter called him "a pagan who lectures often in churches [and] a Paris-trained artist who considers Indian art more significant than anything he learned in school."[23]

The College of Indian Wisdom was held during July and August. Classes were usually conducted outdoors and often included field trips to historic ruins, archaeological sites, and famous pueblos. The courses, all fully accredited by the American Association of Colleges, were taught by a faculty of forty-two. Among them were Edgar L. Hewett, who served as the institute's honorary president, and Clyde Fisher of the American Museum. In addition to Seton's lectures on art and environment, Ina Cassidy offered a course in Indian basketry, Kenneth Chapman lectured on pottery design and symbolism, while natives of San Ildefonso and Santa Clara pueblos taught pottery-making. H. C. Gossard, president of New Mexico Normal College (now New Mexico Highlands University) in Las Vegas, also served on the faculty for a time. Julia Buttree acted as dean of the college and also performed the duties of keeper of the fires in the Woodcraft ceremonials. The institute accepted a limited number of students each year, and as the word spread, applications came from as far away as France and England.[24] At the end of each semester, graduation exercises, complete with diplomas, were held at the kiva. Afterward, each graduate would go up to the "Hill of Memories" and plant a "spirit stone."[25]

Later on, facilities were provided for a children's camp, which usually lasted a month. The children were divided into three age groups and taught facets of Indian culture according to their level of understanding. Here, too, the number admitted was limited usually to approximately thirty per session, so that each could receive personal attention. A flat fee covered all expenses. Among the Indian customs adopted at the camps was the beautiful and simple evening song, with only a drum beat or two as accompaniment. Julia often sang it in the children's camp as a signal for lights out and rest. Soon the adult students came to request the song and responded with equal enthusiasm to the relaxation it brought at the end of the day. With its last note, silence reigned for the remainder of the night.[26]

Between seasons, although busy giving lectures and preparing for the next summer's institute, Seton still found time to observe his beloved wild animals. Recorded observations of animal life were no longer the bulk of his journal entries, but he never lost his desire to be with animals. On occasion, he made special trips to game refuges to observe deer and varieties of game birds.[27] The *Journal of Mammalogy* published Seton's findings on animal behavior, as well as recorded instances of species considered rare or extinct in New Mexico and the Southwest.[28]

Whatever activity he was engaged in, Seton relied heavily on his own intense concentration, which was part of his personal religion. He often referred to the Supreme Being as the "Maker and Ruler of the Universe." Whenever he had problems to solve or important decisions to make, he was known to hold lonely vigils in a high, quiet retreat.[29] Even though the Chief belonged to no established creed, he was occasionally called upon to conduct weddings and funerals, clerical functions he performed with Indian touches. Weddings, in particular, were usually held during sunset at a small shrine erected for that purpose. These were patterned after the "Troth Plightings" used by Woodcraft groups in England. In them, Seton sought to inject "a note of sincerity and variety which takes the triteness out of the often too familiar phrases of the usual rites."[30]

Despite his unorthodox worship, some people looked upon Seton as a true "man of God." Such was the case of Helen McClorman, an elderly widow who had come to Seton Village when it was still under construction to live near her son, who had been hired as the grounds maintenance foreman. Before she died in July, 1932, Mrs. McClorman declared that she "would rather lie under a piñon tree in Seton Village than in a great marble mausoleum anywhere on earth." Her wish was granted. On the Sunday following her death, Seton conducted her funeral, and she was interred on a hill overlooking the village.[31]

As Seton continued to lecture nationwide, many relatives and old cronies back East were attracted to his enterprise. The Chief's naturalist nephew and his wife, Stuart and Eleanor Thompson, came for a visit in 1932 and were immediately impressed with the New Mexico atmosphere. Back home, Stuart promoted his uncle's work and contributed some of his own findings to the *Totem Board*. When Florence Merriam Bailey and her husband visited Seton's college in the summer of 1933, they sent back a favorable report to her brother, C. Hart Merriam, who subsequently subscribed to the magazine. At the 1933 "Century of Progress" World's Fair in Chicago, the Woodcraft League exhibited a model Indian village camp for boys and girls.[32] Even when the Chief was temporarily laid up in the hospital in March, 1935, to undergo a repair job on the hernia operation he had endured in Chicago more than fifty years before, Seton Village continued to expand as funds were made available. By the summer of 1935, it had more than twenty permanent buildings.[33]

Meanwhile, Seton's relationship with Julia Buttree, thirty years his junior, became a permanent one. For fifteen years, they had enjoyed a solid "literary partnership." Her undying support of his dreams and faithful service to the league and institute drew them ever closer together. In 1934, Julia's twenty-one-year marriage to Ted Buttree was annulled; late in November of that year, while in El Paso, Seton filed for a legal divorce from Grace across the border in Juárez. On January 18, 1935, the petition was granted in court at Santa Fe. The lawyer handling the case was Francis C. Wilson, whose distinguished career as U.S. Attorney for the Pueblo Indians was well known. During the 1920s, Wilson had been instrumental in establishing Pueblo land rights and had helped draft the Colorado River Compact in 1928. Indeed, he seemed a logical choice to manage the whole delicate situation for the Chief.[34] Four days later, on January 22, Ernest Thompson Seton and Julia M. Buttree were formally united as husband and wife at the home of Mrs. W. H. Webb in El Paso. For their "honeymoon," they traveled to Los Angeles to give lectures, check up on business affairs, and visit with Frederick Webb Hodge, who had retired from his position at the Smithsonian and moved to California to become curator of the Southwest Museum.[35]

Returning to Seton Village in February, the newlyweds made final preparations to build their "dream house." Always the believer in the simple, the practical, and the picturesque, Seton designed his pueblo-style "castle" complete with the necessary landscaping. Lumber for rafters, handrails, and other wooden fixtures was carefully selected from evergreens growing profusely on their land or pine logs hauled from the mountains above Pecos. With a drawknife, Seton carefully peeled the bark off each tree to be used; when someone suggested that this was in opposition to his philosophy of using natural materials, Seton replied: "Many times have we had to point out the difference between simplicity and crudity. Many of us by nature and by training are devoted to the simple life. But some groups have mistaken simplicity for savagery, and in their enthusiastic desire for the simple life as they see it have been led into some entirely unprofitable boorish customs." Local men were again hired to do the construction work. Julia later told the story of

four young Pueblo Indians who made adobe bricks for the castle. At the
end of one long work day, they entertained the Setons with tribal songs
to the accompaniment of a drum fashioned out of a lard bucket and an
old inner tube. As Mrs. Seton explained, "Indian song is impossible
without a drum."[36]

The castle, upon its completion, contained thirty rooms. Constructed
of adobe on a stone foundation, the central portion of the house ran
from east to west. Long vigas supported the roof. Half of this space was
occupied by bedrooms and the other half by the combination living
room—library and a small inglenook. To the rear of this portion, on the
east, were the kitchen and pantry. Small, single-room second and third
stories were built above the living room. Running north off the central
axis was a long, high-ceilinged room suitable for large gatherings. Here
were housed a portion of the library and many of Seton's works. A long
portal ran the length of the western end of the castle, and a row of small
rooms was located below the main floor on the southern end. Seton had
plenty of space for his studio and museum exhibits. His library, which
eventually numbered nearly 70,000 volumes, was said to be the largest
in New Mexico. Overall, the castle's organic and individualistic nature
testified to the continued presence of its chief architect.[37]

After they moved into their new house, Mrs. Seton recalled:

We laid great store by the little rituals and ceremonials we performed at home
through the years. Every hearth was blessed on its first lighting, each of our
rooms carried on the door the totem of the occupant, no birthday ever passed
without its joyous celebration. There were a number of meaningful customs
which we used at the table—on the face of them trifling perhaps, but won-
drously powerful in establishing and perpetuating an atmosphere of love.

Along the driveways, gates, and paths throughout the Village, Seton
nailed up humorous placards and wood carvings "to surprise me at my
next passing," according to his wife. On a bridge over a dry creek bed,
he tacked up a No Fishing sign, the reason being that it was "a mere
statement of fact." At the southwest corner of the castle patio, a small
shrine was erected for weddings and other ceremonies.[38]

Built on a hill facing west and dominating the Village, Seton Castle
presented an almost feudal atmosphere, and in many ways that system
was benignly carried out. All mail went there for distribution, and personnel problems were generally solved there as well.[39]

Although a graying seventy-four when he married for the second time, Seton thought nothing of dashing from place to place to give programs. Julia, who lectured with him jointly on Indian lore and crafts, became noted for her variety of costumes from different tribes. She especially treasured her white buckskin Sioux costume, deeming it "the most beautiful . . . in existence." One reporter described in detail the format the Setons most often used:

[The audience] listened in child-like delight as the eccentric-looking, gray-haired writer told and acted out in illustrative fashion Indian fairy tales. A story which parallels the American Cinderella story served as a background to Mrs. Seton's performance.

Wearing long black braids and an Indian dress composed of red and white headpiece and red, green, blue and white full-skirted dress, Mrs. Seton sang an Indian lullaby, a travel song, a hunting song, and a death song to the weird accompaniment of an Indian drum. The death song was one given her by an Indian chief who visited them some years ago. This type of song has no parallel in American music but should have. . . . In youth the Indian composes it, and when death comes he stands to sing it if he is able. Few of these songs have been collected because of the feeling of sacredness attached to them.

Changing her costume . . . she told of Indian religions and music and their similarities to the white man. Summing up their religious creed, she said that "there is one great spirit, creator and ruler of all, to whom all are responsible. Man's first duty is the attainment of manhood, consecration of manhood, and service to mankind. The condition after death will be exactly governed by our actions in this world." [40]

Millions of young people in the Great Depression era were just as thrilled with his ability to make a story come alive as their parents had been years before. Sometimes, the Chief and his wife even visited young fans and admirers in hospitals. [41]

Late in November, 1935, the Setons began their first overseas lecture tour together. From El Paso they drove across Texas to Oklahoma City, where Seton was guest of honor at a reunion of Wild West Show veterans at Pawnee Bill's Ranch. After lecturing in Ohio, New York, and Washington, D.C., the couple sailed for France, where they spent their first Christmas as husband and wife "exploring the gastronomic possibilities of the country." On January 22, 1936, they celebrated their first wedding anniversary in London. The occasion was all the more historic in that it coincided with the death of King George V. In all, the whole tour lasted more than five months. [42]

Returning on April 7, the Setons immediately began preparations for the 1936 summer institute. By then, the Village could accommodate 150 children and adults, and the College of Indian Wisdom was providing a unique educational experience for young and old alike. At the same time, it was being used as a sounding board for one of the most important pieces of federal reform legislation to affect the changing West.

CHAPTER 21

Seton Village and the
Indian New Deal

Along with the institute, the Setons continued using their lectures as tools to champion Indian rights. The Chief went so far as to suggest that the federal government give back to the Western nomadic tribes their old prairie hunting grounds, where land could be fenced off and stocked with buffalo herds. The tribes of the desert Southwest, he felt, could support themselves by selling their arts and crafts if the whites would stop sending Indian children to distant schools. By this time, Seton's antipathy toward the Bureau of Indian Affairs had become increasingly obvious. He accused its employees of being totally unsuited to their jobs because they had no real experience with or sympathy for Indians. Seton and his wife thus continually advocated the upgrading of hiring standards in the BIA.[1]

Seton also continued in his opposition to any form of individual allotment. Ever since his first visit to the Hopi mesas in 1914, Seton had argued against attempts on the part of government officials to break up villages on the reservation for reasons of sanitation. He reasoned that, as the experiences of the plains wheat farmers proved, individual land holdings in the West's drier regions led only to solitude, monotony, and eventual despair. A village community with a system of shared land tenure was therefore the only viable system in arid plains and deserts. He argued that such a mild form of socialism was better for the well-being of the populace and that it encouraged greater social intercourse.[2]

Seton also felt that the U.S. Supreme Court should review all Indian treaties and that all land unfairly wrested from the tribes should be restored in every case where possible. He said that all reservation boundaries should be permanently fixed and alterations permitted only by a clear voting majority of the tribe. Furthermore, he felt that each tribe

should be allowed to incorporate and thus hold land as a group enterprise. Such changes would enable the Indians to preserve and protect
what land they had left.[3]

Alongside these legal questions, the Setons continually advocated
preservation of tribal culture. The experience of James Paytiano (Flaming Arrow), a young Acoma Indian, illustrated this concern. Paytiano
reportedly could sing his people's tribal chants "till your spine would
run cold." Before long, tourists complimented him on his voice, and he
began to take singing lessons. His white music teacher, who taught him
songs like "From the Land of Sky Blue Waters," later married him and
renamed him James. One evening, when the couple called on the Setons,
the women requested that he sing. After Paytiano had gone through a
mediocre rendition of white men's compositions about Indians, Julia
handed him a drum and asked him to do his tribe's native chants. As he
complied, his whole personality, as well as the pitch of his voice, suddenly changed. Subsequently, Paytiano took the course in Indian dancing at Seton Institute, and he and his wife "made it big" in show business with their "native" act. "That's what people want," Julia later remarked, "the real thing."[4]

Seton therefore believed the government should publicly acknowledge that Indians possessed many admirable cultural traits which should
be preserved. Since these cultural practices did not violate mankind's
basic laws, he argued that the tribes should have the right to their own
forms of government, religion, and customs. Indian-owned schools,
museums, and local industry would help to save tribal arts from extinction. Finally, he advocated the abolition of Indian boarding schools in
the East, calling them instruments of cultural destruction. Instead, he
felt that each tribe should have the freedom to select its own teachers
and religious leaders.[5]

The majority of Seton's ideas were shared by other reform-minded
people who sought to alter traditional Indian policy. Indeed, the shock
of the Great Depression and its effect on Indians, as reported by Emergency Relief agents, ushered in a national movement of ambitious reform. Its chief spokesman was John Collier, who in 1933 was appointed
commissioner of Indian Affairs under Interior Secretary Harold L.
Ickes.[6]

Seton had first become acquainted with Collier through their mutual
association with Luther and Charlotte Gulick. At that time, Collier was
civic secretary of the People's Institute in New York City. As a leader in

the Camp Fire Girl organization, he served on its National Board of Directors and also wrote its "Fire Makers' Desire" in 1912.[7] Like Seton, Collier believed that of all America's ethnic groups, the Indians knew and used adolescence as "the gateway and endless road to the union of man with man, man with earth, and man with the cosmic mystery." He also recognized Kropotkin's mutual aid theory as the Indians, especially the Pueblos, applied it to their ancient democratic system of government. For Collier, group contributions, diversity, continuity, and solidarity were most important. The white man's technology, he felt, threatened to do away with this harmonious social order. During the 1920s, Collier viewed the efforts of Seton and the Woodcraft League with mounting interest. He later recalled one speech at a luncheon at the New York City Club in 1924, in which "Seton dwelt with insistence and at length upon our United States Indians and their hopes, as representative of the Indians of the Western Hemisphere. His was the first voice to speak of the ill effects, from the Rio Grande to Chile, of our victimization of the U.S. Indians."[8]

As commissioner, Collier lobbied Congress to pass the Indian Reorganization (Wheeler-Howard) Act in 1934. Inspired largely by Collier's personal experiences with the Pueblos, the act reversed the liquidation and allotment of Indian lands, allowed voluntary consolidation of fragmented lands and further purchase of lands, and instituted conservation practices. It also stressed tribal self-help and self-government and provided steps for greater Indian participation in BIA operations. Among the provisions especially pleasing to Seton were the increased emphasis on and support for Indian day schools (public or federal), the establishment of the Indian Arts and Crafts Board, Indian religious freedom, federal-state cooperation in Indian affairs, and the codification of Indian law.[9] While Collier's "Indian New Deal" was not popular among Indians who enjoyed special privileges under individual allotment, the act survived legislative attacks and opened a new era in federal Indian policy.[10]

Collier's efforts received unfailing support from Seton and others who shared his principles. Indeed, the College of Indian Wisdom obtained considerable notice from government agencies as a result of the Indian Reorganization Act. Even before the bill became law, the BIA had ordered nine of its employees to take several of the institute's courses to help them encourage reservation Indians to revive their ancient arts. In 1934, Seton told the *Los Angeles Times*:

We are reviving the Indians' pride in their ancestry, their traditions, their customs and themselves. And now, at long last, we have the government on our side to a greater extent than ever before. In order to supply the tourist demand for cheap souvenirs, the Indians had been forsaking their arts to create purely commercial products. With regained self-respect, and with regained lands which the government is buying back from whites who had stolen the springs and best lands, the Indians are coming into their own once more.[11]

Seton supported the efforts of Natalie Curtis, Mary Austin, Gerald Cassidy, Oliver La Farge, and others seeking to replace fake "store" items with genuine Indian crafts. He took an active interest in regional organizations such as the Indian Arts Fund and the American Association of Indian Affairs, which were dedicated to improving the red man's welfare. He also worked with the Indian Emergency Relief Board. During the short existence of the *Totem Board* at Seton Village, the Chief encouraged his regionalist friends to contribute articles. The book review sections contained mostly favorable commentaries on major works about Indians, such as Stanley Vestal's dramatic biography of Sitting Bull.[12] When F. W. Hodge announced plans to revise his *Handbook of American Indians*, Seton offered his own knowledge on the subject and pointed out certain errors in the first edition. He also gave Hodge a standing invitation to come to his college as a guest lecturer.[13]

John Collier was quick to recognize the importance of Seton's institute in the promotion of Indian culture and education. He eagerly endorsed Seton's lectures and kept him informed of significant breakthroughs resulting from the Indian New Deal. When a sacred "Indian Medicine Bundle" was restored to the Hidatsas, Seton lauded that accomplishment, declaring that the native Americans "have just as much right to their sacred relics as our churches have to their bits of the true cross or relics of the Saints." Many of Collier's colleagues considered Seton "one of our greatest living Americans," and the commissioner of Indian Affairs agreed that it was people like him who helped museums and schools discover and revive lost tribal arts and crafts. Despite Collier's own busy schedule, he was able to make occasional visits to Seton Village and guest appearances at the institute.[14]

To enlist the aid of others in reviving native culture, Seton and his wife published several books on the subject. Julia, in particular, won wide recognition as an authority on various facets of Indian culture. Her first important work was *The Rhythm of the Redman* (1930), a collection about Indian dances from different tribes, first published before her marriage to Seton. The Chief wrote the preface and did the illustrations for this book, showing that he was never too old to learn. His outline of the characteristics of Indian art seemed to suggest that art, after all, did not merely copy nature. He noted that Indian paintings were symbolic rather than realistic; for instance, instead of painting the likeness of a buffalo, the Indian artist produced a symbol of the animal. Perhaps Seton realized that his *Sleeping Wolf*, too, had been symbolic. Influenced to a great extent by Frederick Burton, Frances Densmore, Natalie Curtis, and others, Mrs. Seton emphasized the importance of the dance as part of the Indians' religion and described each ceremony in detail. The BIA later adopted this book as a text for Indians.[15]

Throughout the thirties, Julia turned out more books on the Indian theme, including *Indian Costume Book* (1938) and *Sing, Sing, What Shall I Sing?* (1935). Her *Pulse of the Pueblo* (1939) is a collection of the Setons' personal impressions from visits to different Indian reservations and villages. Many of her Indian tales and myths were first featured in the *Totem Board* and other periodicals before appearing in book form.[16]

The high point in the Setons' Indian rights campaign came in 1936. For years, one of the Chief's favorite lectures had been "The Message of the Redman," in which he listed the shortcomings of white society in comparison with that of the Indians. "Our system," he declared, "has broken down—our civilization is a failure. . . . It makes a millionaire and a million paupers wherever pushed to a conclusion." Essentially, white cultural values were "how much property you have gotten" as opposed to the Indians' "how much service you have rendered to your people." Seton felt that through his summer camps and institutes, his movement was paving the way for a new civilization. "For every Woodcraft camp is more or less an Indian village," he wrote, "a little world of Indian life and thought, a part at least of the Redman's message, with a chance to complete the chapter."[17] Remembering his encounter with the mystic woman in California who had told him he was a reincarnated Indian chief, Seton collaborated with his wife and produced *The Gospel of the Redman*, in which he compared the teachings of the Bible to the native Americans' nature philosophy and religion. In criticizing the white man's materialism, Seton pointed out several instances in history where Indians lived up to certain Christian principles better than did churchgoing whites.[18]

In essence, *The Gospel of the Redman* is a historical summation of the arguments presented in Seton's earlier works. In general, Seton argued, the Indian was more honest than his white frontier counterpart. Violent conflicts largely resulted from whites' deliberate lies or from lack of cultural understanding; Indian depredations, in most cases, had been provoked by the transgressions of whites. In the book's first edition, Seton listed numerous massacres of Indians from Cos Cob to Wounded Knee. In one chapter, he pointed out that torture and scalping were for the most part adopted from the example set by Europeans. Overall, Seton considered the history of Indian-white relations in America a stain on the nation's professed ideals. Although the Indian New Deal was a major step toward rectifying the situation, he feared that the inherent hypocrisy in this difference between ideals and reality would ultimately eradicate the American democratic experiment. Seton was not a Marxist, but he was socialist in that he believed the federal government should play a greater role in the allocation of resources to reduce social inequalities.[19]

Even before its publication, the manuscript evoked mixed reactions. A number of rabbis and Protestant clergymen declared that it paralleled to some extent their own doctrines.[20] Charles Eastman, George Bird Grinnell, and Edgar Hewett all agreed with F. W. Hodge, who felt that Seton had assembled much valuable information that the public needed to know. John Collier commended him: "I have long thought that just such a book was needed and ought to be widely consulted, and I do not think there is anyone so competent to assemble it as yourself."[21] On the other hand, Seton's tendency to exaggerate Indian virtues merited legitimate criticism. Walter S. Campbell, who wrote under the pen name Stanley Vestal, felt that although *The Gospel of the Redman* contained many strong points, it was entirely "too much 'Setonized.'"[22]

Seton's relationship with Stanley Vestal, a University of Oklahoma professor, merits some mention here. As a teenager growing up in the country near the Indian communities around Guthrie and Weatherford, Oklahoma, Vestal had read Seton's columns in the *Ladies' Home Journal*. Inspired, he had organized two Woodcraft tribes, using Southern Cheyenne motifs and giving himself the name Timber Wolf. In a sense, Seton was responsible for Vestal's own rise as an author, for in 1904 the latter had published his first article in *Holiday Magazine for Children*. Entitled "Our Oklahoma Tribe," it related the young writer's experiences as a Woodcraft Indian.[23] From that time on, Vestal's interest in Indians and America's frontier past mounted. Over the years he maintained correspondence with the Chief, and they became close friends. As a more scholarly author of the West, however, Vestal did not allow himself to be swayed by Seton's biases as he critiqued *The Gospel of the Redman*.[24]

It is only fair, however, to consider the overall impact of the book— indeed, all of Seton's Indian writings—on the reading public as well as his purpose in publishing his ideas; his unabashed praise of native life-styles was due to his passionate belief in the worth of a culture other than his own.[25] At any rate, *The Gospel of the Redman* was an immediate best-seller, and several editions were printed through the years. Wherever the Setons lectured at a meeting, copies of the book usually sold out. Many readers were probably astounded with a statement made by Neil Erickson, an old rancher whom Seton interviewed at Douglas, Arizona, in 1935. Born in Sweden, Erickson had come to Arizona in the 1880s as a soldier, taken part in the Geronimo campaign, and then established his ranch in the Chiricahua Mountains near Willcox. At the end of their conversation, he reportedly told Seton: "If I had known what I know now about Indian character, I would have deserted from the American Army and joined up with the Apaches."[26]

The success of Seton's "Indian Bible" was a boost to his own ego as well, for in 1934 he had suffered a few literary setbacks. Although the *Totem Board* was featuring a variety of short stories, informative articles, travel pieces, and book reviews, the onslaught of the Great Depression made the cost of producing a monthly periodical prohibitive, and the Woodcraft League was compelled to stop publication after May, 1934.[27]

In the same year, Seton had compiled the western tall tales he had gathered over the years and sent the manuscript to Bobbs-Merrill in Indianapolis, Indiana. Entitled *The Sheriff of Golden*, the collection was a mixture of Baron Münchausen's adventures and the tall tales of Pecos Bill and other folk heroes. Evidently, Seton was trying to do with the folklore of the Anglo-American frontier what he had done with that of the Indians. As he stated in his introduction, "What the *Arabian Nights* were to the good folks of Araby, these sheriff tales are to the Bronco men of the West." However, authors such as Joe Miller and B. A. Botkin had already published western yarns, and the Bobbs-Merrill editors rejected the manuscript on these grounds, adding that the tales lacked the bombast and bravado of "the cowboy story of Texas" and that they had no unifying theme (beyond having a fictional sheriff as the narrator). Furthermore, as one editor stated: "It is a little startling to read a manuscript from the pen of Mr. Seton filled with such words, frequently used, as 'helluva' and 'sunavabitch' which he explains means 'a very unpleasant person.' It is quite out of the run of his other work."[28]

Such failures were overshadowed by the success of *The Gospel of the Redman*. Besides, Seton's animal stories continued to be popular; Appleton-Century and other New York publishers were turning out new editions of *The Biography of a Silver Fox* and earlier works for a new generation of readers.[29] Seeing this, Seton turned to his favorite genre once again. In 1937, he published *Great Historic Animals, Mainly about Wolves*, a new collection of short stories that had previously appeared in the *Totem Board*. The book's theme reveals Seton's belief in Darwinism; wolves, because of their social structure and behavior, were creatures that greatly interested primitive men. While these animals were a source of nightly terror, only during hard winters or other times of famine were there recorded instances of wolves attacking humans and livestock. Seton goes on to argue that just as dogs and other domestic animals retain certain characteristics and behavior patterns of their wild ancestors, modern man likewise retains certain habits and thought patterns (or "inner impulses") from his primitive forebears.[30]

The wolf stories in *Great Historic Animals* follow the same formula used in the earlier works. Whether the stories are set in Europe or the American West, the themes of man versus nature, chase and pursuit, and the final showdown are prevalent. The accounts of "Courtand" and "La Bête," the two man-killing wolves of France, were taken from an old French book called *La chasse de loup* (1861), a copy of which had been sent to Seton by Kermit Roosevelt.[31] The dog stories "Rincon" and "Carrots" once again explore the intimate relationship between dog and master and utilize Jack London's theme of the wild versus the tame side of nature. In "Hank and Jeff," based on a yarn from the backwoods of Kentucky, Seton embellishes the adage that "no man ever gave up his dog, if it was really truly his dog." Perhaps the book's most unusual story is "The Leopard Lover," Seton's own version of Honoré de Balzac's "Passion in the Desert." It concerns a lost soldier of Napoleon's army and his strange relationship with a female leopard, whose character resembles that of his jealous, long-lost fiancée. In summing up the book's Darwinian theme, Seton stated:

> Those of you who would divide the world into human emotion and (on a far lower plane) animal impulse, have not dipped deep into the wells of truth. You

have barely skimmed those stagnant ponds, those abysses of ignorance, called dictionaries and encyclopedias.

I wish I could take you out with me to sit by the campfires of the old timers, to hear their blasphemous truths, to rake the gold out of garbage bins, to learn the big things that come out of daily, nightly communion, but which are absolutely destroyed by creeds, by orthodoxies, as surely as the Copernican cosmogony was damned by the church folk of his day.[32]

The Darwinian theme is also present in *The Biography of an Arctic Fox*. Originally titled *Katug, the Snow Child*, the story is not only a scientific account based on studies of arctic foxes but also a parable of the Great Depression era and its effects on society. Katug is symbolic of the individualistic American farmer who seeks a mate and a place to settle. Arriving at Orlak, he wins Liagu for his own; they dig a den, set up "housekeeping," and become the parents of five pups. The arctic summer is a time of prosperity, and good hunting enables Katug to provide for his family. Nanook, the polar bear and a borrowed stereotype, is like a feudal baron. He represents the wealthy elite since he always gets the most food. Nevertheless, Katug and Liagu are able to survive and feed their young by using their skill and cunning. The impending depression is symbolized by the appearance of "Old Frothy Jaws," the wolf, who is at the door but because of the parent foxes' advice (based on their instincts), cannot destroy the family and home. As soon as the fox pups are grown up, they leave the den, but heeding the instincts of their parents, like the forewarnings of the small but vocal minority of economic experts who predicted hard times, they bury caches of lemmings to feed on during lean periods.[33]

The hard times finally arrive, in the form of arctic winter storms. Certainly the bleak "Winter of Despair" in 1932–33 could scarcely have been better described. Many animals starve, while others migrate south. Here, Seton's familiarity with the "Okie" migrations to "uncongenial lands . . . till the final remnant is engulfed in a far strange sea" is evident. While the arctic fox family is scattered, Katug and Liagu stay near the lemming caches to tough it out. But as the famine worsens, Katug is compelled to travel long distances to find game. At one point, the foxes dig up one of their caches and are lulled into a false sense of security, like many of the nation's liberal economic forecasters in 1936–37. But soon the "little hot millstones" in Katug's stomach are grinding again. Separated from his mate by the early spring thaws, the white fox stumbles onto an Eskimo hunters' village. Here the scene resembles a big industrial enterprise: the igloos belch clouds of dust-colored smoke. Although the caches of dried fish and seal meat are guarded by the Eskimos' dogs, Katug takes a desperate gamble to get at the fat red meat and relieve his hunger. Unfortunately, the pack spots and easily over-takes him. Before he is killed, the fox tries but fails to pacify the dogs by friendly frolicking; thus the Turnerian farmer, with his ideals, is done in by the dogs of industrialism. But he goes down fighting. The dog leader is cowardly, and Seton compares the pack to pirates and ruffians—per-haps alluding to unemployed industrial workers, many of whom came from the farm to the city and allowed themselves to be "dehumanized" by "the System." The purity and innocence that the white fox symbol-izes cannot survive long in an atmosphere tainted by strikes and vio-lence. In the meantime, Liagu, waiting in vain for her lost mate, rejects the amours of another male for a year, but finally accepts him.[34] Perhaps this last scene reflects Seton's own choice of a new partner and his long-ing for a return to the peace and prosperity of times past. Above all, the tale depicts the age-old struggle between plutocracy and individual democratic instinct. Although he believed in Darwin's theories as ap-plied to natural science, Seton at the same time disliked the plutocratic Republican application of social Darwinism. His inclination toward the New Deal, both the Collier and Roosevelt versions, is subtly revealed.

As was the case with Seton's earlier animal stories, these later books received mixed reviews. Donald Culross Peattie was especially disturbed by *Great Historic Animals*, deeming much of its content erroneous and misleading. Frank Chapman rallied to Seton's defense, however, stating that if he "wants to amuse himself by telling fireside tales of more or less mythical animal heroes, hasn't he earned the right to do so without be-ing burned at the stake?"[35]

While Seton was expressing his sociopolitical views through animal tales, his Village continued to grow as more youth camp leaders, artists, and writers were attracted to the summer institutes. A group known as the Seton Village Poets, with the Chief as their leader, began publishing works derived from their aesthetic view of the New Mexico environ-ment. (Even though he had never published a major poetic work, Seton had made it a lifelong habit to record his deepest feelings in verse.[36] Most of his later poetry was written in the Indian sage tradition, his "Indian Prayer" being a prime example.) One of the institute's high-lights came to be the nighttime outdoor performance of "The Mime of

Creation," a stage show written by Harley B. Alexander and based on the mythic and ritual lore of the Pueblo tribes. Essentially a chanted poem with illustrative tableaux and dances—its characters costumed like the masked Pueblo dancers—the play, with its chorus and musicians, was reminiscent of an ancient Greek drama, but in a native American setting.[37]

The College of Indian Wisdom thus seemed to be on the road to success. But new threats of war appeared on the horizon portending a turn of events that would lead to the institute's sudden death—although not before the Chief had assumed a parent's role once more.

CHAPTER 22

The Last Years

If *The Biography of an Arctic Fox* was indeed Seton's symbolic portrayal of the Great Depression, it was accurate. To the Chief and his likeminded neighbors, the situation of the Dust Bowl refugees plodding across the deserts to an elusive promised land was just another consequence of America's technological revolution. In their eyes, it was small wonder that Californians, themselves reeling from the crisis, often afforded these transients a reception like the one the Eskimo dogs gave Katug.[1] Certainly the Great Crash had brought social disruption and economic chaos to the West; tourism was abruptly curtailed, and many promising cultural activities were stifled as the sales of books and paintings plummeted. Only the motion picture industry proved the exception to this unhappy state of affairs, and the Setons were among the many who sought cheap entertainment and temporary escape in local movie theaters.[2]

But there was hope in those desperate times. Weary of the Hoover administration's empty promises, Americans had voted overwhelmingly in 1932 for the Democratic candidate, Franklin D. Roosevelt. Distantly related to Theodore Roosevelt, Seton's old friend from years past, FDR assured the public that it had "nothing to fear but fear itself." The president almost immediately set the wheels of federal bureaucracy in motion by declaring bank holidays, throwing out the gold standard, and pushing through Congress a series of legislative programs on behalf of the ranchers, farmers, and others affected by the crash.[3]

The West was especially receptive to the New Deal. Along with the federal agricultural programs, Roosevelt gave his wholehearted support to public power projects. Under the Bureau of Reclamation, large portions of the semiarid West were transformed into reservoirs and thriving irrigated farmlands, thus encouraging the construction of new resorts and suburbs. Thousands of unemployed young men found work in the Civilian Conservation Corps and the Works Progress Administration. These agencies improved streets and highways and constructed tourist facilities in state and national parks, monuments, and wilderness areas. Even closer to Seton's interests were the WPA's cultural programs designed to provide employment (and subsistence) for artists, writers, and musicians.[4]

In Seton's New Mexico, the effects of the depression were keenly felt. A poor state to begin with, its economy was virtually paralyzed. The traditional Republican dominance in New Mexico's leadership declined as Democratic "patróns" effectively used relief administration control to gain political clout. While little socioeconomic reform was actually accomplished, New Mexico, like much of the West, became more heavily dependent on the federal government.[5]

Seton cared little about politics except where Indian reforms and wilderness areas were involved, but changes in his personal and social life took up his attention. The depression years saw the passing of several of his old cronies, including Robert Henri, Lincoln Steffens, Gerald Cassidy, George Bird Grinnell, Charles Eastman, Hamlin Garland, and Mary Austin. When Austin, the poetess of the Dry West, died in 1934, the Chief offered a site on a hill near his Village for her grave as an expression of gratitude for her sympathetic friendship (however, according to her wish, her ashes were interred on Mount Picacho outside of Santa Fe).[6] Several younger artistic and literary talents rose to prominence and filled the artistic void she left. Distinguished Eastern visitors, like the poet-playwright Maxwell Anderson, joined the Santa Fe colony for a time and dramatized the Indian-white cultural conflicts that Seton was striving to resolve. To keep up with cultural trends in his adopted state, Seton participated in, among other things, the Poet's Roundup held each summer in Santa Fe.[7]

The Setons' reputation among Indians became almost legendary. Many local tribesmen grew to respect Chief Black Wolf as much as they would their own caciques and medicine men. The family of one "urban Indian" couple, who worked at the Village for a time as house servants, became fast friends of the Setons, who encouraged them to sell their pottery and crafts and to keep their identity as Indians.[8] Seton had an open invitation to swim at the Santa Fe Indian School. Once, when the Setons were in Tulsa, a wealthy old Osage came to them and asked sadly if they would take his son to the institute and teach him the ways of his own people. The Setons also knew the Lujan family of the Taos pueblo and were always delighted to see the Lujan children dance in costume.[9]

Everywhere they spoke, whether at downtown hotels and convention

centers or on college campuses, the Setons received an enthusiastic response. The graying Chief's robust personality left on many an "impression of great vigor."[10]

In the spring of 1937, a delegation of coeds and their sponsors from
Texas Technological College in Lubbock visited Seton Castle by special
invitation. This group was the Ko-Shari Club, a campus women's organization with an Indian theme. Every spring the club made a field trip
to Santa Fe, where they toured the Frijoles Canyon ruins—the setting
of Adolph Bandelier's novel *The Delight Makers*, from which the club's
name was derived—and initiated new members at an ancient kiva. On
this occasion, the Ko-Sharis were so charmed by their hosts and their
work that they arranged to have the Setons speak at their campus in
March of the following year.[11] The positive response of the students
and faculty to the couple's joint lecture on animals and Indian lore
prompted James G. Allen, acting dean of men, to invite them back in
July as part of Texas Tech's summer recreation program. On the appointed afternoon, despite threatening rain, the Chief and his wife gave
their "Message of the Redman" to an audience of four hundred on the
green in front of the college administration building.[12]

In October, 1938, Seton attended a ceremony held in his honor at
New Mexico Highlands University in Las Vegas. At this dedication, led
by university president H. C. Gossard, the student lounge was renamed
the Seton Lounge. In his address, Gossard remarked: "This institution
deeply appreciates the friendship of one of the most famous citizens and
appreciates that here, too, we might have the privilege of using his name
which signifies the character of a strong Western man." The Chief donated seventeen of his paintings and drawings to the university and addressed the student body at Ilfeld Auditorium on the growing problems
of American youth.[13]

The 1938 institute was particularly memorable. By that time the
Woodcraft League had around 80,000 members nationwide. The student enrollment for that year was 176, and many more were turned away
because of limited facilities. Furthermore, Seton Village Press was open
for business, run by Maurice and Marcelle Taylor, who, on invitation
from the Setons, had arrived on January 3 from Cedar Rapids, Iowa.
They had brought with them "three-hundred pounds of foundry type, a
side-lever Chandler & Price press with a 6 by 10 inch chase, and other
bare essentials of printing equipment and paraphernalia," which they
installed in the small adobe print shop.[14]

To the Chief and his wife, however, that summer was special in a personal sense, for in August they became the adoptive parents of two-month-old Beulah. On "the fourteenth sun of the Green Corn (or Red) Moon," Seton celebrated his seventy-eighth birthday with a christening ceremony at the kiva for his adopted daughter. Juan Gonzales of San Ildefonso pueblo performed the clerical rites, using a piñon branch to sprinkle water. At the request of the children at the camp, Beulah was given the Indian name of Payo Pai, or "Summer Flower." For the occasion, Seton prepared a small booklet entitled *The Buffalo Wind* in which—in the poetic style of an Indian orator—he briefly reviewed his life and longing to go into the wilderness. Only two hundred copies of this now priceless edition were printed (in the fashion of Elbert Hubbard's *Roycrofters*) and bound in buffalo hide.[15]

While many people thought it unusual for a man of his age to adopt a baby, Seton did not agree. "Why I know a man who had a daughter at the age of ninety-two," he quipped. His youthful outlook undimmed, the Chief certainly considered Beulah "a real asset." Wherever they traveled, cross-town or cross-country, the Setons carried her in a bassinet in the back of the car. "Twice on the way to New York, we were stopped for speeding," Julia recalled. "Beulah just smiled at the cops, and we got away with it."[16]

The Setons had a stroke of good fortune when they hired Pablita Velarde, an upcoming young artist from Santa Clara pueblo, as nurse and babysitter. After graduating from the Santa Fe Indian School in 1936, Pablita had returned to her home to teach at the pueblo's day school and establish her own art studio. When the Setons hired her to babysit in the summer of 1938, they soon realized her artistic talents and took her along on a four-month lecture tour of the eastern and southern United States. For Pablita, the trip was an awakening. Her first big break as an artist came in 1939 when the National Park Service commissioned her to do the murals in the Museum and Visitors' Center at Bandelier National Monument. The Setons complimented Pablita as a "person of unusual artistic abilities" and encouraged her to continue her work.[17]

As the 1930s drew to a close, the Setons traveled almost continually, preaching the Indians' message, selling books, and recruiting students for the institute. As Julia explained, "We eat, drink, sleep and breathe our work." Their tour through the East in the fall of 1938 was repeated the following year; early in 1940 they took a three-month jaunt through

Mexico in their new Chevrolet, visiting such cities as Monterrey, Ciudad Victoria, Mexico City, Cuernavaca, and Acapulco.[18]

In the meantime, rapid changes occurred in the world around them. Although the Great Depression was ending and prosperity was finally "just around the corner," the world's most destructive global war was about to erupt. The nation was increasingly preoccupied with the mounting threats of Nazi Germany, Fascist Italy, and Imperial Japan. Indeed, the Setons had seen firsthand the results of the Third Reich's "new order" in Germany. The story goes that during their last European tour, Adolf Hitler had sent the Setons a formal invitation to a banquet, along with a request for a private audience. Supposedly, he was interested in comparing his "Hitler Youth" movement with the Boy Scouts and other American youth groups. However, the Chief's antipathy toward militarism and Julia's Jewish blood caused him to decline the Führer's invitation. Soon after their return to Santa Fe, the German chancellor sent the Setons a china tea set, each piece emblazoned with the emblem of the Third Reich, as an apparent diplomatic gesture. Seeing the swastika, a Zuni Indian symbol for good fortune, transformed into a symbol of tyranny must have been particularly disheartening for Seton.[19] His misgivings about Hitler were verified in September, 1939, when the Führer unleashed his dogs of war on Poland.

In the summer of 1940, the Seton Institute had two hundred students and a staff of fifty experts. Although Zoo Lodge had been lost in an oil and gas explosion, the Village now contained thirty buildings. Library books were available for free reference, or they could be checked out for two cents.[20] In short, the Setons had a "going concern" that looked promising and showed no signs of decline—until the nation's attention was diverted toward Hitler's "blitzkrieg" in Europe. No longer could the Setons or their students travel overseas. Already, scores of young men in New Mexico, including some of Seton's employees, were enlisting in the armed forces. Since it required much time and energy to run the children's camp and adult institute, the Setons confessed that during the height of the summer activities they spent almost no time in the castle "except the sleeping hours." For these and other reasons, they reluctantly announced their decision to discontinue the school after that year. As Julia later explained it, "Our lives were getting too full—even for us who thrived on fullness. What with lecturing autumn, winter and spring, the school all summer, we had mighty little time to write."[21]

Indeed, Seton by that time was completing what he considered a lifetime project—his autobiography. As early as 1918, the Chief had seriously contemplated writing the story of his life, and Frank Doubleday and others were encouraging him to do so.[22] By 1935, he had finally prepared a manuscript of his life story and submitted it to several interested New York publishers under the title "My Trail through the Woods." In 1939, Maxwell Perkins, the famed Scribner editor, agreed to publish it, but a lawsuit over an alleged contract made earlier with Farrar and Rinehart delayed publication. Attorneys of the Authors' League settled the dispute out of court, and in the summer of 1940 the manuscript was ready to go to press under the title *Trail of an Artist-Naturalist*.[23]

Originally, Seton had intended to produce a two-volume work, with 1900 as the dividing point, since by then his reputation was established. But after several editings, the manuscript was condensed into one volume. The most noticeable omission from the original manuscript is Seton's account of his role in the founding of the Boy Scouts. He had prepared a chapter on that subject, but shortly before the book went to press, it was withdrawn at his wife's request.[24]

The reasons for this move are not clear, but perhaps Julia was concerned about the prolonged controversy between her husband and the BSA executives. In 1937 a new battle had started with the publication of W. D. Murray's official *History of the Boy Scouts of America*. Although Murray and others had solicited his information, Seton felt that their treatment of him in their book was both inadequate and unfair.[25] Consequently, he vented considerable rage in attempting to straighten out the record. He was joined in this effort by Dan Beard, who put aside past quarrels in his own bid to delete inaccuracies from the book. Responding to Seton's long-standing threat to publish a personal vindication, James West and other executives tried once again to humor him, but their support of Baden-Powell's interpretation of Scouting's origins remained obvious.[26] Indeed, Baden-Powell had prepared a "note for . . . when I am dead" in which he argued his own preeminent role.[27]

Aware of all these things, Julia probably decided that the best way to avoid serious repercussions was to exclude the Boy Scout chapter completely. Had her husband chosen to question Baden-Powell's integrity publicly, he would likely have been subjected to legal proceedings. To the very end, however, Seton remained firmly convinced that his Woodcraft Indians were the roots of the BSA's tree and that their guidelines had been "perverted by a league of Wall Street brokers and reactionary patriots who sacrificed the spontaneity of youth to the blandness of the status quo."[28] Nevertheless, he wisely consented to his wife's action, and considering his enormous popularity among local troops and councils everywhere, it was probably best for all concerned. Even after her husband's death, Julia always sought to maintain "the most cordial relations between the Boy Scouts of America and Seton Village."[29]

Seton's *Trail of an Artist-Naturalist* is thus a somewhat incomplete narrative of his life. In writing it, Seton took the position of a "white Indian" and a naturalist concerned with the literal truth as he saw it. Indeed, the text relies largely on a store of selective, sometimes bitter memories and occasional half-truths, particularly in the narrative of his first trip to New Mexico. In several instances, he used fictional names for people he encountered: Joe and Charley Callis became the Tannerey brothers, and Jack Brooks became Jim Bender. The appearance of the dude deputy, "Chawles Fitzwohltah," and Seton's liberal use of western folklore makes one wonder whether he injected portions of the rejected "Sheriff of Golden" manuscript. The Scribner editors encouraged him along that line by saying, "the more Wild West, the better." While this advice reflected the popularity of Wild West lore, Seton was perhaps seeking to portray, in his own humorous fashion, the myth and reality of the Old West through the character of the dude deputy.[30]

Throughout his autobiography, Seton attempted to turn himself into the symbol of man at one with the animal kingdom. The greater portion of the narrative is devoted to his early field trips and observations in the Canada of his youth. Of his marriage to Grace, Seton wrote only briefly (earlier, he had requested that she not publish anything about him or Julia or his work without giving them "a chance to comment or correct").[31] The appendix contains two of Seton's earliest poems—including his very first, "The Kingbird"—and a brief history of the origins of the Seton surname to help clear up any "controversy and confusion" surrounding his name change.[32]

Despite its weaknesses, the autobiography was, for the most part, well received by Seton's audience. Alan Devoe, editor of *Saturday Review* and a former Woodcraft Indian, felt that "a little complacent self-congratulating is perhaps permissible to an old man who has fought many battles and fought them stoutly."[33] Other fellow Woodcrafters gave Seton positive responses, although a few felt that he had been "a bit too severe" in his treatment of John Burroughs.[34]

The publication of Seton's life story almost coincided with his birthday on August 14, 1940. "I am eighty years old today, and I don't feel it," the Chief wrote in his journal.[35] Despite his age, Seton continued to produce works with both the pen and the brush, his ability to concentrate on and complete one project at a time accounting for his large output. "At times, when he worked on the illustrations for a story that brought back thoughts of some unhappy occurrence," Julia recalled, "I would read to him in order to keep his mind off the memories that were distasteful. This became a custom all through our life together, whenever I found him engaged with a brush or crayon." Many of his drawings and oil paintings were sold to museums and galleries throughout the Southwest. He even tried his hand at sculpture, and although his finished bird and mammal pieces were crude compared with those of expert sculptors, even these rare attempts reflected his genius. Never known to use a typewriter, Seton did all his manuscripts in longhand and always sought to make his point "simply and sincerely."[36] Such was the case with *Trail and Camp-Fire Stories* (1940), a collection of Indian folktales he and Julia had obtained over the years from Pauline Johnson and others, and *Santana, the Hero Dog of France* (1945), his last published animal story in book form. Even when he was busy at his desk, however, Seton never failed to welcome visitors with his customary "How! How!" Indian salutation.[37]

After the "day of infamy" on December 7, 1941, the United States was plunged into the expanding global conflict. For the moment, public attention even in New Mexico shifted away from Indian reforms and the return to harmony with nature that the Setons preached. Their grounds maintenance crew diminished as the workmen joined the fight against the Axis. Of course, the Setons fully supported the war effort by buying and depositing war bonds and conserving commodities, even to the extent of closing down the castle and temporarily moving to a smaller house in the Village. Their lecture engagements were reduced by wartime rationing, but they did make one memorable jaunt to the East Coast in February, 1942. At Greenwich, Seton visited Ann and the grandchildren, who now numbered three with the birth of another daughter, Clemency, by her second husband, Hamilton Chase. He also saw once more his beloved DeWinton estate and Little Peequo cottage. "Oh, how changed is everything," he lamented. In Philadelphia, he received a minor head wound when his car collided with another; Seton was treated and released, but the Chevrolet had to undergo major repairs.[38]

During the summer of 1942, the Setons made plans to establish a boarding school at the Village. A contract between Seton and Dr. John G. Thompson of Gulfport, Mississippi, specified that Seton was to serve as advisor, Thompson as principal, and Mrs. Thompson as nurse. However, these proposals fell through: the Setons were warned that Thompson was a strange, irresponsible person, and sure enough, he took "French leave," owing them a great deal of money and later claiming that he was their nephew. Never again would the Setons conduct a formal school, but they continued to welcome students, artists, and others interested in their lifestyle, and Seton Village Press remained in operation until 1943.[39]

Throughout the war years, the aged Seton recorded in his journal everyday events in the Village and his family. He noted the harsh winters that brought occasional mountain blizzards and often wreaked havoc on the plumbing facilities and gas lines. Seton Village was not far from the state penitentiary, and the Chief recorded one episode in which an escaped prisoner surprised their housemaid. The Setons notified the police, who quickly arrived and scoured the woods. But the convict, who wore a mask, had fled into the night. There were other instances of petty theft and of tenants vacating the premises without paying their rent, but these were few. Most tenants joined with their unorthodox landlord in spirit of friendship and cooperation.

Through the radio and local newspapers, Seton kept up with the war's progress and rejoiced every time "the boys" overseas scored a victory for the Allied cause. June 6, 1944, was memorable not only because of the D-Day landings in Normandy but also because it was Beulah's sixth birthday. When President Roosevelt died on April 12, 1945, Seton noted that all the bars in Santa Fe were closed, while all the churches were open.[40] Strangely enough, he made no mention of the big explosion at the Trinity Site on July 16, 1945, which ushered in the Atomic Age. While the Manhattan Project operated in utter secrecy, it resulted in radical changes for Seton's beloved West: from that time on, New Mexico in particular was to be one of the nation's leading scientific and military defense centers, a far cry from the wilderness that Seton preferred.[41]

Although wartime rationing severely limited their travels after 1942, the Setons continued to present their programs to area Boy Scout troops, Cub Scout packs, and other youth groups. They also met occasionally with the governor and other state officials. Undoubtedly, the welfare of the Indians was their main item of conversation. The formation of the National Congress of American Indians (NCAI) in 1944, in support of John Collier's policies, must have been especially pleasing to the Chief and his wife. With its strong tribal emphasis and inclusion of important tribal officials in its leadership echelon, the NCAI soon became an active pan-Indian organization in which Indians could have more say in their process of acculturation to twentieth-century America.[42]

It was little Beulah who kept Seton Castle lively and brought happiness to her adoptive father during his last years. Energetic and precocious, Beulah undoubtedly evoked memories of Ann's childhood at Wyndygoul. In his journal, Seton recorded several instances of the child's made-up rhymes and bright comments. From the time she was seven months old, Beulah had often appeared with her parents in their programs on Indian song and dance; later she practically stole the show whenever she performed in costume.[43]

Life in Seton Castle reflected a simple family atmosphere. Birthdays, holidays, and other special events were always celebrated, and Christmas was a particularly festive occasion. The castle and other buildings in the Village were surrounded with *luminarias*. After the Christmas Eve dinner, it was time to trim the tree, which was usually set up in the library. One of the Setons' employees or neighbors played Santa Claus and distributed gifts to the neighborhood children. Seton the artist produced his own homemade Christmas cards.[44]

Seton's chieftainship was keenly felt at dinner, especially when guests were present, as he occupied the head of the table in the lofty dining hall. Beulah sat demurely at one side awaiting his request that she ask the Indian blessing. One out-of-state visitor recalled that mealtimes at Seton Castle were a "home scene, cordial and dignified." Sometimes the family dog, Petunia, was seen hovering in the doorway. This black-and-white mongrel had been given to Beulah by her kindergarten teacher as a Christmas present. "Although Seton the naturalist was not keen on dogs," a dinner guest noted, "Seton the father was kind." Several cats, at one time or another, were also among Beulah's beloved companions.

All who dined with, lived near, or worked for the Setons soon found themselves "a part of the scheme, talking freely and naturally." The end of the war better enabled the Chief to keep permanent help around the house. Kitty, the maid and waitress, was especially happy with her job. "Everything was all right in her world now because she and her husband had the desired home for their baby," wrote one visitor. Maurice and Marcelle Taylor and their daughter Lynne were among the resident families who were practically members of Seton's own.[45]

After a meal, Seton and his guests usually retired to the living room dominated by the fireplace and mantel over which was nailed Old Lobo's huge pelt. Here Seton often reminisced about his earlier years, especially his adventures in the wild. J. Frank Dobie, the Texas folklorist, once called on Seton to collect information on coyotes. Later, Dobie recalled how tears came to his host's eyes "as he described the agony of one [coyote] he saw strychnined."[46] At other times, Seton talked of Mark Twain, whose dry humor his own resembled, and of other literary cronies who had since passed on.[47]

Of course, Seton was always glad to hear from relatives and friends back East. He lauded his daughter's success as a writer and was eager for news about the grandchildren. Several times, Ann and her husband visited Seton Village during her travels to gather material for her novels. Part of one book, *The Turquoise*, is set in Santa Fe and is concerned with its history.[48] Seton was especially pleased to learn that some of Ann's works such as *Dragonwyck* were being made into movies.[49]

Seton also kept in touch with his kin in Canada and Chicago. In March, 1944, he was notified of the death of his brother Arthur, with whom he had spent so many of his "golden" days in Manitoba. Yet of all his brothers, George was the one to whom Ernest remained closest. Having retired from the printing business on a comfortable income, George took up golf and won several club tournaments.[50] Another series of letters in the Seton files came from a nephew, Stanley S. Thompson, the son of the Chief's eldest brother, Joseph. Stanley avidly followed his father's footsteps in the real estate business, investing in property not only in Canada but also in Australia and Jamaica. His detailed descriptions of the problems he encountered during and after the war in the Pacific provide an interesting insight into that period.[51] Such correspondence reflected the Setons' sincere interest in the lives of other family members, even though they seldom were able to visit them.

After the war's close the Setons were able to resume their cross-country speaking tours, and early in the spring of 1946, they drove to California for another round of lectures. Despite the rapidly changing styles of entertainment, accelerated by the advent of television, Seton was still widely in demand as a speaker. And he never stopped telling his stories. The Chief represented a bygone age, and his postwar audiences were willingly swept along by sentimental nostalgia.[52] In Los Angeles, the Setons attended the annual dinner of the Woodcraft Rangers as the guests of Manley P. Hall, a noted author and head of the city's Philosophical Research Center.[53]

To the very end, as Ralph Wallace of *Reader's Digest* discovered when he interviewed the Chief in September, 1945, Seton remained strong in body and agile of mind. Having battled ill health, poverty, and public criticism, he lived to be eighty-six years old. Even at that age, Seton continued to write, paint, and even go so far as to reroof his library. Beulah, by then a pixieish seven-year-old, often invited her young friends over to be captivated by his familiar animal tales and Indian legends.[54]

In May, 1946, the Chief and his wife made a brief lecture trip to Colorado Springs. One friend recalled the scene as they drove off in their Chevrolet. Tall, quiet, and studious, Seton wore a Stetson from which his unruly hair "escaped rebelliously." Beside him sat his diminutive but dynamic wife, who was driving. On August 14, they commemorated his eighty-sixth birthday by speaking at Rodey Hall, on the University of New Mexico campus, as part of its summer lecture series. Their topic was the Indians of New Mexico. They planned another 10,000-mile speaking tour for the fall and winter,[55] but that plan was never to materialize.

"My hope is that when my finish comes, it will be a swift one," Seton had once stated in a letter to F. W. Hodge. In July, 1946, realizing that his aging body was betraying his active spirit, he made a will in which he bequeathed the Village and surrounding property to his wife and young daughter.[56] Throughout the summer, he recorded in his diary insignificant things like the weather, the behavior of the car, and a diary record of the water level on the property. The last journal entry was dated September 11, 1946. Meanwhile, he made plans for another book and preparations for another painting. But his desire for a "swift finish" soon came true: On the morning of October 23, 1946, Ernest Thompson Seton died at his beloved Castle. Although "circulatory failure" was initially ruled as the cause of death, an autopsy showed that he had had pancreatic cancer. As he had requested, the funeral on October 25 was followed by cremation in Albuquerque. In death, as in most of his adult life, the Chief was first and foremost an Indian at heart. He chose the type of burial most befitting a Southwestern author who sought to return to the land that he loved.[57]

During the following month, condolences came in from friends and relatives nationwide, and on November 11 a special Woodcraft memorial service was held on the grounds of the public library in Greenwich, Connecticut. Many former Woodcraft Indians and several notables attended, among them Seton's old adversary, James West. The special music included one of the Chief's favorite hymns, "Beulahland," in addition to Indian funeral dirges.[58]

In summarizing the close of Seton's long life, one friend of the family stated:

Ernest Thompson Seton may, as we felt, have changed toward the end, but indisputably he was the same artistic genius whose . . . numerous . . . books have entertained and taught 2,000 readers, young and old; the Ernest Thompson Seton who, nearing his ninetieth year, remains in my memory like the pines of his beloved New Mexico—growing heavenward, straight and strong and useful to the end.[59]

Sometime after his death, an elderly, half-blind Indian who had once worked for Seton came across a framed photograph of him in the castle. Alone, he picked it up and gazed at it in silence. Then gently he drew his hand smoothly over the glass, muttering softly, "Grampapa, Grampapa."[60]

Epilogue

Ernest Thompson Seton remains an enigmatic figure. Personally and politically, he was a divided man. Along with his occasional arrogance and baronial aspirations, he had a genuine compassion for society's underdogs and an undying hatred for competition. In his lifelong quest for the ideal, he stressed mutual aid and believed that if modern man followed the example of the animal kingdom, as the Indians did, the result would be a decentralized, almost utopian society free of war.[1] Because of his failure to attain that ideal in the East, Seton's Village could be looked upon as symbolic of his final attempt to retreat from the world's problems and pressures, an attempt that began with his boyhood escapes from his overbearing father. Perhaps Julia best summed up her late husband's character:

He stands out above all else not as a writer, artist, or student, but as a man. It is the lovable trivia which comes to mind—the intangible foibles, the frailties, the misbehaviors, the peccadillos—all the insignificant things that constituted the warm quality in him, the wholesome spirit that was the foundation of his charm and his greatness. . . . He never could have settled into a rut, for the whole world was his to deal with and to make his own.[2]

And William H. Carr, naturalist and former Woodcraft Indian, wrote: "I have the highest respect for Seton. His particular accomplishments were without equal. He was . . . an egotist, but so what? If anyone rated it, he did. I belonged to the Woodcraft League, but it had to be a one-man show: Seton."[3]

Born into the Victorian era, Seton lived to see the dawn of the Atomic Age. He had watched the world of transportation and communication turn away from horse and buggy, railroad, and telegraph to automobiles, airplanes, radio, and television. It has been argued that Seton is less well known today because of World War II. Coming as it did toward the end of his life, the war shifted public concern away from man's interrelationships with nature; for the moment, Seton's prophetic voice was lost in the distant thunder of guns and bombs threatening to annihilate not only his beloved nature but mankind as well. At the time of his death in 1946, most people were intent on getting back to "business as usual" after the agony and austerity of the conflict.[4] Furthermore, the West that Seton as a young man had seen and experienced was gone. No longer was it a wilderness colony for Wall Street businessmen. No longer was it an intellectual or cultural desert attempting to imitate the older East. With many of America's affluent, mobile populace starting to flock to the "Sun Belt," the region was providing the most innovative segment of the nation's social and cultural life. In the eyes of most Americans, the West was "coming of age." It was developing into a strange mixture of Turnerian independence and economic dependence on Washington.

To Seton and those who thought like him, however, the West paid a high price for its lost innocence. In its role as a pacesetter for the nation, it lost some of its regional distinctiveness and became more like the older regions.[5] Indeed, the postwar boom was little concerned with any environmental movement. "Ecology" was practically an unknown term, and few people at that time even realized that this nation would eventually be "poisoned, polluted and developed off the face of the earth" unless something were done about it. Though Seton had warned of it years before, his preachments were forgotten after 1945. Only later would many join his lament for the past as technology's ugly results became more visible. Indeed, he probably would have gained a sizable following among contemporary environmentalists. As it is, his preservationist philosophy is felt strongly in the bylaws and activities of various wilderness conservation groups, especially the still-active Camp Fire Club of America in Chappaqua, New York.[6]

This is not to say that Seton's contributions to the worlds of literature and social reform were entirely overlooked by the postwar generation. Although the weak, decentralized Woodcraft League gradually fell into oblivion after the death of its founder, several regional groups, notably the Los Angeles–based Woodcraft Rangers, continued to exist through the 1950s; this organization adopted many of the ideas that Seton had employed with the Indian Scouts in New York. Furthermore, many of Seton's principles were incorporated into later government reforms for the Indians. To this day, older members of the Rio Grande Pueblos still speak of Chief Black Wolf with respect and gratitude. And folklorist J. Frank Dobie said of him: "Perhaps no other writer of America has aroused so many people, young people especially, to an interest in our wild animals." As the editors of *Time* wrote: "Ernest Thompson Seton was a man who, in an age of sweeping mechanization, loved the natural earth, its seasons and its creatures, with a rare intensity and an unusual power to communicate his vision to others."[7] In 1967, his name was added to the Honor Roll of the New Mexico Folklore Society.

Recently, some historians have derided Seton as a "drugstore Indian" and accused him of misleading young readers by using "certain Indian-isms that continue no matter how well the English has been acquired."[8] While that may be true, it must be remembered that he was one of a long line of writers who sought to make native Americans universally appealing and invoke in his audience a degree of sympathy for them. Folk singer Peter Seeger was one who was inspired during his child-hood by *Two Little Savages* and other Seton works. Seeger has recalled how, as a boy growing up in the Hudson Valley during the 1920s, he liked to emulate the "little savages" by donning war paint and a loin-cloth, fashioning a tepee shelter, and hunting rabbits with a homemade bow and arrow. "I grew up in a woodland tower," he once quipped. Much of Seeger's music, indeed, reflects his belief in Seton's motto: "Because I have known the torment of thirst, I would dig a well where others may drink."[9]

In the world of natural science as well, Seton's memory lives on. A species of caribou in the wilds of northern Russia is named *Rangifer setoni* in his honor. His early reports on the nests and eggs of Canadian bird species previously unknown are still widely used as references, as is his *Lives of Game Animals*.[10] Roger Tory Peterson, one of America's lead-ing ornithologists and bird artists, patterned the bird drawings for his field guides directly on those of Seton. In his youth, Peterson could easily identify with Yan; like him, he wanted to be free and thus devel-oped his own philosophy after that expounded in *Two Little Savages*.[11] As the English naturalist Henry Chester Tracy argued, Seton brought out the importance of the subjective side of natural science, "inspired with truth as all real art is inspired." While many of Seton's imitators produced "merely romantic stories," his were not "nature faking" but art added to science. Through his literary works and Woodcraft pro-gram, Seton sought "to direct primal impulses toward recreation in natural ways so that they may result in the formation of health and char-acter."[12] In that sense, Seton was a true Progressive.

In recent years, many of Seton's books have enjoyed a revival in popu-larity. New paperback editions of *Wild Animals I Have Known, Lives of the Hunted,* and *Two Little Savages* appeared in the 1970s. Walt Disney Productions based two of its feature-length nature films, "The Legend of Lobo" and "King of the Grizzlies"—however loosely—on Seton's tales of Lobo and Wahb. Certain naturalists have argued that Disney and many television writers overendowed nature's creatures with human traits, whereas Seton wrote strictly as a natural scientist, "living with the creatures of the wild, recording their every activity and portraying them as they existed, each as an intricate part of the earth's ecosystem." [13]

After her husband's death, Julia M. Seton continued lecturing and also held traveling exhibitions of her husband's artwork. In 1947 she began a memorial fund, which she later incorporated into a foundation, to help maintain the castle and other buildings. Over the next twenty years, she published several books on camping and Indian lore and gave guided tours of the castle. [14] All the while, Julia remained a firm supporter of her husband's connections with the Boy Scouts and contributions to natural history. In 1965, she built a smaller house near the Castle in which she could do her "private living." Three years later, another dream for Seton Village came true with the completion and dedication of a nonsectarian chapel symbolizing the Chief's belief in religious universality and freedom of worship. For many years, Mrs. Seton was active in the Santa Fe Community Theater in both acting and directing roles. Almost to the time of her death on April 28, 1975, she remained as vivacious as ever, even after suffering a stroke in 1969. [15]

Grace Gallatin Seton, the Chief's first wife, continued her world travels and campaigns for women's rights throughout the depression and war years. She died in 1959 at the age of eighty-seven. Their daughter, Anya Seton Chase, who resides in Greenwich, has continued her career as a popular author. [16] In the spring of 1960, the centennial anniversary of her father's birth, Anya was in South Shields to visit his birthplace at 43 Wellington Terrace. That evening, while she was in her hotel room, "Home on the Range" was suddenly played on the radio. "I could hear Daddy singing it, as he always did," Anya later wrote to Julia. "It was a reminder of his beloved West and the endings of that wonderful life." [17]

In 1976, as part of the American Bicentennial celebration, the Seton heirs assembled several of the Chief's artworks and other memorabilia into a traveling exhibition entitled "The Wild Animal Friends of Ernest Thompson Seton." After the exhibit was displayed at Osaka and other major Japanese cities for nine months, Seton became a hero among the youth throughout Japan, especially the Boy Scouts, and his books were widely read.[18]

Today, Seton Village, located off Interstate 25 (U.S. 84–85) southeast of Santa Fe, remains New Mexico's chief memorial to its famous adopted son. In 1975 it was designated a National Historic Landmark. The castle, now owned by Beulah (Mrs. Dee Seton Barber) and her family, still contains some of Seton's artwork and library volumes.[19] However, most of the memorabilia were given by his widow to the Ernest Thompson Seton Memorial Library and Museum, opened in 1968 at the Philmont Scout Ranch near Cimarron. Mrs. Seton had felt that the BSA was the best organization to keep and handle the valuable collections: "By giving them in the possession of the Scouts, it completes the circle of Seton's basic thought. Here he was, in the beginning, at the founding of the Boy Scouts, and as a finish to all his years of collecting, his work is back in the hands of the Scouts."[20]

The Seton collections housed there include 3,250 drawings, paintings, and sculpture pieces; more than 2,000 bird and mammal skins (including Lobo's hide); 30,000 volumes from his library; and hundreds of Indian artifacts. There, too, are his numerous awards, among them a scroll and medal given to him by Czar Nicholas II of Russia in honor of his wolf stories and knowledge of wildlife. Photocopies of Seton's daily journals, which he kept from 1879 until six weeks before his death, are also in the library; the originals are housed in the Rare Book Room of the American Museum of Natural History in New York.[21]

Perhaps the most important tribute to Ernest Thompson Seton is the memory of the people who best knew him. To them, he was like so many of his animal heroes: an individual gifted with unique strength and understanding who triumphed over great odds and, in the end, passed away bravely. Like Old Lobo, he would rather have died than give up his freedom. As one author stated: "That spirit seemed appropriate for New Mexico, somehow."[22]

NOTES

PREFACE

1. Calvin Horn, *Climbing a Rainbow*, p. 221.
2. Arthur R. M. Lower, *Canadians in the Making*, p. 273.
3. See John Henry Wadland, *Ernest Thompson Seton: Man in Nature and the Progressive Era, 1880–1915*.

Chapter 1

1. Julia M. Seton, *By a Thousand Fires; Nature Notes and Extracts from the Life and Unpublished Journals of Ernest Thompson Seton*, pp. 2–3, 6; E. T. Seton, *Trail of an Artist-Naturalist*, p. 10.
2. Seton, *Artist-Naturalist*, pp. 6–7; Magdalene Redekop, *The Canadians: Ernest Thompson Seton*, pp. 3–4. This brief biographical sketch is one of a series done on the lives of famous Canadians.
3. Julia Seton, *Thousand Fires*, p. 9.
4. Austin S. Thompson to Ernest Thompson Seton, May 14, 1938, Seton Papers, Seton Castle, Santa Fe, N. Mex., and Seton Memorial Library and Museum, Cimarron, N. Mex. (hereafter cited as SP).
5. Seton to Austin S. Thompson, May 23, 1938, SP; Julia Seton, *Thousand Fires*, pp. 9–10.
6. Wadland, *Man in Nature*, p. 49.
7. Seton, *Artist-Naturalist*, pp. 6, 11.
8. Julia Seton, *Thousand Fires*, pp. 12–19. It is interesting to note that while Joseph was denied a higher education in favor of his father's business, his younger brother Evan was put through Durham University. Joseph received his scholarly knowledge from a private tutor who, among other things, taught him French and took him on a prolonged tour of France. Seton, *Artist-Naturalist*, pp. 5–6.
9. Seton, *Artist-Naturalist*, p. 6; Julia Seton, *Thousand Fires*, pp. 20–23.
10. Seton, *Artist-Naturalist*, p. 8; Redekop, *The Canadians*, p. 4.
11. Julia Seton, *Thousand Fires*, pp. 7–8.
12. An ironic twist of fate occurred when soon after the chicken-slaying episode, Cousin Harry Lee forgave young Ernest by giving him candy while on his way to work in the shipyards. Less than an hour later, Harry was killed in a freak accident. Seton, *Artist-Naturalist*, pp. 9–10.
13. Ibid., p. 11.
14. Edgar McInnis, *Canada: A Political and Social History*, pp. 287–321; Edwin C. Guillet, *Early Life in Upper Canada*, pp. 702–719. Also, see Reginald G. Trotter, *Canadian Federation*.
15. Lower, *Canadians in the Making*, p. 263.

16. Seton, *Artist-Naturalist*, pp. 11–12.

17. Ibid., pp. 12–13; E. T. Seton, *The Preacher of Cedar Mountain*, p. 30.

18. Polly Burfield to Stuart L. Thompson, Feb. 26, 1930, SP; Julia Seton, *Thousand Fires*, pp. 36–41.

19. Seton, *Artist-Naturalist*, pp. 14, 16–22, 34–40.

20. Ibid., pp. 23–24, 41–46; Redekop, *The Canadians*, pp. 5–6.

21. Seton, *Artist-Naturalist*, pp. 43, 53–54.

22. Harry L. Coles, *The War of 1812*, pp. 136–38; Guillet, *Early Life*, pp. 79–116. Also see Edith J. Firth, ed., *The Town of York, 1793–1815*.

23. Lower, *Canadians in the Making*, pp. 304–305.

24. Charles Dudley Warner, "Studies in the South and West, with Comments on Canada, 1889," in *Complete Writings*, p. 506; Lower, *Canadians in the Making*, pp. 304–305. Also see C. Pelham Mulvaney, *Toronto: Past and Present*; Jesse Edgar Middleton, *The Municipality of Toronto: A History*.

25. George Seton Thompson to John Enoch Thompson, Feb. 18, 1917, SP; Polly Burfield to Stuart L. Thompson, Feb. 26, 1930, SP.

26. E. T. Seton, *Two Little Savages*, pp. 173–74.

27. Seton, *Artist-Naturalist*, pp. 53–59, 70–75.

28. Wadland, *Man in Nature*, p. 55.

29. E. T. Seton, "The Spirit of the Woods: A Confession," *Century* 103 (Dec., 1921): 213–14; Julia Seton, *Thousand Fires*, pp. 43–47.

30. E. T. Seton, *Wild Animals I Have Known*, pp. 277–324; Seton, *Artist-Naturalist*, pp. 85–88; Julia Seton, *Thousand Fires*, pp. 53–56, 60–63; Wadland, *Man in Nature*, p. 54.

31. Seton to James L. Baillie, Dec. 2, 1930, SP; E. T. Seton, "The Rat and the Rattlers," *Totem Board* 12 (Mar., 1933): 109–13; *Great Historic Animals*, pp. 171–79; *Artist-Naturalist*, pp. 80–85, 89–96.

32. E. T. Seton, "An Amateur Circus I Once Gave," *Ladies' Home Journal* (hereafter *LHJ*) 33 (Sept., 1916): 57; *Artist-Naturalist*, pp. 60–67; 81, 99–102; Redekop, *The Canadians*, pp. 8, 11–12.

33. Seton, *Two Little Savages*, pp. 14–24, 32–34; *Artist-Naturalist*, pp. 103–107.

34. Seton, *Artist-Naturalist*, pp. 25–26, 97–99, 394–95.

35. Ibid., pp. 108–15; S. E. Read, "Flight to the Primitive: Ernest Thompson Seton," *Canadian Literature* 13 (Summer, 1962): 53–54.

36. E. T. Seton, "More Wild Animals I Have Known: The Boy and the Lynx," *LHJ* 20 (Nov., 1902): 13–14; *Animal Heroes*, pp. 169–204; *Artist-Naturalist*, pp. 117–25.

37. Seton, *Artist-Naturalist*, pp. 126–30; John G. Samson, ed., *The Worlds of Ernest Thompson Seton*, p. 43.

38. E. T. Seton, Unpublished Autobiography MS, n.d., SP; Seton to Charlotte Schreiber, Dec. 19, 1900, SP; Seton, *Artist-Naturalist*, p. 130; Wadland, *Man in Nature*, pp. 56–72.

39. Seton, *Two Little Savages*, p. 176; Wadland, *Man in Nature*, pp. 60–62.

40. Seton, *Artist-Naturalist*, pp. 130–31.

41. Seton, "Spirit of the Woods," p. 214; Read, "Flight to the Primitive," p. 46.

Chapter 2

1. Seton, *Artist-Naturalist*, pp. 135, 142.
2. Samson, ed., *Worlds of Seton*, pp. 26–27.
3. E. T. Seton Journal, I, 6–11, originals in American Museum of Natural History, New York City, photocopies in Seton Library, Cimarron, New Mexico; Seton, *Artist-Naturalist*, pp. 136–40, 144–45; Wadland, *Man in Nature*, pp. 65–69.
4. E. T. Seton, "The Plan of My Life," London, March 7, 1881, unpublished MS, SP.
5. Seton Journal, I, 59; Seton, *Artist-Naturalist*, pp. 145–47; Wadland, *Man in Nature*, pp. 70–71.
6. Seton, *Artist-Naturalist*, pp. 148–53; Julia Seton, *Thousand Fires*, p. 18.
7. J. R. Dymond to Seton, March 30, 1927, SP; Seton to Dymond, April 14, 1927, SP; Seton to Baillie, Dec. 2, 1930, SP; Seton Journal, I, 153; E. T. Seton, "On Journal Keeping," *Bird-Lore* 4 (Nov.–Dec., 1902): 175–76.
8. Wadland, *Man in Nature*, pp. 73, 75.
9. Chester Martin, *"Dominion Lands" Policy*, pp. 141, 161–62; McInnis, *Canada*, pp. 331–35.
10. Seton Journal, I, 30–37; Wadland, *Man in Nature*, pp. 74–75.
11. Seton, *Artist-Naturalist*, pp. 153–65.
12. Seton Journal, I, 59–87; Seton, *Artist-Naturalist*, pp. 168–74, 189; E. T. Seton, *Life-Histories of Northern Animals* I, 3–34, 46, 140.
13. Seton, *Artist-Naturalist*, pp. 174–79.
14. E. T. Seton, "The Master Plowman of the West," *Century* 68 (June, 1904): 300–307; E. T. Seton, *Lives of Game Animals* IV, 395–418.
15. E. T. Seton, *Animal Tracks and Hunter Signs*, pp. 17–20; Redekop, *The Canadians*, pp. 24–25.
16. Seton, *Wild Animals I Have Known*, pp. 131–64; *Life-Histories* II, 807.
17. Seton, *Artist-Naturalist*, pp. 210–13; Julia Seton, *Thousand Fires*, pp. 210–14. After completing his printer's apprenticeship, George had moved to Chicago in 1879. He, along with their cousin (and adopted sister) Polly Burfield, helped Ernest recuperate: George S. Thompson to J. Enoch Thompson, Feb. 18, 1917, SP; George S. Thompson to Seton, October 7, 1942, SP.
18. Seton Journal, I, 153ff; Julia Seton, *Thousand Fires*, p. 85.
19. See Robert Miller Christy, *Manitoba Described*; Seton, *Artist-Naturalist*, pp. 144, 226–28.
20. W. L. Morton, *Manitoba: A History*, p. 199; George F. G. Stanley, *The Birth of Western Canada: A History of the Riel Rebellions*, pp. 3–192.
21. E. T. Seton, "How Wapoos Won His Rifle," *Totem Board* 12 (June, 1933): 215–19. Seton wrote this embellished account in poetry the day after the courier, Wapoos, arrived after traveling twenty-five hours nonstop. Although the actual

event occurred in July, Seton made the poem a winter journey "to incorporate the hardships of another run well-known to me." Apparently, the traders considered this a usual feat among the Indians. E. T. Seton and Julia M. Seton, *The Gospel of the Redman*, p. 38.

22. Seton, *Artist-Naturalist*, pp. 237–38.

23. Seton Journal, I, 153–208.

24. Seton to William S. Thompson, December 20, 1912, SP.

25. William W. Whitelock, "Ernest Seton-Thompson," *Critic* 29 (Oct., 1901): 324.

26. For brief biographies of Seton's Canadian art colleagues, see J. Russell Harper, *Early Painters and Engravers in Canada*, pp. 46, 334; Colin S. Mac-Donald, comp., *A Dictionary of Canadian Artists* I, 38–39, III, 582–83.

27. Seton to H. H. Hatten, n.d., SP; Seton, *Artist-Naturalist*, pp. 246–47.

Chapter 3

1. E. T. Seton, "The Prairie Chicken or Sharptailed Grouse, *Pedioecetes phasianellus* (Baird)," *Proceedings of the Canadian Institute* I (1879–83): 405–12.

2. Seton, *Artist-Naturalist*, p. 246.

3. Seton to George Blake, May 4, 1884, SP; Seton, *Artist-Naturalist*, pp. 166, 222. Coues, long noted for his scientific expeditions to the American frontier, was teaching anatomy at his alma mater, Columbia College in Washington, D.C., at the time Seton wrote him. In 1884 he produced a second edition of his *Key*. Paul R. Cutright and Michael J. Brodhead, *Elliott Coues: Naturalist and Frontier Historian*, pp. 77–90, 138–77, 256–58.

4. Spencer F. Baird to Seton, Feb. 15, 1883, March 2, 1883, SP.

5. Seton, *Artist-Naturalist*, p. 247; Wadland, *Man in Nature*, pp. 86–88. Also see W. H. Dall, *Spencer Fullerton Baird: A Biography*; Kier B. Sterling, *Last of the Naturalists: The Career of C. Hart Merriam*.

6. Seton Journal I, 210ff; *Artist-Naturalist*, pp. 250–55.

7. Seton, *Life-Histories* I, 140; *Artist-Naturalist*, pp. 255–61.

8. Seton, *Artist-Naturalist*, pp. 261–62.

9. E. T. Seton, "A Carberry Deer Hunt," *Forest and Stream* 26 (June 3, 1886): 366–68; Seton, *Artist-Naturalist*, pp. 261–65; Redekop, *The Canadians*, pp. 27–29.

10. Seton Journal, I, 216ff; *Artist-Naturalist*, pp. 269–75; "The Trail of the Sandhill Stag," *Scribner's Magazine* 26 (Aug., 1899): 191–204.

11. Seton, *Artist-Naturalist*, p. 239.

12. Wadland, *Man in Nature*, pp. 84–85.

13. Morton, *Manitoba*, pp. 199–205, 211–13; T. R. Weir, "Pioneer Settlement of Southwest Manitoba, 1879–1901," *Canadian Geographer* 8 (1964): 64–71; Stanley, *The Birth of Western Canada*, pp. 44–326.

14. Seton Journal II, 36; Wadland, *Man in Nature*, p. 75.

15. E. T. Seton, "Nest and Habits of the Connecticut Warbler (*Oporornis agilis*)," *Auk* I (Apr., 1884): 192–93; "Manitoban Notes," *Auk* 2 (Jan., 1885):

21–24; "The Swallow-tailed Flycatcher in Manitoba and at York Factory," *Auk* 2 (Apr., 1885): 218; "Nest and Eggs of the Philadelphia Vireo," *Auk* 2 (July, 1885): 305–306; "The Western Grebe in Manitoba," *Auk* 2 (July, 1885): 314; "Interesting Records from Toronto, Canada," *Auk* 2 (Oct., 1885): 334–37; "The Birds of Western Manitoba," *Auk* 3 (Apr., 1886): 145–56; "The Birds of Western Manitoba: Conclusion," *Auk* 3 (July, 1886): 320–29; "The Birds of Western Manitoba: Addenda," *Auk* 3 (Oct., 1886): 453; "Occurrence of the Evening Grosbeak (*Coccothraustes vespertina*) at Toronto, Canada," *Auk* 4 (July, 1887): 256–57; "Evening and Pine Grosbeaks in Ontario," *Auk* 7 (Apr., 1890): 211.

16. C. Hart Merriam to Seton, June 12, 1884, SP.

17. Frank M. Chapman, "In Memoriam: Joel Asaph Allen," *Auk* 39 (Jan., 1922): 1–14; H. W. Henshaw, "In Memoriam: William Brewster," *Auk* 37 (Jan., 1920): 1–23; Seton, *Artist-Naturalist*, pp. 285, 292.

18. John A. Garraty, *The New Commonwealth*, p. 287.

19. *St. Nicholas* was begun in 1873 by Roswell Smith, founder of the Century Company. He selected Mary Mapes Dodge, author of *Hans Brinker*, as its editor. Frank L. Mott, *A History of American Magazines* III, 500–505.

20. Seton, *Artist-Naturalist*, pp. 280–81; Cutright and Brodhead, *Elliott Coues*, p. 236.

21. E. T. Seton, "Outlines of Ornithology," *Proceedings of the Canadian Institute* 3 (June, 1886): 180; "Strawberry Finch," *Transactions of the Canadian Institute* (*Trans. Can. Inst.*), 1 (1889–90): 41–42; "*Sturnella magna* Wintering near Toronto," *Trans. Can. Inst.* 1 (1889–90): 42; "Disappearance of Forest Birds," *Trans. Can. Inst.* 1 (1889–90): 47; "*Linota cannabrua* at Toronto," *Trans. Can. Inst.* 1 (1889–90): 54–55; "Rare Birds in Toronto University Museum," *Trans. Can. Inst.* 1 (1889–90): 55–56; "Spring Notes," *Trans. Can. Inst.* 1 (1889–90): 41–42; "First *Sialia sialis* at Lorne Park," *Trans. Can. Inst.* 1 (1889–90): 56; Wadland, *Man in Nature*, p. 91.

22. Arthur S. Thompson to Seton, October 6, 1886, SP; Morton, *Manitoba*, p. 266.

23. Seton Journal II, 12–35. One interesting habit that Seton adopted was the use of a red muffler in place of a fur cap for headgear. His argument was that a cap "muffles both eyes and ears beyond possibility of use; even at twenty below, the top of the head is unpleasantly hot." In addition, the red scarf saved him from being mistaken for prey. E. T. Seton, "A Record of Failures: Part I" and "Part II," *Forest and Stream* 28 (Mar. 24 and 31, 1887): 178–79, 198.

24. Seton Journal II, 20; *Artist-Naturalist*, p. 282.

25. Morton, *Manitoba*, p. 266.

26. Seton to H. H. Hatten, n.d., SP; Julia Seton, *Thousand Fires*, pp. 101–102. This theme is explored in depth in Leo Marx, *The Machine in the Garden*.

27. Stanley, *Birth of Western Canada*, pp. 327–407; Redekop, *The Canadians*, pp. 30–31.

28. Seton, *Artist-Naturalist*, pp. 282–83.

29. Seton Journal II, 62, 101; "Nights with the Coons," *Forest and Stream* 30 (July 19, 1888): 518–20.

30. Seton Journal, II 96, 108, 140.

31. Seton, *Wild Animals I Have Known*, 53–127, 167–202, 277–324; *Bannertail, the Story of a Gray Squirrel*.

32. Seton to Mary Mapes Dodge, April 12, 1887, Sept. 31, 1887, Oct. 10, 1887, May 21, 1889; also, original handwritten MSS of "The Drummer of Snowshoes," "Tracks in the Snow," "The Pintail," and "The Ovenbird," all in Henry E. Huntington Library (HL), San Marino, Calif.

33. E. T. Seton, "Moose and Bear Queries," *Forest and Stream* 26 (June 24, 1886): 427; "Canadian Game and Fish Resorts," *Forest and Stream*, 28 (Feb. 10, 1887): 42–43; "Do Squirrels Hibernate?" *Forest and Stream*, 28 (Feb. 10, 1887): 65; "Hibernation of the Hare," *Forest and Stream*, 28 (April 7, 1887): 226; "An Exhibition of Snakes," *Forest and Stream*, 28 (June 16, 1887): 451; "Ontario Game Laws," *Forest and Stream*, 30 (Mar. 29, 1888): 185; "The Big Buck We Didn't Shoot," *Forest and Stream*, 37 (Sept., 10, 1891): 143. Also, see A. K. Fisher, "In Memoriam: George Bird Grinnell," *Auk* 56 (Jan., 1939): 1–12.

34. Frank M. Chapman, *Autobiography of a Bird Lover*, pp. 63, 77; "Naturalist, Artist, Author, Educator," *Bird-Lore* 37 (July, 1935): 245–47; "In Memoriam: Louis Agassiz Fuertes, 1874–1927," *Auk* 47 (Jan., 1928): 1–26.

35. Robert Ridgway to Seton, Oct. 12, 1887, Dec. 7, 1888, May 20, 1889, SP; Seton Journal II, 162; Harry C. Oberholser, "Robert Ridgway: A Memorial Appreciation," *Auk* 47 (Apr., 1933): 159–69.

36. E. T. Seton, "Domestication of the Buffalo," *Forest and Stream* 26 (July 8, 1886): 467; W. T. Hornaday to Seton, May 4, 1889, May 7, 1889, May 22, 1889, May 24, 1889, SP; W. T. Hornaday, "The Extermination of the American Bison, with a Sketch of Its Discovery and Life History," *Annual Report of the Board of Regents of the Smithsonian Institution, 1887, Part II*, pp. 394–96, pls. VI, XI, XII, XIII; Wadland, *Man in Nature*, pp. 237–38.

37. Seton to Charles E. Bendire, Dec. 26, 1889, Jan. 19, 1890, Bendire Papers, Library of Congress, Manuscript Division (hereafter LC), Washington, D.C. Charles E. Bendire, a retired U.S. Army major and a member of the AOU, was honorary curator of oology at the Smithsonian. At the time, he was preparing his own study on North American birds, which he published in 1892. Seton's notes proved useful to him in several instances. See Charles E. Bendire, *Life Histories of North American Birds with Special Reference to Their Breeding Habits and Eggs*. References to Seton are on pp. 64, 103, 161.

38. Seton to G. Brown Goode, June 17, 1891, July 6, 1891, SP; Ridgway to Seton, June 30, 1891, SP; Seton to Ridgway, July 15, 1891, SP; Seton Journal, II, 241–42; Wadland, *Man in Nature*, pp. 95–100.

39. E. T. Seton, "The Birds of Manitoba," *Proceedings of the United States National Museum* 13 (May 29, 1891): 457–643; Journal II, 242.

40. Seton, *Artist-Naturalist*, p. 249.

41. McIlwraith—a Hamilton, Ontario, businessman—was recognized as Canada's senior ornithologist. At first, he had deemed the Seton monograph to be hasty and premature; later, he employed Seton to illustrate his own *Birds of Ontario*. Seton to Thomas McIlwraith, May 4, 1885, SP. Macoun's surveys and experiments, made between 1872 and 1882, determined the fertility and suitabil-

ity of the Manitoba prairie for agriculture, as well as the most feasible route for the Canadian Pacific Railway. In his book, *Manitoba and the Great North-West*, Macoun argued that the Canadian prairies were not an extension of the "Great American Desert" as was earlier believed. Through him Seton first learned that prairies, like forests, contained a wide diversity of flora and fauna. John Macoun to Seton, July 4, 1892, Aug. 25, 1892, Sept. 2, 1892, Oct. 29, 1909, Jan. 13, 1910, SP; Wadland, *Man in Nature*, pp. 78, 97. Also see John and James Macoun, *Catalogue of Canadian Birds*.

42. Seton and his brother Joe later sank $800 into further property investments in Toronto's Waverly and Lake Park districts. These schemes were not entirely successful; Seton came out with only $550, as opposed to Joe's $1,000. Yet Joe was said to have been a poor businessman, not always able to repay his debts. Seton to William S. Thompson, Dec. 20, 1912, SP; Seton Journal II, 238; Seton, *Artist-Naturalist*, p. 283.

Chapter 4

1. Wadland, *Man in Nature*, pp. 101–102.

2. Seton, *Artist-Naturalist*, pp. 284–85, 291–92. Seton had first heard of Wolf through Daniel Giraud Elliott in New York. Wolf had taught Elliott the art of reproducing plumage through variant imbrication and had illustrated his *Life and Habits of Wild Animals* (1873). Undoubtedly, Elliott, and later Wolf, passed these techniques on to Seton. See A. H. Palmer, *Life of Joseph Wolf*; Walter Gilbey, *Animal Painters of England*.

3. Seton Journal, II, 238; Seton to Gerald Christy, Dec., 1891, and Seton to "Whomever it May Concern," n.d., both in Humanities Research Center (hereafter HRC), University of Texas, Austin, Tex.

4. Seton to "Rufus," Dec. 13, 1890, Dec. 17, 1890, Dec. 31, 1890, Jan. 7, 1891, SP; Seton, "A Visit of Satan," MS, SP. "Rufus" was Henry Milford Steele, art director for *Scribner's* magazine, who hailed from Oswego, New York. Judging from their tone, these "Rufus Letters," a weekly account of Seton's first two years in Paris, were probably intended for publication. Steele and Julia M. Seton later recopied several of the letters, and some of the originals are missing. Wadland, *Man in Nature*, pp. 107–110.

5. Wadland, *Man in Nature*, p. 114. Also, see Robert Henri, *The Art Spirit*, and William Innes Homer, *Robert Henri and His Circle*.

6. A. A. Anderson, *Experiences and Impressions: The Autobiography of Colonel A. A. Anderson*, pp. 46–50.

7. Wadland, *Man in Nature*, pp. 115–16.

8. Seton to "Rufus," Dec. 27, 1890, Jan. 14, 1891, SP. Gérôme, one of Europe's most famous genre painters, had earlier taught the radical American artist Thomas Eakins. He was not entirely averse to painting animals, particularly dogs, although at this point in his career, Gérôme focused his attention on human subjects. Of all the French artists, he alone showed particular interest in Seton's portfolio. Wadland, *Man in Nature*, pp. 111–12. Also see Albert Boime, *The Academy and French Painting in the Nineteenth Century*, and Gerald M.

Ackerman, "Gérôme: Reassessing a Scorned Painter," *Art News* 72 (Jan., 1973): 32–35.

9. Seton Journal, II, 238–42; "An Expedition to Mehalaland," *Pall Mall Budget*, July 23, 1891, copy in SP.

10. Seton Journal, II, 245, 249–59; Seton to Gerald Christy, June 27, 1894, HRC; E. T. Seton, "How Bull-Fighting Was Suppressed in France," *Our Animal Friends* 24 (Feb., 1897): 128–29.

11. Seton, with characteristic humor, recalled: "As I grew old enough to enjoy the standard nursery tales, my favorites were 'Red Riding Hood and the Wolf' and 'The Wolf and the Seven Kids.' Though, low be it spoken—and I tell it with a sense of guilt—in each, I had a measure of sympathy for the wolf. I felt that his case was not properly presented; he acted strictly within the law, and on each occasion he got a very raw deal." Seton, *Artist-Naturalist*, p. 8.

12. E. T. Seton, "The Winnipeg Wolf," *LHJ* 20 (Dec., 1902): 11; Seton, *Wild Animals I Have Known*, pp. 158–64.

13. Redekop, *The Canadians*, p. 33.

14. Seton Journal, II, 241. Seton boasted of the fact that *The Sleeping Wolf* was accepted over Robert Henri's entries, *Les Roches* and *Paysage*. The truth of the matter was that the jury preferred realism and genre over the impressionism toward which Henri leaned. Seton, *Artist-Naturalist*, pp. 286–87; Homer, *Robert Henri*, pp. 59–60. During the years that followed, the original of *The Sleeping Wolf* somehow disappeared from public view and knowledge. In 1963, however, Julia Seton learned that it had turned up in the private art collection of a Toronto man. This gentleman offered to sell it to her, and she eagerly accepted. *The Sleeping Wolf*, with its original frame, still hangs in Seton Castle. Julia Seton, *Thousand Fires*, p. 239.

15. Seton Journal, II, 246; *Artist-Naturalist*, pp. 287–89; Wadland, *Man in Nature*, pp. 122–25.

16. E. T. Seton, "'Sport' in France, 1," *Forest and Stream* 38 (June 16, 1892): 560; "'Sport' in France, 2," *Forest and Stream* 38 (June 23, 1892): 586; "'Sport' in France, 3," *Forest and Stream* 38 (June 30, 1892): 611.

17. Seton Journal, II, 262.

18. Seton Journal, IV, 120–30; *Artist-Naturalist*, pp. 284, 298–300.

19. Seton to Christy, June 22, 1892, HRC.

20. Seton Journal, IV, 130, 164, 172–74, 308; *Artist-Naturalist*, p. 299; E. T. Seton, "Notes of a Trip to Manitoba," Parts 1 and 2, *Forest and Stream* 41 (Nov., 18 and 25, 1893): 424–25, 446–48.

21. Seton, *Artist-Naturalist*, pp. 297–98. For accounts of Elizabeth Taylor's expedition, see Grace Lee Nute, "Paris to Peel's River in 1892," *Beaver* 278 (Mar., 1948): 19–23; "Down North in 1892," *Beaver*, 278 (June, 1948): 42–46; "To Edmonton in 1892," *Beaver* 281 (June, 1950): 3–5. Her father's early years in the consulate are documented in Hartwell Bowsfield, ed., *The James Wickes Taylor Correspondence, 1859–1870*.

22. When Seton received his appointment, no limit was set on the term of office. Subsequently, the charter was never revoked. For the rest of his life, then, even after he had become an American citizen, Seton could still boast that he

was "an official of the Canadian Government." Seton Journal, II, 271–74; Manitoba, Department of the Provincial Secretary, Order-in-Council 4214, 1893; Julia Seton, *Thousand Fires*, pp. 103–104; Wadland, *Man in Nature*, pp. 132–33.

23. *Toronto Globe*, Feb. 16, 1893; Seton Journal, II, 273; *Artist-Naturalist*, pp. 289–90; Pauline Johnson to Seton, Aug. 2, 1905, Aug. 17, 1905, SP; Marcus Van Steen, *Pauline Johnson: Her Life and Work*, pp. 16–18.

24. Joan Murray, *Ontario Society of Artists: 100 Years*, pp. 10, 54; Wadland, *Man in Nature*, p. 125.

25. *Toronto Globe*, Mar. 30, 1893.

26. William Brymner to Seton, April 6, 1893, SP; Franklin Brownell to Seton, April 3, 1893, SP; Robert Harris to Seton, Mar. 16, 1893, April 4, 1893, SP; E. T. Seton, copy of L. R. O'Brien's Opinion, MS note, n.d., SP.

27. John C. to Seton, Mar. 31, 1893, SP. For the role of the newspapers in the controversy, see Hector Charlesworth, *Candid Chronicles: Leaves from the Notebook of a Canadian Journalist*, pp. 334–35.

28. Alfred Selwyn to J. S. Larke, Mar. 14, 1893, SP; Selwyn to Seton, Mar. 20, 1893, SP; Larke to Selwyn, Mar. 15, 1893, SP; Larke to J. N. Kirchoffer, Mar. 27, 1893, SP; Frank Smith to Auguste Angers, April 7, 1893, SP.

29. Seton Journal, II, 274; Seton to Angers, April 10, 1893, SP.

30. Robert Harris to Seton, April 10, 1893, SP; William Brymner to Seton, May 15, 1893, SP; Seton, *Artist-Naturalist*, p. 290; Charlesworth, *Candid Chronicles*, p. 335.

31. Seton Journal, II, 274–79.

32. For a more detailed analysis of the controversy, see Wadland, *Man in Nature*, pp. 125–42.

33. Seton to William S. Thompson, Oct. 31, 1897, SP.

Chapter 5

1. Frederick Jackson Turner, "The Significance of the Frontier in American History," in the American Historical Association's *Annual Report for 1893*, pp. 199–227; also in Turner, *The Frontier in American History*, pp. 1–38; John Opie, "Learning to Read the Pioneer Landscape: Braudel, Eliade, Turner, and Benton," *Great Plains Quarterly* 2 (Winter, 1982): 23.

2. David Lowenthal, "The Pioneer Landscape: An American Dream," *Great Plains Quarterly* 2 (Winter, 1982): 6–7.

3. See Philip Ashton Rollins, *The Cowboy: An Unconventional History of Civilization on the Old-Time Cattle Range*.

4. Seton Journal, II, 290; *Artist-Naturalist*, pp. 303–304.

5. Seton to Fitz-Randolph, Oct. 6, 1893, copy in Seton Journal, V.

6. Seton Journal, II, 290; *Artist-Naturalist*, p. 306.

7. Seton Journal, V, 1–9.

8. Thomas J. Caperton, *Rogue: Being an Account of the Life and High Times of Stephen W. Dorsey, United States Senator and New Mexico Cattle Baron*, pp. 36–38.

9. New Mexico Writers' Project, *New Mexico: A Guide to the Colorful State*, pp. 301–302.

10. E. T. Seton, "Four Months in New Mexico," MS in SP; Julia Seton, *Thousand Fires*, p. 111. Also see H. Allen Anderson, "Ernest Thompson Seton's First Visit to New Mexico, 1893–1894," *New Mexico Historical Review* 56 (Oct., 1981): 369–83. The following section on Seton's New Mexico venture is a slightly expanded version of that essay.

11. Seton, *Artist-Naturalist*, p. 314.

12. A. W. Thompson to Seton, Dec. 21, 1943, SP.

13. Seton Journal, V, 9–15; "Four Months in New Mexico," SP; Julia Seton, *Thousand Fires*, pp. 112–13.

14. Seton Journal, V, 21. For a history of the Cross L, see C. L. Douglas, *Cattle Kings of Texas*, pp. 289–98.

15. The roadrunner, a member of the cuckoo family and the state bird of New Mexico, was known during that time largely by its Spanish name, *paisano*. Seton Journal, V, 39.

16. Seton pointed out that in the wild, prairie dogs did not live in crowded "towns"; normally, their mounds were fifty or more feet apart. Seton Journal, V, 29; "Four Months in New Mexico," SP; Julia Seton, *Thousand Fires*, pp. 114–15.

17. E. T. Seton, "The Kangaroo Rat," *Scribner's* 27 (April, 1900): 426–27; *Lives of the Hunted*, pp. 11, 256.

18. Seton Journal, V, 30–32, 36; *Animal Tracks and Hunter Signs*, pp. 105–106. Also see E. T. Seton, *Wild Animals at Home*, pp. 104–106.

19. Seton, *Game Animals* I, 302.

20. E. T. Seton, "The King of Currumpaw: A Wolf Story," *Scribner's* 23 (Nov. 1894): 618.

21. J. Evetts Haley, *The XIT Ranch of Texas*, pp. 161–64.

22. Seton, *Game Animals* I, 307.

23. In one incident, which Seton used to illustrate his animal communications theory, he came upon a coyote that had taken some bait at one of his "drags" and was having convulsions because of strychnine poisoning. When the naturalist rode up to shoot it, the coyote suddenly vomited up all it had eaten and ran off, gradually working the paralysis out of its legs. Seton concluded that the animal "would ever after know and fear the smell of strychnine" and teach others of its kind to do the same. Seton, *Artist-Naturalist*, p. 309. Seton later incorporated this incident into his short story, "Tito: The Story of the Coyote That Learned How"; Seton, *Lives of the Hunted*, pp. 290–91.

24. Seton, "Four Months in New Mexico," SP; Julia Seton, *Thousand Fires*, p. 115.

25. Seton later wrote his initial reaction to the tragedy: "What right, I asked, has man to inflict such horrible agony on fellow beings, merely because they do a little damage to his material interests? It is not right; it is horrible—horrible—hellish!" *Artist-Naturalist*, p. 310.

26. A. W. Thompson to Seton, Dec. 21, 1943, SP.

27. Telephone interview with Lousie Wells of Clayton, N. Mex., Mar., 1980.

28. Seton Journal, V, 112, 176–78.

29. Seton, *Wild Animals I Have Known*, pp. 237–38.

30. Seton Journal, V, 122–28, 132; *Life-Histories*, I, 294–96.

31. Seton Journal, V, 82, 208. Cattle afflicted with "lumpy jaw," a malady caused by a parasite, were not considered marketable. Thus Seton learned how to spot and cut out "lumpy jaws" whenever he needed cattle for bait. *Artist-Naturalist*, pp. 307–308.

32. Seton Journal, V, 72; *Artist-Naturalist*, pp. 324–25. Theodore Roosevelt, during his Western experiences in the Dakota Badlands, likewise considered the Winchester the best rifle available: Theodore Roosevelt, *Hunting Trips of a Ranchman*, p. 27.

33. A. W. Thompson to Seton, Dec. 21, 1943, SP; Seton, *Artist-Naturalist*, pp. 374–75.

34. Seton Journal, V, 39; *Artist-Naturalist*, pp. 318–19.

35. Seton, *Artist-Naturalist*, p. 322.

36. Seton further enhanced his story by saying that the deputy apprehended the Callises the next day. Joe was sentenced to fifteen years in prison and Charley, five. They had served only one year, however, when "politics took the right turn" and both were pardoned. Soon after their release, Seton supposedly received a letter from the outlaw wolfer: "Dear friend: We are out of the pen O.K. Come on back and we'll have some more fun on the Canadian." Seton, *Artist-Naturalist*, pp. 323–24.

37. Seton Journal, II, 305, V, 84–104.

38. Wadland, *Man in Nature*, pp. 209–10.

39. Seton Journal, V, 11; *Artist-Naturalist*, p. 331.

40. New Mexico Writers' Project, *New Mexico*, p. 302. "Lobo," the Spanish noun for "wolf," was usually styled "loafer" by the cowboys. Seton Journal, V, 136; Haley, *The XIT Ranch*, pp. 161–62.

41. Seton Journal, V, 11.

42. Seton, *Lives of the Hunted*, pp. 233–34.

43. Seton Journal, V, 210.

44. Seton, *Game Animals* I, 314.

45. Seton Journal, V, 210.

46. Merriam to Seton, Feb. 5, 1895, SP; Ralph Wallace, "Wild Animals He Has Known," *Reader's Digest* 49 (Sept., 1946): 59.

47. Hornaday to Seton, Dec. 22, 1896, SP.

48. Seton to Charles F. Lummis, May 7, 1901, Lummis papers (hereafter LP), Southwest Museum Library (SWML), Los Angeles, California; E. T. Seton, "The True Story of a Little Gray Rabbit," *St. Nicholas* 17 (Oct., 1890): 953–55; Seton, *Lives of the Hunted*, p. 11.

49. Seton Journal, V, 9.

50. Redekop, The Canadians, pp. 38–39.

51. Seton, "The King of Currumpaw," pp. 627–28; Seton, *Artist-Naturalist*, pp. 334–39; Wadland, *Man in Nature*, pp. 210–14.

Chapter 6

1. Seton Journal, II, 297; Seton to Christy, June 27, 1894, HRC.

2. F. W. Hodge to Seton, Sept. 2, 1893, SP; Seton to Hodge, Oct. 9, 1893,

May 5, 1894, July 6, 1894, Hodge Collection (HC), SWML; Hodge to Seton, Jan. 6, 1894, HC; Miller Christy to Hodge, Dec. 2, 1895, Jan. 23, 1896, HC; Seton to Hodge, Feb. 15, 1908, HC. Thomas Hutchins was chief factor at the Hudson's Bay Company post at Albany during the 1770s and 1780s, and played an important role in the various expeditions sent out to estalish new posts and locate new sources of fur. E. E. Rich, *Hudson's Bay Company, 1670–1870*, II, 34, 44, 94, 110.

3. Seton Journal, II, 305; *Artist-Naturalist*, pp. 343–44.

4. Seton Journal, II, 309, 311.

5. E. T. Seton, Lecture no. 1, "The Practical Application of Anatomy by the Great Animaliers," MS notes, n.d., SP; *Artist-Naturalist*, p. 291.

6. Seton, *Artist-Naturalist*, p. 292.

7. Seton Journal, II, 308; Macmillan and Company to Seton, Jan. 1, 1895, Jan. 9, 1895, SP.

8. Seton, "The King of Currumpaw," pp. 624, 627.

9. Macmillan and Company to Seton, Feb. 21, 1895, SP. According to Muybridge, given the results of his famous photographic series, the camera or "sun picture" of a horse in motion shows that what we think we see (the "brain picture") is not really there. It only looks as though the horse's feet never touch the ground. See Van Deren Coke, *The Painter and the Photograph from Delacroix to Warhol*, pp. 156–59; Wadland, *Man in Nature*, pp. 148–53.

10. E. T. Seton, *Studies in the Art Anatomy of Animals*; Lecture no. 1, SP; Wadland, *Man in Nature*, pp. 153–54.

11. E. T. Seton, "The Baron and the Wolves," *Forest and Stream* 47 (Dec. 26, 1896): 504–506; Seton Journal, II, 309–11.

12. Edward Detaille to Seton, n.d., SP; Seton, *Artist-Naturalist*, p. 291.

13. Wadland, *Man in Nature*, pp. 156–64. Several of Seton's impressionist-style paintings are feature in Samson, *Worlds of Seton*.

14. Wadland, *Man in Nature*, pp. 160–62.

15. Seton Journal, II, 247–48, 311.

16. Seton Journal, II, 290; Caroline Fitz-Randolph to Seton, March 13, 1895, Sept. 20, 1895, Nov. 10, 1895, SP.

17. Seton to H. H. Hatten, n.d., SP; Seton, *Artist-Naturalist*, pp. 136, 246; Julia Seton, *Thousand Fires*, pp. 101–102.

18. Seton to Christy, Oct. 8, 1895, HRC; Seton Journal II, 312–13; *Artist-Naturalist*, p. 343; "Chronicle and Comment," *Bookman* 9 (Mar., 1899): 9–10.

Chapter 7

1. G. Edward White, *The Eastern Establishment and the Western Experience: The West of Frederic Remington, Theodore Roosevelt, and Owen Wister*, pp. 1–7, 77–144.

2. Cutright and Brodhead, *Elliott Coues*, pp. 339–94.

3. White, *Eastern Establishment*, pp. 171–202.

4. Ibid., pp. 184–86. Also, see Wadland, *Man in Nature*, pp. 447–61.

5. Seton Journal, II, 313; *Artist-Naturalist*, pp. 344, 349.

6. Seton to Charles E. Bendire, Oct. 19, 1896, Bendire Papers, LC.

7. Seton Journal, II, 313; Seton, *Artist-Naturalist*, pp. 344–45; Chapman, *Bird Lover*, pp. 77, 83–84. Also, see Chapman, *Bird Life* and *Handbook of Birds of Eastern North America*.

8. Seton to Gerald Christy, July 30, 1896, Oct. 21, 1896, HRC; Seton to J. E. Davis, May 28, 1897, SP; Seton, *Artist-Naturalist*, pp. 345–49.

9. Seton, *Artist-Naturalist*, p. 351; Hamlin Garland, *Roadside Meetings*, pp. 320–27.

10. Julia Seton, *Thousand Fires*, p. 131; Paul R. Cutright, *Theodore Roosevelt, the Naturalist*, pp. 33–37.

11. Seton, *Artist-Naturalist*, p. 351. Soon afterward, in the spring of 1897, Roosevelt was appointed as assistant secretary of the Navy under McKinley. Henry F. Pringle, *Theodore Roosevelt: A Biography*, pp. 93–106, 115–21.

12. Hiram M. Chittenden, *The Yellowstone National Park*, p. 105; Aubrey L. Haines, *The Yellowstone Story*, I, 203–204.

13. George Bird Grinnell and Charles Sheldon, eds., *Hunting and Conservation*, pp. 534–35; Theodore Roosevelt, *Works* I, xvii–xviii; Edmund Morris, *The Rise of Theodore Roosevelt*, pp. 383–87; Wadland, *Man in Nature*, pp. 230–31.

14. See, e.g., G. B. Grinnell, "Wolves and Wolf Nature," in *Trail and Camp-Fire*, pp. 152–203.

15. Theodore Roosevelt to Seton, March 23, 1897, SP; Madison Grant, "The Origin of the New York Zoological Society," in Grinnell and Roosevelt, *Trail and Camp-Fire*, pp. 317–20.

16. Wadland, *Man in Nature*, pp. 232–33; Frank Gruber, *Zane Grey*, p. 43.

17. E. T. Seton, "The New Sportsman," *Recreation* 10 (Jan., 1899): 39–40; "Chanticleer vs. Egret," *Forest and Stream* 49 (Oct. 9, 1897): 283; Kenneth Fowler, "The Story of the Camp Fire Club," *Field and Stream* 15 (Nov., 1910): 601–15.

18. Grace Gallatin Seton, *A Woman Tenderfoot*, pp. 15–58; Julia Seton, *Thousand Fires*, p. 117.

19. Seton Journal, VI, 9–10; Garland to Seton, June 27, 1897, SP; Hamlin Garland, *A Daughter of the Middle Border*, pp. 38–39. Garland lived among the Sioux, Crow, and Northern Cheyenne for the next month before going on to Seattle. His observations, which invoked in him greater sympathy for the Indians, were incorporated into several of his subsequent works, most notably his novel *The Captain of the Gray Horse Troop*. See Joseph B. McCulloch, *Hamlin Garland*, p. 23.

20. Seton Journal, VI, 11–13; Jack E. Haynes, *Haynes Guide: Handbook of Yellowstone National Park*, p. 31. Also, see Rudyard Kipling, *From Sea to Sea*, pp. 62–72.

21. Haines, *Yellowstone Story* II, 162–65, 454–55; George S. Anderson, *Report of the Superintendent of Yellowstone National Park to the Secretary of the Interior*.

22. Haines, *Yellowstone Story* II, 105.

23. Samuel B. M. Young, *Report of the Acting Superintendent of the Yellowstone National Park to the Secretary of the Interior, 1897*; Haines, *Yellowstone Story* II, 455.

24. E. T. Seton, "Elkland, 3: Old-Timers," *Recreation* 7 (Nov., 1897): 369–70.

25. Chittenden, *Yellowstone*, p. 333; Rollins, *The Cowboy*, pp. 303, 346, 361; Richard A. Bartlett, *Nature's Yellowstone*, pp. 28–29; Haines, *Yellowstone Story* I, 304–305, II, 238.

26. Seton Journal, VI, 17; Julia Seton, *Thousand Fires*, p. 117.

27. Haines, *Yellowstone Story* I, 318; II, 50, 68–69.

28. Seton, *Life-Histories* I, 240–41.

29. Seton Journal, VI, 25, 35; *Wild Animals at Home*, pp. 64–65, 82–83.

30. Seton, "Elkland, 2: The Beaver Pond," *Recreation* 7 (Oct., 189?): 286–90; *Life-Histories* II, 979–80; *Wild Animals at Home*, pp. 22–23.

31. E. T. Seton, "Chink: The Development of a Pup," *Youth's Companion* 75 (Jan. 17, 1901): 28–29; *Lives of the Hunted*, pp. 179–93; *Wild Animals at Home*, pp. 8–11, 139–41.

32. Seton, "Old-Timers," pp. 369–72; Rollins, *The Cowboy*, pp. vii, 52, 75, 110–11, 363, 365–67; Haines, *Yellowstone Story* I, 68, 71, 81, 217, 246, 249, 303.

33. Julia Seton, *Thousand Fires*, p. 118. One bordello in Gardiner was said to have figured prominently in Jane's "old-age assistance plan." Haines, *Yellowstone Story* II, 179, 405 n30. For an analysis of Calamity Jane as a dime novel heroine, see Henry Nash Smith, *Virgin Land; The American West as Symbol and Myth*, pp. 117–18.

34. Anderson, *Experiences and Impressions*, pp. 4–6.

35. Seton Journal, VI, 33, 45.

36. Ibid., VI, 52; Julia Seton, *Thousand Fires*, pp. 117–18.

37. Seton Journal, VI, 56; *Wild Animals at Home*, p. 92.

38. Haines, *Yellowstone Story* II, 116–17.

39. E. T. Seton, "Elkland, 5: Puss and the Bear," *Recreation* 8 (Jan., 1898): 33–34; "Johnny Bear," *Schribner's* 28 (Dec., 1900): 658–71; *Wild Animals at Home*, pp. 204–10.

40. Seton Journal, VI, 71; *Wild Animals at Home*, pp. vi, 166; G. G. Seton, *A Woman Tenderfoot*, pp. 210–13. Also see H. Allen Anderson, "Ernest Thompson Seton in Yellowstone Country," *Montana* 34 (Spring, 1984): 46–59.

41. J. W. Watson, "Report of Crow Agency," in *Report of the Secretary of the Interior* II, 180–84; E. A. Burbank, *Burbank among the Indians*, pp. 147–63; Howard R. Lamar, ed., *Reader's Encyclopedia of the American West*, p. 138.

42. G. G. Seton, *A Woman Tenderfoot*, pp. 217–43; Burbank, *Among the Indians*, pp. 218–19.

43. Seton Journal, VI, 85; Grace Gallatin Seton, *Nimrod's Wife*, pp. 213–15; Julia Seton, *Thousand Fires*, pp. 121–22. Seton's *Sign Talk* contains much of what he learned from White Swan.

44. Seton Journal, VI, 90–145; "Ernest Thompson Seton's Boys: Part 5, Tee-pees," *LHJ* 19 (Sept., 1902): 15; Burbank, *Among the Indians*, p. 219. The portrait of Sharpnose hung for years in Seton Castle but was later purchased by Manley P. Hall of Los Angeles. Julia Seton, *Thousand Fires*, pp. 122–23.

45. E. T. Seton, *The Book of Woodcraft and Indian Lore*, pp. 475–78; Julia M. Seton, *The Pulse of the Pueblo*, pp. 141–45; Julia Seton, *Thousand Fires*, p. 122.

46. Plenty-Coup's exploits during his earlier life are recounted in Frank B. Linderman, *Plenty-Coups: Chief of the Crows*.

47. G. G. Seton, *Nimrod's Wife*, pp. 217–19; Seton, *The Book of Woodcraft*, pp. 485–88; Burbank, *Among the Indians*, pp. 158–59; Julia Seton, *Pulse of the Pueblo*, pp. 157–61; Julia Seton, *Thousand Fires*, pp. 123–24.

48. G. G. Seton, *Nimrod's Wife*, pp. 222–27.

49. See Donald Dresden, *The Marquis de Mores: Emperor of the Badlands*.

50. Theodore Roosevelt, *Ranch Life and the Hunting Trail*. Also see William W. Sewall, *Bill Sewall's Story of T. R.*; Hermann Hagedorn, *Roosevelt in the Badlands*; Lincoln Lang, *Ranching with Roosevelt*.

51. Ray H. Mattison, "Roosevelt and the Stockmen's Association," *North Dakota History* 17 (Apr., and July, 1950): 73–95; 117–207; Carleton Putnam, *Theodore Roosevelt: The Formative Years*, pp. 595–96; Morris, *Rise of Roosevelt*, pp. 292–95.

52. Federal Writers' Project, *North Dakota: A Guide to the Northern Prairie State*, p. 285; Elwyn B. Robinson, *History of North Dakota*, pp. 185, 188.

53. Bruce Nelson, *Land of the Dacotahs*, p. 196; Pringle, *Theodore Roosevelt*, p. 66; Putnam, *Formative Years*, pp. 308–309, 323–25; Dresden, *Marquis de Mores*, pp. 45–48, 62–64, 69.

54. G. G. Seton, *A Woman Tenderfoot*, pp. 248–52.

55. Seton Journal, VI, 89; *Life-Histories* II, 870; *Game Animals* I, 315–16; Julia Seton, *Thousand Fires*, p. 126.

56. Seton Journal, VI, 146; *Life-Histories* I, 220; *Wild Animals at Home*, pp. 159–62.

57. Seton Journal, VI, 11, 146; G. G. Seton, *A Woman Tenderfoot*, pp. 248, 252–63; Evelyn King, "Cattle Queens of the West," *Persimmon Hill* 14 (1984): 16–17, 19.

58. Seton Journal, VI, 146; G. G. Seton, *A Woman Tenderfoot*, pp. 267–90.

59. Seton Journal, VI, 146; *Life-Histories* II, 870.

60. Seton, "Elkland, 1," *Recreation* 7 (Sept., 1897): 199–201; "Elkland, 6: Duels," *Recreation* 8 (Feb., 1898): 117–19; Michael Frome, *Whose Woods These Are: The Story of the National Forests*, pp. 28–30.

61. Seton, "Old Timers," p. 369.

62. Roosevelt to Seton, Oct. 26, 1897; Nov. 1, 1897; Nov. 18, 1897, Theodore Roosevelt Papers (TRP), LC. Also, see Roosevelt, *Works*, vols. 8, 9.

63. Julia Seton, *Thousand Fires*, p. 119; Redekop, *The Canadians*, p. 45. Also, see Robert F. Berkhofer, Jr., *The White Man's Indian*, pp. 113–75.

64. Seton, "Old Timers," p. 372; Journal, VI, 39.

Chapter 8

1. Seton, "Birds of Western Manitoba: Addenda," 453; *Artist-Naturalist*, pp. 391–93; Julia Seton, *Thousand Fires*, pp. 8–11.

2. Robert Seton to Seton, Nov. 3, 1898, SP; Seton to Robert Seton, Dec. 12, 1898, Dec. 16, 1898, SP; Robert Seton, *An Old Family: or, the Setons in Scotland and America*; Seton, *Artist-Naturalist*, pp. 4, 354.

3. Whitelock, "Ernest Seton-Thompson," p. 30.

4. Legal notice of name change, *New York Evening Journal*, Oct. 29, 1901; *Los Angeles Times*, Jan. 23, 1934; Seton, *Artist-Naturalist*, p. 393.

5. E. T. Seton, "Why the Chickadee Goes Crazy Once a Year," *Our Animal Friends* (hereafter cited as *OAF*) 21 (Sept., 1893): 17–18; "Not Caught Yet," *OAF* 21 (Dec., 1893): 89; "The Goldenrod," *OAF* 21 (Aug., 1894): 280–81; "The Wood Rabbit or Hare," *OAF* 22 (Nov., 1894): 65; "How Bull-Fighting Was Suppressed in France," *OAF* 24 (Feb., 1897): 128–29; "Playing Pretend," *OAF* 23 (Nov., 1895): 65–66; "The Wood-Duck," *OAF* 24 (July, 1897): 256–57; "The Yellowleg and the Hens," *OAF* 25 (Nov., 1897): 64–65; "The Wood Thrush," *OAF* 25 (May, 1898): 207–208; "The Wolf Question," *Recreation* 8 (Feb., 1898): 126–27; "What Is a True Sportsman?" *Forest and Stream* 47 (Sept. 26, 1896): 245; "The Timmer Doodle," *Recreation* 7 (Dec., 1897): 445–46; "Some More about Wolves," *Forest and Stream* 48 (Mar. 6, 1897): 183–84; "Poem Addressed to a Brass Paper Weight in the Form of a Mouse," *Recreation* 8 (Feb., 1898): 153.

6. E. T. Seton, "The Birds That We See," *Scribner's* 13 (June, 1893): 759–76; "Silverspot," *Scribner's* 23 (Feb., 1898): 212–18.

7. Seton, *Artist-Naturalist*, pp. 351–52; Mabel Osgood Wright to Seton, Nov. 11, 1896, SP; Merriam to Seton, Dec. 15, 1898, SP; Arthur H. Scribner to Seton, May 4, 1899, SP; Joel Chandler Harris, quoted in "Chronicle and Comment," pp. 9–10; Mabel Osgood Wright, *Four-Footed Americans and Their Kin.* Seton also did the illustrations for J. H. Stickney's *Bird World.*

8. Harold U. Faulkner, *Politics, Reform and Expansion*, pp. 69–70; Joseph E. Gould, *The Chautauqua Movement*, pp. 97–99.

9. Roosevelt to Seton, April 18, 1898, TRP; J. A. Allen to Seton, March 19, 1898, SP; W. M. R. French to Seton, May 13, 1899, SP; Seton, *Artist-Naturalist*, pp. 356–57.

10. Seton to Christy, July 4, 1898, June 20, 1901, HRC; Seton "To Whom it May Concern," n.d., HRC; Wilbur L. Davidson to Seton, July 11, 1908, July 25, 1908, August 21, 1098, SP; D. S. Paterson to Seton, Jan. 31, 1910, SP; W. C. Glass to Seton, Oct. 30, 1910, SP.

11. J. C Scorer to Seton, Dec. 9, 1908, SP; George S. Thompson to Seton, Sept. 16, 1909, Oct. 16, 1909, Oct. 14, 1910, SP; Seton, *Artist-Naturalist*, p. 357.

12. Seton Journal, VII, 1–2; *Artist-Naturalist*, p. 359.

13. G. G. Seton, *A Woman Tenderfoot*, pp. 19, 25, 51.

14. Ibid., pp. 61–72; Seton Journal, VII, 2–3.

15. G. G. Seton, *A Woman Tenderfoot*, pp. 75–95.

16. Seton Journal, VII, 13–28; *Life-Histories* I, 248; *Artist-Naturalist*, pp. 359–60, 363; G. G. Seton, *A Woman Tenderfoot*, pp. 99–111, 131, 142, 163–74, 185–206; Roosevelt, *Works* II, 240–41; Morris, *Rise of Roosevelt*, pp. 409–10.

17. E. T. Seton, "The Natural History of the Ten Commandments," *Century* 75 (Nov., 1907): 32–33; *Life-Histories* I, 244–46; G. G. Seton, *A Woman Tenderfoot*, pp. 177–81.

18. Seton, *Artist-Naturalist*, pp. 363–66; "Berry and the Mustang," *Totem Board* 11 (Sept., 1932): 415–17.

19. G. G. Seton, *A Woman Tenderfoot*, pp. 115–28.

20. Ibid., pp. 206–208; Seton Journal, VII, 29; Anderson, *Experiences and Impressions*, pp. 1–2, 202–204.

21. Anderson, *Experiences and Impressions*, pp. 202–19.

22. W. D. Pickett, "Four-Bears Creek," *Forest and Stream* 80 (Oct. 18, 1913): 488; Anderson, *Experiences and Impressions*, pp. 1–6, 71–73; Seton, *Game Animals* II, 63, 66.

23. G. G. Seton, *A Woman Tenderfoot*, pp. 185, 193–94, 208–209; Seton, *Life-Histories* II, 1032; Anderson, *Experiences and Impressions*, pp. 189–90.

24. Seton Journal, VII, 33.

25. Seton, *Wild Animals at Home*, p. 175.

26. James MacArthur, "Wolf Thompson and His Wild Animals," *Bookman* 9 (Mar., 1899): 72.

Chapter 9

1. E. T. Seton, *The Trail of the Sandhill Stag*; Frank H. Scott to Seton, May 8, 1899, SP; Scott to Seton, May 2, 1899, Seton to Scott, May 3, 1899, Memorandum of Agreement between Seton and the Century Company, Dec. 27, 1899, all in Seton correspondence, Lilly Library (LL), Indiana University, Bloomington, Ind.; E. T. Seton, "The Biography of a Grizzly: Part 1, The Cubhood of Wahb," *Century* 59 (Nov., 1899): 25–40; "Part 2, The Days of His Strength," *Century* 59 (Dec., 1899): 200–12; "Part 3, The Waning of Wahb," *Century* 59 (Jan., 1900): 351–62; E. T. Seton, *Biography of a Grizzly*.

2. Seton to Madison Grant, Jan. 18, 1897, Nov. 21, 1899, Nov. 22, 1899, SP; Allan Brooks to Seton, Jan. 25, 1899, SP; Seton to S. P. Langley, April 3, 1899, SP; E. T. Seton, "Communication Regarding the Needs of Artists in the Zoological Park," *First Annual Report of the New York Zoological Society*; "A School of Animal Painting and Sculpture in the New York Zoological Park," *Second Annual Report of the N.Y. Zoological Society*, pp. 69–75; "The National Zoo at Washington, Part 1," *Century* 59 (Mar., 1900): 649–60; "Part 2," *Century* 60 (May, 1900): 1–10; "The National Zoo at Washington: A Study of Its Animals in Relation to Their Natural Environment," *Annual Report of the Board of Regents of the Smithsonian Institution, 1901*, pp. 617–99, 170–76; Wadland, *Man in Nature*, pp. 240–41.

3. Seton Journal, VII, 53–94; G. G. Seton, *A Woman Tenderfoot*, pp. 293–311.

4. Seton is credited with the discovery of a now extinct subspecies of caribou, *Rangifer taradus dawsoni*, on the Queen Charlotte Islands. A second subspecies which he claimed to have discovered, *Rangifer montanus*, was later grouped under the former. E. T. Seton, "*Rangifer dawsoni*: Preliminary Description of a New Caribou from Queen Charlotte's Islands," *Ottawa Naturalist* 13 (Feb., 1900); 257–61; "Preliminary Description of a New Caribou," *Ottawa Naturalist* 13 (Aug., 1899): 129–30; Wadland, *Man in Nature*, p. 274.

5. Seton Journal, VII, 95–105.

6. E. T. Seton, *Monarch, the Big Bear of Tallac*, pp. 13–14, 201–14; *Life-Histories* II, 1041–44. Monarch was named after William Randolph Hearst, the "Mon-

arch of the Dailies," under whom Kelly worked. For Hearst's role in the episode, see W. A. Swanberg, *Citizen Hearst*, p. 65.

7. Seton, "The National Zoo at Washington, Part 2," pp. 1–4.

8. Justin Kaplan, *Lincoln Steffens: A Biography*, pp. 6–7; Seton Journal,
VII, 108.

9. Seton Journal, VII, 108–109; G. G. Seton, *Nimrod's Wife*, pp. 26–32.

10. Roosevelt, *Works* I, 93.

11. G. G. Seton, *Nimrod's Wife*, pp. 33–47.

12. Seton Journal, VII, 110–31; *Wild Animals at Home*, pp. 192–98; G. G.
Seton, *Nimrod's Wife*, pp. 48–51.

13. Seton Journal, VII, 132–33; *Animal Tracks and Hunter Signs*, p. 90.

14. Seton Journal, VII, 134–77.

15. Ibid., VII, 179–89; G. G. Seton, *Nimrod's Wife*, pp. 55–80.

16. Seton Journal, VII, 191–247.

17. Seton to Miss Annie Field, Feb. 5, 1900, LL; Frank H. Scott to Seton,
Feb. 6, 1900, LL; Seton to Scott, May 5, 1900, LL; Seton to G. D. Seymour,
Mar. 3, 1900, May 1, 1900, Seymour Papers, Yale University Library, New
Haven, Conn.

18. "Note on Ernest Seton-Thompson," *Bookman* 13 (Mar., 1901): 4–5.

19. E. T. Seton, "The Myth of the Song Sparrow," *Bird-Lore* 1 (Apr., 1899):
59; "The Origin of Dick Cissel," *Bird-Lore*, 2 (June, 1900): 88; "A Welcome Superstition," *Bird-Lore* 2 (Oct., 1900): 166; Chapman, *Bird Lover*, p. 187.

20. Seton Journal, VIII; *Life-Histories* I, 203–206.

21. E. T. Seton, "The Legend of the White Reindeer," *Century* 63 (Nov.,
1901): 79–89.

22. Gerald D. Nash, *The American West in the Twentieth Century*, pp. 12–13.

Chapter 10

1. Lester F. Ward, *Psychic Factors of Civilization*, pp. 133–37, 260–80, and
Outlines of Sociology, p. 193; George E. Mowry, *The Era of Theodore Roosevelt*,
pp. 15–21.

2. Alfred Kazin, *On Native Grounds*, p. 15n; Mowry, *Era of Roosevelt*, pp. 32–
33.

3. Walter Lippmann, *Drift and Mastery*, pp. 266–73, 285, 333.

4. Wadland, *Man in Nature*, p. 167.

5. Peter J. Schmitt, *Back to Nature: The Arcadian Myth in Urban America*,
p. viii; Read, "Flight to the Primitive," p. 51; Wadland, *Man in Nature*, pp. 166–
69; Redekop, *The Canadians*, p. 47.

6. See, e.g., William H. Magee, "The Animal Story: A Challenge in Technique," *Dalhousie Review* 44 (Summer, 1964): 156–64; James Polk, "Ernest
Thompson Seton" in *Wilderness Writers*, pp. 16–60, and "Lives of the Hunted,"
Canadian Literature 53 (Summer, 1972): 51–59; Patricia Morley, "Seton's Animals," *Journal of Canadian Fiction* 2 (Summer, 1973): 195–98.

7. Seton, *Animal Heroes*, pp. 259–86; *Wild Animal Ways*, pp. 123–40; *Wild*

Animals I Have Known, pp. 148–64, 249–73, 316–20; *Lives of the Hunted*, pp. 191–93; Polk, "Lives of the Hunted," p. 54.

8. E. T. Seton, *The Biography of a Silver Fox*, pp. 203–209; *Monarch*, pp. 201–14; *Animal Heroes*, pp. 163–65; *Lives of the Hunted*, pp. 287–93.

9. Seton, *Wild Animals I Have Known*, pp. 197–202; "The Waning of Wahb," pp. 351–62; Read, "Flight to the Primitive," p. 51; Polk, "Lives of the Hunted," p. 53. Seton received his information on Death Gulch from Professor T. R. Jagger, who made studies and took photographs—including one of a dead grizzly—at the site in 1897. Although few large animals have actually died from the concentrated noxious gases, bodies of rodents and birds have often been found there. T. R. Jagger, Jr., "Death Gulch, a Natural Bear Trap," *Science Monthly* 6 (Feb., 1899): 5–6; Seton, *Life-Histories* II, 1049–50; Bartlett, *Nature's Yellowstone*, p. 29.

10. Chase and confrontation, as well as the untamed nature of outlaw heroes, are standard fare in countless formula westerns. Max Brand, for example, uses a black outlaw stallion and wolf dog to symbolize the wild nature of his Homeric outlaw hero, Whistling Dan Barry. A chase scene in which Barry barely escapes the taming forces of civilization is, in some ways, remarkably similar to those of Seton's animal heroes. See Max Brand, *The Seventh Man*, pp. 174–206; Robert Easton, *Max Brand, the Big "Westerner,"* pp. 65–75.

11. Seton, *Sandhill Stag*, pp. 91–93; *Lives of the Hunted*, pp. 83–96; Polk, "Lives of the Hunted," p. 56.

12. Seton, *Wild Animals I Have Known*, p. 208; *Lives of the Hunted*, pp. 221–22.

13. Seton, *Game Animals* II, 28. Seton agreed with many of his contemporaries that sheepherding was a lowly, dirty occupation. Unlike real "shepherds" (such as those in Scotland and England), the Mexican sheepmen whom Seton observed in New Mexico and California did not see their flocks as "loved and loving followers." He noted the peculiarities of their business, commented on the sheep's stupidity, and mentioned that the Mexicans had no guns "or very poor ones, so that the wolves were little afraid of these men." Seton, *Wild Animals I Have Known*, pp. 29–30; *Monarch*, pp. 89–97, 104; *Artist-Naturalist*, p. 335.

14. Seton, *Animal Heroes*, pp. 268, 286.

15. Ibid., pp. 67–70; Redekop, *The Canadians*, p. 47.

16. Seton obtained this story, which reportedly occurred in 1871 near Winnipeg, from his old friend G. W. Fraser. Seton Journal, IX, 114–15; *Wild Animals at Home*, pp. 116–30.

17. Seton, *Silver Fox*, pp. 205–209.

18. Ibid., p. 140; *Animal Heroes*, pp. 245–56.

19. *St. Paul* (Minnesota) *Dispatch*, April 1, 1902; Seton, *Life-Histories* II, 1041–44; *Game Animals* I, 314–15; Seton to James C. Torrey, Jan. 6, 1905, HL.

20. Anderson, *Experiences and Impressions*, pp. 186–94. Contrary to Seton's characterization of Wahb as a loner, the Meeteetse giant reportedly had a mate, which Anderson also shot. While Seton's bear was compiled from several grizzly reports and observations, it is probable that *The Biography of a Grizzly* was pub-

lished prior to the shooting of Wahb; Anderson gives no specific dates, however.

21. Texas folklorist J. Frank Dobie compiled legends and reports of pacing white mustang stallions from various regions of the West, but at the time of Dobie's publication, Seton was the only one to write of a black outlaw pacer. See J. Frank Dobie, *The Mustangs*, pp. 143–70.

22. Seton, *Wild Animals I Have Known*, p. 239; *Artist-Naturalist*, p. 362. Dobie later recounted several other instances of wild mustangs leaping off cliffs or drowning in bogs and rivers to avoid capture. Dobie, *The Mustangs*, pp. 182–91; Lang, *Ranching with Roosevelt*, pp. 296–99.

23. See, e.g., Zane Grey, *Wildfire*, and *The Last of the Plainsmen*, pp. 109–22.

24. MacArthur, "Wolf Thompson," p. 72; Whitelock, "Ernest Seton-Thompson," p. 324; Lincoln Steffens, *Autobiography of Lincoln Steffens*, p. 440.

25. Seton to Charles F. Lummis, May 26, 1901, LP; Lummis to Seton, Oct. 21, 1903, LP; Seton to Lummis, Jan. 28, 1915, LP; Lummis to Seton, June 9, 1910, SP; Seton, *Wild Animals I Have Known*, dedication; "To 'Jim,'" *Outing Magazine* 36 (Apr., 1900): 44.

26. Seton to Katharine M. Johnson, Jan. 19, 1908, HRC; Grace G. Seton to Roosevelt, Dec. 30, 1911, TRP; Elon Huntington Hooker to Grace G. Seton, Oct. 6, 1912, SP.

27. "Note on Ernest Seton-Thompson," 4–5.

28. MacArthur, "Wolf Thompson," p. 9; C. S. Osburn to Seton, Nov. 1, 1899, SP; David Starr Jordan to Lummis, Oct. 16, 1899, copy in SP.

29. Seton, *Artist-Naturalist*, p. 353; Julia Seton, *Thousand Fires*, p. 245.

30. Wadland, *Man in Nature*, p. 216.

31. Seton Journal IX, 87; Theodore Roosevelt, *The Letters of Theodore Roosevelt*, ed. Elting E. Morison, III, 59.

32. Seton to Frank N. Doubleday, Apr. 1, 1899, Dec. 23, 1899, SP; Edward Bok, *The Americanization of Edward Bok*, pp. 160–80, 190–250; Mott, *American Magazines* IV, 545; Schmitt, *Back to Nature*, pp. 30–31.

33. E. T. Seton, "The Wild Animal Play," *LHJ* 17 (July, 1900): 3–4, 28; *The Wild Animal Play for Children*. Seton remarked in a letter that Kipling was such a poor speaker that he sometimes broke down on the platform. Seton to Lummis, May 7, 1901, LP. Since he wanted the "pen world" to become aware of these facts, it is obvious that his ego was much inflated at the time of this composition.

34. E. T. Seton, "A Wild Animal Bed Quilt," *LHJ* 22 (Jan., 1905): 9.

35. Seton, *Lives of the Hunted*, pp. 125–59.

36. Mark Sullivan, *Our Times* II, 445; Cutright, *Roosevelt, the Naturalist*, pp. 102–103; Julia Seton, *Thousand Fires*, p. 119. The success of the teddy bear allegedly enabled Morris Michton to form the Ideal Toy Corporation. John L. Eliot, "T. R.'s Wilderness Legacy," *National Geographic* 162 (Sept., 1982): 359.

Chapter 11

1. Seton to Elbert Hubbard, June 19, 1903, HRC.

2. Anderson, *Experiences and Impressions*, pp. 123–28; Hamlin Garland, *Companions on the Trail*, p. 195.

3. F. W. Halsey, "Ernest Seton-Thompson in Bryant Park, N.Y.," *American Authors and Their Homes*, pp. 281–92; Whitelock, "Ernest Seton-Thompson," pp. 320–22; Garland, *Companions on the Trail*, p. 182.

4. Steffens, *Autobiography*, pp. 436–37, 440, 583–84.

5. Wadland, *Man in Nature*, p. 308; Redekop, *The Canadians*, p. 51.

6. E. T. Seton, "The Story of Wyndygoul," *Country Life in America* (hereafter *CLIA*) 16 (Sept., 1909): 505–508, 540, 542, 544; Seton, *Game Animals*, IV, 579, 873; Seton, *Artist-Naturalist*, p. 377; Lida Rose McCabe, "At Wyndygoul with Ernest Thompson Seton," *Book Buyer* 25 (Aug., 1902): 22; Schmitt, *Back to Nature*, p. 27.

7. William Brewster to Seton, April 8, 1902, April 20, 1902, April 25, 1902, May 10, 1903, May 17, 1903, SP.

8. W. Beach Thomas, "A Wonderful Home: How a Great Naturalist Lives," *London Daily Mail*, Nov. 29, 1909; E. T. Seton, "Making a Hollow Tree and What Came into It: Bulletin 1," *CLIA* 15 (Nov., 1908): 47, 84; "Bulletin 2," *CLIA* 15 (Dec., 1908): 226; "Bulletin 3," *CLIA* 15 (Jan., 1909): 310; "Bulletin 4," *CLIA* 15 (Feb., 1909): 414; "Bulletin 5," *CLIA* 15 (Mar., 1909): 542; "Bulletin 6," *CLIA* 15 (Apr., 1909): 658, 660; "Bulletin 7," *CLIA* 16 (July, 1909): 354, 356; "Bulletin 8," *CLIA* 16 (Aug., 1909): 455; "Bulletin 9," *CLIA* 16 (Sept., 1909): 552; "Bulletin 10," *CLIA* 16 (Oct., 1909): 662; "The Hollow Tree," *CLIA* 20 (Sept., 1911): 88 and *Bird-Lore* 11 (Jan., 1909): 1–3; "Further Annals of a Hollow Tree," *CLIA* 22 (Oct., 1912): 64, 66.

9. Myra Emmons, "With Ernest Seton-Thompson in the Woods," *LHJ* 18 (Sept., 1901): 3–4; Wadland, *Man in Nature*, p. 309n.

10. E. T. Seton, "The Story of Wyndygoul," *CLIA* 16 (Aug., 1909): 446–48; Leland M. Roth, *A Concise History of American Architecture*, p. 200.

11. E. T. Seton, "The House That Is Mine," *House and Garden* 44 (Oct., 1923): 62, 114; "Achieving the Picturesque in Building," *CLIA* 35 (Oct., 1918): 44–47.

12. E. T. Seton, "If Da Vinci Came to Town," *American City* 5 (Nov., 1911): 252–54.

13. McCabe, "At Wyndygoul," p. 22; Seton, "The House That Is Mine," p. 62.

14. Seton to Elbert Hubbard, June 22, 1908, HRC.

15. McCabe, "At Wyndygoul," pp. 21–22.

16. Seton, "The House That Is Mine," p. 116; *Artist-Naturalist*, p. 377.

17. Emmons, "With Ernest Seton-Thompson," p. 3; McCabe, "At Wyndygoul," pp. 27–28; E. T. Seton, "The Wild Geese of Wyndygoul," *CLIA* 28 (Apr., 1916): 19–21.

18. McCabe, "At Wyndygoul," pp. 26, 28; Seton, "On Journal Keeping," p. 76. Vols. XXII and XXIII of Seton's journals contain much on the animals of Wyndygoul.

19. J. Walter Jones, *Fur Farming in Canada*, pp. 98, 147; E. T. Seton, "Raising Fur Bearing Animals for Profit," *CLIA* 9 (Jan. 1906): 294–97; "The Annals of a Fur Farm: Chapter 1," *CLIA* 23 (Nov., 1912): 38–40; "Chapter 2," *CLIA* 23 (Dec., 1912): 61–62; "Chapter 3," *CLIA* 23 (Jan., 1913): 30–32; "Practical Fur

Farming: Part 1," *Field and Stream* 18 (Mar., 1914): 1146–51; "Part 2, The Care and Feeding of Skunks," *Field and Stream* 18 (Apr., 1914): 1299–1302; "Part 3, The Diseases and Breeding of Skunks," *Field and Stream* 19 (May, 1914): 19–24; "Part 4, Marking and Disarming," *Field and Stream* 19 (July, 1914): 296–99; "Part 5, Marketing Skins," *Field and Stream* 19 (Aug., 1914): 391–94; "Part 6, Mink Farming, with a Footnote on Skunk Raising," *Field and Stream* 19 (Nov., 1914): 746–51; "Part 7, Marten Farming," *Field and Stream* 19 (Jan., 1915): 923–25.

20. Seton Journal, XXV, 130–31; *Game Animals* II, 360–67; *New York Tribune*, Sept. 8, 1919. Although Seton kept a few red foxes in his menagerie, he never raised silver foxes because breeders were too expensive, and the fur, though valuable, was not very durable. E. T. Seton, "Is Our Fur Supply in Danger?" *World's Work* 47 (Mar., 1924): 495–98; "Is the World's Fur Supply in Danger?" *World Today* 45 (Feb., 1925): 200–203.

21. Seton to Robert Underwood Johnson, Jan. 25, 1907, HRC; Seton Journal, IX, 4–13.

22. Emmons, "With Ernest Seton-Thompson," p. 4; Whitelock, "Ernest Seton-Thompson," p. 320; Wadland, *Man in Nature*, pp. 312–13.

23. Lincoln Steffens, *The Letters of Lincoln Steffens*, ed. Ella Winter and Granville Hicks, I, 154; Steffens, *Autobiography*, p. 436; Homer, *Robert Henri*, pp. 102, 118, 121. Frederic Remington recalled one time when John Twachtman sketched the newly erected entrance gates to Wyndygoul in 1900. In so doing, he drew two lines through each "S" in the Seton monogram to make dollar signs. Peggy Samuels and Harold Samuels, *Frederic Remington: A Biography*, pp. 403–404.

24. Seton to Richard LeGallienne, Jan. 14, 1905, Dec. 25, 1905, HRC; E. T. Seton, quoted in Havelock Ellis, *My Life: Autobiography of Havelock Ellis*, p. 479; Wadland, *Man in Nature*, p. 314.

25. Seton to Hubbard, June 24, 1914, HRC; Freeman Champney, *Art and Glory: The Story of Elbert Hubbard*, pp. 3–5.

26. Seton to James Whitcomb Riley, Dec. 6, 1903, Seton Correspondence, LL.

27. Garland, *Companions on the Trail*, pp. 182–83.

28. Ibid., p. 11; Franklin Walker, *Frank Norris: A Biography*, p. 268; Ernest Marchand, *Frank Norris: A Study*, p. 171n.

29. Catalogue of the American Art Association Anderson Galleries, Jan. 29–30, 1936, item 131; Telegram from Seton to Mark Twain, Nov., 30, 1905, both in Mark Twain Papers, Bancroft Library (BL), University of California, Berkeley, California. The copper placard is in the Anya Seton Papers, Boston University Library, Boston, Mass. Also, see Justin Kaplan, *Mr. Clemens and Mark Twain*, pp. 439–40.

30. Hamlin Garland, *Crumbling Idols: Twelve Essays on Art Dealing Chiefly with Literature, Painting and the Drama*, ed. Jane Johnson, pp. 7–17, 97–124; Donald Pizer, Introduction and Editorial Note, in Hamlin Garland, *Hamlin Garland's Diaries*, pp. xi–xii.

31. Seton to Garland, May 15, 1897, SP; Wadland, *Man in Nature*, pp. 314–16.

32. Seton to Edwin Markham, Aug. 13, 1919; Seton to Anna Catharine Markham, Nov. 6, 1921, HRC.

33. See, e.g., David Starr Jordan, *Imperial Democracy, A Check List of the Fishes and Fishlike Vertebrates of North and Middle America*, and *The Fur-Seals and Fur-Seal Islands of the North Pacific Ocean*.

34. Seton Journal, IX, 96; Jordan to Lummis, Oct. 16, 1899, copy in SP; David Starr Jordan, *The Days of a Man: Being Memories of a Naturalist, Teacher and Minor Prophet of Democracy* I, 474; Edward McNall Burns, *David Starr Jordan: Prophet of Freedom*, pp. 1–37.

35. Charles F. Lummis, *A Tramp across the Continent*.

36. Nash, *American West*, pp. 51–52.

37. Seton Journal, IX, 98; Dudley Gordon, *Charles F. Lummis: Crusader in Corduroy*, pp. 157–73; Turbese Lummis Fiske and Keith Lummis, *Charles F. Lummis: The Man and His West*, pp. 97–102.

38. Seton to Lummis, May 26, 1901, Aug. 2, 1901, Oct. 24, 1901, Oct. 21, 1903, April 21, 1906, June 5, 1910, June 30, 1910, Jan. 6, 1915, Jan. 28, 1915, LP; Lummis to Seton, June 9, 1910, SP; Edward R. Bingham, *Charles F. Lummis: Editor of the Southwest*, p. 142.

39. Seton Journal, IX, 98–99; Lummis to Seton, Oct. 15, 1909, Oct. 27, 1909, SP.

40. Lummis to Seton, Nov. 1, 1912, Dec. 3, 1912, SP; Seton to Lummis, n.d., SP; Seton to Lummis, Sept. 26, 1911, LP.

41. Augusta Fink, *I-Mary: A Biography of Mary Austin*, pp. 7–112.

42. Seton to Mary Austin, Nov. 27, 1930, T. M. Pearce Collection, Special Collections (SC). University of New Mexico, Albuquerque, N. Mex.; Mary Austin, *Earth Horizon*, pp. 296–97; Mary Austin, *Literary America, 1903–1934; The Mary Austin Letters*, ed. T. M. Pearce, p. 222; Nash, *American West*, pp. 52–53.

43. Seton to Mary Austin, May 11, 1915, HL.

44. Seton Journal, XI, 37; "Little Warhorse: The Story of a Jackrabbit," *LHJ* 21 (June, 1904): 13–14; *Game Animals* IV, 662, 742, 755–61; *Animal Tracks and Hunter Signs*, pp. 62, 67.

45. Seton Journal, IX, 66. While in Manitoba during the 1880s, Seton had made his first buffalo observations of a herd in the vicinity of Stoney Mountain near Winnipeg. This herd, said to be the earliest attempt at domesticating buffalo, was owned by S. L. Bedson. In 1888, Bedson sold his buffalo to Jones, who added them to his herd near Garden City, Kan., a town that he had helped found. Seton, *Life-Histories* I, 298–99; Hornaday, "Extermination of the American Bison," p. 458. Also see C. J. Jones with Col. Henry Inman, *Buffalo Jones' Forty Years of Adventure*; Robert Easton and Mackenzie Brown, *Lord of Beasts: The Saga of Buffalo Jones*, pp. 1–84.

46. Ernest Harold Baynes to Seton, Nov. 25, 1905, SP; J. W. Crawford to Seton, Dec. 18, 1909, Dec. 23, 1909, SP; Clayton W. Old to Seton, Oct. 19, 1910, SP; Charles S. Bird to Roosevelt, Feb. 6, 1911, TRP; Bird to Seton, Feb. 6, 1911, TRP.

47. Seton Journal, IX, 69–96.

48. Seton Journal, X, 6ff; "The Fantail, Flagtail, or Gazelle Deer, *Odocoileus*

taxanus. Mearns," *Recreation* 10 (Jan., 1899): 59–60; *Game Animals*, III, 320–22.

49. Seton Journal, X, 164; G. G. Seton, *Nimrod's Wife*, pp. 187–211. Seton later concluded that the "fantail" was really the dwarf whitetail of Arizona, whose range was thought to have extended into the Northern Rockies prior to 1920. *Game Animals* III, 322.

50. Seton Journal, XII, 20–136; *Life-Histories* I, 131; *Wild Animals at Home*, pp. 155–63; G. G. Seton, *Nimrod's Wife*, pp. 81–167, 176–82.

51. G. G. Seton, *Nimrod's Wife*, pp. 128–29.

52. Seton Journal, XII, 63; "The Story of Coaly-Bay," *May Court Magazine* (Feb., 1909): 5–11; *Wild Animal Ways*, pp. vi–vii, 3–16.

Chapter 12

1. Charles G. D. Roberts, *The Kindred of the Wild*, and *The Watchers of the Trail*, p. v; "Ernest Thompson Seton," *Bookman* 45 (Dec., 1913): 147–48; W. J. Keith, *Charles G. D. Roberts*, p. 87; Wadland, *Man in Nature*, pp. 170–72.

2. Seton to Charles G. D. Roberts, Jan. 22, 1899, SP; Seton to Gertrude Pringle, Nov. 20, 1926, SP; Gertrude Pringle to Seton, Nov. 23, 1926, SP; Gertrude Pringle to William Arthur Deacon, Nov. 23, 1926, copy in SP; Garland, *Companions on the Trail*, p. 183.

3. E. T. Seton, "Introduction to Famous Animal Stories," MS notes, n.d., SP; "Introduction to the Volume of Animal Stories in the Young Folks' Library," MS notes, n.d., SP; Wadland, *Man in Nature*, p. 168.

4. George S. Hellman, "Animals in Literature," *Atlantic Monthly* 87 (Mar., 1901): 391–92.

5. Seton, *Lives of the Hunted*, p. 11; Whitelock, "Ernest Seton-Thompson," pp. 322–23; Nancy Bell, "The Work of Ernest Seton-Thompson," *Humane Review* 4 (Apr., 1903): 11–20.

6. W. J. Long, *School of the Woods: Some Life Studies of Animal Instincts and Animal Training*, and "The Modern School of Nature Study and Its Critics," *North American Review* 176 (May, 1903): 689–90; Seton, *Artist-Naturalist*, pp. 367, 371; Wadland, *Man in Nature*, pp. 179–81. An example of healing strictly by instinct occurs when Wahb, the outlaw grizzly, licks and massages a bullet wound to prevent infection. Seton, *Biography of a Grizzly*, pp. 70–71.

7. Henry Fairfield Osborn, *Impressions of Great Naturalists*, pp. 185–87, 190; Clyde Fisher, "John Burroughs," *Totem Board* 12 (July, 1933): 276–84.

8. John Burroughs, "Real and Sham Natural History," *Atlantic Monthly* 91 (Mar., 1903): 298–309; Clara Barrus, *The Life and Letters of John Burroughs* II, 49; Wadland, *Man in Nature*, pp. 182–83.

9. Brewster to Seton, March 4, 1903, March 23, 1903, SP; E. T. Seton, "New Music from the Old Harp," *Century* 60 (Aug., 1900): 639; *Artist-Naturalist*, pp. 367–68.

10. Andrew Carnegie, *The Autobiography of Andrew Carnegie*, p. 281; Seton, *Artist-Naturalist*, pp. 368–71; Brewster to Seton, April 1, 1903, May 20, 1905, SP.

11. John Burroughs, *Camping and Tramping with Roosevelt*; Cutright, *Roose-*

velt, the Naturalist, pp. 104–17. Also see William Frederic Bode, *The Life and Letters of John Muir* II, 411–12.

12. John Burroughs to Seton, Aug. 1, 1908, Mar. 25, 1920, June 10, 1920, July 5, 1920, Oct. 11, 1920, SP; Seton to Burroughs, Mar. 21, 1920, Mar. 27, 1920, June 7, 1920, June 14, 1920, June 30, 1920, Oct. 7, 1920, SP; Barrus, *Life of John Burroughs* II, 87–88, 251–52, 396–97; Wadland, *Man in Nature,* pp. 185–86. Also see John Burroughs, "The Literary Treatment of Nature," *Atlantic Monthly* 94 (July, 1904): 42.

13. Roosevelt to Caspar Whitney, June 7, 1901, in Roosevelt, *Letters* III, 89; Garland, *Companions on the Trail,* 205.

14. Theodore Roosevelt, "Nature Fakers," *Everybody's* 17 (Sept., 1907): 428; Edward B. Clark, "Roosevelt and the Nature Fakirs," *Everybody's* 16 (June, 1907): 771, 774; Sullivan, *Our Times* III, 146–51; Wadland, *Man in Nature,* pp. 186–87.

15. Clarence Hawkes, *Shovelhorns,* p. v; Seton, *Artist-Naturalist,* p. 353; Zane Grey, quoted in Carlton Jackson, *Zane Grey,* p. 138.

16. *New York World,* May 24, 1907; Lyman T. Abbott, *The Outlook* (June 8, 1907): 263; Sullivan, *Our Times* III, 149, 154–55; Chapman, *Bird Lover,* p. 183; Cutright, *Roosevelt, the Naturalist,* pp. 129–39; William Morton Wheeler, "Woodcock Surgery," *Science* 19 (Feb. 26, 1904): 348; W. J. Long, "Science, Nature and Criticism," *Science* 19 (May 13, 1904): 760–67.

17. Edward B. Clark, "Real Naturalists on Nature Faking," *Everybody's* 17 (Sept., 1907): 423–27; Frank M. Chapman, "The Case of William J. Long," *Science* 19 (Mar. 4, 1904): 387–89; Schmitt, *Back to Nature,* pp. 45–55.

18. Robert M. Yerkes to Seton, Jan. 7, 1909, SP; Henry R. Carey to Seton, Nov. 12, 1912, SP.

19. Chapman, *Bird Lover,* pp. 182–83; John H. Wadland to Ellie ——, April 18, 1975, copy in SP. Long later claimed that he was himself "fairly well-known as a naturalist before Seton was ever heard of." Sullivan, *Our Times* III, 147n.

20. Seton to Roosevelt, Mar. 9, 1901, TRP; Roosevelt to Seton, Mar. 13, 1901, TRP; Grace G. Seton to Roosevelt, Feb. 17, 1909, TRP; Roosevelt to Grace G. Seton, Feb. 19, 1909, TRP; Seton to Charles H. Horton, Mar. 22, 1910, SP.

21. Chapman, *Bird Lover,* p. 182; Seton, *Artist-Naturalist,* p. 373; Cutright, *Roosevelt, the Naturalist,* pp. 128–32.

22. Seton, "The Natural History of the Ten Commandments," p. 27; Wadland, *Man in Nature,* pp. 227–28. Among the works of Ernst Haeckel that Seton probably read were *The History of Creation, The Evolution of Man, The Riddle of the Universe at the Close of the Nineteenth Century,* and *The Wonders of Life.*

23. Contract between Seton and the Century Company, Nov. 30, 1903, and Frank H. Scott to Seton, Dec., 7, 1903, Appleton-Century MSS, LL; E. T. Seton, "Fable and Woodmyth: Part 1," *Century* 67 (Nov., 1903): 35–39; "Part 2," *Century* 67 (Dec., 1903): 276–79; "Part 3," *Century* 67 (Jan., 1904): 346–51; "Part 4," *Century* 67 (Feb., 1904): 496–500; "Part 5," *Century* 67 (Mar., 1904): 750–56; *Woodmyth and Fable.*

24. E. T. Seton, "The Wapiti and His Antlers," *Scribner's* 39 (Jan., 1906): 15–33; "The Moose and His Antlers," *Scribner's* 39 (Feb., 1906): 157–58; "The

Caribou and His Kindred," *Scribner's* 39 (Apr., 1906): 426–43; "The Prong-Horned Antelope," *Scribner's* 40 (July, 1906): 33–49; "The White-Tailed (Virginian) Deer and Its Kin," *Scribner's* 40 (Sept., 1906): 321–41; "The American Bison or Buffalo," *Scribner's* 40 (Oct., 1906): 385–405; "The Habits of Wolves: Including Many Facts about Animal Marriage," *American* 64 (Oct., 1907): 636–45; "The Snow-Shoe Rabbit," *Everybody's* 16 (May, 1907): 599–608; "The Merry Chipmunk," *Success* 10 (May, 1907): 328–31, 368–70; "Dogs of Song," *Success* 10 (Aug., 1907): 537–39, 562–63; Wadland, *Man in Nature*, pp. 229, 266.

25. Seton to Roosevelt, Jan. 20, 1909, SP; Roosevelt to Seton, Jan. 22, 1909, SP; Julia Seton, *Thousand Fires*, p. 119.

26. George H. Measham to Seton, April 2, 1901, Aug. 30, 1901, Sept. 16, 1901, SP; E. W. Darby to Seton, July 20, 1906, SP; Seton to D. C. Cameron, Dec. 7, 1910, SP; G. Huntington to Seton, Sept. 14, 1910, SP; G. O. Shields to Seton, Oct. 28, 1910, SP; Verein Nahrschutz-Park to Seton, Nov. 16, 1909, SP.

27. Seton, *Life-Histories* I, 144; G. G. Seton, *Nimrod's Wife*, pp. 271–388.

28. E. A. Preble, *A Biological Investigation of the Hudson Bay Region*; E. A. Preble to Seton, Jan. 1, 1908, July 11, 1908, July 29, 1908, Aug. 4, 1908, Sept. 15, 1908, Oct. 4, 1908, Nov. 11, 1908, SP; Merriam to Seton, July 16, 1908, July 24, 1908, SP; Seton to Merriam, July 23, 1908, SP.

29. Easton and Brown, *Lord of Beasts*, pp. 117–18. Also see E. T. Seton, "The Arctic Prairies: Part 1, The Land of the Buffalo," *Scribner's* 48 (Nov., 1910): 513–32; "Part 2, The Land of the Caribou," *Scribner's* 48 (Dec., 1910): 725–34; "Part 3, The Land of the Caribou (cont'd.)," *Scribner's* 49 (Jan., 1911): 61–72; "Part 4, The Land of the Musk-Ox," *Scribner's* 49 (Feb., 1911): 207–23; *The Arctic Prairies*.

30. Seton, *The Arctic Prairies*, pp. v, 61–69. Preble's original journal of the venture is included among the Seton journals in the American Museum.

31. Memorandum from commissioner, Northwest Mounted Police, Regina, May 6, 1907, SP; Harry V. Radford to Seton, Aug. 28, 1908, SP; Seton, *The Arctic Prairies*, pp. 223, 235.

32. Seton to Edward F. Bigelow, Dec. 16,1909, SP; Seton, *Life-Histories* I, vii; Wadland, *Man in Nature*, pp. 292–93.

33. Gifford Pinchot to Seton, Nov. 16, 1909, SP; Madison Grant to Seton, Feb. 25, 1910, SP; Brewster to Seton, Nov. 21, 1909, SP; Chapman to Seton, Nov. 26, 1909, SP; J. A. Allen to Seton, Nov. 16, 1909, Nov. 29, 1909, SP; H. F. Osborn to Seton, Dec. 17, 1909, SP; Roosevelt to Seton, Jan. 6, 1911, SP; Hornaday to Seton, Nov. 26, 1909, Nov. 30, 1909, SP; Merriam to Seton, Nov. 29, 1909, SP; Seton to Roosevelt, Dec. 31, 1910, TRP.

34. Hornaday to Seton, Aug. 27, 1908, SP; Barrus, *Life of John Burroughs*, p. 187; Seton, *Artist-Naturalist*, pp. 371–73.

35. Frank H. Scott to Seton, Jan. 23, 1908, Appleton-Century MSS, LL; Edward Bok to Seton, Dec. 11, 1909, SP; Seton to Bok, Dec. 13, 1909, SP; Bigelow to Seton, Dec. 22, 1909, SP; Seton to Robert L. Peary, Dec. 21, 1909, SP; E. T. Seton, "How Long Do Animals Live?" *LHJ* 27 (Aug., 1910): 6; *Artist-Naturalist*, p. 373.

36. Merriam to Seton, April 3, 1910, SP. For an in-depth analysis of Seton's impact and contributions to the natural sciences, see Wadland, *Man in Nature*, pp. 228–97.

37. Wadland, *Man in Nature*, p. 297; Redekop, *The Canadians*, pp. 48–49.

38. *Winona Morning Independent*, Dec. 12 and 20, 1902, copies in Seton Journal, XII, 164; Sullivan, *Our Times*, I, 582.

Chapter 13

1. Seton to Frank Scott, Jan. 24, 1908, Appleton-Century MSS, LL.

2. J. Enoch Thompson to Seton, July 31, 1909, SP; Stuart L. Thompson to Seton, Aug. 25, 1908, Dec. 30, 1908, May 2, 1911, Sept. 28, 1911, SP; Stuart L. Thompson to Julia M. Seton, Jan. 27, 1947, SP; Seton, *Animal Tracks and Hunter Signs*, pp. 62, 77.

3. John Higham, "The Reorientation of American Culture in the 1890s," in *American Civilization*, ed. Eugene Drozdowski, pp. 266–68; Nash, *American West*, p. 53; Theodore Roosevelt, *The Strenuous Life: Essays and Addresses*, pp. 1–21.

4. G. Stanley Hall, *Adolescence: Its Psychology and Its Relations to Physiology, Anthropology, Sociology, Sex, Crime, Religion and Education* II, 60–61, 220–21, 228–29; Wadland, *Man in Nature*, pp. 335–72.

5. Seton, *Book of Woodcraft*, pp. 3–8; Thomas O'Connor, "Ernest Thompson Seton: The American Indian as Youth Model," 1974 (MS in author's possession), pp. 1–2; Wadland, *Man in Nature*, pp. 301, 369–72.

6. Seton, *Two Little Savages*, pp. 55–61; *Book of Woodcraft*, p. 572; Seton and Seton, *Gospel of the Redman*, p. 31.

7. E. T. Seton, "A History of the Boy Scouts," MS, n.d., p. 2, SP; "Spirit of the Woods," pp. 213–15; *Artist-Naturalist*, pp. 355–56, 375; O'Connor, "Youth Model," pp. 4–6.

8. E. T. Seton, "A History of the Woodcraft Movement: An Interview," MS copy, n.d., SP; "History of the Boy Scouts," pp. 10–11; "Spirit of the Woods," pp. 215–16; Wadland, *Man in Nature*, pp. 345–79.

9. E. T. Seton, "The Scouting Mind," MS copy, n.d., SP; *The American Boy Scout: The Official Handbook of Woodcraft for the Boy Scouts of America*, pp. xi–xii; O'Connor, "Youth Model," pp. 6–7.

10. Julia Seton, *Thousand Fires*, pp. 120–21.

11. Seton Journal, XI, 92–138; James R. Walker to Seton, Aug. 10, 1902, copy in Journal XI; Walker to Seton, Sept. 13, 1910, Sept. 21, 1910, July 15, 1914, SP. Also see James R. Walker, *The Sun Dance and Other Ceremonies of the Oglala Division of the Teton Dakota*.

12. Seton Journal IX, 101–108, 142–43, 172–75; "Sitting Bull Recalled," *Manitoba Free Press*, July 11, 1901.

13. Roosevelt, *Works* I, 16, 371–73; Edward Wagenknecht, *The Seven Worlds of Theodore Roosevelt*, pp. 229–30; Morris, *Rise of Roosevelt*, pp. 310–11.

14. C. F. Lummis Journal, entry for Dec. 12, 1901, LP; Gordon, *Crusader in*

Corduroy, pp. 11–21; Fiske and Lummis, *Charles F. Lummis*, pp. 112–17. Also see
C. F. Lummis, "My Brother's Keeper," *Land of Sunshine* 11–12 (Aug., 1899–
Feb., 1900).

15. Charles A. Eastman, *The Indian Today*, pp. 109–10; Hazel W. Hertzberg,
The Search for an American Indian Identity: Modern Pan-Indian Movements,
pp. 39–42. Also see Raymond Wilson, "Charles Alexander Eastman (Ohiyesa):
Santee Sioux," Ph.D. diss., University of New Mexico, 1977; Anna Lee Stens-
land, "Charles Alexander Eastman: Sioux Storyteller and Historian," *American
Indian Quarterly* 3 (Autumn, 1977): 199–208.

16. Seton to William H. Taft, Oct. 15, 1912, SP; Seton, *Artist-Naturalist*,
p. 275; Wadland, *Man in Nature*, pp. 328–29.

17. E. M. Ruttenber, *History of the Indian Tribes of Hudson's River*, pp. 103–
104, 112–19; F. W. Hodge et al., *Handbook of American Indians North of Mexico* II,
913, 929; Seton and Seton, *Gospel of the Redman*, pp. 53–54. Seton gave the date
of the massacre as December 24, 1641; however, judging from the accounts of
Ruttenber and Hodge, 1643 is probably the accurate date. The colonists destroyed two of three stockaded villages, or "castles," in the Greenwich area, thus
accounting for the high Indian casualties. The third village remained for several
decades. While Seton charged the "pious settlers" with murdering innocent,
peaceful Indians, the Wappinger tribes equally shared the blame. In 1642 a band
of Sinawas attacked the plantation of Anne Hutchinson, the famous religious
dissenter, at Pelham's Neck, New York. Only two of her children survived that
massacre.

18. Emmons, "With Ernest Seton-Thompson," p. 4; McCabe, "At Wyndygoul," p. 24.

19. The original Lummis House Book is in the Lummis Papers, SWML;
Seton's poem and logo are among the facsimiles from the House Book repro-
duced in Fiske and Lummis, *Charles F. Lummis*, pp. 170–71; Seton to Garland,
May 15, 1897, SP; Seton to Lummis, May 12, 1901, LP. Among the early works on
Indian symbolism and mythology with which Seton was obviously familiar
were Garrick Mallery, "Picture Writing of the American Indians," in *Tenth Annual Report of the Bureau of Ethnology to the Secretary of the Smithsonian Institution, 1888–89*, pp. 483–87; Ellen Russell Emerson, *Indian Myths*, pp. 32–40.

20. Wadland, *Man in Nature*, pp. 316–17; Bronwen J. Cohen, "Nativism and
Western Myth: The Influence of Nativist Ideas on the American Self-Image,"
Journal of American Studies 8 (Apr., 1974): 23–39.

21. E. T. Seton, *Boy Scouts of America: A Handbook of Woodcraft, Scouting and
Lifecraft*, pp. 1–2; Garland, *Companions on the Trail*, pp. 14–15; and "The Red
Man's Present Needs," *North American Review* 174 (Apr., 1902): 487–88; Lonnie
E. Underhill and Daniel F. Littlefield, Jr., eds., *Hamlin Garland's Observations
on the American Indian, 1895–1905*, pp. 30–31. Also, see Hamlin Garland, *Book of
the American Indian*.

22. Seton, "Woodcraft Movement: An Interview"; O'Connor, "Youth
Model," p. 10.

23. Henry George, *Progress and Poverty*; Seton and Seton, *Gospel of the Redman*, pp. 26, 28–30. Also see Peter Kropotkin, "The Morality of Nature," *Nine-*

teenth Century, 57 (Mar., 1905): 407–26, and *Mutual Aid: A Factor in Evolution*, ed. Paul Avrich.

24. Lewis Henry Morgan, *League of the Ho-de-no-sau-nee, or Iroquois* and *Ancient Society, or, Researches in the Lines of Human Progress from Savagery through Barbarism to Civilization*; Carl Resek, *Lewis Henry Morgan, American Scholar*, pp. 21–24; Seton, *Book of Woodcraft*, p. 573; Wadland, *Man in Nature*, pp. 319–20. Morgan's works also influenced the leftist teachings of Friedrich Engels, but as Wadland points out, the German philosopher's extrapolations probably did little to sway Seton's beliefs.

25. Seton, *Book of Woodcraft*, pp. 9, 51–53, 572; Brian Morris, "Ernest Thompson Seton and the Origins of the Woodcraft Movement," *Journal of Contemporary History* 5 (1970): 194.

26. W. A. Jones to Seton, Feb. 3, 1902, SP; Wadland, *Man in Nature*, p. 321.

Chapter 14

1. Seton to Doubleday, Apr. 1, 1899, Dec. 23, 1899, SP; Bok to Seton, July 18, 1901, May 25, 1903, SP; Seton to Bok, June 3, 1903, SP; Seton, "History of the Boy Scouts," p. 19, SP; E. T. Seton, "Ernest Thompson Seton's Boys: Part 1, Trailing," *LHJ* 19 (May, 1902): 15, 41; "Part 2, The Second Chapter on Tracks," *LHJ* 19 (June, 1902): 15; "Part 3, Playing 'Injun,'" *LHJ* 19 (July, 1902): 17; "Part 4, Archery," *LHJ* 19 (Aug., 1902): 16; "Part 5, Tepees," *LHJ* 19 (Sept., 1902): 15; "Part 6, Woodcraft Indians and Getting Lost," *LHJ* 19 (Oct., 1902): 14; "Part 7, Freezing," *LHJ* 19 (Nov., 1902): 15.

2. Although there is some discrepancy in Seton's publications as to the exact date of that first campout, several of the original Woodcraft Indians later recalled its being on Easter weekend. E. T. Seton, "Organized Boyhood: The Boy Scout Movement, Its Purposes and Laws," *Success Magazine* 13 (Dec., 1910): 804; *Artist-Naturalist*, pp. 377–78; T. Wyckoff, "Interview with Seton Indians in Greenwich, Conn., September 22, 1966," MS copy in SP; Penny Bott, *Seton's Indians: Oral History Interview with Leonard S. Clark*, pp. 5–6.

3. E. T. Seton, "The Boy Scouts in America," *Outlook* 95 (July 23, 1910): 631–32; "Seton's Boys: Part 5," p. 15; McCabe, "At Wyndygoul," p. 26.

4. Seton, "Spirit of the Woods," p. 219; Wadland, *Man in Nature*, pp. 340–41.

5. Bott, *Seton's Indians*, p. 7.

6. E. T. Seton, "Laws of the Seton Indians," *Association Boys*, 4 (June, 1905): 100–102; "Boy Scouts in America," p. 633; *Artist-Naturalist*, pp. 378–82; Wadland, *Man in Nature*, pp. 342–43.

7. Seton Journal XIII, 86a; Wyckoff, "Interview with Seton Indians"; Bott, *Seton's Indians*, pp. 10, 13, 20–21, 35, 41. Promotions and instructions for the "deer hunt," which required knowledge of the animal's anatomy, include Seton, "Seton's Boys: Part 4," p. 16; *Two Little Savages*, pp. 140–46; "The Revival of the Bow and Arrow," *CLIA*, 7 (Jan., 1905): 273–75; "A New Deer Hunt with the Bow," *CLIA* 7 (Feb., 1905): 370–71; *Book of Woodcraft*, pp. 199–202.

8. Ruttenber, *Tribes of Hudson's River*, p. 50.

9. Seton, "Seton's Boys: Part 5," p. 15; "Emergency Foods in the Northern Forest," *CLIA* 6 (Sept., 1904): 438–40; "Invitation to a Woodcraft Camp, 10th Sun of the Rose Moon (June), 1906," SP.

10. Bott, *Seton's Indians*, pp. 44, 46; Schmitt, *Back to Nature*, p. 107; Wadland, *Man in Nature*, p. 339.

11. Seton, "Setons' Boys: Part 5," p. 14.

12. E. T. Seton, *How to Play Indian; The Red Book; The Birch Bark Roll of the Woodcraft Indians;* Seton to J. Ray Peck, June 1, 1905, American Literature MSS, LL; Wyckoff, "Interview with Seton Indians," SP.

13. E. T. Seton, "Two Little Savages: Part 1," *LHJ* 20 (Jan., 1903): 11–12; "Part 2," *LHJ* 20 (Feb., 1903): 11–12; "Part 3," *LHJ* 20 (Mar., 1903): 13–14; "Part 4," *LHJ* 20 (Apr., 1903): 11–12; "Part 5," *LHJ* 20 (May, 1903): 11–12; "Part 6," *LHJ* 20 (June, 1903): 11–12; "Part 7," *LHJ* 20 (July, 1903): 11–12; "Part 8," *LHJ* 20 (Aug., 1903): 15–16, 32; Julia Seton, *Thousand Fires*, p. 245.

14. Seton, *Two Little Savages*, pp. 56, 116–21, 249–58; Read, "Flight to the Primitive," pp. 48, 54.

15. See, e.g., Hamlin Garland, *Main Traveled Roads*.

16. Seton, *Two Little Savages*, pp. 38–39, 62–70, 75–88, 130, 163, 220–27; Read, "Flight to the Primitive," p. 55; Wadland, *Man in Nature*, pp. 338–39.

17. "Are You a Seton Indian?" *New York Herald*, Oct. 11, 1903; "Indians at Wyndygoul," *Greenwich News*, Oct. 23, 1903; Charles G. D. Roberts, "The Home of a Naturalist," *CLIA* 5 (Dec., 1903): 155; W. W. Storms, "The Woodcraft Indians," *Holiday Magazine for Children* 3 (Oct., 1904): 76–79.

18. E. T. Seton, "The League of the Seton Indians," MS notes, n.d., SP; Seton to Copper Eagle, July 28, 1908, SP.

19. E. T. Seton, "The Twelve Secrets of the Woods," *Craftsman* 30 (June, 1916): 232–33; Wadland, *Man in Nature*, pp. 344–45, 358–59.

20. E. T. Seton, *The Forester's Manual; or, the Forest Trees of Eastern North America; Book of Woodcraft*, pp. 327–467; Bott, *Seton's Indians*, p. 18.

21. E. T. Seton, "Stories on the Tree-Trunks," *CLIA* 6 (May, 1904): 37–39, 90; "How to Stuff a Bird," *CLIA* 6 (July, 1904): 267–69; "What to Do When Lost in the Woods," *CLIA* 6 (Aug., 1904): 359; "The Woodcrafter and the Stars," *CLIA* 7 (Nov., 1904): 61; "Blazes and Indian Signs," *CLIA* 7 (April, 1905): 632–34; "The Oldest of All Writing—Tracks," *CLIA* 17 (Dec., 1909): 169–73, 242, 244, 246, 248, 250; "How to Study a Bird," *Bird-Lore* 6 (Nov.–Dec., 1904): 181–84; *Book of Woodcraft*, pp. 281–84.

22. Burroughs to Roosevelt, July, 1906, and Aug. 27, 1906, quoted in Barrus, *Life of John Burroughs* II, 97, 116; Seton to Roosevelt, Sept. 11, 1906, TRP; Roosevelt to Seton, Mar. 3, 1907, TRP; Seton to Roosevelt, Mar. 8, 1907, SP; Seton, *American Boy Scout*, p. 34; *The Woodcraft Manual for Boys: The Fifteenth Birch Bark Roll*, p. ix.

23. Pauline Johnson to Seton, Aug. 2, 1905, Aug. 17, 1905, SP; Walter McCraye to Seton, April 2, 1913, SP; E. T. Seton, Introduction, in Pauline Johnson, *The Shagganappi*, pp. 5–7; *Artist-Naturalist*, p. 290; Walter McCraye, *Pauline Johnson and Her Friends*, pp. 52–53, 61–62.

24. Charles Mair, *Tecumseh, a Drama, and Canadian Poems*, pp. 201–202;

Pauline Johnson, *Toronto World*, Mar. 22, 1892, quoted in Norman Shrive, *Charles Mair: Literary Nationalist*, p. 191.

25. Seton to F. W. Hodge, Jan. 16, 1929, SP; Seton, "History of the Boy Scouts," p. 19; *Book of Woodcraft*, 525; Seton and Seton, *Gospel of the Redman*, pp. 78–80; Seton, *Artist-Naturalist*, p. 376; Wadland, *Man in Nature*, pp. 323–26.

26. James. O. Dorsey, "A Study of Siouan Cults," in *Eleventh Annual Report of the Bureau of Ethnology to the Secretary of the Smithsonian Institution, 1889–90*, pp. 351–553; Frances Densmore to Seton, May 30, 1911, Sept. 20, 1918, SP; Charles Hofman, ed., *Frances Densmore and American Indian Music: A Memorial Volume*; Seton, *Book of Woodcraft*, pp. 26, 38; *Woodcraft Manual for Boys*, p. 73.

27. Seton to Lummis, Sept. 28, 1903, LP; Lummis to Seton, Oct. 12, 1903, LP; Seton to Hodge, Apr. 8, 1902, Jan. 4, 1907, Jan. 21, 1907, Feb. 18, 1907, Feb. 27, 1907, Mar. 26, 1907, Mar. 28, 1907, Apr. 10, 1907, Nov. 18, 1907, HC; Grace G. Seton to Hodge, Feb. 28, 1903, HC; Fiske and Lummis, *Charles F. Lummis*, 114–15.

28. Edward S. Curtis to Seton, Jan. 25, 1910, SP; Natalie Curtis to Seton, Feb. 4, 1904, Jan. 15, 1910, June 17, 1911, March 29, 1916, SP; Seton to Natalie Curtis, Jan. 8, 1910, SP; Edward S. Curtis, *The North American Indian*, ed. F. W. Hodge; Natalie Curtis, *The Indian's Book: An Offering by the American Indians of Indian Lore, Musical and Narrative, to Form a Record of the Songs and Legends of Their Race*; Alice Fletcher, *Indian Story and Song from North America*; Seton, *Book of Woodcraft*, pp. 61–62; *Woodcraft Manual for Boys*, pp. 9, 26, 71, 76.

29. F. R. Burton to Seton, Mar. 19, 1905, SP; Seton to W. T. Talbot, Apr. 12, 1905, SP; Garland, *Companions on the Trail*, p. 196; F. R. Burton, *American Primitive Music; with Especial Attention to the Songs of the Ojibways*.

30. Seton and Seton, *Gospel of the Redman*, p. vii; Seton, *The Buffalo Wind*.

31. Seton to W. T. Talbot, April 12, 1905, SP; Seton to C. A. Shenck, Sept. 8, 1910, SP; H. H. Fiske to Seton, Aug. 11, 1910, SP.

32. Jean Holloway, *Hamlin Garland: A Biography*, p. 181.

33. Seton Journal, XIII, 105; Bott, *Seton's Indians*, pp. 44–45.

34. Seton, *Arctic Prairies*, p. 10; *Silver Fox*, p. 3; *Wild Animal Ways*, pp. 23–24, 124.

35. Samson, *Worlds of Seton*, p. 100; Seton, *Wild Animals at Home*, p. 107, pl. 24; *Game Animals* II, pl. 57.

36. Seton Journal XX, 18, 166; Hornaday to Seton, n.d., SP; George S. Thompson to Seton, June 10, 1911, SP. One of George's favorite stories concerning Ann was about her asking, at age seven, why her parents did not go to church on Sunday. Seton replied evasively that probably it was because they had had too much of it when they were young. With her parents' blessings, Ann and the governess spent the next several Sundays trying out every church in town. Finally Ann settled for the Christian Science congregation, to which her Grandmother Gallatin belonged. George S. Thompson to J. Enoch Thompson, Feb. 18, 1917, SP.

37. Seton to Sarah Splint, Dec. 20, 1909, SP; Seton to George J. Fisher, Sept. 5, 1926, SP; M'Cready Sykes, "Let's Play Indian: Making a New American Boy through Woodcraft," *Everybody's* 23 (Oct., 1910): 481.

38. Seton, "History of the Boy Scouts," p. 10; *Woodcraft Manual for Boys*, pp. 33, 163–64; Miller Jordan to Seton, Jan. 4, 1910, July 21, 1910, Sept. 9, 1913, SP; Howard Bradstreet to Seton, Sept. 6, 1908, Dec. 7, 1908, Dec. 29, 1909, July 7, 1910, SP.

39. Open letter from Howard Bradstreet, Jan. 11, 1910, SP; Seton to E. M. Robinson, Oct. 13, 1934, SP; Ethel Josephine Dorgan, *Luther Halsey Gulick, 1865–1918*, pp. 100, 112–25, 141–42; Seton, "History of the Boy Scouts," p. 53; Wadland, *Man in Nature*, pp. 407–410.

40. Helen Buckler et al., *Wo-He-Lo: The Story of Camp Fire Girls*, pp. 19–20.

Chapter 15

1. Daniel Carter Beard, *Hardly a Man Is Now Alive: The Autobiography of Dan Beard*, pp. 351–61; Wadland, *Man in Nature*, pp. 304, 411. Beard's career in youth work and emergence as the Boy Scouts' folk hero is examined in Allan Richard Whitmore, "Beard, Boys and Buckskins: Daniel Carter Beard and the Preservation of the American Pioneer Tradition," Ph.D. diss., Northwestern University, 1970.

2. Joseph Knowles, *Alone in the Wilderness*, pp. 239–53, 286; Roderick Nash, *Wilderness and the American Mind*, pp. 147–149.

3. Morris, "Origins of Woodcraft," p. 194; Paul Wilkinson, "English Youth Movements, 1908–1930," *Journal of Contemporary History* 4 (Apr., 1969): 3–23; J. O. Springhall, "The Boy Scouts, Class and Militarism in Relation to English Youth Movements, 1908–1930," *International Review of Social History* 16 (1971): 125–58.

4. David Irving Macleod, "Good Boys Made Better: The Boy Scouts of America, Boys' Brigades and YMCA Boys' Work, 1880–1920," Ph.D. diss., University of Wisconsin, 1973, pp. 214, 218, 289, and *Building Character in the American Boy: The Boy Scouts, YMCA and Their Forerunners, 1870–1920*, pp. 29–59.

5. Wadland, *Man in Nature*, pp. 298–306, 447–61.

6. Seton to Gerald Christy, June 20, 1901, Feb. 1, 1902, Apr. 4, 1904, HRC; William Y. Knight to Seton, n.d., SP; Seton, "History of the Boy Scouts," p. 40.

7. Interrogatories . . . administered to Lt. Gen. Sir Robert S. S. Baden-Powell of London, England; Baden-Powell's testimony given May 24, 1918, at the U.S. Consulate in London in the case of Boy Scouts of America v. United States Boy Scouts, Supreme Court, New York County, copy in SP; Robert S. S. Baden-Powell, *Aids to Scouting for NCO's and Men*, and *Scouting and Youth Movements*, pp. 22–24; E. E. Reynolds, *The Scout Movement*, pp. 4–6; Robert Lacour-Gayet, *A History of South Africa*, p. 215.

8. Seton to Christy, Mar. 20, 1906, HRC; Wyckoff, "Interview with Seton Indians; Bott, *Seton's Indians*, p. 18.

9. Robert S. S. Baden-Powell to Seton, Aug. 1, 1906, SP; E. T. Seton, "History of the Scouting Movement," MS notes, n.d., SP; "Woodcraft Movement: An Interview"; "History of the Boy Scouts," p. 41; Lord Roberts to Baden-Powell, May 18, 1906, quoted in E. K. Wade, *Twenty-one Years of Scouting: The*

Official History of the Boy Scout Movement from Its Inception, p. 41; William Hill-court, *Baden-Powell: The Two Lives of a Hero*, pp. 257–57; Wadland, *Man in Nature*, pp. 388–91.

10. Baden-Powell to Seton, Oct. 31, 1906, SP; Seton to Baden-Powell, Nov. 3, 1906, SP; Seton to Lord Roberts, Dec. 8, 1906, SP; Seton, "Woodcraft Movement: An Interview."

11. Robert S. S. Baden-Powell, *Boy Scouts: A Suggestion*, copy in SP; Baden-Powell to Seton, Nov. 3, 1906, Nov. 6, 1906, Nov. 10, 1906, Nov. 23, 1906, Dec. 4, 1906, Dec. 11, 1906, SP.

12. Baden-Powell to Seton, June 17, 1907, Dec. 3, 1907, Jan. 24, 1908, Feb. 13, 1908, Feb. 24, 1908, SP; Robert S. S. Baden-Powell, *Scouting for Boys: A Handbook for Instruction in Good Citizenship*. Also, see Wade, *Twenty-one Years*, pp. 35–53; Baden-Powell, *Scouting and Youth Movements*, pp. 24–27; Wadland, *Man in Nature*, pp. 393–98.

13. Baden-Powell to Seton, March 2, 1908, March 14, 1908, SP; Seton to Baden-Powell, April 24, 1910, SP; E. T. Seton, "Note," MS note, 1940, in SP; "History of the Boy Scouts," p. 44.

14. Seton, "Woodcraft Movement: An Interview"; William Y. Knight to Seton, n.d., SP.

15. Baden-Powell to Seton, June 17, 1907, July 9, 1908, SP; International Press Service to W. T. Porter, June 22, 1908, copy in SP; Seton, "History of the Boy Scouts," p. 42; Wadland, *Man in Nature*, pp. 399–403.

16. Seton, "Woodcraft Movement: An Interview."

17. Baden-Powell, *Scouting and Youth Movements*, p. 30.

18. Baden-Powell to Seton, Nov. 10, 1906, May 31, 1910, SP; Seton to Baden-Powell, April 24, 1910, June 24, 1910, SP; Seton, "History of the Boy Scouts," pp. 45–49; Hillcourt, *Baden-Powell*, pp. 270, 282.

19. Seton to Baden-Powell, Sept. 30, 1909, Dec. 10, 1910, SP; Seton to Bok, Dec. 13, 1909, SP; Baden-Powell to Seton, Jan. 17, 1910, SP; Baden-Powell to H. C. Roberts, Sept. 3, 1909, copy in SP. Also, see Baden-Powell, *Scouting for Boys*, pp. 9, 18, 70, 76, 91, 117, 139–40, 171; Wadland, *Man in Nature*, pp. 403–405.

20. H. W. Lanier to Seton, Aug. 11, 1908, Aug. 25, 1908, SP; Luther H. Gulick to Seton, Sept. 21, 1909, SP; Harvey L. Smith to Seton, Sept. 22, 1909, SP.

21. Daniel Carter Beard, "The Boy Scouts of America,: *American Review of Reviews* 44 (Oct. 1911): 432, 437, and *Hardly a Man*, pp. 353–54; Wyckoff, "Interview with Seton Indians."

22. Robert S. S. Baden-Powell, "Educational Possibilities of the Boy Scouts' Training," *Nineteenth Century* 70 (Aug. 1911): 300; Seton to Edmund Seymour, Jan. 11, 1919, SP; Caspar Hodgson to Seton, Feb. 3, 1920, SP; M. V. O'Shea to Seton, May 2, 1920, May 7, 1920, June 18, 1920, SP; Seton to Colin H. Livingstone, June 7, 1920, SP.

23. Ralph D. Blumenfeld, editor of Arthur Pearson's *Daily Express*, seemed to verify Seton's fears in his article, "The Boy Scouts," *Outlook* 95 (July 23, 1910):

617–29. Seton to Baden-Powell, June 24, 1910, SP; William B. Kelsey to Seton, Sept. 18, 1910, SP; E. M. Robinson to F. P. Gignilliat, Nov. 2, 1910, copy in SP; Wadland, *Man in Nature*, pp. 411–414

24. Wade, *Twenty-one Years*, p. 127; W. D. Murray, *As He Journeyed: The Autobiography of William D. Murray*, pp. 346–47, and *The History of the Boy Scouts of America*, pp. 1–27; Schmitt, *Back to Nature*, pp. 108–10; Seton to Crump, July 22, 1941, SP; James E. West to Seton, July 29, 1941, SP. Also see Edgar M. Robinson, *The Early Years: The Beginnings of Work with Boys in the Young Men's Christian Association*. In 1915, Boyce founded the "Lone Scouts," a boys' organization that brought Scouting principles to isolated rural communities. At one time, its membership numbered more than a half million. In 1924 it merged with the BSA as the Department of Rural Scouting. Lucien W. Emerson to Julia M. Seton, Oct. 17, 1959, SP.

25. Murray, *As He Journeyed*, p. 347, and *History of the Boy Scouts*, pp. 27–32; Robinson to Seton, Oct. 4, 1934, SP; Seton to Robinson, Oct. 13, 1934, SP; Wadland, *Man in Nature*, 414–18.

26. Seton to Baden-Powell, May 20, 1910, June 13, 1910, June 24, 1910, Sept. 17, 1910, SP; Baden-Powell to Seton, Sept. 24, 1910, SP; Seton to F. M. Barton, June 30, 1910, SP; W. B. Forbush to Seton, June 22, 1910, SP; Baden-Powell to Doubleday, Page, July 5, 1910, July 31, 1910, Sept. 12, 1910, copies in SP.

27. Robinson to Seton, July 26, 1910, Oct. 4, 1934, SP; Seton to Robinson, Oct. 13, 1934, SP; Miller Jordan to Seton, Sept. 19, 1910, SP; Robinson to E. M. Willis, n.d., copy in SP; Murray, *As He Journeyed*, p. 347, and *History of the Boy Scouts*, p. 33.

28. Sarah Splint to Seton, June 25, 1910, SP; Dan Beard to Seton, Sept. 19, 1910, SP; John L. Alexander to Seton, Aug. 10, 1910, SP; George Dugan to Seton, Sept. 16, 1910, SP; W. T. Hornaday to Seton, June 26, 1910, June 30, 1910, Nov. 10, 1910, SP; Seton to Edmund Seymour, Dec. 2, 1918, SP; Daniel Carter Beard, "The Boy Scouts," *Outlook* 95 (July 23, 1910): 696–97.

29. Baden-Powell to Seton, Sept. 24, 1910, SP; Seton to Baden-Powell, Sept. 17, 1919, SP; Seton to Robinson, Aug. 10, 1940, SP.

30. Roosevelt to Seton, Sept. 23, 1910, SP.

31. Alexander to Seton, Sept. 29, 1910, SP; Edward L. Wertheim to Seton, Oct. 11, 1910, SP; Caspar Whitney to Seton, Oct. 13, 1910, SP; Seton to Whitney, Oct. 17, 1910, SP; S. S. Aplin to Seton, Oct. 14, 1910, SP; Murray, *History of the Boy Scouts*, p. 36.

32. Dan Beard to "Mr. Thompson," n.d., SP.

33. Wyckoff, "Interview with Seton Indians"; Murray, *History of the Boy Scouts*, pp. 54–64.

34. Seton to Arthur B. Reeve, Oct. 28, 1910, SP; H. Chessman Kittredge to Seton, June 26, 1911, SP; Baden-Powell to Seton, Jan. 31, 1911, Feb. 3, 1911, SP; Murray, *As He Journeyed*, p. 348; *Boy Scouts of America: The Official Handbook for Boys*.

35. W. D. Murray, George Pratt, and A. A. Jameson to Seton, Aug. 15, 1912, SP; Seton to the Editorial Board, Aug. 25, 1912, SP; Murray to Seton, Dec. 21, 1911, SP.

36. Seton to Alexander, Jan. 13, 1913, SP; Alexander to Seton, Oct. 27, 1914, SP; Lee Hanmer to Seton, Dec. 5, 1913, Jan. 8, 1914, SP; Philip D. Fagens to Seton, Dec. 9, 1913, Jan. 3, 1914, SP; E. C. Bishop to Seton, Dec. 30, 1913, SP; Baden-Powell to Seton, Mar. 3, 1913, Mar. 10, 1913, Mar. 12, 1913, April 17, 1913, May 9, 1913, SP.

37. Seton to Elbert Hubbard, Jan. 29, 1912, HRC; Seton to Col. Edwin Emerson, Feb. 8, 1913, HL; Seton to John D. Phelan, Dec. 24, 1913, BL; Seton to the Editorial Board of the BSA, Aug. 25, 1912; Seton to the president and Executive Board of the BSA, Nov. 21, 1912, SP.

38. See Wadland, *Man in Nature*, pp. 419–32.

39. E. T. Seton, *Rolf in the Woods*, p. vii.

40. Charles Stewart to Seton, May 23, 1911, SP; Seton, *Rolf in the Woods*, pp. vii–viii, 375–411. Also see Roosevelt, *Works X*.

41. Seton, *Rolf in the Woods*, pp. 12–48, 286–312, 322–74, 412–37; Read, "Flight to the Primitive," pp. 48, 53.

42. H. W. Lanier to Seton, Oct. 12, 1909, SP; Theodore Dreiser to Seton, Sept. 12, 1910, SP; Seton to Dreiser, Sept. 27, 1910, SP; E. T. Seton, "Scouting: Number 1," *American Boy (AB)*, 12 (July, 1911): 5, 21; "Number 2," *AB* 12 (Aug., 1911): 4–5; "Number 3," *AB* 12 (Sept. 1911): 3–4; "Number 4," *AB* 12 (Oct., 1911): 3–4; "Number 5," *AB* 12 (Nov., 1911): 6, 29; "Number 6," *AB* 12 (Dec., 1911): 3, 31; "Number 7," *AB* 13 (Jan., 1912): 3, 31; "Number 8," *AB* 13 (Feb., 1912): 3, 26; "Number 9," *AB* 13 (Mar., 1912):3, 27; "Number 10," *AB* 13 (Apr., 1912): 7, 27.

43. E. T. Seton, "Smoke Signals, Sign Talk and Totems," *Boy's Life (BL)* 3 (Dec., 1912): 24; "Peace and Patrol Names," *BL* 3 (Jan., 1913): 21; "The Indian Sign Language for Boy Scouts," *BL* 4 (Feb., 1913): 15; "The Badger Who Was Brother to a Boy," *BL* 3 (Nov., 1913): 12–13, 34; Murray, *As He Journeyed*, p. 349.

44. E. T. Seton, "Around the Camp Fire: 1," *BL* 3 (Oct., 1913): 13; "2," *BL* 3 (Dec., 1913): 28; "3," *BL* 4 (Jan., 1914): 20; "4," *BL* 4 (Mar., 1914): 20; "5," *BL* 4 (Apr., 1914): 23; "6," *BL* 4 (May, 1914): 24; "7," *BL* 4 (June, 1914): 26; "8," *BL* 4 (Sept., 1914): 24; "A Greeting from the Chief Scout," *BL* 4 (Jan., 1914): 2; Wadland, *Man in Nature*, pp. 433–37.

45. Anna A. MacDonald to Seton, Dec. 27, 1911, SP; Seton to Anna Mac-Donald, Dec. 29, 1911, SP.

46. Seton to Robert Underwood Johnson, Oct. 10, 1912, HRC; Robert Underwood Johnson, *Remembered Yesterdays*, pp. 239ff, 287; Nash, *Wilderness and the American Mind*, pp. 130–31, 158–59.

Chapter 16

1. Buckler, *Wo-He-Lo*, p. 5; Wyckoff, "Interview with Seton Indians"; Bott, *Seton's Indians*, p. 37.

2. Buckler, *Wo-He-Lo*, pp. 11, 15, 26–27; Schmitt, *Back to Nature*, p. 110.

3. Buckler, *Wo-He-Lo*, pp. 29–32; *Girl Scout Handbook*, pp. 13–18; Gladys D. Schultz and Daisy G. Lawrence, *Lady from Savannah: The Life of Juliette Low*, pp. 293–380.

4. *The Book of the Camp Fire Girls*, pp. 19–103; Buckler, *Wo-He-Lo*, pp. 45–46, 90; Macleod, *Building Character*, pp. 50–51, 132.

5. Buckler, *Wo-He-Lo*, pp. 100–101, 121–122.

6. Seton Journal, XXI, 68–72; Seton to Lummis, Sept. 2, 1915, LP; Arthur E. Bestor to Seton, Aug. 19, 1910, SP; Buckler, *Wo-He-Lo*, p. 119; Seton and Seton, *Gospel of the Redman*, p. 32.

7. F. R. Barlow to Seton, n.d., SP; Christy to Seton, Sept. 23, 1910, SP; D. S. Paterson to Seton, Jan. 31, 1910, SP: Lecture Tour Itinerary for Seton in Canada, Nov. 7–26, n.d., SP.

8. E. T. Seton, "The Narrowest Escape I Ever Had from a Wild Beast," *Farm and Fireside* 46 (Jan., 1922): 13, 34, 35, 37; "The Chillingham Bull," *Totem Board* 12 (Apr., 1933): 131–138; *Great Historic Animals, Mainly about Wolves*, pp. 27–39.

9. Commissioner of the Legion of Frontiersmen to Seton, July 31, 1908, SP; Frank Atherton to Seton, n.d., SP.

10. George S. Thompson to Seton, Dec. 7, 1912; Frank H. Powers to Seton, Nov. 27, 1912, SP; Buckler, *Wo-He-Lo*, pp. 101, 121.

11. Seton, "The House That Is Mine," p. 63; Hamlin Garland, *My Friendly Contemporaries*, 38–59.

12. Seton Journal, XXIII, 26; A. J. Hanna, "A Bibliography of the Writings of Irving Bacheller," *Rollins College Bulletin* 35 (Sept., 1939): 8; Garland, *My Friendly Contemporaries*, p. 75; Steffens, *Autobiography*, p. 584.

13. Seton to the Executive Council [Board], BSA, June 21, 1914, SP; Frank Presbrey, "The Associate Editors of *Boys' Life*," *BL* 4 (May, 1914): 6; Murray, *As He Journeyed*, p. 348; Macleod, "Good Boys Made Better," pp. 268–69.

14. Doubleday to Seton, Aug. 19, 1914, SP; Seton to West, July 18, 1914, SP; Boy Scouts of America *The Official Handbook for Boys*, rev. ed. Interestingly enough, although Doubleday lost the 1914 edition to Grosset and Dunlap, he was able to regain rights to the manual after Seton's exit from the BSA. Wadland, *Man in Nature*, pp. 437–39.

15. Alexander to West, Sept. 22, 1914, Oct. 27, 1914, copies in SP; Alexander to Seton, Oct. 27, 1914, Dec. 7, 1914, SP; Julia Seton, *Thousand Fires*, p. 132; Wadland, *Man in Nature*, pp. 439–41.

16. Seton Journal, XXIII, 8; Seton to Grace G. Seton, Jan. 31, 1915, quoted in Wadland, *Man in Nature*, p. 441; Seton to E. S. Martin, Mar. 6, 1934, SP.

17. Seton to Charles C. Jackson, May 12, 1915, SP; Seton to West, Aug. 14, 1937, SP; West to Seton, Aug. 27, 1937, SP; "Ernest Thompson Seton's Statement Answered by Executive Board of the National Council," *New York Times*, Dec. 11, 1915; Wadland, *Man in Nature*, p. 442.

18. Seton, *Artist-Naturalist*, p. 349; Julia Seton, *Thousand Fires*, p. 134; Redekop, *The Canadians*, p. 58.

19. Seton Journal, XXIII, 10, 19. While aboard the *Lusitania*, Seton penned the following statement on a picture postcard of the liner: "To the Boy Scouts of the Panhandle: Ho Scouts:—Some of my best days were spent riding in the Panhandle. It is a glorious country, one of the best in the world for Scouting. So I hope you will rise to your chance and become the best Scouts in the World. Greetings from Ernest Thompson Seton, Chief Scout."

The Chief Scout had indeed visited the Texas Panhandle during his early pro-
motional campaigns and met with several interested residents, including the
pioneer rancher Charles Goodnight. In 1912, W. A. Warner of Claude, Texas, had
organized the first Scout troop west of the Mississippi, and it was probably to
them that Seton wrote this note of encouragement. The postcard, dated Feb. 5,
1915, and bearing Seton's wolf-track signature, was eventually obtained by T. D.
Hobart, manager of the JA Ranch and executor of the Cornelia Adair estate.
For years it was displayed on the mantel in the JA headquarters in Armstrong
County. The original framed card is now in the interview files of the Panhandle-
Plains Museum Library. Walter Owens to J. Evetts Haley, March 20, 1929, Haley
Correspondence, 1924–34, Panhandle-Plains Museum Library and Archives,
Canyon, Tex. Also, see Armstrong County Historical Association, *A Collection
of Memories: A History of Armstrong County*, p. 365.

20. E. T. Seton, Untitled statement re World War I, Nov. 2, 1917, in Poems of
the Great War, original MSS in HRC; Garland, *My Friendly Contemporaries*,
p. 59; Sullivan, *Our Times* V, 114; Champney, *Art and Glory*, pp. 194–96.

21. Roosevelt to West, Nov. 30, 1915, in Roosevelt, *Letters* VIII, 992–93. Also
see Hermann Hagedorn, *The Roosevelt Family of Sagamore Hill*, pp. 359–376.
Roosevelt's indictment was probably aimed more directly at David Starr Jordan
and those who shared his pacifistic views. Jordan was one of two vice-presidents
elected to the BSA Executive Board in 1910. He served in that position until
1916, when he resigned. Although neither he nor Murray gave any reason for his
resignation, it is likely, judging from Jordan's antiwar stance, that he did so
under pressure. Jordan, *Days of a Man*, p. 543; Murray, *History of the Boy Scouts*,
pp. 47, 93; Burns, *David Starr Jordan*, pp. 78–108.

22. "Seton Still Insists on Quitting Scouts," *New York Times*, Dec. 6, 1915;
"West Says Seton Is Not a Patriot," *New York Times*, Dec. 7, 1915.

23. Seton to Beard, Nov. 26, 1915, Dec. 22, 1938, SP; Beard to Seton, Nov. 30,
1915, SP; Wadland, *Man in Nature*, pp. 443–45.

24. "Why Mr. Seton Is Not Chief Scout," *BL* 6 (Jan., 1916): 28.

25. Wadland, *Man in Nature*, pp. 442–43, 445; Redekop, *The Canadians*,
pp. 58–59.

Chapter 17

1. Haynes, *Haynes Guide*, pp. 160–61; Haines, *Yellowstone Story* II, 238, 242,
267–71, 458.

2. Seton Journal, XXI, 145; *Wild Animals at Home*, pp. 72–75; Julia M. Seton,
Pulse of the Pueblo, pp. 203–209; Haines, *Yellowstone Story* II, 447; Joseph G.
Rosa, *The West of Wild Bill Hickok*, p. 196.

3. L. M. Brett to Seton, Dec. 2, 1912, SP; Seton, *Wild Animals at Home*,
pp. 87–88, 93–94, 210. Devil's Kitchen, the interior of an extinct hot spring,
had for years a wooden stairway that allowed visitors access, but in 1939 it was
removed because of the potential danger from noxious gases. Haynes, *Haynes
Guide*, p. 47. Seton returned to Yellowstone in the winter of 1913–14 to pho-

tograph animals such as elk and bighorn sheep in their snowy settings. Many of these were later featured in his *Lives of Game Animals*.

4. Seton Journal, XXI, 106–22; "Owner Sticks," *Totem Board* 11 (Dec., 1932): 537–39; Julia Seton, *Thousand Fires*, p. 122.

5. Julia Seton, *Pulse of the Pueblo*, pp. 148–51, 197–202.

6. Wadland, *Man in Nature*, p. 349.

7. George Bird Grinnell to Seton, July 3, 1906, Aug. 14, 1908, Oct. 29, 1908, SP. Also see George Bird Grinnell, "The Indian on the Reservation," *Atlantic Monthly* 89 (Feb., 1899): 263, and *The Story of the Indian*.

8. Garland, *My Friendly Contemporaries*, p. 59; Wilson, "Charles Alexander Eastman," p. 187.

9. Charles A. Eastman to Seton, Oct. 11, 1912, SP; Seton to Eastman, Oct. 15, 1912, SP; Seton to Taft, Oct. 15, 1912, SP.

10. Seton to Lummis, Jan. 12, 1912, April 25, 1912, LP; E. T. Seton, unpublished fragment, n.d., SP; *Arctic Prairies*, pp. 22–23; *Book of Woodcraft*, p. 10.

11. Seton, *Book of Woodcraft*, pp. 45–47, 55–59, 536. Also see James Mooney, "The Ghost Dance Religion and the Sioux Outbreak of 1890," *Fourteenth Annual Report of the Bureau of Ethnology to the Secretary of the Smithsonian Institution*, pp. 641–1136. Among the accounts of army officers Seton used to construct his arguments were John G. Bourke's *On the Border with Crook* (1891) and Oliver O. Howard's *Famous Indian Chiefs I Have Known* (1908).

12. Seton, *Book of Woodcraft*, pp. 12–13, 24, 50–51, 58, 572–73; Wadland, *Man in Nature*, pp. 330–33. Also, see Charles A. Eastman, *The Soul of the Indian: An Interpretation*.

13. See Edgar B. Bronson, *Reminiscences of a Ranchman*; Seton, *Book of Woodcraft*, pp. vi, 548–71. A more recent sympathetic treatment of Dull Knife's flight is Mari Sandoz, *Cheyenne Autumn*.

14. Seton to Hodge, May 23, 1912, July 16, 1912, Aug. 12, 1912, Nov. 21, 1913, HC; Grinnell to Seton, Dec. 3, 1912, SP; Seton to Hubbard, Dec. 30, 1912, HRC. Also see Robert G. Valentine, "Making Good Indians," *Sunset* 24 (June, 1910): 598–611.

15. Seton to the Editor, *New York Herald*, Dec. 27, 1912, SP.

16. Seton Journal, XXI, 178–79, XXII, 146–51.

17. Seton Journal, XXIII, 47–56. As agent, Seger was known for his sympathetic treatment of his Cheyenne and Arapaho charges and for his pragmatic stance regarding Indian education. John H. Seger, *Early Days Among the Cheyenne and Arapahoe Indians*, ed. Stanley Vestal; Jack T. Rairdon, "John Homer Seger: The Practical Indian Educator," *Chronicles of Oklahoma* 34 (Summer, 1956): 203–16.

18. Seton Journal, XXIII, 58–69. Sheldon Parsons, New York–born portrait and landscape artist, had come to New Mexico in 1912 for his health. In 1918 he became director of the State Art Museum in Santa Fe. Van Deren Coke, *Taos and Santa Fe: The Artist's Environment, 1882–1942*, p. 30.

19. Seton to Ina S. Cassidy, Sept. 2, 1915, Cassidy Scrapbook, BL. Gerald Cassidy, a New York commercial artist, won notice in New Mexico for his postcards and travel posters for the Santa Fe Railroad, as well as for his landscapes and

Indian portraits. In 1915 he was awarded a grand-prize gold medal for his murals in the Indian Arts Building of the Panama-California Exposition in San Diego. Coke, *Taos and Santa Fe*, p. 29; A. M. Gibson, *The Santa Fe and Taos Colonies: Age of the Muses, 1900–1942*, p. 32.

20. Seton Journal, XXIII, 70–84. Also see Frances Gillmor and Louisa W. Wetherill, *Traders to the Navajos*.

21. Seton Journal, XXIII, 85–88; Fiske and Lummis, *Charles F. Lummis*, p. 141.

22. Seton Journal, XXIII, 138–69.

23. *Tulsa Daily World*, June 23, 1936; Seton and Seton, *Gospel of the Redman*, p. 30.

24. Wadland, *Man in Nature*, p. 461.

25. Seton Journal, XXIII, 39; Seton to Mary Austin, May 11, 1915, Apr. 6, 1916, Apr. 26, 1917, HL.

Chapter 18

1. *New York Tribune*, Sept. 18, 1919; Seton, *Artist-Naturalist*, p. 349.

2. Merle Curti, *The Growth of American Thought*, pp. 663–66.

3. Murray, *History of the Boy Scouts*, pp. 101–36; Buckler, *Wo-He-Lo*, pp. 145–65; Macleod, *Building Character*, pp. 79–84.

4. John Collier, *Indians of the Americas*, p. 144.

5. Hertzberg, *American Indian Identity*, pp. 31–38, 59–173; Wilson "Charles Alexander Eastman," pp. 186–215.

6. E. T. Seton, *The Manual of the Woodcraft Indians*, 14th edition, p. v; Wadland, *Man in Nature*, pp. 356–58.

7. E. T. Seton, "Woodcraft Extolled as the Science That Makes Men: A Gospel for Out-of-Doors," *Current Opinion* 73 (Oct., 1922): 461–64.

8. Seton to E. M. Robinson, Feb. 21, 1928, SP; E. T. Seton, Spiritual Thrift, Number 2: Helping to Develop Democracy with Nature's Aid Through the Woodcraft League," *Touchstone* 1 (June, 1917): 119.

9. Seton to Hodge, Mar. 16, 1916, HC; Seton to Mary Austin, April 26, 1917, HL.

10. E. T. Seton, "The Honors, Exploits or Coups of the Seton Indians," pp. 1–6, MS in SWML; *Manual of the Woodcraft Indians*, pp. 13, 17.

11. E. T. Seton, *Manual of the Brownies, the Little Lodge of the Woodcraft League of America*; Lester S. Thomas, "Sweat Lodge Ceremony," *Totem Board* 12 (Oct., 1933): 401–06.

12. E. T. Seton, Sport, MS Notes, SP; "The Honors, Exploits or Coups of the Seton Indians," p. 7; Wadland, *Man in Nature*, pp. 362–63. For an example of the decrease in the athletics category, compare Seton's *American Boy Scout* (1910) with his *Woodcraft Manual for Boys* (1917 edition). Also, see E. T. Seton, "Hunting with the Camera," *Recreation* 8 (April, 1898): 263–64.

13. E. T. Seton, "Introduction to the Beast and Bird Section of the Volume on Nature Study," MS notes, n.d., SP; Seton, "On Nature Study" in *The Library of Natural History*, ed. Richard Lydekker, p. v; Wadland, *Man in Nature*, p. 370.

14. Seton, *Book of Woodcraft*, pp. 12–13; Wadland, *Man in Nature*, pp. 331–32. The spiritual side of modern ecology has been a subject of recent analysis. Seton's view was similar to that of Saint Francis of Assisi, who believed in the equality of all God's creatures. The Franciscan doctrine of the animal soul, however, was based not on pantheism but on a "unique sort of pan-psychism of all things animate and inanimate, designed for he glorification of their transcendent Creator, who in the ultimate gesture of cosmic humility, assumed flesh, lay helpless in a manger, and hung dying on a scaffold." See Lynn White, Jr., "The Historical Roots of Our Ecologic Crisis," in *Dynamo and Virgin Reconsidered*, pp. 75–94; Weston La Barre, *The Ghost Dance: Origins of Religion*.

15. Seton, *Book of Woodcraft*, pp. 108–43, 172–95, 468–508. Prior to his visits to the Navajo Country in 1914, Seton relied mostly on Washington Matthews, "Navajo Weavers," *Third Annual Report of the Bureau of Ethnology to the Secretary of the Smithsonian Institution, 1881–82*, pp. 375–91.

16. E. T. Seton, *The Woodcraft Manual for Girls*; *Woodcraft Boys, Woodcraft Girls: How to Begin*.

17. Seton, "Spirit of the Woods," pp. 222–23; "Woodcraft Extolled," pp. 461–64.

18. See E. T. Seton, "How the Giant Cactus Came" and "The Singing Hawk"; John B. May, "The Sport of Bird Banding," all in *Totem Board* 10 (May, 1927): 3–5, 10.

19. Seton to Mary Austin, April 26, 1917, Jan. 13, 1919, HL.

20. E. T. Seton, "Coaly-Bay, the Outlaw Horse," *Collier's* 56 (Jan. 22, 1916): 10–11; *Wild Animal Ways*, pp. 12–16.

21. Seton, *Cedar Mountain*, pp. 30, 68.

22. Ibid., pp. 4–52.

23. Ibid., pp. 229, 329–30. For a comparison, see Owen Wister, *The Virginian*, pp. 297–318.

24. Schmitt, *Back to Nature*, p. 143; Susan Wood, "Ralph Connor and the Tamed West," in *The Westering Experience in American Literature: Bicentennial Essays*, ed. Merrill Lewis and L. L. Lee, pp. 199–205.

25. Seton, *Cedar Mountain*, p. 77.

26. Ibid., pp. 163, 246–47, 315–17.

27. Ibid., p. 419.

28. Garrick Mallery, "Sign Language among North American Indians, Compared with That among Other Peoples and Deaf Mutes," in *First Annual Report of the Bureau of Ethnology to the Secretary of the Smithsonian Institution, 1879–80*, pp. 269–552; William Philo Clark, *The Indian Sign Language*.

29. Hodge to Seton, Oct. 20, 1910, Mar. 4, 1916, Aug. 23, 1916, Dec. 11, 1916, SP; Seton to Hodge, Mar. 23, 1916, May 25, 1916, Sept. 6, 1916, SP; Hodge to Cato Sells, May 17, 1916, SP; Hodge to J. W. Dortch, May 23, 1916, SP; Seton to Hodge, Apr. 21, 1914, Mar. 13, 1916, HC; Wadland, *Man in Nature*, p. 330.

30. Seton to Hodge, Dec. 19, 1916, Mar. 26, 1917, HC. Francis La Flesche, an Omaha Indian and a colleague of Alice Fletcher, was noted for his ethnological and sociological studies of his tribe. See Francis La Flesche, "An Indian Allotment," *Independent* 52 (Nov. 8, 1900): 2686–88; Alice C. Fletcher and Francis La

Flesche, "The Omaha Tribe," in *Annual Report of the Bureau of American Ethnology, 1905–06*.

31. Seton to Hodge, Dec. 3, 1918, Jan. 11, 1919, HC; Seton, *Sign Talk*. Also see William C. Stokoe, *Semiotics and Human Sign Languages*.

32. Seton to Hodge, May 25, 1916, Jan. 11, 1919, HC; Hodge to Seton, May 26, 1916, Jan. 29, 1932, HC. Also, see Henry R. Schoolcraft, *Historical and Statistical Information Respecting the History, Conditions, and Prospects of the Indian Tribes of the United States*; Frances S. Nichols, comp., *Index to Schoolcraft's 'Indian Tribes of the United States.'*

33. Buckler, *Wo-He-Lo*, pp. 165–66; Wilson, "Charles Alexander Eastman," p. 203.

34. Seton to Charles Lathrop Pack, Jan. 12, 1927, HRC; E. T. Seton, "Teddy's Obituary" quoted in Julia Seton, *Thousand Fires*, p. 135. It is interesting to note that while Kermit offered his services to the Woodcraft League, his brother, Theodore Roosevelt, Jr., was elected to the BSA National Executive Board in 1919. As a vice-president on the board, Ted Roosevelt served on various committees and at one time or another was chairman of the Personnel and the Health and Safety committees. Murray, *History of the Boy Scouts*, pp. 179, 360–61, 370.

35. See E. W. Nelson, "Larger North American Mammals," *National Geographic* 30 (Nov., 1916): 385–472; Nelson, "Smaller Mammals of North America," *National Geographic* 33 (May, 1918): 371–493; Nelson, *Wild Animals of North America*.

36. E. T. Seton, "Migrations of the Gray Squirrel," "For a Methodic Study of Life Histories of Mammals," "Does the *Cuterebra* Ever Emasculate Its Host?" *Journal of Mammalogy* (hereafter *JM*) 1 (Feb., 1920): 53–58, 67–69, 94–95; "Notes on the Breeding Habits of Captive Deermice," "Food of the Red Fox," "Acrobatic Skunks," "Bobcats and Wild Turkeys," *JM* 1 (May, 1920): 134–138, 140; "The Mole-Mouse, Potato-Mouse, or Pine-Mouse," *JM* 1 (Aug., 1920): 185; "The Jaguar in Colorado," *JM* 1 (Nov., 1920): 241; "The Sea Mink," *JM* 2 (Aug., 1921): 168; "Gray Squirrels and Nuts," *JM* 2 (Nov., 1921): 41; "More Acrobatic Skunks," *JM* 3 (Feb., 1922): 53; "The Magpie as a Sentinel for Rabbits," *JM* 3 (May, 1922): 119; "The Value of Moles," *JM* 4 (Feb., 1923): 51; "The Mane on the Tail of the Gray-Fox," *JM* 4 (Aug., 1923): 180–82; "On the Study of Scatology," *JM*, 6 (Feb., 1925): 47–49; "The Prairie Dogs (*Cynomys ludovicianus*) at Washington Zoo," *JM* 7 (Aug., 1926): 229–30.

37. E. T. Seton, "Recent Bird Records for Manitoba," *Auk* 25 (Oct., 1908): 450–54.

38. E. T. Seton, "On the Popular Names of Birds," *Auk* 28 (Apr., 1919): 229–35; "Why Do Birds Bathe? Part 1," *Bird-Lore* 22 (Nov.–Dec., 1920): 334–35; "Part 2," *Bird-Lore* 23 (May–June, 1921): 124–37; "What Do Birds Signal with Their Tails?" *Bird-Lore* 23 (Nov.–Dec., 1921): 286–87; "Early Bird Banding," *Auk* 38 (Oct., 1921): 611.

39. Elbert Hubbard II to Seton, May 1, 1919, June 6, 1919, June 20, 1919, HRC; Seton to Hubbard, May 16, 1919, June 1, 1920, July 4, 1920, Sept. 3, 1920, HRC.

40. Seton Journal, XXV, 61.

41. Ibid., XXV, 62–65; E. T. Seton, "Wild Life and the Motor Car," *JM* 2 (Aug., 1921): 240.

42. Seton Journal, XXV, 65–70.

43. See Charles A. R. Campbell, *Bats, Mosquitoes and Dollars*.

44. E. T. Seton, "A Roving Band of Say's Bats," *JM* 3 (Feb., 1922): 52; *Life-Histories* II, 1147–1200.

45. E. T. Seton, "The Story of Atalapha, a Winged Brownie," *Scribner's* 59 (Apr., 1916): 441–58; *Wild Animal Ways*, pp. 143–207.

46. Campbell, *Bats, Mosquitoes and Dollars*, pp. 96, 132.

47. Seton Journal, XXV, 68–69; *Game Animals* IV, 859–63.

Chapter 19

1. Lincoln Steffens, *The World of Lincoln Steffens*, ed. Ella Winter and Herbert Shapiro, p. 47.

2. Frederick Lewis Allen, *Only Yesterday*, pp. 15–125.

3. Hertzberg, *American Indian Identity*, pp. 213–14, 239–94, 302.

4. Seton, *Artist-Naturalist*, p. 358.

5. E. T. Seton, "Why Wear Clothes?" *Hearst's* (Aug., 1920): 21, 73.

6. E. T. Seton, *Woodland Tales*.

7. Seton Journal, XXV, 65–67.

8. E. T. Seton, "Bannertail, the Story of a Gray Squirrel: Part 1," *LHJ* 39 (Feb., 1922): 13, 157–58; "Part 2," *LHJ* 39 (Mar., 1922): 141–42: "Part 3," *LHJ* 39 (Apr., 1922): 177–78, "Part 4," *LHJ* 39 (May, 1922): 149–50.

9. Seton to George L. Wheelock, April 19, 1919, Dec. 28, 1921, Appleton-Century MSS, LL: Frank Crane, quoted in *National Geographic* 42 (Dec., 1922): 569.

10. Seton to Gelett Burgess, Jan. 24, 1921, Jan. 27, 1921, Burgess Collection, Seton Correspondence, BL: Seton to S. C. G. Walkins, Jan. 31, 1924. Collier Papers, Yale University Library (YUL), New Haven, Conn.

11. Lummis to Seton, Mar. 22, 1919; LP; Seton to Lummis, Feb. 3, 1922, LP; Ad for First Annual Woodcraft Potlatch on Feb. 27, 1922, LP; Seton Journal, XXV, 131–35.

12. Seton Journal, XXV, 135–42; "Minutes of the Woodcraft Executive Council," n.d., MS in SP.

13. E. T. Seton, "Dipo: Sprite of the Desert," *Century* 105 (Nov., 1922): 106–15; "The Story of Carrots," *Farm and Fireside*, 47 (June, 1923): 12, 13, 30, 31, 33; "Rincon, or the Call in the Night," *Totem Board* 12 (Aug., 1933): 295–303; *Great Historic Animals*, pp. 55–59.

14. Seton Journal, XXV, 166–80.

15. Seton to Upton Sinclair, April 1, 1923, April 18, 1923, June 6, 1923, Sinclair MSS, LL.

16. Buckler, *Wo-He-Lo*, p. 128.

17. E. T. Seton, *Trail and Camp-Fire Stories*, ed. Julia M. Seton, p. ix.

18. Therese La Farge, "The Indefatigable, Indestructible Julia Seton," *Santa Fe News*, Oct. 9, 1969.

19. Seton Journal, XXV, 187, 189; *Santa Fe News*, Oct. 9, 1969.

20. Seton, *Artist-Naturalist*, p. 387.

21. Seton to Gerald Christy, June 6, 1922, June 9, 1922, June 22, 1925, July 6, 1925, Sept. 12, 1925, Mar. 18, 1926, HRC; Arthur Todhunter to Christy, Sept. 11, 1925, HRC.

22. Seton Journal, XXV, 165; Julia Seton, *Thousand Fires*, pp. 162–65.

23. Seton to Grace G. Seton, May 14, 1924, SP; Grace G. Seton to Seton, Oct. 8, 1924, SP; Seton to W. English Walling, Dec. 13, 1925, HL; E. T. Seton, "Holy Smoke!" *Rotarian* 45 (Aug., 1934): 9–11, 57.

24. Seton to Grace G. Seton, May 14, 1924, SP; Garland, *Diaries*, pp. 252–53.

25. See, e.g., "The Lament of the Owl," in Seton, *Woodland Tales*, p. 226.

26. Seton Journal, XXV, 183; Grace G. Seton to Seton, April 5, 1923, Sept. 27, 1923, SP; Anya Seton Autobiographical Sketch, n.d., SP.

27. Seton to Lummis, Feb. 27, 1924, LP; John C. Devlin and Grace Naismith, *The World of Roger Tory Peterson*, p. 29.

28. Seton to Lummis, Jan. 21, 1924, Feb. 27, 1924, May 19, 1924, LP; Lummis to Seton, Jan. 28, 1924, May 3, 1924, LP; Seton to W. L. Finley, Oct. 24, 1923, Nov. 24, 1923, HRC.

29. Julia Seton, *Thousand Fires*, p. 244.

30. Lummis to Seton, Mar. 6, 1924, LP.

31. Seton to Gerald Christy, Mar. 4, 1926, HRC; Robert Ingersoll Brown to Seton, n.d., SP; Vilhjalmer Stefanson to Seton, Feb. 2, 1931, SP; Seton, *Artist-Naturalist*, p. 386; Julia Seton, *Thousand Fires*, pp. 243–44.

32. Donald Culross Peattie, "Nature and Nature Writers," *Saturday Review* 16 (Aug. 28, 1937): 10–11; William Vogt, "Popularizing Nature," *Saturday Review* 16 (Sept. 18, 1937): 9.

33. Seton to Livingstone, Apr. 9, 1926, SP; Livingstone to Seton, Apr. 17, 1926, SP; West to Seton, Apr. 20, 1926, SP; Murray, *History of the Boy Scouts*, pp. 169–70, 315.

34. Livingstone to Seton, April 23, 1926, SP; West to Seton, April 27, 1926, May 3, 1927, SP; Seton to West, Apr. 28, 1926, May 12, 1927, SP; Bolton Smith to Seton, May 4, 1926, SP.

35. Seton to Walter W. Head, Aug. 16, 1926, SP; Wadland, *Man in Nature*, pp. 381–83.

36. West to Seton, Jan. 7, 1927, Oct. 27, 1927, SP; Seton to West, Oct. 25, 1927, SP; Setom to Mortimer Schiff, June 27, 1927, Mar. 1, 1928, Mar. 11, 1928, SP; Wadland, *Man in Nature*, p. 383.

37. A. G. Knebel, *Four Decades with Men and Boys, p. 181; Murray, History of the Boy Scouts* p. 428, Howard Hopkins, *A History of the YMCA in North America*, pp. 462–63; Macleod, "Good Boys Made Better," pp. 237–41.

38. Robinson to Seton, June 24, 1927, Oct. 6, 1928, Nov. 6, 1934, SP; Seton to Robinson, Oct. 11, 1928, SP; Robinson to W. D. Murray, copy in SP; Wadland, *Man in Nature* p. 384.

39. E. T. Seton, "Some Prints of Leaves," *Nature* 2 (Sept., 1923): 142–43, 191; "They're Still Wild in Spots," *Collier's* 76 (Aug. 1, 1925): 12–13.

40. Julia Seton, *Thousand Fires*, pp. 148–60.

300   Notes

41. Seton to C. L. Pack, Jan. 12, 1927; Arthur N. Pack to W. L. Finley, Jan. 21, 1927, HRC.
42. See American Museum of Natural History bulletins, 1913–33.
43. Seton to C. L. Pack, Jan. 12, 1927, HRC; Seton to W. L. and Irene Finley, Mar. 9, 1928, HRC.
44. Seton to Grace G. Seton, May 14, 1924, SP; Wadland, *Man in Nature*, p. 464.
45. Schmitt, *Back to Nature*, pp. 102–105; Morris, "Seton and the Woodcraft Movement," pp. 188–94.
46. Grace G. Seton to Seton, Nov. 2, 1922, Dec. 8, 1922, Aug. 22, 1923, Sept. 27, 1923, Oct. 8, 1924, Oct. 12, 1924, Apr. 30, 1927, July 16, 1927, July 26, 1927, Aug. 6, 1927, SP.
47. Grace G. Seton to Seton, April 7, 1923, SP; Grace Gallatin Seton, *A Woman Tenderfoot in Egypt, Chinese Lanterns,* and *Yes, Lady Saheb: A Woman's Adventurings with Mysterious India*; Seton, *Artist-Naturalist*, p. 349.
48. Redekop, *The Canadians*, p. 59.
49. Grace G. Seton to Seton, April 19, 1923, SP; Seton to Grace G. Seton, Dec. 14, 1929, SP.
50. Seton to Grace G. Seton, May 14, 1924, SP; Samson, *Worlds of Seton*, p. 101.
51. Carey McWilliams, *The New Regionalism in American Literature*; Nash, *American West*, pp. 116–17.
52. Hanna, "Bibliography of Irving Bacheller," pp. 5–9; Wilson, "Charles Alexander Eastman," pp. 187–89, 250.
53. Hamlin Garland, *Afternoon Neighbors*, pp. 537–89; *Santa Fe New Mexican*, June 26, 1940. Also, see T. M. Pearce, *The Beloved House*.
54. B. A. Botkin, *Folk-Say: A Regional Miscellany*, pp. 14, 16–17; Nash, *American West*, pp. 117–19.
55. Morris, "Seton and the Woodcraft Movement," p. 194.
56. Seton to Lummis, June 1, 1927; Lummis to Seton, June 8, 1927, LP.
57. Seton Journal, XXVI, 1–16; Julia Seton, *Pulse of the Pueblo*, pp. 177–89, 200–202.
58. Seton Journal XXVI, 18–24; *Denver Post*, Aug., 1, 1927.
59. Seton Journal, XXVI, 26–34.
60. *Albuquerque Journal*, Aug. 29, 1927; John Collier, *American Indian Ceremonial Dances*, p. 8; Gibson, *Santa Fe and Taos Colonies*, pp. 31–32.
61. Seton Journal, XXVI, 34–102.
62. Seton to Mary Austin, Sept. 15, 1927, HL.
63. Seton, *The Buffalo Wind*; Seton, *Artist-Naturalist*, pp. 297, 386; Samson, *Worlds of Seton*, p. 101.

Chapter 20

1. Samson, *Worlds of Seton*, p. 122.
2. T. M. Pearce, *Mary Hunter Austin*, pp. 50–51, 64–65; Joshua C. Taylor, *The Fine Arts in America*, pp. 184–85; Nash, *American West*, pp. 120–25.

3. Julia Seton, *Pulse of the Pueblo*, pp. 180–82; Hertzberg, *American Identity*, pp. 201–202; Berkhofer, *The White Man's Indian*, pp. 179–80.

4. Wilcomb E. Washburn, *The Indian in America*, pp. 252–53; Berkhofer, *The White Man's Indian*, pp. 180–82.

5. "A Prophet on the Hill," *Santa Fe New Mexican*, Mar. 20, 1931; D. W. Meinig, *Southwest: Three Peoples in Geographical Change, 1600–1970*, pp. 100–101.

6. Seton to Mary Austin, Dec. 6, 1927, Oct., 2, 1928, Dec. 13, 1928, HL; Fink, *I-Mary*, pp. 223–49. Also see Mary Austin, *The American Rhythm: Studies and Re-expressions of American Songs*, and *Children Sing in the Far West*.

7. Seton, "Minutes of the Woodcraft Executive Council," n.d., SP.

8. Lummis to Seton, Oct. 10, 1927; Seton to the Lummis Family, Dec. 6, 1928, LP.

9. Seton Journal, XXVII–XXVIII, 8; Seton to Mary Austin, Oct. 30, 1928, HL; *Los Angeles Herald*, Feb. 16, 1929.

10. Survey of Sebastian de Vargas Grant, March, 1927, copy in Manuel A. Sanchez Papers, New Mexico State Records Center and Archives (NMSRC), Santa Fe, New Mexico.

11. Seton to Mary Austin, Dec. 13, 1928, Aug. 13, 1929, Sept. 18, 1929, Sept. 26, 1929, Nov. 29, 1929, Dec. 10, 1929, Dec. 20, 1929, HL; Julia Seton, *Thousand Fires*, pp. 251–53.

12. Julia Seton, *Thousand Fires*, pp. 251–53.

13. Grace G. Seton to Seton, Apr. 14, 1931, Anya Seton Papers, Boston University Library; Grace G. Seton to Seton, Apr. 14, 1931, Anya Seton Papers, Boston University Library; Grace G. Seton to Seton, Mar. 7, 1928, Nov. 30, 1929, Dec. 3, 1929, Dec. 9, 1929, SP; Seton Journal, XXVII–XXVIII, 6; XXIX–XXX, 9ff; *Santa Fe New Mexican*, June 27, 1931.

14. Anya Seton, Autobiographical Sketch, n.d., copy in SP; *My Theodosia*.

15. Seton to William S. Thompson, Dec. 20, 1912, SP; William S. Thompson to Seton, Aug. 13, 1927, SP; Seton to George S. Thompson, Dec. 25, 1925, SP; Stuart L. Thompson to Seton, June 4, 1928, SP; Seton to Stuart L. Thompson, June 28, 1928, SP.

16. Richard Greenwood, Description of Seton Village, Jan. 14, 1975, National Historic Landmark No. 7c, MS in National Park Service, Southwestern Regional Office, Santa Fe, N. Mex.

17. Seton Journal, XXIX–XXX, 4–10; Julia M. Seton to J. G. Thompson, July 13, 1942, SP; "Ernest Thompson Seton Lecture," *El Palacio* 30 (May 20, 1931): 235–36.

18. Seton to Mary Austin, Nov. 27, 1930, HL; Julia Seton, *Thousand Fires*, p. 134.

19. Greenwood, Description of Seton Village; F. Beatrice MacIntyre, "The Paleface Chief," *New Mexico Magazine* 24 (Apr., 1948): 25. Also, see Richard White, "The Cultural Landscape of the Pawnees," *Great Plains Quarterly* 2 (1982): 31–39.

20. E. T. Seton, "The Song of the Porcupine," *JM* 13 (May, 1932): 168–69.

21. Julia Seton, *Thousand Fires*, p. 252; Gibson, *Santa Fe and Taos Colonies*, p. 157.

22. Seton to Mary Austin, Apr. 15, 1931, HL; E. T. Seton, "The Woodcraft League or College of Indian Wisdom," *Homiletic Review* 101 (June, 1931): 434–39.

23. *Santa Fe New Mexican*, Mar. 20, 1931; *New Mexico Candle* (Las Vegas), July 6, 1932; *Los Angeles Times*, Jan. 23, 1934.

24. Seton to F. W. Hodge, Feb. 2, 1932, HC; *Santa Fe New Mexican*, July 25, 1932; Gibson, *The Santa Fe and Taos Colonies*, pp. 157–58.

25. Seton Journal, XXXI–XXXII, July 30, 1933. Note: Seton's later journals, beginning with 1933, contain no page numbers. Therefore, these will be cited with the date(s) of entry.

26. *Tulsa* (Oklahoma) *Tribune*, June 23, 1936; Claudia Boynton, "The Man Who Made Lobo Famous," 1967, p. 6, MS photocopy in SP.

27. Seton Journal, XXIX–XXX, 93–94.

28. E. T. Seton, "Two Records for New Mexico," *JM* 12 (May, 1931): 166; "Occurrence of the Least Weasel near Denver," *JM* 14 (Feb., 1933): 70.

29. MacIntyre, "The Paleface Chief," p. 35.

30. Seton Journal, XXIX–XXX, 94; Julia Seton, *Thousand Fires*, pp. 196–99. At a typical English Woodcraft "Troth Plighting," the bride and groom wore green jerkins. The ceremony was performed by the "Headman," who asked the couple, "Are you both agreed to keep the trail for service of the people" to which they replied, "Aye." "Your trails have run together; your trail is one," the Headman continued. The wedding guests, also in Robin Hood green, gathered around the totem of which the groom was a member. These Troth Plightings contained elements of medieval Celtic as well as American Indian tradition. Seton felt that the English Woodcrafters' emphasis on ritual helped evoke some "intensely interesting ceremonies, full of the Woodcraft spirit in its highest, noblest sense." E. T. Seton, "The Troth Plighting of Desmos and White Lion," *Totem Board* 12 (June, 1933): 222–26.

31. E. T. Seton, Address at the Grave of Helen McClorman, July 2, 1932, SP; Julia Seton, *Thousand Fires*, pp. 199–202.

32. C. Hart Merriam to Seton, Oct. 9, 1933, SP; Stuart L. Thompson to Julia M. Seton, Dec. 31, 1945, SP; Stuart L. Thompson, "The Seeing Eye," *Totem Board* 11 (Nov., 1932): 482–83; Thompson, "The Warbler in the Vine," *Totem Board* 12 (Apr., 1933): 160–61; Thompson, "The Charm of Sound," *Totem Board* 13 (Jan. 1934): 29–30; E. T. Seton, "Woodcraft at the World's Fair," *Totem Board* 11 (Dec., 1932): 578.

33. Seton Journal, XXXIII–XXXIV, Mar., 1935; Francis C. Wilson to W. J. Lucas, Mar. 5, 1935, Francis C. Wilson Papers, NMSRC; Julia Seton, *Thousand Fires*, p. 210; *Los Angeles Times*, Jan. 23, 1934.

34. Seton Journal, XXXI–XXXII, Nov. 21, 1934; Journal, XXXIII–XXXIV, Jan. 18, 1935. Wilson to Lucas, Dec. 14, 1934, Apr. 3, 1935, Apr. 24, 1935; Lucas to Wilson, Apr. 2, 1935, Apr. 22, 1935, Apr. 30, 1935; B. M. Webster to Wilson, Feb. 18, 1935, Mar. 2, 1935, Apr. 6, 1935, Apr. 29, 1935, May 9, 1935; Wilson to Webster, Feb. 22, 1935, Feb. 26, 1935, Apr. 3, 1935, Apr. 11, 1935, Apr. 24, 1935, May 2, 1935, Jan. 2, 1935; Grace G. Seton to Wilson, Apr. 10, 1935; Lucas to Seton,

Apr. 22, 1935; Divorce Proceedings, Ernest Thompson Seton vs. Grace Gallatin Seton, 1935, all in Wilson Papers, NMSRC. See also Seton, *Artist-Naturalist*, p. 350; Alan Dickson, "The Professional Life of Francis C. Wilson of Santa Fe: A Preliminary Sketch," *New Mexico Historical Review*, 51 (Jan., 1976): 35–55.

35. Seton Journal, XXXIII–XXXIV, Jan. 22, 1935, Jan. 31, 1935; *El Paso Times*, Jan. 23, 1935.

36. MacIntyre, "The Paleface Chief," p. 35; Julia Seton, *Pulse of the Pueblo*, pp. 25–27; Julia Seton, *Thousand Fires*, p. 257.

37. Greenwood, Description of Seton Village.

38. Julia M. Seton, "Impressions," *Ernest Thompson Seton's America*, ed. Farida Wiley, pp. xi–xii; *Thousand Fires*, p. 196.

39. MacIntyre, "The Paleface Chief," p. 35.

40. *Lubbock Morning Avalanche*, Mar. 4, 1938.

41. Seton Journal, XXXIII–XXXIV, Feb. 8, 1935; *Los Angeles Times*, Jan. 23, 1934.

42. Seton Journal, XXXIII–XXXIV, Nov. 15, 1935–Apr. 7, 1936; Julia Seton, *Thousand Fires*, p. 34.

Chapter 21

1. Seton to Capt. Rodney Berg, Jan. 12, 1928, SP; O'Connor, "Youth Model," p. 16.

2. E. T. Seton, "The Indian Question," MS, SP; Julia Seton, *Pulse of the Pueblo*, pp. 101–104.

3. Seton, "The Indian Question"' O'Connor, "Youth Model," p. 17.

4. *Daily Oklahoman*, June 25, 1936. James Paytiano is also noted for his collection of tribal legends, *Flaming Arrow's People*.

5. Seton, "The Indian Question."

6. Washburn, *The Indian in America*, p. 253.

7. Buckler, *Wo-He-Lo*, pp. 36, 44–45, 153.

8. John Collier, *From Every Zenith: A Memoir and Some Essays on Life and Thought*, p. 159, and *American Indian Ceremonial Dances*, pp. 185–89; Berkhofer, *The White Man's Indian*, pp. 182–88. Also see Kenneth R. Philip, "John Collier and the American Indian, 1920–1945," in *Essays on Radicalism in Contemporary America*, ed. Leon B. Blair, pp. 63–80.

9. Hertzberg, *American Indian Identity*, p. 287–89; Berkhofer, *The White Man's Indian*, pp. 182–88. Also see Kenneth R. Philip, "John Collier and the Crusade to Protect Indian Religious Freedom," *Journal of Ethnic Studies* 1 (Spring, 1973): 22–28.

10. Hertzberg, *American Indian Identity*, p. 289; Washburn, *The Indian in America*, pp. 255–57.

11. *Los Angeles Times*, Jan. 23, 1934.

12. Seton Journal, 31–32: July 18, 1933; Seton to Mary Austin, Mar. 3, 1932, HL; Seton to John Collier, Oct. 11, 1937, and Collier to Seton, Dec. 6, 1937, Collier Papers, YUL; *Santa Fe New Mexican*, June 26, 1940; Oliver La Farge, "An

Art That Is Really American," *Totem Board* 12 (Apr., 1933): 139–45; E. T. Seton, "Review of Stanley Vestal's *Sitting Bull*," *Totem Board* 12 (May, 1933); 207–208; Ina S. Cassidy, "The Shalako at Zuni," *Totem Board* 12 (June, 1933): 246.

13. Seton to Hodge, Jan. 26, 1932, Feb. 2, 1932, Jan. 3, 1933, July 31, 1936, HC; Julia M. Seton to Hodge, June 3, 1936, June 8, 1936, HC; Hodge to Julia M. Seton, June 5, 1936, HC.

14. Seton Journal, XXXI–XXXII, July 12, 1933. John Collier to Ellsworth Jaeger, Aug. 10, 1935; Seton to Collier, Aug. 16, 1935; Winifred Pomeroy to Seton, Oct. 15, 1937; Seton to Collier, Jan. 18, 1938; Collier to Seton, Mar. 1, 1938; Thomas V. Flannery to Collier, Nov. 30, 1938; Winifred Pomeroy to Flannery, Dec. 3, 1938, all in Collier Papers, YUL. See also Collier, *Indians of the Americas*, p. 144.

15. Julia M. Buttree (Seton), *The Rhythm of the Redman*; *El Paso Times*, Jan. 23, 1935; Redekop, *The Canadians*, p. 60.

16. Julia M. Seton to John Collier, Aug. 10, 1939; Kristie Sather to Julia M. Seton, Aug. 15, 1939, both in Collier Papers, YUL. Also see Julia M. Seton, *Sing, Sing, What Shall I Sing?* and *Indian Costume Book*.

17. E. T. Seton, "The Message of the Redman," *Totem Board* 11 (Jan. 1932): 6–36; "Plumes from the Thunder Bird: The Redman's Message," *Totem Board* 12 (May, 1933): 203–205.

18. Seton, *Book of Woodcraft*, pp. 572–73; *Seton and Seton, Gospel of the Redman*, pp. xvi, 105; O'Connor, "Youth Model," pp. 12–13.

19. Seton to Hodge, June 12, 1936, HC; Seton and Seton; *Gospel of the Redman*, pp. 51–57, 65; O'Connor, "Youth Model," pp. 11–12, 15.

20. Seton and Seton, *Gospel of the Redman*, p. vii.

21. Seton to Hodge, Sept. 6, 1935, HC; Hodge to Seton, Sept. 19, 1935, HC; Collier to Seton, May 15, 1935, SP.

22. Walter S. Campbell (Stanley Vestal), *The Book Lover's Southwest*, p. 110.

23. Walter Stanley Campbell, "Our Oklahoma Tribe," *Holiday Magazine for Children*, 1904 (exact date and page unknown).

24. Ray Tassin, *Stanley Vestal: Champion of the Old West*, 35–36, 48, 54–55.

25. Seton and Seton, *Gospel of the Redman*, p. xvi; O'Connor "Youth Model," p. 18.

26. Seton Journal, XXXIII–XXXIV, Feb. 8, 1935; Seton and Seton, *Gospel of the Redman*, p. 31; Thomas V. Flannery to John Collier, Nov. 30, 1938, Collier Papers, YUL; Elizabeth Lochrie to Seton, June 18, 1940, SP.

27. Wadland, *Man in Nature*, p. 464.

28. Betsy Larabee and Anne Ross, critiques of "The Sheriff of Golden" by Ernest Thompson Seton, Bobbs-Merrill MSS, LL.

29. Seton to Albert Bigelow Paine, Nov. 5, 1931, HL; Seton to L. W. Sanders, Feb. 13, 1935, Feb. 23, 1935, Feb. 12, 1936, Appleton-Century MSS, LL.

30. Seton, *Great Historic Animals*, pp. v–xi, 61–91.

31. Seton Journal, XXIX–XXX, 92

32. Seton, *Great Historic Animals*, pp. 105–19, 133–47, 205–23, 291–311, 313–20.

33. E. T. Seton, *The Biography of an Arctic Fox*, pp. 15–70; Allen, *Only Yesterday*, pp. 283–84, 320–25.

34. Seton, *Arctic Fox*, pp. 71–126; William E. Leuchtenberg, *Franklin D. Roosevelt and the New Deal*, pp. 18–40, 138–39, 231–51.

35. Peattie, "Nature and Nature Writers," pp. 10–11; Frank M. Chapman, "A Champion of Ernest Thompson Seton," *Saturday Review* 16 (Oct. 2, 1937): 9.

36. Seton Journal, 31–32: Aug. 30, 1933; Julia Seton, *Thousand Fires*, p. 116.

37. E. T. Seton et al., *Pictographs of the Old Southwest*, pp. 7, 14–25; Julia Seton, *Thousand Fires*, pp. 128–30.

Chapter 22

1. Seton, *Arctic Fox*, 110–119; Nash, *American West*, pp. 145–46, 177–78.

2. Seton Journal, XXXI–XXXII: Nov. 21, Dec. 31, 1934; 33–34: July 2, 1935.

3. Frederick Lewis Allen, *Since Yesterday*, pp. 83–103.

4. Leuchtenberg, *Roosevelt and the New Deal*, pp. 125–28; Nash, *American West*, pp. 155–61, 183–86.

5. Warren A. Beck, *New Mexico: A History of Four Centuries*, pp. 311–15.

6. Pearce, *Beloved House*, pp. 214, 217; Fink, *I-Mary*, pp. 250–60.

7. Marta Weigle and Kyle Fiore, *Santa Fe and Taos: The Writer's Era, 1916–1941*, pp. 39, 46; Nash, *American West*, pp. 176–80.

8. Julia Seton, *Pulse of the Pueblo*, pp. 65–78.

9. Seton Journal, XXXI–XXXII: July 11, 20, 1933; *Daily Oklahoman*, June 25, 1936.

10. T. M. Pearce to H. Allen Anderson, Sept. 14, 1981, SC.

11. *La Ventana* (Texas Tech), 1937; *Lubbock Morning Avalanche*, Mar. 3, 1938; *The Toreador* (Texas Tech), Mar. 2, 1938.

12. Sueanna Hammerly to James G. Allen, May 12, 1938, June 27, 1938; Allen to Sueanna Hammerly, June 30, 1938; Allen to Seton, May 16, 1938, May 19, 1938, June 1, 1938; Texas Technological College, Summer School Recreation Program for July 5–8, 1938, all in Southwest Collection, Texas Tech University, Lubbock, Tex. *Lubbock Morning Avalanche*, July 7, 1938; *Toreador*, July 8, 1938; Seton Journal, XXXIII–XXXIV, July 6–7, 1938.

13. *New Mexico Candle*, Oct. 13, 1938.

14. *Lubbock Morning Avalanche*, Mar. 4, 1938. Clark Kimball quoted in Marta Weigle, "Publishing in Santa Fe, 1915–40," *El Palacio* 90 (Anniversary Issue, 1984): 14–15.

15. Seton Journal, XXXIII–XXXIV, Aug. 14, 1938.

16. *New York World Telegram*, Nov. 19, 1938.

17. Pablita Velarde, or "Tse Tsan" ("Golden Dawn"), has become nationally known for her intricate paintings of Pueblo life. She has also made jewelry and published several books, all illustrated by her own hand, on Indian folklore, notably *Old Father, the Story Teller*, a collection of stories she had heard as a child from her father and other relatives. Married in 1943, she remained a lifelong friend of the Setons, "I go to see [Julia] whenever I can," Tse Tsan said in 1964.

Lela Waltrip and Rufus Waltrip, *Indian Women: Thirteen Who Played a Part in the History of America from Earliest Days to Now*, pp. 149–62.

18. Seton Journal, XXXV, Jan.–Mar., 1940; *New York World Telegram*, Nov. 19, 1938.

19. Seton, *Woodland Tales*, p. 158. The tea set is still in the possession of Mrs. Dee Seton Barber at Seton Castle. For analytical studies of the Hitler Youth, as compared with English and American youth movements, see Hubert S. Lewin, "Hitler Youth and the Boy Scouts of America: A Comparison of Aims," *Human Relations* 1 (1947): 206–27; John R. Gillis, "Conformity and Rebellion: Contrasting Styles of English and German Youth, 1900–1933," *History of Education Quarterly* 13 (Fall, 1973): 249–60.

20. Seton Journal, XXXIII–XXXIV, Feb. 9, 1938; Julia M. Seton to J. G. Thompson, July 13, 1943, SP.

21. Seton to F. W. Hodge, June 8, 1936, HC; Julia Seton, *Thousand Fires*, p. 262.

22. F. N. Doubleday to Seton, Oct. 18, 1918, SP.

23. Lois Dwight Cole to Seton, Nov. 19, 1935, SP; Seton to Simon & Schuster, Dec. 4, 1935, SP; Maria Leiper to Seton, Oct. 22, 1937, SP: John Farrar to Seton, Jan. 24, 1938, SP; Seton to Scribner, Aug. 10, 1939, SP; Maxwell Perkins to Seton, Sept. 28, 1939, May 1, 1940, SP; Stanley M. Rinehart to Scribner, Jan. 20, 1940, SP; Seton to attorneys of Authors' League, Apr. 4, 1940, SP.

24. Seton to Scribner, Aug. 10, 1939, SP; Perkins to Seton, Jan. 4, 1940, SP; Perkins to Julia M. Seton, May 9, 1940, SP; Julia M. Seton to Perkins, May 13, 1940, SP.

25. Seton to James West, March 6, 1931, SP; West to Seton, June 29, 1937, SP; E. S. Martin to Seton, March 2, 1934, SP; E. M. Robinson to Seton, Jan. 17, 1935, SP; Seton to W. D. Murray, March 12, 1935, SP; Murray to Seton, March 13, 1935, SP.

26. Seton to West, Oct. 11, 1937, Aug. 9, 1940, Sept. 7, 1940, Oct. 1, 1940, Oct. 22, 1940, Nov. 30, 1940, SP; West to Seton, Oct. 20, 1937, Oct. 14, 1940, SP; Robinson to Seton, Feb. 20, 1939, Mar. 12, 1939, Sept. 15, 1943, SP; Robinson to Julia M. Seton, Feb. 13, 1941, SP; Seton to Murray, Aug. 16, 1938, SP; Murray to Seton, July 26, 1938, Aug. 26, 1938, SP; Martin to Seton, Sept. 16, 1938, SP; R. H. Vitalius to Seton, Mar. 20, 1942, SP; Beard to Seton, Nov. 4, 1938, Jan. 30, 1940, May 28, 1940, SP; Seton to Beard, May 23, 1940, SP; Beard to Cyril Clemens, Mar. 22, 1938, SP; Wadland, *Man in Nature*, pp. 380–81.

27. Robert S. S. Baden-Powell, "Note for office to keep in case of revival of arguments later when I am dead. R. B-P. 17. 12.13" quoted in Reynolds, *The Scout Movement*, pp. 2–3; Baden-Powell to Seton, Aug. 8, 1939, SP; West to Seton, Oct. 14, 1940, SP; Wadland, *Man in Nature*, p. 385.

28. E. T. Seton, Scouting and Woodcraft, "Submitted to C. J. Carlson, Jan. 16, 1930 and accepted by him with 2 emendations," MS notes, n.d., SP; "For Union of Woodcraft and Boy Scouts," MS notes, n.d., SP; "Memorandum Regarding Woodcraft and Boy Scouts," MS notes, n.d., SP; Wadland, *Man in Nature*, pp. 385–86.

29. Julia Seton, *Thousand Fires*, p. 250.

30. Perkins to Seton, Jan. 4, 1940, SP; Seton, *Artist-Naturalist*, pp. 311–30.

31. Seton to Anya Seton Chase, May 19, 1939, SP; Redekop, *The Canadians*, p. 60.

32. Perkins to Seton, Dec. 20, 1939, SP; Seton to Perkins, March 20, 1940, SP; Seton, *Artist-Naturalist*, pp. 391–98.

33. Alan Devoe, "Artistic Wilderness," *Saturday Review* 23 (Dec. 7, 1940): 18.

34. Seton to John Stuart Groves, Feb. 4, 1941, HRC; A. L. Byron-Curtiss to Seton, Dec. 17, 1941, SP; Seton, *Artist-Naturalist*, pp. 367–73.

35. Seton Journal, XXXV, Aug. 14, 1940.

36. Ibid., Sept., 1945; Wiley, *Seton's America*, p. ix; Jack Samson, "Seton, America's Forgotten Naturalist," *Field and Stream* 78 (April, 1974): 63.

37. Seton, *Trail and Camp-Fire Stories* and *Santana, the Hero Dog of France*; Wiley, *Seton's America*, p. ix. MacIntyre, "The Paleface Chief," p. 25.

38. Seton Journal, XXXV: Feb. 23–27, Aug. 27, Sept. 23, 1942.

39. Julia M. Seton to J. G. Thompson, July 13, 1942, SP; Mrs. Leonard S. Allen to Julia M. Seton, Aug. 20, 1942, SP: Julia M. Seton to Director of Associated School Services, Mar. 3, 1942, SP; Director of Associated School Services to Julia M. Seton, Feb. 25, 1942, SP; Weigle, "Publishing in Santa Fe," p. 15.

40. Seton Journal, XXXV, Dec., 1943–Feb., 1946.

41. Nash, *American West*, pp. 206–209.

42. Seton Journal, XXXV, Apr. 11, 1945; Stan Steiner, *The New Indians, pp. 107, 223*; Hertzberg, *American Indian Identity*, p. 289.

43. Seton Journal, XXXV, Jan. 22, 1942, Mar. 16, May 11, 1943; *Santa Fe New Mexican*, June 26, 1940.

44. Seton Journal, XXXIII–XXXIV, Dec., 1939.

45. Ibid., XXXV, Dec., 1943, Jan. 2, 1944; MacIntyre, "The Paleface Chief," p. 37. The Taylors published several poems and articles on regional folklore and recipes. See Weigle, "Publishing in Santa Fe," p. 15.

46. J. Frank Dobie, *The Voice of the Coyote*, pp. 93–94.

47. MacIntyre, "The Paleface Chief," p. 35.

48. Seton Journal, XXXV, Oct., 1943. See Anya Seton, *The Turquoise*.

49. Anya Seton Chase to Seton, July 15, 1943, July 25, 1945, SP; Seton to Anya Seton Chase, July 19, 1943, SP; MacIntyre, "The Paleface Chief," p. 35. One successful movie based on an Anya Seton novel was *Dragonwyck* (1946), which starred Gene Tierney and Vincent Price: see Anya Seton, *Dragonwyck*.

50. Jessie Fullerton to Seton, Apr. 7, 1941, SP; Alan S. Thompson to Seton, Apr. 11, 1943, SP; Anna S. Thompson to Seton, Mar. 13, 1944, SP; Gertrude Pringle to Julia M. Seton, May 27, 1945, Dec. 11, 1945, SP; George S. Thompson to Seton, Sept. 8, 1938, Sept. 25, 1940, May 13, 1942, Aug. 9, 1942, Oct. 7, 1942, SP; Seton to George S. Thompson, May 15, 1942, SP.

51. Stanley Seton Thompson to Julia M. Seton, Mar. 12, 1941, Apr. 22, 1941, June 9, 1941, Nov. 24, 1943, Nov. 30, 1945, Jan. 18, 1946, Feb. 22, 1946, Apr. 17, 1946, Apr. 24, 1946, June 5, 1946, June 12, 1946, July 1, 1946, July 30, 1946, Nov. 5, 1946, SP.

52. Redekop, *The Canadians*, p. 60.

53. Seton Journal, XXXV, Feb.–Mar., 1946; *Pasadena* (California) *Star-News*, Oct. 23, 1946.

54. Seton Journal, XXXV, Sept. 7, 1945; Ralph Wallace to Seton, n.d., 1946, SP; Wallace, "Wild Animals He Has Known," p. 59.

55. MacIntyre, "The Paleface Chief," p. 37; *Summer Lobo* (University of New Mexico), Aug. 9, 1946; *Albuquerque Tribune*, Aug. 12, Aug. 15, 1946; T. M. Pearce to H. Allen Anderson, Sept. 14, 1981, SC.

56. Seton to F. W. Hodge, Sept. 6, 1935, HC; Last Will and Testament of Ernest Thompson Seton, July 31, 1946, copies in C. Quintana Collection No. 99, NMSRC. A copy of the will is also in the Appleton-Century MSS, LL.

57. Seton Journal, XXXV, July 1–Sept. 11, 1946; *Albuquerque Tribune*, Oct., 23, 1946; *Daily Current-Argus* (Carlsbad, N. Mex.), Oct. 23, 1946; *Pasadena Star-News*, Oct. 23, 1946; "Necrology," *New Mexico Historical Review* 22 (Jan., 1947): 107; John A. Garraty and Edward T. James, eds., *Dictionary of American Biography*, supp. 4, 1946–50, p. 737. In 1960, in honor of Seton's 100th birthday and Santa Fe's 350th anniversary, Julia planned to fly a plane over the Village and scatter his ashes. Anya Seton Chase to Julia M. Seton, May 23, 1960, June 27, 1960, SP; Julia M. Seton to Anya Seton Chase, May 31, 1960, SP.

58. Stanley S. Thompson to Julia M. Seton, Nov. 5, 1946, SP; Anya Seton Chase to Julia M. Seton, Nov. 11, 1946, SP.

59. MacIntyre, "The Paleface Chief," p. 37.

60. Boynton, "The Man Who Made Lobo Famous," p. 6.

Epilogue

1. Wadland, *Man in Nature*, p. viii.

2. Wiley, *Seton's America*, pp. xi–xii.

3. W. H. Carr, quoted in Samson, "Forgotten Naturalist," p. 193.

4. Ibid., p. 194.

5. Nash, *American West*, pp. 213–62. Also, see Neil Morgan, *Westward Tilt*.

6. Samson, *Worlds of Seton*, p. 17; Ron Arnold, *At the Eye of the Storm: James Watt and the Environmentalists*, pp. 143–56.

7. *Time*, Nov. 4, 1946, p. 30; J. Frank Dobie, *Life and Literature of the Southwest* p. 156.

8. Raymond W. Stedman, *Shadows of the Indian*, p. 72.

9. David King Dunaway, *How Can I Keep From Singing: Pete Seeger*, p. 72.

10. Wallace, "Wild Animals He Has Known," pp. 61, 63.

11. Roger Tory Peterson, *A Field Guide to the Birds*, p. v; Devlin and Naismith, *World of Roger Tory Peterson* pp. 16–19, 62, 66. Peterson's bird paintings are also influenced, to a great extent, by Louis Agassiz Fuertes.

12. Henry Chester Tracy, *American Naturalists*, pp. 233, 242.

13. Samson, "Forgotten Naturalist," p. 194.

14. Stuart L. Thompson to Julia M. Seton, Jan. 27, 1947, SP; Julia M. Seton to Anya Seton Chase, Apr. 28, 1960, SP; "A New Series of Lectures by Mrs.

Julia M. Seton," brochure from Seton Village, 1948, copy in SWML. Also, see Julia M. Seton, *Indian Creation Stories, American Indian Arts*, and *The Quandary of Youth*.

15. Julia M. Seton to Spud Johnson, Oct. 4, 1963, HRC; *Santa Fe New Mexican*, June 24, 1965, July 11, 1968, April 29, 1975; *Santa Fe News*, Oct. 9, 1969.

16. Grace Gallatin Seton, *Magic Waters*, and *Poison Arrows*. Most of Grace G. Seton's papers and manuscripts are located in the Grace G. Seton Collection, Sophia Smith Collection, Women's History Archive, Smith College, Northampton, Mass. Also, see Anya Seton, *The Hearth and Eagle, Foxfire, Katharine, The Mistletoe and Sword, The Winthrop Woman, Devil Water, Avalon, Green Darkness*, and *Smouldering Fires*.

17. Anya Seton Chase to Julia M. Seton, Apr. 9, 1960, SP.

18. *Viva* (Santa Fe), Jan. 25, 1976.

19. Greenwood, Description of Seton Village.

20. *Santa Fe New Mexican*, Aug. 15, 1968.

21. MacIntyre, "The Paleface Chief," p. 35.

22. Horn, *Climbing a Rainbow*, p. 222; Garraty and James, eds. *Dictionary of American Biography* IV, 736.

BIBLIOGRAPHY

Manuscript Collections and Other Unpublished Material

Allen, James G. Papers. Southwest Collection, Texas Tech University, Lubbock, Tex.

Bendire, Charles E. Papers. Library of Congress (LC), Manuscript Division, Washington, D.C.

Cassidy, Gerald. Scrapbooks, 1905–32. Bancroft Library (BL), University of California, Berkeley, Calif.

Collier, John. Papers. Yale University Library (YUL), New Haven, Conn.

Greenwood, Richard. Description of Seton Village, January 14, 1975. National Historic Landmark No. 7c, MS in National Park Service, Southwest Regional Office, Santa Fe, N. Mex.

Haley, J. Evetts. Correspondence, 1924–34. Panhandle-Plains Museum Library and Archives, Canyon, Tex.

Hodge, Frederick Webb. Papers (HC). Southwest Museum Library (SWML), Los Angeles, Calif.

Lummis, Charles F. Papers (LP). Southwest Museum Library (SWML), Los Angeles, Calif.

O'Connor, Thomas. "Ernest Thompson Seton: The American Indian as Youth Model," 1974. Unpublished MS in author's possession.

Pearce, T. M. Papers. Special Collections (SC), General Libraries, University of New Mexico, Albuquerque, N. Mex.

Quintana, C. Papers. New Mexico State Records Center and Archives (NMSRC), Santa Fe, N. Mex.

Roosevelt, Theodore. Papers (TRP). Library of Congress (LC), Manuscript Division, Washington, D.C.

Sanchez, Manuel A. Papers. New Mexico State Records Center and Archives (NMSRC), Santa Fe, N. Mex.

Seton, Anya. Papers. Mugar Memorial Library, Boston University, Boston, Mass.

Seton, Ernest Thompson. Correspondence. Bancroft Library (BL), University of California, Berkeley, Calif.

———. Correspondence. Lilly Library (LL), Indiana University, Bloomington, Ind.

———. Journals, 1879–1946. 36 MS vols. American Museum of Natural History, New York. Photocopy in Seton Library, Cimarron, N. Mex.

———. Manuscripts and Correspondence. Humanities Research Center (HRC), University of Texas, Austin, Tex.

———. Manuscripts and Correspondence. Huntington Library (HL), San Marino, Calif.

Seton, Ernest Thompson, and Julia Moss Seton. Papers. (SP). Seton Castle, Santa Fe, N. Mex., and Philmont Museum, Cimarron, N. Mex.

Seton, Grace Gallatin (Thompson). Papers. Sophia Smith Collection, Women's History Archive, Smith College, Northampton, Mass.

Seymour, George D. Papers. Yale University Library (YUL). New Haven, Conn.

Wilson, Francis C. Papers. New Mexico State Records Center and Archives (NMSRC), Santa Fe, N. Mex.

Dissertations

Macleod, David Irving. "Good Boys Made Better: The Boy Scouts of America, Boys' Brigades and YMCA Boys' Work, 1880–1920." Ph.D. dissertation, University of Wisconsin, 1973.

Whitmore, Allan Richard. "Beard, Boys and Buckskins: Daniel Carter Beard and the Preservation of the American Pioneer Tradition." Ph.D. dissertation, Northwestern University, 1970.

Wilson, Raymond. "Charles Alexander Eastman (Ohiyesa): Santee Sioux." Ph.D. dissertation, University of New Mexico, 1977.

Published Works of Ernest Thompson Seton

In 1925, Seton's publishers produced a bibliography (*Ernest Thompson Seton: A Biographical Sketch Done by Various Hands to Which Is Attached a Complete Bibliography of the Works of This Author* [Garden City, N.Y.: Doubleday, Page, 1925]), which contained several errors. The following list of Seton's published articles, notes, short stories, poems, books, and illustrations is complete with the possible exception of Seton's writings for the *Totem Board*, extant copies of which are extremely difficult to locate; the most comprehensive collection known is in the Library of Congress. Moreover, since many *Totem Board* articles are unsigned, it is difficult to determine which ones are attributable to Seton; therefore, only those articles from issues that I was able to find and examine are included. All Seton items are grouped under three headings: Contributions to Other Works, Articles and Short Stories, and Books; articles, short stories, and books are listed in alphabetical order by title, with the name Seton was using at the time shown in parentheses. Only the first editions of books have been cited, except where there has been a change in title or in content.

Contributions to Other Works

Bailey, Florence Augusta. *Birds of Village and Field*. Boston: Houghton, Mifflin, 1898. (Illustrations by Ernest Thompson Seton.)

Century Company. *The Century Dictionary: An Encyclopedic Lexicon of the English Language*. Compiled by William Dwight Whitney. 6 vols. New York: Century, 1889–91. (Illustrations by Ernest Thompson Seton.)

Chapman, Frank M. *Bird Life*. New York: Appleton, 1900. (Illustrations by Ernest Thompson Seton.)

————. *Handbook of Birds of Eastern North America*. New York: Appleton, 1895. (Illustrations by Ernest Thompson Seton.)

Charles Scribner's Sons. *Pictures by Popular American Artists Selected from "Scribner's Magazine."* New York: Scribner, 1900. (Illustrations by Ernest Thompson Seton.).

Grinnell, George Bird. "Climbing for White Goats." *Scribner's* 15 (May, 1894): 644–48. (Illustrations by Ernest Thompson Seton.)

————. "Wolves and Wolf Nature." In *Trail and Camp-Fire*. Edited by George Bird Grinnell and Theodore Roosevelt. (New York: Forest and Stream, 1897): 152–203. (Illustrations by Ernest Thompson Seton.)

Hoffman, Ralph. *Bird Portraits*. Boston: Ginn, 1901. (Illustrations by Ernest Thompson Seton.)

Hornaday, William T. "The Extermination of the American Bison, with a Sketch of Its Discovery and Life History." *Annual Report of the Board of Regents of the Smithsonian Institution, 1887: Report of the United States National Museum, Part II*. Washington, D.C.: GPO, 1889), 367–548. (Illustrations by Ernest Thompson Seton.)

Johnson, E. Pauline. *The Shagganappi*. Introduction by Ernest Thompson Seton. Toronto: William Briggs, 1913.

Macoun, John. *The Autobiography of John Macoun, M.A.* Introduction by Ernest Thompson Seton. Ottawa: Ottawa Field Naturalists' Club, 1922.

Medsger, Oliver Perry. *Edible Wild Plants*. Introduction by Ernest Thompson Seton. New York: Macmillan, 1939.

Nelson, E. W. "Larger North American Mammals." *National Geographic* 30 (November, 1916): 385–472. (Illustrations by Ernest Thompson Seton.)

————. "Smaller Mammals of North America." *National Geographic* 33 (May, 1918): 371–493. (Illustrations by Ernest Thompson Seton.)

————. *Wild Animals of North America*. Washington, D.C.: National Geographic Society, 1918. (Illustrations by Ernest Thompson Seton.)

Pratt, Alice Day. *Animals of a Sagebrush Ranch*. Foreword by Ernest Thompson Seton. New York: Rand McNally, 1938.

Stickney, J. H. *Bird World*. Boston: Ginn, 1898. (Illustrated by Ernest Thompson Seton.)

Wright, Mabel Osgood. *Four-Footed Americans and Their Kin*. Edited by Frank M. Chapman. New York: Macmillan, 1898. (Illustrations by Ernest Thompson Seton.)

Articles and Short Stories

"Achieving the Picturesque in Building." (Ernest Thompson Seton) *Country Life in America* 35 (October, 1918): 44–47.

"Acrobatic Skunks." (Ernest Thompson Seton) *Journal of Mammalogy* 1 (May, 1920): 140.

"Additions to the List of Manitoba Birds." (Ernest E. Thompson) *Auk* 10 (January, 1893): 49–50.

"An Amateur Circus I Once Gave." (Ernest Thompson Seton) *Ladies' Home Journal* 33 (September, 1916): 57.

"The American Bison or Buffalo." (Ernest Thompson Seton) *Scribner's* 40 (October, 1906): 385–405.

"The Angel of the Night." (Ernest Thompson Seton) *Totem Board* 11 (May, 1932): 231–32.

"The Annals of a Fur Farm, Chapter 1." (Ernest Thompson Seton) *Country Life in America* 23 (November, 1912): 38–40.

"The Annals of a Fur Farm, Chapter 2." (Ernest Thompson Seton) *Country Life in America* 23 (December, 1912): 61–62.

"The Annals of a Fur Farm, Chapter 3." (Ernest Thompson Seton) *Country Life in America* 23 (January, 1913): 30–32.

"The Arctic Prairies: Part 1, The Land of the Buffalo." (Ernest Thompson Seton) *Scribner's* 48 (November, 1910): 513–32.

"The Arctic Prairies: Part 2, The Land of the Caribou." (Ernest Thompson Seton) *Scribner's* 48 (December, 1910): 725–34.

"The Arctic Prairies: Part 3, The Land of the Caribou (cont'd.)" (Ernest Thompson Seton) *Scribner's* 49 (January, 1911): 61–72.

"The Arctic Prairies: Part 4, The Land of the Musk-Ox." (Ernest Thompson Seton) *Scribner's* 49 (February, 1911): 207–23.

"Arnaux, the Homing Pigeon." (Ernest Thompson Seton) *Ladies' Home Journal* 22 (April, 1905): 13–14.

"Around the Camp Fire: 1." (Ernest Thompson Seton) *Boys' Life* 3 (October, 1913): 13.

"Around the Camp Fire: 2." (Ernest Thompson Seton) *Boys' Life* 3 (December, 1913): 28.

"Around the Camp Fire: 3." (Ernest Thompson Seton) *Boys' Life* 4 (January, 1914): 20.

"Around the Camp Fire: 4." (Ernest Thompson Seton) *Boys' Life* 4 (March, 1914): 20.

"Around the Camp Fire: 5." (Ernest Thompson Seton) *Boys' Life* 4 (April, 1914): 23.

"Around the Camp Fire: 6." (Ernest Thompson Seton) *Boys' Life* 4 (May, 1914): 24.

"Around the Camp Fire: 7." (Ernest Thompson Seton) *Boys' Life* 4 (June, 1914): 26.

"Around the Camp Fire: 8." (Ernest Thompson Seton) *Boys' Life* 4 (September, 1914): 24.

"Around the Camp Fire: 9." (Ernest Thompson Seton) *Boys' Life* 4 (October, 1914): 16, 25.

"Around the Camp Fire: 10." (Ernest Thompson Seton) *Boys' Life* 4 (December, 1914): 24.

"The Badger Who Was Brother to a Boy." (Ernest Thompson Seton) *Boys' Life* 3 (November, 1913): 12–13, 34.

"Bannertail, the Story of a Gray Squirrel: Part 1." (Ernest Thompson Seton) *Ladies' Home Hournal* 39 (February, 1922): 13, 157–58.

"Bannertail, the Story of a Gray Squirrel: Part 2." (Ernest Thompson Seton) *Ladies' Home Journal* 39 (March, 1922): 141–42.

"Bannertail, the Story of a Gray Squirrel: Part 3." (Ernest Thompson Seton) *Ladies' Home Journal* 39 (April, 1922): 177–78.

"Bannertail, the Story of a Gray Squirrel: Part 4." (Ernest Thompson Seton) *Ladies' Home Journal* 39 (May, 1922): 149–50.

"The Baron and the Wolves." (Ernest Seton Thompson) *Forest and Stream* 47 (December 26, 1896): 504–506.

"Bear and Moose Queries." (Ernest E. T. Seton) *Forest and Stream* 26 (June 24, 1886): 427.

"Berry and the Mustang." (Ernest Thompson Seton) *Totem Board* 11 (September, 1932): 415–17.

"The Big Buck We Didn't Shoot." (Ernest E. Thompson) *Forest and Stream* 37 (September 10, 1891): 143.

"Billy, the Big Wolf: Part 1." (Ernest Thompson Seton) *Ladies' Home Journal* 22 (August, 1905): 5–6.

"Billy, the Big Wolf: Part 2." (Ernest Thompson Seton) *Ladies' Home Journal* 22 (September, 1905): 10, 49.

"The Biography of a Grizzly: Part 1, The Cubhood of Wahb." (Ernest Seton-Thompson) *Century* 59 (November, 1899): 25–40.

"The Biography of a Grizzly: Part 2, The Days of His Strength." (Ernest Seton-Thompson) *Century* 59 (December, 1899): 200–12.

"The Biography of a Grizzly: Part 3, The Waning of Wahb." (Ernest Seton-Thompson) *Century* 59 (January, 1900): 351–62.

"Bird Records from Great Slave Lake Region: A Preliminary List of Birds Observed by My 1907 Expedition into the Arctic Barren Grounds of Canada." (Ernest Thompson Seton) *Auk* 25 (January, 1908): 68–74.

"The Birds of Manitoba." (Ernest E. Thompson) *Proceedings of the United States National Museum* 13 (May 29, 1891): 457–643.

"The Birds of Western Manitoba." (Ernest E. T. Thompson) *Auk* 3 (April, 1886): 145–56.

"The Birds of Western Manitoba: Conclusion." (Ernest E. T. Thompson) *Auk* 3 (July, 1886): 320–29.

"The Birds of Western Manitoba: Addenda." (Ernest E. Thompson) *Auk* 3 (October, 1886): 453.

"The Birds That We See." (Ernest E. Thompson) *Scribner's Magazine* 13 (June, 1893): 759–76.

"Blazes and Indian Signs." (Ernest Thompson Seton) *Country Life in America* 7 (April, 1905): 632–34.

"Bobcats and Wild Turkeys." (Earnest Thompson Seton) *Journal of Mammalogy* 1 (May, 1920): 140.

"'Bow Skirmish' or 'Arrow Fight'" (Ernest Thompson Seton) *Forest and Stream* 79 (November 30, 1912): 693.

"The Boy Scouts in America." (Ernest Thompson Seton) *Outlook* 95 (July 23, 1910): 630–35.

"Boy Scout Initiations." (Ernest Thompson Seton) *Boys' Life* 3 (January, 1913): 19.

"Building a Log Cabin." (Ernest Thompson Seton) *Country Life in America* 8 (May, 1905): 79–80.

"Canadian Game and Fish Resorts." (Ernest E. Thompson) *Forest and Stream* 28 (February 10, 1887): 42–43.

"A Carberry Deer Hunt." (Ernest E. T. Seton) *Forest and Stream* 26 (June 3, 1886): 366–68.

"The Caribou and His Kindred." (Ernest Thompson Seton) *Scribner's* 39 (April, 1906): 426–43.

"Chanticleer vs. Egret." (Ernest Seton Thompson) *Forest and Stream* 49 (October 9, 1897): 283.

"Chicaree." (Ernest Thompson Seton) *World Outlook* 5 (December, 1919): 38–39.

"The Chillingham Bull." (Ernest Thompson Seton) *Totem Board* 12 (April, 1933): 131–38.

"Chink: The Development of a Pup." (Ernest Seton-Thompson) *Youth's Companion* 75 (January 17, 1901): 28–29.

"Coaly-Bay, the Outlaw Horse." (Ernest Thompson Seton) *Collier's* 56 (January 22, 1916): 10–11.

"Comments on the Art Anatomy of Animals." *Quartier Latin* 2 (1897): 177.

"Communication Regarding the Needs of Artists in the Zoological Park." (Ernest Seton Thompson) *First Annual Report of the New York Zoological Society.* New York: New York Zoological Society, 1897.

"Courtand, The King Wolf of France." (Ernest Thompson Seton) *Totem Board* 12 (December, 1933): 465–82.

"Critical Note on Mr. J. B. Tyrrell's Paper, Entitled 'Catalogue of the Mammalia of Canada Exclusive of the Cetacea.'" (Ernest E. Thompson) *Proceedings of the Canadian Institute* 7 (October, 1889): 178–80.

"Dipo: Sprite of the Desert." (Ernest Thompson Seton) *Century* 105 (November, 1922): 106–15.

"Directive Coloration of Birds." (Ernest Seton Thompson) *Auk* 14 (October, 1897): 395–96.

"Disappearance of Forest Birds." (Ernest E. Thompson) *Transactions of the Canadian Institute* 1 (1889–90): 47.

"Do Squirrels Hibernate?" (Ernest E. Thompson) *Forest and Stream* 28 (February 10, 1887): 65.

"Does the *Cuterebra* Ever Emasculate Its Host?" *Journal of Mammalogy* 1 (February, 1920): 94–95.

"Dogs of Song." (Ernest Thompson Seton) *Success Magazine* 10 (August, 1907): 537–39, 562–63.

"Domestication of the Buffalo." (Ernest E. T. Thompson) *Forest and Stream* 26 (July 8, 1886): 467.

"Domino Reynard of Goldur Town: Part 1." *Century* 77 (December, 1908): 208–219.

"Domino Reynard of Goldur Town: Part 2." (Ernest Thompson Seton) *Century* 77 (January, 1909): 374–89.

"Domino Reynard of Goldur Town: Part 3." (Ernest Thompson Seton) *Century* 77 (February, 1909): 545–54.

"The Drummer on Snowshoes." (Ernest E. Thompson) *St. Nicholas* 14 (April, 1887): 414–17.

"Early Bird Banding." (Ernest Thompson Seton) *Auk* 38 (October, 1921): 611.

"Elephant Hunting in New York." (Ernest Thompson Seton) *Four Track News* 9 (December, 1905): 469–70.

"Elkland, 1." (Ernest Seton Thompson) *Recreation* 7 (September, 1897): 199–201.

"Elkland, 2: The Beaver Pond." (Ernest Seton Thompson) *Recreation* 7 (October, 1897): 286–90.

"Elkland, 3: Old-Timers." (Ernest Seton Thompson) *Recreation* 7 (November, 1897): 369–72.

"Elkland, 4: Flies and Weather." (Ernest Seton Thompson) *Recreation* 7 (December, 1897): 456–57.

"Elkland, 5: Puss and the Bear." (Ernest Seton Thompson) *Recreation* 8 (January, 1898): 33–34.

"Elkland, 6: Duels." (Ernest Seton Thompson) *Recreation* 8 (February, 1898): 117–19.

"Emergency Foods in the Northern Forest." (Ernest Thompson Seton), *Country Life in America* 6 (September, 1904): 438–40.

"English Names of Mammals." (Ernest Thompson Seton) *Journal of Mammalogy* 1 (February, 1920): 104–105.

"Ernest Thompson Seton's Boys: Part 1, Trailing." (Ernest Thompson Seton) *Ladies' Home Journal* 19 (May, 1902): 15, 41.

"Ernest Thompson Seton's Boys: Part 2, The Second Chapter on Tracks." (Ernest Thompson Seton) *Ladies' Home Journal* 19 (June, 1902): 15.

"Ernest Thompson Seton's Boys: Part 3, Playing 'Injun.'" (Ernest Thompson Seton) *Ladies' Home Journal* 19 (July, 1902): 17.

"Ernest Thompson Seton's Boys: Part 4, Archery." (Ernest Thompson Seton) *Ladies' Home Journal* 19 (August, 1902): 16.

"Ernest Thompson Seton's Boys: Part 5, Teepees." (Ernest Thompson Seton) *Ladies' Home Journal* 19 (September, 1902): 15.

"Ernest Thompson Seton's Boys: Part 6, Woodcraft Indians and Getting Lost." (Ernest Thompson Seton) *Ladies' Home Journal* 19 (October, 1902): 14.

"Ernest Thompson Seton's Boys: Part 7, Freezing." (Ernest Thompson Seton) *Ladies' Home Journal* 19 (November, 1902): 15.

"Evening and Pine Grosbeaks in Ontario." (Ernest E. Thompson) *Auk* 7 (April, 1890): 211.

"The Evolutionary Force of a Wide Range." (Ernest Thompson Seton) *Journal of Mammalogy* 3 (August, 1922): 167–69.

"An Exhibition of Snakes." (Ernest E. Thompson) *Forest and Stream* 28 (June 16, 1887): 451.

"Fable and Woodmyth: Part 1." (Ernest Thompson Seton) *Century* 67 (November, 1903): 35–39.

"Fable and Woodmyth: Part 2." (Ernest Thompson Seton) *Century* 67 (December, 1903): 276–79.

"Fable and Woodmyth: Part 3." (Ernest Thompson Seton) *Century* 67 (January, 1904): 346–51.

"Fable and Woodmyth: Part 4." (Ernest Thompson Seton) *Century* 67 (February, 1904): 496–500.

"Fable and Woodmyth: Part 5." (Ernest Thompson Seton) *Century* 67 (March, 1904): 750–56.

"The Fantail, Flagtail, or Gazelle Deer, *Odocoileus texanus*. Mearns." (Ernest Thompson Seton) *Recreation* 10 (January, 1899): 59–60.

"Fauna of Manitoba." (Ernest Thompson Seton) In *British Association Handbook*. Winnipeg: British Association, 1909.

"A Fifth Avenue Troubadour." (Ernest Seton-Thompson) *Ladies' Home Journal* 18 (October, 1901): 13–14.

"First *Sialia sialis* at Lorne Park." (Ernest E. Thompson.) *Transactions of the Canadian Institute* 1 (1889–90): 56.

"Food of the Red Fox." (Ernest Thompson Seton) *Journal of Mammalogy* 1 (May, 1920): 140.

"For a Methodic Study of Life Histories of Mammals." (Ernest Thompson Seton) *Journal of Mammalogy* 1 (February, 1920): 67–69.

"Forest Secrets—The Soul Song of Baba-Moss-Anib." (Ernest Thompson Seton) *Country Life in America* 20 (July, 1911): 39–42, 66, 68.

"Further Annals of a Hollow Tree." (Ernest Thompson Seton) *Country Life in America* 22 (October, 1912): 64, 66.

"The Goldenrod." (Ernest E. Thompson) *Our Animal Friends* 21 (August, 1894): 280–81.

"Gray Squirrels and Nuts." (Ernest Thompson Seton) *Journal of Mammalogy* 2 (November, 1921): 41.

"The Great North West." (Ernest E. T. Seton) *Herts and Essex Observer* March 24, 1883.

"A Greeting From the Chief Scout." (Ernest Thompson Seton) *Boys' Life* 4 (January, 1914): 2.

"The Habits of Wolves: Including Many Facts about Animal Marriage." (Ernest Thompson Seton) *American Magazine* 64 (October, 1907): 636–45.

"Hank and Jeff." (Ernest Thompson Seton) *Totem Board* 11 (July–August, 1932): 315–20, 370–74.

"Hibernation of the Hare." (Ernest E. Thompson) *Forest and Stream* 28 (April 7, 1887): 226.

"The Hollow Tree." (Ernest Thompson Seton) *Bird-Lore* 11 (January, 1909): 1–3; *Country Life in America* 20 (September, 1911): 88.

"Holy Smoke!" (Ernest Thompson Seton) *Rotarian* 45 (August, 1934): 9–11), 57.

"A Horned Cow Elk." (Ernest Seton Thompson) *Forest and Stream* 48 (February 20, 1897): 145.

"The House That Is Mine." (Ernest Thompson Seton) *House and Garden* 44 (October, 1923): 62, 63, 112, 114, 116.

"How Bull-Fighting Was Suppressed in France." (Ernest E. S. Thompson) *Our Animal Friends* 24 (February, 1897): 128–29.

"How Long Do Animals Live?" (Ernest Thompson Seton) *Ladies' Home Journal* 27 (August, 1910): 6.

"How the Giant Cactus Came." (Ernest Thompson Seton) *Totem Board* 10 (May, 1927): 3–4.

"How the New Slang Came." (Ernest Thompson Seton) *Totem Board* 12 (February, 1933): 51–61.

"How to Get Cool Water." (Ernest Thompson Seton) *Boys' Life* 3 (May, 1913): 17.

"How to Make a Fire by Rubbing Sticks." (Ernest Thompson Seton) *Country Life in America* 6 (June, 1904): 145–46, 204.

"How to Study a Bird." (Ernest Thompson Seton) *Bird-Lore* 6 (November–December, 1904): 181–84.

"How to Stuff a Bird." (Ernest Thompson Seton) *Country Life in America* 6 (July, 1904): 267–69.

"How Wapoos Won His Rifle." (Ernest Thompson Seton) *Totem Board* 12 (June, 1933): 215–19.

"Hunting with the Camera." (Ernest Thompson Seton) *Recreation* 8 (April, 1898): 263–64.

"Hybrid *Pinicola enncleator + Carpidacus purpureus*." (Ernest E. Thompson) *Auk* 11 (January, 1894): 1–3.

"If Da Vinci Came to Town." (Ernest Thompson Seton) *American City* 5 (November, 1911): 252–54.

"The Indian Sign Language for Boy Scouts." (Ernest Thompson Seton) *Boys' Life* 3 (February, 1913): 15.

"Indian Words in Common Use." (Ernest Thompson Seton) *Forest and Stream* (July 8, 1911): 55.

"The Injun's Christmas Spree." (Ernest Seton Thompson) *International*, January, 1899, pp. 35–36.

"Intercommunication of Wolves." (Ernest Seton Thompson) *Forest and Stream* 48 (January 23, 1897): 64–65.

"Interesting Records from Toronto, Canada." (Ernest E. T. Seton) *Auk* 2 (October, 1885): 334–37.

"An Interview with Whitman's Spirit." (Ernest Seton Thompson) *Recreation* 6 (June, 1897): 480.

"Is Our Fur Supply in Danger?" (Ernest Thompson Seton) *World's Work* 47 (March, 1924): 491–502.

"Is the World's Fur Supply in Danger?" (Ernest Thompson Seton) *World Today* 45 (February, 1925): 200–203.

"The Jaguar in Colorado." (Ernest Thompson Seton) *Journal of Mammalogy* 1 (November, 1920): 241.

"Johnny Bear." (Ernest Seton-Thompson) *Scribner's Magazine* 28 (December, 1900): 658–71.

"Joy Comes with a Job Well Done." (Ernest Thompson Seton) *New York American*, November 8, 1922, 10.

"The Kangaroo Rat." (Ernest Seton-Thompson) *Scribner's* 27 (April, 1900): 418–27.

"The King of Currumpaw: A Wolf Story." (Ernest E. Thompson) *Scribner's* 16 (November, 1894): 618–28.

"Krag, the Kootenay Ram: Part 1." (Ernest Seton-Thompson) *Scribner's* 29 (June, 1901): 693–707.

"Krag, the Kootenay Ram: Part 2." (Ernest Seton-Thompson) *Scribner's* 30 (July, 1901): 43–51.

"Krag, the Kootenay Ram." (Ernest Thompson Seton) *Reader's Digest* 79 (July, 1961): 162–65.

"La Bête, the Beast Wolf of Gevandan." (Ernest Thompson Seton) *Totem Board* 13 (March–April, 1934): 83–93, 123–32.

"The Last of the Irish Wolves." (Ernest Thompson Seton) *Totem Board* 12 (September, 1933): 335–41.

"Laws of the Seton Indians." (Ernest Thompson Seton) *Association Boys* 4 (June, 1905): 99–108.

"A Legend of the Bloodroot." (Ernest Seton-Thompson) 36 (May, 1900): 177.

"The Legend of the White Reindeer. (Ernest Seton-Thompson) *Century* 63 (November, 1901): 79–89.

"The Leopard Lover." (Ernest Thompson Seton) *Totem Board* 13 (January–February, 1934): 3–8, 43–48.

"*Linota cannabrua* at Toronto." (Ernest E. Thompson) *Transactions of the Canadian Institute* 1 (1889–90): 54–55.

"A List of Fishes Known to Occur in Manitoba." (Ernest Seton-Thompson) *Forest and Stream* 51 (September 10, 1898): 214.

"A List of the Big Game in North America." (Ernest Seton Thompson) *Forest and Stream* 51 (October 8, 1898): 285–86.

"A List of the Mammals of Manitoba." (Ernest E. Thompson) *Transactions of the Manitoba Historical and Scientific Society* 23 (May, 1886): 1–26.

"A List of the Turtles, Snakes and Batrachians of Manitoba." (Ernest Thompson Seton) *Ottawa Naturalist* 32 (November, 1918): 79–83.

"Little Burnt All-Over." (Ernest Thompson Seton) *American Girl* 8 (April, 1924): 5, 6, 7, 26, 27.

"Little Marie and the Wolves." (Ernest Thompson Seton) *Totem Board* 12 (July, 1933): 255–62.

"Little Warhorse: The Story of a Jack Rabbit." (Ernest Thompson Seton) *Ladies' Home Journal* 21 (June, 1904): 13–14.

"Lobo." (Ernest Thompson Seton) *Golden Book* 12 (July, 1930): 58–65.

"Lobo, King of the Currumpaw." (Ernest Thompson Seton) *Reader's Digest* 41 (November, 1942): 103–106.

"Locality, Date and Name with Observations." (Ernest Thompson Seton) *Journal of Mammology* 1 (February, 1920): 107.

"The Lovers and the Shining One: A Prose Poem." (Ernest Thompson Seton) *Scribner's* 61 (June, 1917): 751–53.

"Lure of the Wild: The Story of a Dog." (Ernest Thompson Seton) *Coronet* 36 (September, 1954): 123–28.

"The Mackenzie River Ghost." (Ernest Thompson Seton) *Boys' Life* 28 (December, 1938): 16–17.

"The Magpie as Sentinel for Rabbits." (Ernest Thompson Seton) *Journal of Mammalogy* 3 (May, 1922): 119.

"Making a Hollow Tree and What Came into It: Bulletin 1." (Ernest Thompson Seton) *Country Life in America* 15 (November, 1908): 47. 84.

"Making a Hollow Tree and What Came into It: Bulletin 2." (Ernest Thompson Seton) *Country Life in America* 15 (December, 1908): 226.

"Making a Hollow Tree and What Came into It: Bulletin 3." (Ernest Thompson Seton) *Country Life in America* 15 (January, 1909): 310.

"Making a Hollow Tree and What Came into It: Bulletin 4." (Ernest Thompson Seton) *Country Life in America* 15 (February, 1909): 414.

"Making a Hollow Tree and What Came into It: Bulletin 5." (Ernest Thompson Seton) *Country Life in America* 15 (March, 1909): 542.

"Making a Hollow Tree and What Came into It: Bulletin 6." (Ernest Thompson Seton) *Country Life in America* 15 (April, 1909): 658, 660, 662, 664.

"Making a Hollow Tree and What Came into It: Bulletin 7." (Ernest Thompson Seton) *Country Life in America* 16 (July, 1909): 354, 356.

"Making a Hollow Tree and What Came into It: Bulletin 8." (Ernest Thompson Seton) *Country Life in America* 16 (August, 1909): 455.

"Making a Hollow Tree and What Came into It: Bulletin 9." (Ernest Thompson Seton) *Country Life in America* 16 (September, 1909): 552.

"Making a Hollow Tree and What Came into It: Bulletin 10." (Ernest Thompson Seton) *Country Life in America* 16 (October, 1909): 662.

"Making Permanent Records of Animal Tracks." (Ernest Thompson Seton) *Country Life in America* (June, 1905): 228–29.

"The Making of Silly Billy." (Ernest Thompson Seton) *National Sunday Magazine*, January 23, 1916, p. 620.

"Mammals of the Yellowstone Park." (Ernest Seton-Thompson) *Recreation* 8 (May, 1898): 365–71.

"The Mane on the Tail of the Gray Fox." (Ernest Thompson Seton) *Journal of Mammology* 4 (August, 1923): 180–82.

"A Manitoban Blizzard." (Ernest E. T. Seton) In Robert Miller Christy, ed., *Manitoba Described*, pp. 57–58. London: Wyman and Sons, 1885.

"Manitoban Notes." (Ernest E. T. Seton) *Auk* 2 (January, 1885): 21–24.

"The Master Plowman of the West." (Ernest Thompson Seton) *Century* 68 (June, 1904): 300–307.

"The Merry Chipmunk." (Ernest Thompson Seton) *Success* 10 (May, 1907): 328–31, 368–70.

"The Message of the Redman." (Ernest Thompson Seton) *Totem Board* 11 (January, 1932): 6–36.

"Migrations of the Gray Squirrel (*Sciurus carolinensis*)." (Ernest Thompson Seton) *Journal of Mammalogy* 1 (February, 1920): 53–58.

"Modern Adaptations." (Ernest Thompson Seton) *Totem Board* 11 (February, 1932): 86–87.

"The Mole-Mouse, Potato-Mouse, or Pine-Mouse." (Ernest Thompson Seton) *Journal of Mammology* 1 (August, 1920): 185.

"Monarch the Grizzly: Part 1." (Ernest Thompson Seton) *Ladies' Home Journal* 21 (February, 1904): 5–6, 47.

"Monarch the Grizzly: Part 2." (Ernest Thompson Seton) *Ladies' Home Journal* 21 (March, 1904): 13–14.

"Monarch the Grizzly: Part 3."(Ernest Thompson Seton) *Ladies' Home Journal* 21 (April, 1904): 15–16, 60.

"Moose and Bear Queries."(Ernest E. T. Seton) *Forest and Stream* 26 (June 24, 1886): 427.

"The Moose and His Antlers." (Ernest Thompson Seton) *Scribner's* 39 (February, 1906): 157–78.

"More about the Scream (of the Panther). (Ernest E. Thompson) *Forest and Stream* 39 (November 17, 1892): 421.

"More about the Yak." (Ernest Thompson Seton) *Country Life in America* 21 (December, 1911): 44.

"More Acrobatic Skunks." (Ernest Thompson Seton) *Journal of Mammology* 3 (February, 1922): 53.

"More Wild Animals I Have Known: The Boy and the Lynx." (Ernest Thompson Seton) *Ladies' Home Journal* 20 (November, 1903): 13–14.

"Mother Love in the Cows of the Western Range." (Ernest Seton-Thompson) *Breeder's Gazette* 38 (December 19, 1900): 947–48.

"The Mother Teal and the Overland Route." (Ernest Seton-Thompson) *Ladies' Home Journal* (July, 1901): 5–6.

"The Myth of the Song Sparrow." (Ernest Seton Thompson) *Bird-Lore* 1 (April, 1899): 59.

"The Narrowest Escape I Ever Had from a Wild Beast." (Ernest Thompson Seton) *Farm and Fireside* 46 (January, 1922): 13, 34, 35, 37.

"The Nation Awaits a Song." (Ernest Thompson Seton) *New York Tribune*, December 1, 1918.

"The National Zoo at Washington: Part 1." (Ernest Seton Thompson) *Century* 59 (March, 1900): 649–60.

"The National Zoo at Washington: Part 2." (Ernest Seton Thompson) *Century* 60 (May, 1900): 1–10

"The National Zoo at Washington: A Study of Its Animals in Relation to Their Natural Environment." (Ernest Thompson Seton) *Annual Report of the Board of Regents of the Smithsonian Institution, 1901*, 697–716. Washington, D.C.: GPO, 1902.

"The Natural History of the Ten Commandments." (Ernest Thompson Seton) *Century* 75 (November, 1907): 24–33.

"Nature and Human Nature." (Ernest Thompson Seton) *Nature* 3 (May, 1924): 279–80, 318.

"Nest and Eggs of the Philadelphia Vireo." (Ernest E. T. Seton) *Auk* 2 (July, 1885): 305–306.

"Nest and Habits of the Connecticut Warbler (*Oporornis agilis*) (Ernest E. T. Thompson) *Auk* 1 (April, 1884): 192–93.

"A New Deer Hunt with the Bow." (Ernest Thompson Seton) *Country Life in America* 7 (February, 1905): 370–71.

"New Music from the Old Harp." (Ernest Seton-Thompson) *Century* 60 (August, 1900): 639.

"The New Sportsman." (Ernest Seton Thompson) *Recreation* 10 (January, 1899): 39–40.

"Nights with the Coons." (Ernest E. Thompson) *Forest and Stream* 30 (July 19, 1888): 518–20.

"Not Caught Yet." (Ernest E. Thompson) *Our Animal Friends* 21 (December, 1893): 89.

"Notes for Observation of Habits of Birds." (Ernest Seton Thompson) *Osprey* 4 (September, 1899): 6–8.

"Notes of a Trip to Manitoba: Part 1." (Ernest E. Thompson) *Forest and Stream* 41 (November 18, 1893): 424–25.

"Notes of a Trip to Manitoba: Part 2." (Ernest E. Thompson) *Forest and Stream* 41 (November 25, 1893): 446–48.

"Notes on Snapper." (Ernest Thompson Seton) *Forest and Stream* 90 (September, 1920): 499.

"Notes on the Breeding Habits of Captive Deermice." (Ernest Thompson Seton) *Journal of Mammology* 1 (May, 1920): 134–38.

"Notes on the English Sparrow." (Ernest E. Thompson) *Forest and Stream* 30 (April 5, 1888): 204–205.

"Occurrence of the Evening Grosbeak (*Coccothraustes vespertina*) at Toronto, Canada." (Ernest E. Thompson) *Auk* 4 (July, 1887): 256–57.

"Occurrence of the Least Weasel (*Mustela rixora*) near Denver." (Ernest Thompson Seton) *Journal of Mammology* 14 (February, 1933): 70.

"The Oldest of all Writing—Tracks." (Ernest Thompson Seton) *Country Life in America* 17 (December, 1909): 169–73, 242, 244, 246, 248, 250.

"On Architecture." (Ernest E. T. Seton) *Toronto Truth*, April 4, 1885.

"On Journal Keeping." (Ernest Thompson Seton) *Bird-Lore* 4 (November–December, 1902): 175–76.

"On Nature Study." (Ernest Seton-Thompson) In *The Library of Natural History*. Edited by Richard Lydekker, pp. iii–vii. New York: Saalfield, 1904.

"On the Popular Names of Birds." (Ernest Thompson Seton) *Auk* 28 (April, 1919): 229–35.

"On the Study of Scatology." (Ernest Thompson Seton) *Journal of Mammalogy* 6 (February, 1925): 47–49.

"On the Use of Faunal Lists." (Ernest E. Thompson) *Proceedings of the Canadian Institute* 7 (1888–89); 275–80.

"Ontario Game Laws." (Ernest E. Thompson) *Forest and Stream* 30 (March 29, 1888): 185.

"Organized Boyhood: The Boy Scout Movement, Its Purposes and Its Laws." (Ernest Thompson Seton) *Success* 13 (December, 1910): 804, 805, 843, 849.

"The Origin of Dick Cissel." (Ernest Seton-Thompson) *Bird-Lore* 2 (June, 1900): 88.

"Our Canadian Birds: Paper 1." (Ernest E. T. Seton) *Canadian Science Monthly* 1 (June, 1884): 55–57.

"Our Canadian Birds: Paper 2." (Ernest E. T. Seton) *Canadian Science Monthly* 1 (July–August, 1884): 74–78.

"Our Canadian Birds: Paper 3." (Ernest E. T. Seton) *Canadian Science Monthly* 1 (September, 1884): 108–12.

"Our Canadian Birds: Paper 4." (Ernest E. T. Seton) *Canadian Science Monthly* 1 (October, 1884): 130–35.

"Our Canadian Birds: Paper 5." (Ernest E. T. Seton) *Canadian Science Monthly* 2 (February, 1885): 19–21.

"Outlines of Ornithology." (Ernest E. T. Seton) *Proceedings of the Canadian Institute* 3 (June, 1886): 180.

"The Ovenbird." (Ernest E. Thompson) *St. Nicholas* 17 (April, 1890): 520–21.

"Owner Sticks." (Ernest Thompson Seton) *Totem Board* 11 (December, 1932): 537–39.

"The Pack Rat." (Ernest E. S. Thompson) *Quartier Latin* 1 (1896): 25.

"Peace and Patrol Names." (Ernest Thompson Seton) *Boys' Life* 3 (January, 1913): 21.

"The Peace Daughters of King Capilano." (Ernest Thompson Seton) *Totem Board* 11 (November, 1932): 517–25.

"The Pintail." (Ernest E. Thompson) *St. Nicholas* 15 (September, 1888): 826–27.

"Playing Pretend." (Ernest E. Thompson) *Our Animal Friends* 23 (November, 1895): 65–66.

"Plumes from the Thunder Bird: The Redman's Message." (Ernest Thompson Seton) *Totem Board* 12 (May, 1933): 203–205.

"Poem Addressed to a Brass Paper Weight in the Form of a Mouse." (Ernest Seton Thompson) *Recreation* 8 (February, 1898): 153.

"A Poetic Exchange of Compliments." (Ernest Seton Thompson) *Recreation* 10 (February, 1899): 106.

"Poison Ivy." (Ernest Thompson Seton) *Boys' Life* 3 (July, 1913): 31.

"The Porcupine at Home." (Ernest Thompson Seton) *Country Life in America* 17 (February, 1910): 415–16.

"Practical Fur Farming: Part 1." (Ernest Thompson Seton) *Field and Stream* 18 (March, 1914): 1146–51.

"Practical Fur Farming: Part 2, The Care and Feeding of Skunks." (Ernest Thompson Seton) *Field and Stream* 18 (April, 1914): 1299–1302.

"Practical Fur Farming: Part 3, The Diseases and Breeding of Skunks." (Ernest Thompson Seton) *Field and Stream* 19 (May, 1914): 19–24.

"Practical Fur Farming: Part 4, Marking and Disarming." (Ernest Thompson Seton) *Field and Stream* 19 (July, 1914): 296–99.

"Practical Fur Farming: Part 5, Marketing Skins." (Ernest Thompson Seton) *Field and Stream* 19 (August, 1914): 391–94.

"Practical Fur Farming: Part 6, Mink Farming, with a Foot Note on Skunk Raising." (Ernest Thompson Seton) *Field and Stream* 19 (November, 1914): 746–51.

"Practical Fur Farming: Part 7, Marten Farming." (Ernest Thompson Seton) *Field and Stream* 19 (January, 1915): 923–25.

"The Prairie Chicken." (Ernest E. T. Seton) *Transactions of the Manitoba Historical and Scientific Society* 14 (May, 1884): 13–18.

"The Prairie Chicken or Sharptailed Grouse, *Pedioecetes phasianellus* (Baird)." (Ernest E. T. Seton) *Proceedings of the Canadian Institute* 1 (1879–83): 405–12.

"The Prairie Dogs (*Cynomys ludovicianus*) at Washington Zoo." (Ernest Thompson Seton) *Journal of Mammalogy* 7 (August, 1926): 229–30.

"Prairie Fires." (Ernest E. T. Seton) In *Annual Report of the Manitoba Department of Agriculture and Statistics, 1883*, 491–92. Winnipeg: Queen's Printer, 1883.

"Prairie Fires." (Ernest E. T. Seton) *Transactions of the Manitoba Historical and Scientific Society* (March, 1884): 13–14.

"Preliminary Description of a New Caribou. *Rangifer montanus*." (Ernest Seton-Thompson) *Ottawa Naturalist* 13 (August, 1899): 129–30.

"The Prong-Horned Antelope." (Ernest Thompson Seton) *Scribner's* 40 (July, 1906): 33–49.

"The Protection of Birds in France." (Ernest E. Seton Thompson) *Our Animal Friends* 26 (November, 1898): 56–58.

"Raising Fur-Bearing Animals for Profit." *Country Life in America* 9 (January, 1906): 294–97.

"*Rangifer dawsoni*, Preliminary Description of a New Caribou from Queen Charlotte's Islands." (Ernest Seton-Thompson) *Ottawa Naturalist* 13 (February, 1900) 257–61.

"Rare Birds in Toronto University Museum." (Ernest E. Thompson) *Transactions of the Canadian Institute* 1 (1889–90); 55–56.

"The Rat and the Rattlers." (Ernest Thompson Seton) *Totem Board* 12 (March, 1933): 109–13.

"Recent Bird Records for Manitoba." (Ernest Thompson Seton) *Auk* 25 (October, 1908):450–54.

"Recognition Marks of Birds." (Ernest Seton-Thompson) *Bird-Lore* 3 (November-December 1901): 187–89.

"A Record of Failures: Part 1." (Ernest E. Thompson) *Forest and Stream* 28 (March 24, 1887): 178–79.

"A Record of Failures: Part 2." (Ernest E. Thompson) *Forest and Stream* 28 (March 31, 1887): 198.

"Reply to a Puritan's Denunciation of *The Decameron*." (Ernest E. S. Thompson) *Quartier Latin* 2 (1897): 210.

"Reply to Mr. Tyrrell's Note." (Ernest E. Thompson) *Proceedings of Canadian Institute* 7 (1888–89): 285–86.

"Report of the Occurrence of the Evening Grosbeak (*Coccothraustes vespertina*) in Ontario during the Winter of 1889–90." (Ernest E. Thompson) *Transactions of the Canadian Institute* 3 (December, 1892): 111.

"Review of Stanley Vestal's *Sitting Bull*." (Ernest Thompson Seton) *Totem Board* 12 (May, 1933): 207–208.

"The Revival of the Bow and Arrow." (Ernest Thompson Seton) *Country Life in America* 7 (January, 1905): 273–75.

"Rincon, or the Call in the Night." (Ernest Thompson Seton) *Totem Board* 12 (August, 1933): 295–303.

"The Road to Fairyland." (Ernest Thompson Seton) *St. Nicholas* 31 (December, 1903): 103.

"The Rocky Mountain Goat." (Ernest Thompson Seton) In *Records of North American Big Game*. Edited by Prentiss N. Gray. New York: Derrydale Press, 1932.

"A Roving Band of Say's Bats." (Ernest Thompson Seton) *Journal of Mammology* 3 (February, 1922): 52.

"The Ruminants of the North-West." (Ernest E. T. Seton) *Proceedings of the Canadian Institute* 3 (February, 1886): 113–17.

Thompson, Ernest Seton. "A School of Animal Painting and Sculpture in the New York Zoological Park." (Ernest Seton Thompson) In *Second Annual Report of the New York Zoological Society*, 69–75. New York: New York Zoological Society, 1898.

"Scouting: Number 1." (Ernest Thompson Seton) *American Boy* 12 (July, 1911): 5,21.

"Scouting: Number 2." (Ernest Thompson Seton) *American Boy* 12 (August, 1911): 4–5.

"Scouting: Number 3." (Ernest Thompson Seton) *American Boy* 12 (September, 1911): 3–4.

"Scouting: Number 4." (Ernest Thompson Seton) *American Boy* 12 (October, 1911): 3–4.

"Scouting: Number 5." (Ernest Thompson Seton) *American Boy* 12 (November, 1911): 6, 29.

"Scouting: Number 6." (Ernest Thompson Seton) *American Boy* 12 (December, 1911): 3, 31.

"Scouting: Number 7." (Ernest Thompson Seton) *American Boy* 13 (January, 1912): 3, 31.

"Scouting: Number 8." (Ernest Thompson Seton) *American Boy* 13 (February, 1912)" 3, 26.

"Scouting: Number 9." (Ernest Thompson Seton) *American Boy* 13 (March, 1912): 3, 27.

"Scouting: Number 10." (Ernest Thompson Seton) *American Boy* 13 (April, 1912): 7, 27.

"Scouting on the Train." (Ernest Thompson Seton) *Boys' Life* 3 (May, 1913): 22.

"The Screech-Owl." (Ernest E. Thompson) *St. Nicholas* 17 (March, 1890): 432–33.

"The Sea Mink, *Mustela macrodon* (Prentiss)." (Ernest Thompson Seton) *Journal of Mammalogy* 2 (August, 1921): 168.

"The Sea Otter." (Ernest Thompson Seton) In *The Book of Naturalists: An Anthology of the Best Natural History*. Edited by William Beebe. New York: Knopf, 1945.

"The Seeing Eye—Wildwood Food." (Ernest Thompson Seton) *Totem Board* 12 (July, 1933): 286.

"The Secrets of the Trail." (Ernest Thompson Seton) *Country Life in America* 8 (June, 1905): 202–205.

"Shishoka." (Ernest Thompson Seton) *Boys' Life* 35 (February, 1945): 8–9, 40.

"Silverspot." (Ernest E. Thompson) *Scribner's* 23 (February, 1898): 212–18.

"The Singing Hawk." (Ernest Thompson Seton) *Totem Board* 10 (May, 1927): 5.

"The Slum Cat." (Ernest Thompson Seton) *Ladies' Home Journal* 21 (August, 1904): 9–10.

"The Small Sanctuary." (Ernest Thompson Seton) *Totem Board* 13 (January, 1934): 17–21.

"Smoke Signals, Sign Talk and Totems." (Ernest Thompson Seton) *Boys' Life* 2 (December, 1912): 24.

"Snap, the Bull-Terrier: The Story of a Christmas Dog." (Ernest Thompson Seton) *Ladies' Home Journal* 21 (December, 1903): 10, 49.

"The Snow-Shoe Rabbit." (Ernest Thompson Seton) *Everybody's* 16 (May, 1907): 599–608.

"Some Famous Wolves of France." (Ernest Seton-Thompson) *Collier's* 26 (October, 1900): 6.

"Some More about Wolves." (Ernest Seton Thompson) *Forest and Stream* 48 (March 6, 1897): 183–84.

"Some Prints of Leaves." (Ernest Thompson Seton) *Nature* 2 (September, 1923): 142–43, 191.

"The Song of the Porcupine (*Erethizon epixanthum*)." (Ernest Thompson Seton) *Journal of Mammalogy* 13 (May, 1932): 168–69.

"The Song of the Prairie Lark." (Ernest E. Thompson) *American* 7 (April, 1888): 717–20.

"The Song Sparrow: An Investigation of His Life History." (Ernest E. Thompson) *Forest and Stream* 30 (April 19, 1888): 244.

"The Spirit of the Woods." (Ernest Thompson Seton) *Century* 103 (December, 1921): 213–24.

"Spiritual Thrift, Number 2: Helping to Develop Democracy with Nature's Aid through the Woodcraft League." (Ernest Thompson Seton) *Touchstone* 1 (June, 1917): 119–22.

"'Sport' in France, 1." (Ernest E. Thompson) *Forest and Stream* 38 (June 16, 1892): 560.

"'Sport' in France, 2." (Ernest E. Thompson) *Forest and Stream* 38 (June 23, 1892): 586.

"'Sport' in France, 3." (Ernest E. Thompson) *Forest and Stream* 38 (June 30, 1892): 611.

"Spring Notes." (Ernest E. Thompson) *Transactions of the Canadian Institute* 1 (1889–90): 60.

"Stories on the Tree Trunks." (Ernest Thompson Seton) *Country Life in America* 6 (May, 1904): 37–39, 90.

"The Story of Atalapha, a Winged Brownie." (Ernest Thompson Seton) *Scribner's* 59 (April, 1916): 441–58.

"The Story of Carrots." (Ernest Thompson Seton) *Farm and Fireside* 47 (June, 1923): 12, 13, 30, 31, 33.

"The Story of Coaly-Bay." (Ernest Thompson Seton) *May Court*, February, 1909, pp. 5–11.

"The Story of Two Pots." (Ernest Thompson Seton) *Totem Board* 11 (May, 1932): 197–99.

"The Story of Wyndygoul." (Ernest Thompson Seton) *Country Life in America* 16 (August, 1909): 399–404, 446, 448, 450.

"The Story of Wyndygoul." (Ernest Thompson Seton) *Country Life in America* 16 (September, 1909): 505–508, 540, 542, 544.

"The Strange Animals of Tibet." (Ernest E. Thompson) *Forest and Stream*, 42 (April 14, 1894): 311–312.

"Strawberry Finch." (Ernest E. Thompson) *Transactions of the Canadian Institute* 1 (1889–90): 41–42.

"The Striped Gopher, *Spermophilus tredecemilineatus* (Mitchell)." (Ernest E. T. Seton) In *Annual Report of the Manitoba Department of Agriculture and Statistics, 1882*, 169–72. Winnipeg: Queen's Printer, 1882.

"*Sturnella magna* Wintering near Toronto." (Ernest E. Thompson) *Transactions of the Canadian Institute* 1 (1889–90): 42.

"The Swallow-Tailed Flycatcher in Manitoba and at York Factory." (Ernest E. T. Seton) *Auk* 2 (April, 1885): 218.

"Tail Glands of the *Canidae*." (Ernest Thompson Seton) *Journal of Mammology* 3 (August, 1923): 180–82.

"Thanksgiving and the Yule-Log." (Ernest Thompson Seton) *Country Life in America* 19 (November, 1910): 37.

"They're Still Wild in Spots." (Ernest Thompson Seton) *Collier's* 76 (August 1, 1925): 12–13.

"The Timmer-Doodle." (Ernest Seton Thompson) *Recreation* 7 (December, 1897): 445–46.

"Tito: The Story of a Coyote That Learned How: Part 1." (Ernest Seton-Thompson) *Scribner's* 28 (August, 1900): 131–45.

"Tito: The Story of a Coyote That Learned How: Part 2." (Ernest Seton-Thompson) *Scribner's* 28 (September, 1900): 316–25.

"To 'Jim.' (Ernest Seton-Thompson) *Outing* 36 (April, 1900): 44.

"Tracks in the Snow." (Ernest E. Thompson) *St. Nicholas* 15 (March, 1888): 338–41.

"The Trail of the Sandhill Stag." (Ernest Thompson Seton) *Scribner's* 26 (August, 1899): 191–204.

"The Troth Plighting of Desmos and White Lion." (Ernest Thompson Seton) *Totem Board* 12 (June, 1933): 222–26.

"The True Story of a Little Gray Rabbit." (Ernest E. Thompson) *St. Nicholas* 17 (October, 1890): 953–55.

"The True Story of Daddy Binks." (Ernest Thompson Seton) *Recreation* 16 (January, 1902): 19–20.

"The Twelve Secrets of the Woods." (Ernest Thompson Seton) *Craftsman* 30 (June, 1916): 231–39, 329–31.

"Two Little Savages: Part 1." (Ernest Thompson Seton) *Ladies' Home Journal* 20 (January, 1903): 11–12.

"Two Little Savages: Part 2." (Ernest Thompson Seton) *Ladies' Home Journal* 20 (February, 1903): 11–12.

"Two Little Savages: Part 3." (Ernest Thompson Seton) *Ladies' Home Journal* 20 (March, 1903): 13–14.

"Two Little Savages: Part 4." (Ernest Thompson Seton) *Ladies' Home Journal* 20 (April, 1903): 11–12.

"Two Little Savages: Part 5." (Ernest Thompson Seton) *Ladies' Home Journal* 20 (May, 1903): 11–12.

"Two Little Savages: Part 6." (Ernest Thompson Seton) *Ladies' Home Journal* 20 (June, 1903): 11–12.

"Two Little Savages: Part 7." (Ernest Thompson Seton) *Ladies' Home Journal* 20 (July, 1903): 11–12.

"Two Little Savages: Part 8." (Ernest Thompson Seton) *Ladies' Home Journal* 20 (August, 1903): 15–16, 32.

"Two Records for New Mexico." (Ernest Thompson Seton) *Journal of Mammalogy* 12 (May, 1931): 166.

"Two Successful Fur Farms." (Ernest Thompson Seton) *Country Life in America* 20 (September, 1911): 39–40.

"The Unseen Fiddlers." (Ernest Thompson Seton) *Totem Board* 12 (September, 1933): 367–69.

"The Value of Moles." (Ernest Thompson Seton) *Journal of Mammology* 4 (February, 1923): 51.

"The Wapiti and His Antlers." (Ernest Thompson Seton) *Scribner's* 39 (January, 1906): 15–33.

"The Waterhen or Gallinule." (Ernest E. S. Thompson) *Our Animal Friends* 27 (September, 1899): 14–15.

"A Welcome Superstition." (Ernest Seton-Thompson) *Bird-Lore* 2 (October, 1900): 166.

"The Western Grebe in Manitoba." (Ernest E. T. Seton) *Auk* 2 (July, 1885): 314.

"The Western Meadow-Lark." (Ernest E. Thompson) *St. Nicholas* 16 (November, 1888): 63–64.

"What Do Birds Signal with Their Tails?" (Ernest Thompson Seton) *Bird-Lore* 23 (November–December, 1921): 286–87.

"What Is a True Sportsman?" (Ernest Thompson Seton [Sloat Hall]) *Forest and Stream* 47 (September 26, 1896): 245.

"What to Do When Lost in the Woods." (Ernest Thompson Seton) *Country Life in America* 6 (August, 1904): 359.

"The White Man's Last Opportunity." (Ernest Thompson Seton) *Canada West* 3 (April, 1908): 525–32.

"The White-Tailed (Virginian) Deer and Its Kin." (Ernest Thompson Seton) *Scribner's* 40 (September, 1906): 321–41.

"Why Do Birds Bathe? Part 1." (Ernest Thompson Seton) *Bird-Lore* 22 (November–December, 1920): 334–35.

"Why Do Birds Bathe? Part 2." (Ernest Thompson Seton) *Bird Lore* 23 (May–June, 1921): 124–37.

"Why the Chickadee Goes Crazy Once a Year." (Ernest E. Thompson) *Our Animal Friends* 21 (September, 1893): 17–18.

"Why Wear Clothes?" (Ernest Thompson Seton) *Hearst's,* August, 1920, pp. 21, 73; *Totem Board* 11 (June, 1932): 245–65.

"A Wild Animal Bed Quilt." (Ernest Thompson Seton) *Ladies' Home Journal* 22 (January, 1905): 9.

"The Wild Animal Play." (Ernest Seton-Thompson) *Ladies' Home Journal* 17 (July, 1900): 3–4, 28.

"The Wild Geese of Wyndygoul." *Country Life in America* 28 (April, 1916): 19–21.

"Wild Life and the Motor Car." (Ernest Thompson Seton) *Journal of Mammalogy* 2 (August, 1921): 240.

"Wild Rice." (Ernest E. Thompson) *Forest and Stream* 39 (August 25, 1892): 157–58.

"Wild Ways of Tame Beasts." (Ernest Thompson Seton) *Totem Board* 12 (January, 1933): 3–20.

"The Windigo." (Ernest Thompson Seton) *Totem Board* 11 (December, 1932): 562–68.

"The Winnipeg Wolf." (Ernest Thompson Seton) *Ladies' Home Journal* 20 (December, 1902): 11–12.

"The Wolf and the Man." (Ernest Thompson Seton) *Totem Board* 11 (May, 1932): 220–24.

"The Wolf and the Primal Law." (Ernest Thompson Seton) *Totem Board* 12 (October, 1933): 379–84.

"The Wolf on the Running Board." (Ernest Thompson Seton) *Totem Board* 13 (May, 1934): 163–65.

"The Wolf Question." (Ernest Seton Thompson) *Recreation* 8 (February, 1898): 126–27.

"The Wood-Duck." (Ernest E. S. Thompson *Our Animal Friends* 24 (July, 1897): 256–57.

"The Wood Rabbit or Hare." (Ernest E. Thompson) *Our Animal Friends* 22 (November, 1894): 65.

"The Wood Thrush." (Ernest E. Thompson) *Our Animal Friends* 25 (May, 1898): 207–208.

"Woodcraft Extolled as the Science That Makes Men: A Gospel for Out-of-Doors." (Ernest Thompson Seton) *Current Opinion,* 73 (October, 1922): 461–64.

"Woodcraft at the World's Fair." (Ernest Thompson Seton) *Totem Board* 11 (December, 1932): 578.

"The Woodcraft League or College of Indian Wisdom." (Ernest Thompson Seton) *Homiletic Review* 101 (June, 1931): 434–39.

"The Woodcrafter and the Stars." (Ernest Thompson Seton) *Country Life in America* 7 (November, 1904): 61.

"The World's Most Wonderful Zoo." (Ernest Seton-Thompson) *London Daily Express,* August 16, 1901.

"Wosca and Her Valiant Cub." (Ernest Thompson Seton) *Totem Board* 12 (November, 1933): 434–48.

"The Yak: A North American Opportunity." (Ernest Thompson Seton) *Country Life in America* 15 (February, 1909): 354–56.

"The Yellowleg and the Hens." (Ernest E. S. Thompson) *Our Animal Friends* 25 (November, 1897): 64–65.

Books

The American Boy Scout: The Official Handbook of Woodcraft for the Boy Scouts of America. (Ernest Thompson Seton) New York: Doubleday, Page, 1910.

Animal Heroes. (Ernest Thompson Seton) New York: Scribner, 1905.

Animal Tracks and Hunter Signs. (Ernest Thompson Seton) Garden City, N.Y.: Doubleday, 1958.

Animals. (Ernest Thompson Seton) Garden City, N.Y.:Doubleday, Page, 1926.

Animals Worth Knowing. (Ernest Thompson Seton) Garden City, N.Y.: Doubleday, Doran, 1934.

The Arctic Prairies. (Ernest Thompson Seton) New York: Scribner, 1911.

Bannertail, the Story of a Gray Squirrel. (Ernest Thompson Seton) New York: Scribner, 1922.

The Best of Ernest Thompson Seton. (Ernest Thompson Seton) Edited by W. Kay Robinson. London: Hodder and Stoughton, 1949.

The Biography of an Arctic Fox. (Ernest Thompson Seton) New York: Appleton-Century, 1937.

The Biography of a Grizzly. (Ernest Seton Thompson) New York: Century, 1900.

The Biography of a Silver Fox or *Domino Reynard of Goldur Town.* (Ernest Thompson Seton) New York: Century, 1909.

The Birch Bark Roll of the Woodcraft Indians. (Ernest Thompson Seton) New York: Doubleday, Page, 1906. (Published in several editions from 1906 to 1931; each edition is distinctive.)

The Book of Woodcraft and Indian Lore. (Ernest Thompson Seton) New York: Doubleday, Page, 1912. (Published, with alterations, in several subsequent editions.)

Boy Scouts of America: A Handbook of Woodcraft, Scouting and Lifecraft. (Ernest Thompson Seton) New York: Doubleday, Page, 1910.

The Brownie Wigwam. (Ernest Thompson Seton) New York: Woodcraft League of America, 1921.

The Buffalo Wind. (Ernest Thompson Seton) Santa Fe: Seton Village Press, 1938.

Ernest Thompson Seton's America. (Ernest Thompson Seton) Edited by Farida A. Wiley. New York: Devin-Adair, 1954.

Famous Animal Stories. Edited by Ernest Thompson Seton. New York: Brentanos, 1932.

The Forester's Manual; or, the Forest Trees of Eastern North America. (Ernest Thompson Seton) Garden City, N.Y.: Doubleday, Page, 1910.

The Gospel of the Redman: An Indian Bible. (Ernest Thompson Seton and Julia M. Seton) Garden City, Doubleday, Doran, 1936.

Great Historic Animals, Mainly about Wolves. (Ernest Thompson Seton) New York: Scribner, 1937.

How to Play Indian. (Ernest Thompson Seton) Philadelphia: Curtis, 1903.

Johnny Bear, Lobo and Other Stories. (Ernest Thompson Seton) New York: Scribner, 1935.

Katug, the Snow Child. (Ernest Thompson Seton) New York: Appleton-Century, 1927.

Krag and Johnny Bear. (Ernest Thompson Seton) New York: Scribner, 1902.

Life-Histories of Northern Animals. (Ernest Thompson Seton) 2 vols. New York: Scribner, 1909.

Lives of Game Animals. (Ernest Thompson Seton) 4 vols. Garden City, N.Y.: Doubleday, Page, 1925–28.

Lives of the Hunted. (Ernest Thompson Seton) New York: Scribner, 1901.

Lobo. (Ernest Thompson Seton) Philadelphia: Pennsylvania Institution for the Instruction of the Blind, 1900.

Lobo, Rag, and Vixen. (Ernest Seton Thompson) New York: Scribner, 1899.

The Manual of the Woodcraft Indians. 14th edition. (Ernest Thompson Seton) Garden City, N.Y.: Doubleday, Page, 1915.

Manual of the Brownies, the Little Lodge of the Woodcraft League of America. New York: Woodcraft League of America, Inc., 1922.

Monarch, the Big Bear of Tallac. (Ernest Thompson Seton) New York: Scribner, 1907.

The Natural History of the Ten Commandments. (Ernest Thompson Seton) New York: Scribner, 1907.

Pictographs of the Old Southwest. (Ernest Thompson Seton) Santa Fe, N. Mex.: Seton Village Press, 1937.

The Preacher of Cedar Mountain. (Ernest Thompson Seton) New York: Doubleday, Page, 1917.

Raggylug. (Ernest Seton-Thompson) Philadelphia: Pennsylvania Institution for the Instruction of the Blind, 1900.

The Red Book. (Ernest Thompson Seton) New York, 1904.

The Red Lodge. (Ernest Thompson Seton) New York, 1912.

Redruff. (Ernest Seton-Thompson) Philadelphia: Pennsylvania Institution for the Instruction of the Blind, 1900.

Rolf in the Woods. (Ernest Thompson Seton) New York: Doubleday, Page, 1911.

Santana: The Hero Dog of France. (Ernest Thompson Seton) Los Angeles: Phoenix Press, 1945.

Sign Talk. (Ernest Thompson Seton) Garden City, N.Y.: Doubleday, Page, 1918.

Studies in the Art Anatomy of Animals. (Ernest E. Thompson) London: Macmillan, 1896.

The Ten Commandments in the Animal World. (Ernest Thompson Seton) Garden City, N.Y.: Doubleday, Page, 1923.

Trail and Camp-Fire Stories. (Ernest Thompson Seton) Edited by Julia M. Seton. New York: Appleton-Century, 1940.

Trail of an Artist-Naturalist: The Autobiography of Ernest Thompson Seton. (Ernest Thompson Seton) New York: Scribner, 1940.

The Trail of the Sandhill Stag. (Ernest Seton-Thompson) New York: Scribner, 1899.

Two Little Savages: Being the Adventures of Two Boys Who Lived as Indians Do and What They Learned. (Ernest Thompson Seton) New York: Doubleday, Page, 1903.

The War Dance and the Fire-Fly Dance. (Ernest Thompson Seton) New York: Doubleday, Page, 1910.

The Wild Animal Play for Children. (Ernest Thompson Seton) Philadelphia: Curtis, 1900; New York: Doubleday, Page, 1900.

Wild Animal Ways. (Ernest Thompson Seton) Garden City, N.Y.: Doubleday, Page, 1916.

Wild Animals at Home. (Ernest Thompson Seton) Garden City, N.Y.: Doubleday, Page, 1913.

Wild Animals I Have Known. (Ernest Seton Thompson) New York: Scribner, 1898.

Wild Animals I Have Known. (Ernest Seton-Thompson) Louisville, Ky.: American Printing House for the Blind, 1900.

Woodcraft Boys, Woodcraft Girls, How to Begin. (Ernest Thompson Seton) New York, 1915.

The Woodcract Manual for Boys: The Fifteenth Birch Bark Roll. (Ernest Thompson Seton) New York: Doubleday, Page, 1917.

The Woodcraft Manual for Girls. (Ernest Thompson Seton) New York: Doubleday, Page, 1916.

Woodland Tales. (Ernest Thompson Seton) Garden City, N.Y.: Doubleday, Page, 1921.

Woodmyth and Fable. (Ernest Thompson Seton) New York: Century, 1905.

Secondary Works on Ernest Thompson Seton

Articles

Anderson, H. Allen. "Ernest Thompson Seton's First Visit to New Mexico, 1893–1894." *New Mexico Historical Review* 56 (October, 1981): 369–86.

———. "Ernest Thompson Seton in Yellowstone Country." *Montana: The Magazine of Western History* 34 (Spring, 1984): 46–59.

The Animal Story." *Edinburgh Review* 214 (July, 1911): 94–118.

Atwood, Margaret. "Animal Victims." In *Survival: A Thematic Guide to Canadian Literature*, 69–86. Toronto: Anansi, 1972.

Bell, Nancy. "The Work of Ernest Seton Thompson." *Humane Review* 4 (April, 1903); 11–20.

Bodsworth, Fred. "The Backwoods Genius with the Magic Pen." *Maclean's* 72 (June 6, 1959): 22, 32, 34, 38, 39, 40.

Buckham, John Wright. "The Modern School of Nature Interpretation." *Book Buyer* 20 (March, 1900): 108–13.

Burroughs, John. "Real and Sham Natural History." *Atlantic Monthly* 91 (March, 1903): 298–309.

Chapman, Frank M. "A Champion of Ernest Thompson Seton." *Saturday Review* 16 (October 2, 1937): 9.

———. "Naturalist, Artist, Author, Educator." *Bird-Lore* 37 (July, 1935): 245–47.

Chesley, Albert M. "Laws of the Seton Indians." In *Social Activities for Men and Boys*, 261–69. New York: Association Press, 1919.

"Chronicle and Comment." *Bookman* 6 (March, 1899): 9–10.

Devoe, Alan. "Artistic Wilderness." *Saturday Review* 23 (December 7, 1940): 18.

———. "Mr. Mother Nature." *Saturday Review* 37 (March 6, 1954): 20–21.

Emmons, Myra. "Ernest Seton Thompson—Artist, Naturalist, Writer." *Recreation* 6 (May, 1897): 315–30.

———. "With Ernest Seton-Thompson in the Woods." *Ladies' Home Journal* 18 (September, 1901): 3–4.

"Ernest Seton-Thompson: Artist, Naturalist, Writer." *Book News Monthly* 18 (May, 1900): 490–92.

"Ernest Thompson Seton." *Bookman* 45 (December, 1913): 147–48.

"Ernest Thompson Seton." In *Current Biography, 1943*, pp. 685–88. New York: H. W. Wilson, 1944.

"Ernest Thompson Seton." In John A. Garraty and Edward T. James, eds. *Dictionary of American Biography*, Supp. 4, 1946–50. pp. 735–37. New York: Scribner, 1974.

"Ernest Thompson Seton." In *National Cyclopedia of American Biography*, 1950 edition. XXVI, 68–69. New York: James T. White, 1950.

"Ernest Thompson Seton Lecture." *El Palacio* 30 (May 20, 1931): 235–36.

Green, Roger Lancelyn. "Ernest Thompson Seton." *Junior Bookshelf* 24 (December, 1960): 341–46.

Halsey, F. W. "Ernest Thompson Seton: In Bryant Park, N.Y." In *American Authors and Their Homes*, pp. 281–92. New York: James Pott, 1901.

Helgeland, Glenn B. "The National Wildlife Federation's Conservation Hall of Fame: Ernest Thompson Seton." *National Wildlife* 6 (August, 1968): 24–25.

Hellman, George S. "Animals in Literature." *Atlantic Monthly* 87 (March, 1901): 391–97.

Lucas, Alec W. "Nature Writers and the Animal Story." In *Literary History of Canada: Canadian Literature in English*. Edited by Carl F. Klinck et al. Toronto: University of Toronto Press, 1965.

MacArthur, James. "Wolf Thompson and His Wild Animals." *Bookman* 9 (March, 1899): 71–74.

McCabe, Lida Rose. "At Wyndygoul with Ernest Thompson Seton." *Book Buyer* 25 (1902): 21–28.

MacIntyre, F. Beatrice. "The Paleface Chief." *New Mexico* 24 (April, 1948): 25, 35, 37.

Magee, William H. "The Animal Story: A Challenge in Technique." *Dalhousie Review* 44 (Summer, 1964): 156–64.

Moore, Margaret. "Getting Acquainted with Ernest Thompson Seton." *Normal Instructor and Primary Plans* 38 (October, 1929): 68–70.

Morley, Patricia. "Seton's Animals." *Journal of Canadian Fiction* 2 (Summer, 1973)" 195–98.

Morris, Brian. "Ernest Thompson Seton and the Origins of the Woodcraft Movement." *Journal of Contemporary History* 5 (1970): 183–94.

"Necrology." *New Mexico Historical Review* 22 (January, 1947): 107.

"Note on Ernest Seton-Thompson." *Bookman* 13 (March, 1901): 4–5.

Peattie, Donald Culross. "Nature and Nature Writers." *Saturday Review*, 16 (August 28, 1937): 10–11.

"People Who Interest Us: Ernest Thompson Seton, Who Has Organized the Boy Scout Movement in the United States." *Craftsman* 19 (October, 1910): 67.

Pigott, T. Digby. "A Canadian Naturalist." *Living Age* 232 (January 25, 1902): 222–25.

Polk, James. "Lives of the Hunted." *Canadian Literature* 53 (Summer, 1972): 51–59.

Porier, Michael. "The Animal Story in Canadian Literature: E. Thompson Seton and Charles G. D. Roberts." *Queen's Quarterly* 34 (January-March, 1927): 298–312; 34 (April-June, 1927): 398–419.

Read, S. E. "Flight to the Primitive: Ernest Thompson Seton." *Canadian Literature* 13 (Summer, 1962): 45–57.

Reid, Russell. "Ernest Thompson Seton." *Museum Review* 2 (January, 1947): 1–5.

Rhodenizer, V. B. "Nature Writers 1: Writers of Animal Stories." *A Handbook of Canadian Literature*, pp. 111–18. Ottawa: Graphic Publishers, 1930.

Roberts, Charles G. D. "The Home of a Naturalist." *Country Life in America* 5 (December, 1903): 153–55.

"Salute to an Old Friend." *Saturday Evening Post* 211 (December 31, 1938): 22.

Samson, Jack. "Seton: America's Forgotten Naturalist." *Field and Stream* 78 (April, 1974): 60–63, 191–94.

Sanford, Chester M., and Grace A. Owen. "Ernest Thompson Seton." In *Modern Americans: A Biographical School Reader for the Upper Grades*, pp. 187–94. Chicago: Laurel, 1918.

Stevenson, Lionel. "Nature in Canadian Prose." In *Appraisals of Canadian Literature*. Toronto: Macmillan, 1926.

Storms, W. W. "The Woodcraft Indians." *Holiday Magazine for Children* 3 (October, 1904): 76–79.

Sykes, M'Cready. "Let's Play Indian: Making a New American Boy through Woodcraft." *Everybody's* 23 (October, 1910): 473–83.

Tracy, Henry Chester. "Ernest Thompson Seton." In *American Naturists*, pp. 233–43. New York: E. P. Dutton, 1930.

Vogt, William. "Popularizing Nature." *Saturday Review* 16 (September 18, 1937): 9.

Wallace, Ralph. "Wild Animals He Has Known." *Reader's Digest* 49 (September, 1946): 59–63.

Whitelock, William W. "Ernest Seton-Thompson." *Critic* 39 (October, 1901): 320–25.

"Why Mr. Seton Is Not Chief Scout." *Boys' Life* 6 (January, 1916): 28.
Zahniser, Howard. "Nature in Print." *Nature* 34 (January, 1941); 7, 50.
————. "Nature in Print." *Nature* 46 (November, 1953): 450–51.

Books

Bott, Penny. *Seton's Indians: Oral History Interview with Leonard S. Clark.* Greenwich, Conn.: Greenwich Library, 1976.
Garst, Shannon, and Warren Garst. *Ernest Thompson Seton.* New York: Messner, 1959.
Polk, James. *Wilderness Writers.* Toronto: Clarke, Irwin, 1972.
Redekop, Magdalene. *The Canadians: Ernest Thompson Seton.* Don Mills, Ont.: Fitzhenry and Whiteside, 1979.
Samson, John G., ed. *The Worlds of Ernest Thompson Seton.* New York: Knopf, 1976.
Wadland, John Henry. *Ernest Thompson Seton: Man in Nature and the Progressive Era, 1880–1915.* New York: Arno, 1978.

Books by Anya Seton

Avalon. Boston: Houghton Mifflin, 1965.
Devil Water. Boston: Houghton Mifflin, 1962.
Dragonwyck. Boston: Houghton Mifflin, 1944.
Foxfire. Boston: Houghton Mifflin, 1951.
Green Darkness. Boston: Houghton Mifflin, 1973.
The Hearth and Eagle. Boston: Houghton Mifflin, 1948.
Katharine. Boston: Houghton Mifflin, 1954.
The Mistletoe and Sword. Garden City, N.Y.: Doubleday, 1955.
My Theodosia. Boston: Houghton Mifflin, 1941.
Smouldering Fires. Garden City, N.Y.: Doubleday, 1975.
The Turquoise. Boston: Houghton Mifflin, 1946.
The Winthrop Woman. Boston: Houghton Mifflin, 1958.

Books by Grace Gallatin (Thompson) Seton

Chinese Lanterns. New York: Dodd, Mead, 1924.
Magic Waters. New York: E. P. Dutton, 1933.
Nimrod's Wife. London: Archibald, Constable, 1907.
Poison Arrows. London: J. Gifford, 1938.
A Woman Tenderfoot. New York: Doubleday, Page, 1900.
A Woman Tenderfoot in Egypt. New York: Dodd, Mead, 1923.
Yes, Lady Saheb: A Woman's Adventures with Mysterious India. London: Hodder and Stoughton, 1925.

Works by Julia M. Buttree (Seton)

Articles

"The Blanket Dance. *Totem Board* 12 (March, 1933): 122.
"Beading." *Totem Board* 11 (March, 1932): 97–120.
"The Ceremony of the Spirit Stones." *Totem Board* 11 (December, 1932): 540–41.
"Dyes of the Redman." *Totem Board* 11 (February, 1932): 154–67.
"Feather Work." *Totem Board* 12 (September, 1933): 353–61.
"Foods of the Omaha and Chippewa." *Totem Board* 11 (October, 1932): 443–54.
"Grouse Dance." *Totem Board* 11 (April, 1932): 186–88.
"Habitations of the Indians." *Totem Board* 11 (February, 1932): 45–85.
"Sweat Baths." *Totem Board* 12 (October, 1933): 394–400.
"Tanning." *Totem Board* 12 (November, 1933): 419–33.

Books

Seton, Julia M. *American Indian Arts.* New York: Ronald Press, 1962.
———. *By a Thousand Fires: Nature Notes and Extracts from the Life and Un-published Journals of Ernest Thompson Seton.* New York: Doubleday, 1967.
———. *Indian Costume Book.* Santa Fe: Seton Village Press, 1938.
———. *Indian Creation Stories.* Santa Fe, N. Mex.: Seton Village Press, 1952.
———. *The Pulse of the Pueblo.* Santa Fe, N. Mex.: Seton Village Press, 1939.
———. *The Quandry of Youth.* Santa Fe, N. Mex.: Seton Village Press, 1966.
Buttree, Julia M. *The Rhythm of the Redman.* New York: A. S. Barnes, 1930.
Seton, Julia M. *Sing, Sing, What Shall I Sing?* Santa Fe., N. Mex.: Seton Village Press, 1935.

Newspapers and Newsmagazines

Albuquerque *Journal.* August 29, 1927.
Albuquerque *Tribune.* August 12, 1946; August 15, 1946; October 23, 1946.
The *Daily Current-Argus* (Carlsbad, N. Mex.). October 23, 1946.
The *Daily Oklahoman* (Oklahoma City, Okla.). June 25, 1936.
Denver *Post.* June 25, 1936.
El Paso *Times.* January 23, 1935.
Greenwich *News.* October 23, 1903.
Los Angeles *Herald.* February 16, 1929.
Los Angeles *Times.* January 23, 1934.
Lubbock *Morning Avalanche.* March 3, 1938; March 4, 1938; July 7, 1938.
Manitoba Free Press. July 11, 1901.
New Mexico *Candle* (Las Vegas). July 6, 1932; October 13, 1938.
New York *Herald.* October 11, 1903.
New York *Times.* December 6, 1915; December 7, 1915.
New York *Tribune.* September 18, 1919.
New York *World,* May 24, 1907.
New York *World Telegram.* November 19, 1938.

Pasadena (California) *Star-News*. October 23, 1946.

St. Paul (Minnesota) *Dispatch*. April 1, 1902.

Santa Fe *New Mexican*. March 20, 1931; June 27, 1931; June 26, 1940; June 24, 1965; August 15, 1968.

Santa Fe *News*. October 9, 1969.

The *Summer Lobo* (University of New Mexico). August 9, 1946.

Time. November 4, 1946.

The *Toreador* (Texas Technological College). March 2, 1938; July 8, 1938.

Toronto *Globe*. March 30, 1893.

Tulsa *Daily World*. June 23, 1936.

Tulsa *Tribune*. June 23, 1936.

Viva (Santa Fe). January 25, 1976.

Winona (Wisconsin) *Morning Independent*. December 12, 1902; December 20, 1902.

Other Secondary Sources

Articles

Ackerman, Gerald M. "Gérôme: Reassessing a Scorned Painter." *Art News* 72 (January, 1973): 32–35.

Bacon, Lucy. "Indian Independence through Tribal Arts." *Totem Board* 12 (March, 1933): 99–108.

Baden-Powell, Robert S. S. "Educational Possibilities of the Boy Scouts' Training." *Nineteenth Century* 70 (August, 1911): 293–305.

Beach, Thomas W. "A Wonderful Home: How a Great Naturalist Lives." *London Daily Mail*, November 29, 1909.

Beard, Daniel Carter. "The Boy Scouts." *Outlook* 95 (July 23, 1910): 696–97.

———. "The Boy Scouts of America." *American Review of Reviews* 44 (October, 1911): 429–38.

Blumenfeld, Ralph D. "The Boy Scouts." *Outlook* 95 (July 23, 1910): 617–29.

Burroughs, John. "The Literary Treatment of Nature." *Atlantic Monthly* 94 (July, 1904): 38–43.

———. "Roosevelt as a Nature Lover and Observer." *Outlook* 86 (July 13, 1904): 547–53.

Campbell, Walter Stanley. "Our Oklahoma Tribe." *Holiday Magazine for Children*, 1904.

Cassidy, Ina S. "The Shalako at Zuni." *Totem Board* 12 (June, 1933): 246.

Chapman, Frank M. "The Case of William J. Long." *Science*, 19 (March 4, 1904): 387–89.

———. "In Memoriam: Joel Asaph Allen." *Auk* 39 (January, 1922): 1–14.

———. "In Memoriam: Louis Agassiz Fuertes." *Auk* 47 (January, 1928): 1–26.

Clark, Edward B. "Roosevelt on the Nature Fakirs." *Everybody's* 16 (June, 1907): 770–74.

———. "Real Naturalists on Nature Faking." *Everybody's* 17 (September, 1907): 423–27.

Cohen, Bronwen J. "Nativism and Western Myth: The Influence of Nativist Ideas on the American Self-Image." *Journal of American Studies* 8 (April, 1974): 23–39.

Dickson, B. Alan. "The Professional Life of Francis C. Wilson of Santa Fe: A Preliminary Sketch." *New Mexico Historical Review* 51 (January, 1976): 35–55.

Dorsey, James O. "A Study of Siouan Cults." In *Eleventh Annual Report of the Bureau of Ethnology to the Secretary of the Smithsonian Institution, 1889–90*, 351–553. Washington: GPO, 1894.

Eliot, John L. "'T. R.'s Wilderness Legacy." *National Geographic* 162 (September, 1982): 340–62.

Fisher, A. K. "In Memoriam: George Bird Grinnell." *Auk* 56 (January, 1939): 1–2.

Fisher, Clyde. "John Burroughs." *Totem Board* 12 (July, 1933): 276–84.

Fletcher, Alice C., and Francis La Flesche. "The Omaha Tribe." In *Annual Report of the Bureau of American Ethnology, 1905–06*. Washington, D.C.: GPO, 1911.

Fowler, Kenneth. "The Story of the Camp Fire Club." *Field and Stream* 15 (November, 1910): 601–15.

Garland, Hamlin. "The Red Man's Present Needs." *North American Review* 174 (April, 1902): 476–88.

Gillis, John R. "Conformity and Rebellion: Contrasting Styles of English and German Youth, 1900–1933." *History of Education Quarterly* 13 (Fall, 1973): 249–60.

Grinnell, George Bird. "The Indian on the Reservation." *Atlantic Monthly* 89 (February, 1899): 263.

Hanna, A. "A Bibliography of the Writings of Irving Bacheller." *Rollins College Bulletin* 35 (September, 1939).

Henshaw, H. W. "In Memoriam: William Brewster." *Auk* 37 (January, 1922): 1–23.

Higham, John. "The Reorientation of American Culture in the 1890s." In *American Civilization*. Edited by Eugene Drozdowski. Glenview, Ill.: Scott, Foresman, 1972.

Jagger, T. R., Jr. "Death Gulch, A Natural Bear Trap." *Science Monthly* 6 (February, 1899): 5–6.

King, Evelyn. "Cattle Queens of the West." *Persimmon Hill* 14 (1984): 8–21.

Kropotkin, Peter. "The Morality of Nature." *Nineteenth Century* 57 (March, 1905): 406–26.

La Farge, Oliver. "An Art That Is Really American." *Totem Board* 12 (April, 1933): 139–45.

La Flesche, Francis. "An Indian Allotment." *Independent* 52 (November 8, 1900): 2686–88.

Lewin, Herbert S. "Hitler Youth and the Boy Scouts of America: A Comparison of Aims." *Human Relations* 1 (1947): 206–77.

Long, William J. "The Modern School of Nature Study and Its Critics." *North American Review* 176 (May, 1903): 688–98.

————. "Science, Nature and Criticism." *Science* 19 (May 13, 1904): 760–67.

Lowenthal, David. "The Pioneer Landscape: An American Dream." *Great Plains Quarterly* 2 (Winter, 1982): 5–19.

Lummis, Charles F. "My Brother's Keeper." *Land of Sunshine* 11–12 (August, 1899–February, 1900).

Mallery, Garrick. "Picture Writing of the American Indians." In *Tenth Annual Report of the Bureau of Ethnology to the Secretary of the Smithsonian Institution, 1888–89.* pp. 25–822. Washington: GPO, 1893.

————. "Sign Language among North American Indians, Compared with That among Other Peoples and Deaf Mutes." In *First Annual Report of the Bureau of Ethnology to the Secretary of the Smithsonian Institution, 1879–80*, pp. 269–552. Washington: GPO, 1881.

Matthews, Washington. "Navajo Weavers." In *Third Annual Report of the Bureau of Ethnology to the Secretary of the Smithsonian Institution, 1881–82.* pp. 375–91. Washington: GPO, 1884.

Mattison, Ray H. "Roosevelt and the Stockmen's Association." *North Dakota History* 17 (April, July, 1950): 73–95, 117–207.

May, John B. "The Sport of Bird Banding." *Totem Board* 10 (May, 1927): 10.

Mooney, James. "The Ghost Dance Religion and the Sioux Outbreak of 1890." In *Fourteenth Annual Report of the Bureau of Ethnology to the Secretary of the Smithsonian Institution, 1892–93*, pp. 641–1136. Washington: GPO, 1894.

Nute, Grace Lee. "Down North in 1892." *Beaver* 278 (June, 1948): 42–46.

————. "Paris to Peel's River in 1892." *Beaver* 278 (March, 1948): 19–23.

————. "To Edmonton in 1892." *Beaver* 281 (June, 1950): 3–5.

Oberholser, Harry C. "Robert Ridgway: A Memorial Appreciation." *Auk* 50 (April, 1933): 159–69.

Opie, John. "Learning to Read the Pioneer Landscape: Braudel, Eliade, Turner, and Benton." *Great Plains Quarterly* 2 (Winter, 1982): 20–30.

Philip, Kenneth R. "John Collier and the Crusade to Protect Indian Religious Freedom," *Journal of Ethnic Studies* 1 (Spring, 1973): 22–28.

Pickett, W. D. "Four-Bears Creek." *Forest and Stream* 80 (October 18, 1913): 488.

Presby, Frank. "The Associate Editors of *Boys' Life*." *Boys' Life* 4 (May, 1914): 6.

Rairdon, Jack T. "John Homer Seger: The Practical Indian Educator." *Chronicles of Oklahoma* 34 (Summer, 1956): 203–216.

Roosevelt, Theodore. "Nature Fakers." *Everybody's* 17 (September, 1907): 427–30.

Shrive, Norman. "What Happened to Pauline?" *Canadian Literature* 13 (Summer, 1962): 25–38.

Springhall, J. O. "The Boy Scouts, Class and Militarism in Relation to British Youth Movements, 1908–1930." *International Review of Social History* 16 (1971): 125–58.

Stensland, Anna Lee. "Charles Alexander Eastman: Sioux Storyteller and Historian." *American Indian Quarterly* 3 (Autumn, 1977): 199–208.

Thomas, Lester S. "Sweat Lodge Ceremony." *Totem Board* 12 (October, 1933): 401–406.

Thompson, Stuart L. "The Charm of Sound." *Totem Board* 13 (January 1934): 29–30.

———. "The Seeing Eye." *Totem Board* 11 (October, 1932): 482–83.

———. "The Warbler in the Vine." *Totem Board* 12 (April, 1933): 160–61.

Turner, Frederick Jackson. "The Significance of the Frontier in American History." In *American Historical Association Annual Report for 1893*, pp. 199–227. Washington: GPO, 1894.

Valentine, Robert G. "Making Good Indians." *Sunset* 24 (June, 1910): 598–611.

Watson, J. W. "Report of Crow Agency." In *Report of the Secretary of the Interior*. 5 vols. Washington: GPO, 1897.

Weigle, Marta. "Publishing in Santa Fe, 1915–40." *El Palacio* 40 (Anniversary Issue, 1984): 10–19.

Weir, T. R. "Pioneer Settlement of Southwest Manitoba, 1879–1901." *Canadian Geographer* 8 (1964): 64–71.

Wheeler, William Norton. "Woodcock Surgery." *Science* 19 (February 26, 1904): 347–50.

White, Richard. "The Cultural Landscape of the Pawnees." *Great Plains Quarterly* 2 (Winter, 1982): 31–39.

Wilkinson, Paul. "English Youth Movements, 1908–1930." *Journal of Contemporary History* 4 (April, 1969): 3–23.

Wood, Susan. "Ralph Connor and the Tamed West." In *The Westering Experience in American Literature: Bicentennial Essays*. Edited by Merrill Lewis and L. L. Lee, pp. 199–205. Bellingham, Wash.: Western Washington University, 1977.

Books

Allen, Frederick Lewis. *Only Yesterday*. New York: Harper, 1931.

———. *Since Yesterday*. New York: Harper, 1940.

Anderson, A. A. *Experiences and Impressions: The Autobiography of Colonel A. A. Anderson*. New York: Macmillan, 1933.

Anderson, George S. *Report of the Superintendent of Yellowstone National Park to the Secretary of the Interior*. Washington, D.C.: GPO, 1896.

Armstrong County Historical Association. *A Collection of Memories: A History of Armstrong County*. Hereford, Tex.: Pioneer Publishers, 1965.

Arnold, Ron. *At the Eye of the Storm: James Watt and the Environmentalists*. Chicago: Regnery Gateway, 1982.

Austin, Mary. *The American Rhythm: Studies and Re-expressions of American Songs*. New York: Harcourt, Brace, 1923.

———. *Children Sing in the Far West*. Boston: Houghton Mifflin, 1928.

———. *Earth Horizon*. New York: Literary Guild, 1932.

———. *Literary America, 1903–1934: The Mary Austin Letters*. Edited by T. M. Pearce. Westport, Conn.: Greenwood Press, 1979.

Baden-Powell, Robert S. S. *Aids to Scouting for NCO's and Men*. London: Gale and Polden, 1909.

———. *Scouting and Youth Movements*. New York: Jonathan Cape, 1931.

———. *Scouting for Boys*. London: C. Arthur Pearson, 1909.

————. *Scouting for Boys: A Handbook for Instruction in Good Citizenship*. London: Horace Cox, 1908.

Barrus, Clara. *The Life and Letters of John Burroughs*. 2 vols. Boston: Houghton Mifflin, 1925.

Bartlett, Richard. *Nature's Yellowstone*. Albuquerque: University of New Mexico Press, 1974.

Beard, Daniel Carter. *Hardly a Man Is Now Alive: The Autobiography of Dan Beard*. New York: Doubleday, Doran, 1939.

Beck, Warren A. *New Mexico: A History of Four Centuries*. Norman: University of Oklahoma Press, 1962.

Bendire, Charles E. *Life Histories of North American Birds with Special Reference to Their Breeding Habits and Eggs*. Smithsonian Institution, National Museum, Special Bulletin No. 1. Washington, D.C.: GPO, 1892.

Berkhofer, Robert F., Jr. *The White Man's Indian*. New York: Random House, 1978.

Bingham, Edward R. *Charles F. Lummis: Editor of the Southwest*. San Marino, Calif.: Huntington Library, 1955.

Blair, Leon D., ed. *Essays on Radicalism in Contemporary America*. Austin: University of Texas Press, 1973.

Bode, William Frederic. *The Life and Letters of John Muir*. 2 vols. Boston: Houghton Mifflin, 1924.

Boime, Albert. *The Academy and French Painting in the Nineteenth Century*. London: Phaidon, 1971.

Bok, Edward. *The Americanization of Edward Bok: The Autobiography of a Dutch Boy Fifty Years After*. New York: Scribner, 1920.

The Book of the Camp Fire Girls. New York: Camp Fire Girls, Inc., 1929.

Botkin, B. A. *Folk-Say: A Regional Miscellany*. Norman: University of Oklahoma Press, 1929.

Bowsfield, Hartwell, ed. *The James Wickes Taylor Correspondence, 1859–1870*. Winnipeg: Manitoba Record Society, 1968.

Boy Scouts of America. *Boy Scouts of America: The Official Handbook for Boys*. Garden City, N.Y.: Doubleday, Page, 1911.

————. *The Official Handbook for Boys*. Rev. ed. New York: Grosset and Dunlap, 1914.

Brand, Max. *The Seventh Man*. New York: Dodd, Mead, 1921.

Bronson, Edgar B. *Reminiscences of a Ranchman*. New York: McClure, 1908.

Buckler, Helen, et al. *Wo-He-Lo: The Story of Camp Fire Girls*. New York: Holt, Rinehart and Winston, 1961.

Burbank, Edward Ayer. *Burbank among the Indians*. Caldwell, Idaho: Caxton, 1946.

Burns, Edward McNall. *David Starr Jordan: Prophet of Freedom*. Stanford, Calif.: Stanford University Press, 1953.

Burroughs, John. *Camping and Tramping with Roosevelt*. Boston: Houghton Mifflin, 1906.

Burton, Frederick R. *American Primitive Music: with Especial Attention to the Songs of the Ojibways*. New York: Moffet, Yard, 1909.

Campbell, Charles A. R. *Bats, Mosquitoes and Dollars*. Boston: Stratford, 1925.

Campbell, Walter S. *The Book Lover's Southwest*. Norman: University of Oklahoma Press, 1955.

Caperton, Thomas J. *Rogue! Being an Account of the Life and High Times of Stephen W. Dorsey, U.S. Senator and New Mexico Cattle Baron*. Santa Fe: Museum of New Mexico Press, 1978.

Carnegie, Andrew. *The Autobiography of Andrew Carnegie*. Boston: Houghton Mifflin, 1920.

Champney, Freeman. *Art and Glory: The Story of Elbert Hubbard*. New York: Crown, 1968.

Chapman, Frank M. *Autobiography of a Bird-Lover*. New York: Appleton-Century, 1933.

———. *Handbook of Birds of Eastern North America*. New York: Dover Books, 1966.

Charlesworth, Hector. *Candid Chronicles: Leaves from the Notebook of a Canadian Journalist*. Toronto: Macmillan, 1925.

Chittenden, Hiram M. *The Yellowstone National Park*. Cincinnati, Ohio: Robert Clarke, 1895.

Christy, Robert Miller. *Manitoba Described*. London: Wyman, 1885.

Clark, William Philo. *The Indian Sign Language*. Philadelphia: L. R. Hamersly, 1885.

Coke, Van Deren. *The Painter and the Photograph from Delacroix to Warhol*. Albuquerque: University of New Mexico Press, 1972.

———. *Taos and Santa Fe: The Artist's Environment, 1882–1942*. Albuquerque: University of New Mexico Press, 1963.

Coles, Harry L. *The War of 1812*. Chicago: University of Chicago Press, 1965.

Collier, John. *American Indian Ceremonial Dances*. New York: Bounty Books, 1949.

———. *From Every Zenith: A Memoir and Some Essays on Life and Thought*. Denver, Sage Books, 1963.

———. *Indians of the Americas*. New York: Mentor, 1947.

Curti, Merle. *The Growth of American Thought*. New York: Harper and Row, 1964.

Curtis, Edward S. *The North American Indian*. Edited by F. W. Hodge. 20 vols. Cambridge: Cambridge University Press, 1907–1930.

Curtis, Natalie. *The Indian's Book: An Offering by the American Indians of Indian Lore, Musical and Narrative, to Form a Record of the Songs and Legends of Their Race*. New York: Harper, 1907.

Cutright, Paul Russell. *Theodore Roosevelt, the Naturalist,* New York: Harper, 1956.

Cutright, Paul Russell, and Michael J. Broadhead. *Elliott Coues: Naturalist and Frontier Historian*. Chicago: University of Chicago Press, 1981.

Dall, W. H. *Spencer Fullerton Baird: A Biography*. Philadelphia: Lippincott, 1915.

Devlin, John C., and Grace Naismith. *The World of Roger Tory Peterson*. New York: Times Books, 1977.

Dobie, J. Frank. *Life and Literature of the Southwest*. Dallas: Southern Methodist University Press, 1952.

————. *The Mustangs*. Boston: Little, Brown, 1952.

————. *The Voice of the Coyote*. Boston: Little, Brown, 1949.

Dorgan, Ethel Josephine. *Luther Halsey Gulick, 1865–1918*. New York: Teachers' College, Columbia University, 1934.

Doubleday, Frank N. *The Memoirs of a Publisher*. Garden City, N.Y.: Doubleday, 1972.

Douglas, C. L. *Cattle Kings of Texas*. Fort Worth: Branch-Smith, 1968.

Dresden, Donald. *The Marquis de Mores: Emperor of the Badlands*. Norman: University of Oklahoma Press, 1970.

Dunaway, David King. *How Can I Keep from Singing: Pete Seeger*. New York: McGraw-Hill, 1981.

Eastman, Charles A. *The Indian Today*. Garden City, N.Y.: Doubleday, Page, 1915.

————. *The Soul of the Indian: An Interpretation*. Boston: Houghton Mifflin, 1911.

Easton, Robert. *Max Brand, the Big "Westerner."* Norman: University of Oklahoma Press, 1970.

Easton, Robert and Mackenzie Brown. *Lord of Beasts: The Saga of Buffalo Jones*. Tucson: University of Arizona Press, 1961.

Ellis, Havelock. *My Life: Autobiography of Havelock Ellis*. Boston: Houghton Mifflin, 1939.

Emerson, Ellen Russen. *Indian Myths*. Boston: J. R. Osgood, 1884.

Faulkner, Harold U. *Politics, Reform and Expansion*. New York: Harper, 1959.

Federal Writers' Project. *North Dakota: A Guide to the Northern Prairie State*. New York: Oxford University Press, 1950.

Fink, Augusta. *I-Mary: A Biography of Mary Austin*. Tucson: University of Arizona Press, 1983.

Firth, Edith, J., ed. *The Town of York, 1793–1815*. Toronto: Champlain Society, 1962.

Fiske, Turbese Lummis, and Keith Lummis. *Charles F. Lummis: The Man and His West*. Norman: University of Oklahoma Press, 1975.

Fletcher, Alice. *Indian Story and Song from North America.* Boston: Small, Maynard, 1900.

Frome, Michael. *Whose Woods These Are: The Story of the National Forests*. New York: Doubleday, 1962.

Garraty, John A. *The New Commonwealth*. New York: Harper and Row, 1968.

Garland, Hamlin. *Afternoon Neighbors*. New York: Macmillan, 1934.

————. *Book of the American Indian*. New York: Harper, 1923.

————. *The Captain of the Gray Horse Troop*. New York: Harper, 1902.

————. *Companions on the Trail*. New York: Macmillan, 1931.

————. *Crumbling Idols: Twelve Essays on Art Dealing Chiefly with Literature, Painting and the Drama*. Edited by Jane Johnson. Cambridge, Mass.: Harvard University Press, 1960.

————. *A Daughter of the Middle Border*. New York: Grosset and Dunlap, 1921.

————. *Hamlin Garland's Diaries*. Edited by Donald Pizer. San Marino, Calif.: Huntington Library, 1968.

————. *Main Traveled Roads*. New York: Signet, 1962.

————. *My Friendly Contemporaries*. New York: Macmillan, 1932.

————. *Roadside Meetings*. New York: Macmillan, 1930.

George, Henry. *Progress and Poverty*. New York: D. Appleton, 1880.

Gibson, Arrell M. *The Santa Fe and Taos Colonies: Age of the Muses, 1900–1942*. Norman: University of Oklahoma Press, 1983.

Gilbey, Sir Walter. *Animal Painters of England*. 3 vols. London: Vinton, 1900–11.

Gillmor, Frances, and Louisa Wade Wetherill. *Traders to the Navajos*. Albuquerque: University of New Mexico Press, 1953.

Girl Scout Handbook. New York: Girl Scouts of the U.S.A., 1947.

Gordon, Dudley. *Charles F. Lummis: Crusader in Corduroy*. Los Angeles: Cultural Assets Press, 1972.

Gould, Joseph E. *The Chautauqua Movement*. Albany: State University of New York Press, 1961.

Grey, Zane. *The Last of the Plainsmen*. New York: Outing, 1908.

————. *Wildfire*. New York: Harper and Row, 1917.

Gridley, Marion E. *Indians of Today*. Chicago: Indian Council Fire, 1947.

Grinnell, George Bird. *The Passing of the Great West: Selected Papers of George Bird Grinnell*. Edited by John F. Reiger. New York: Winchester Press, 1972.

————. *The Story of the Indian*. New York: D. Appleton, 1902.

Grinnell, George Bird, and Theodore Roosevelt, eds. *Trail and Camp-Fire*. New York: Forest and Stream, 1897.

Grinnell, George Bird, and Charles Sheldon, eds. *Hunting and Conservation*. New Haven, Conn. Yale University Press, 1925.

Gruber, Frank. *Zane Grey*. New York: World, 1978.

Guillet, Edwin C. *Early Life in Upper Canada*, Toronto: Ontario Publishing, 1933.

Haeckel, Ernst. *The Evolution of Man*. 2 vols. New York: H. L. Fowle, 1897.

————. *The History of Creation*. London: H. S. King, 1876.

————. *The Riddle of the Universe at the Close of the Nineteenth Century*. New York: Harper, 1900.

————. *The Wonders of Life*. London: Watts, 1905.

Hagedorn, Hermann. *The Roosevelt Family of Sagamore Hill*. New York: Macmillan, 1954.

————. *Roosevelt in the Badlands*. Boston: Houghton Mifflin, 1921.

Haley, J. Evetts. *The XIT Ranch of Texas*. Norman: University of Oklahoma Press, 1953.

Hall, G. Stanley. *Adolescence: Its Psychology and Its Relations to Physiology, Anthropology, Sociology, Sex, Crime, Religion and Education*. 2 vols. New York: D. Appleton, 1904.

Haines, Aubrey L. *The Yellowstone Story*. 2 vols. Boulder: Colorado Associated University Press, 1977.

Hampton, H. Duane. *How the U.S. Calvary Saved Our National Parks*. Bloomington: Indiana University Press, 1971.

Harper, J. Russell. *Early Painters and Engravers in Canada*. Toronto: University of Toronto Press, 1970.

Hawkes, Clarence. *Shovelhorns*. New York: Scribner, 1909.

Haynes, Jack E. *Haynes Guide: Handbook of Yellowstone National Park*. 49th edition. Bozeman, Mont.: Haynes, 1947.

Henri, Robert. *The Art Spirit*. Philadelphia: Lippincott, 1930.

Hertzberg, Hazel W. *The Search for an American Indian Identity: Modern Pan-Indian Movements*. Syracuse, N.Y.: Syracuse University Press, 1971.

Hillcourt, William. *Baden-Powell: The Two Lives of a Hero*. London: Heinemann, 1964.

Hodge, F. W., et al. *Handbook of American Indians North of Mexico*. 2 vols. Washington, D.C.: GPO, 1907–10.

Hofman, Charles, ed. *Frances Densmore and American Indian Music; A Memorial Volume*. New York: Museum of the American Indian, Heye Foundation, 1968.

Holloway, Jean. *Hamlin Garland: A Biography*. Austin: University of Texas Press, 1960.

Homer, William Innes. *Robert Henri and His Circle*. Ithaca, N.Y.: Cornell University Press, 1969.

Hopkins, C. Howard. *A History of the YMCA in North America*. New York: Association Press, 1951.

Horn, Calvin. *Climbing a Rainbow*. Albuquerque: Horn and Wallace, 1966.

Jackson, Carlton. *Zane Grey*. New York: Twayne, 1973.

Johnson, Robert Underwood. *Remembered Yesterdays*. Boston: Houghton Mifflin, 1923.

Jones, C. J., with Col. Henry Inman. *Buffalo Jones' Forty Years of Adventure*. Topeka: Crane and Company, 1899.

Jones, J. Walter. *Fur Farming in Canada*. 2nd edition. Ottawa: Canada Commission of Conservation, 1914.

Jordan, David Starr. *A Check List of the Fishes and Fishlike Vertebrates of North and Middle America*. Washington, D.C.: GPO, 1896.

———. *The Days of a Man: Being Memories of a Naturalist, Teacher and Minor Prophet of Democracy*. 2 vols. Yonkers-on-Hudson, N.Y.: World Book Company, 1922.

———. *The Fur-Seals and Fur-Seal Islands of the North Pacific Ocean*. 4 vols. Washington, D.C.: GPO, 1898–99.

Kaplan, Justin. *Lincoln Steffens: A Biography*. New York: Simon and Schuster, 1974.

———. *Mr. Clemens and Mark Twain*. New York: Simon and Schuster, 1966.

Kazin, Alfred. *On Native Grounds*. New York: Reynal and Hitchcock, 1942.

Keith, W. J. *Charles G. D. Roberts*. Toronto: Copp Clark, 1969.

Kipling, Rudyard. *From Sea to Sea*. New York: Doubleday and McClure, 1899.

Knebel, A. G. *Four Decades with Men and Boys*. New York: Association Press, 1936.

Knowles, Joseph. *Alone in the Wilderness*. Boston: Small, Maynard, 1913.

Kropotkin, Peter. *Mutual Aid: A Factor in Evolution*. Edited by Paul Avrich. New York: New York University Press, 1972.

La Barre, Weston. *The Ghost Dance: Origins of Religion*. New York: Delta, 1972.

Lacour-Gayet, Robert. *A History of South Africa*. London: Cassell, 1970.

Lamar, Howard R., ed. *Reader's Encyclopedia of the American West*. New York: Crowell, 1977.

Lang, Lincoln. *Ranching with Roosevelt*. Philadelphia: Lippincott, 1926.

Leuchtenberg, William E. *Franklin D. Roosevelt and the New Deal*. New York: Harper and Row, 1963.

Linderman, Frank B. *Plenty-Coups: Chief of the Crows*. Lincoln: University of Nebraska Press, 1962.

Lippmann, Walter. *Drift and Mastery*. New York: M. Kennerley, 1914.

Long, William J. *School of the Woods: Some Life Studies of Animal Instincts and Animal Training*. Boston: Ginn, 1902.

Lower, Arther R. M. *Canadians in the Making*. Toronto: Longmans, Green and Company, 1958.

Lummis, Charles F. *The Land of Poco Tiempo*. New York: Scribner, 1893.

———. *A Tramp across the Continent*. New York: Scribner, 1892.

MacDonald, Colin S., comp. *A Dictionary of Canadian Artists*. 4 vols. Ottawa: Canadian Paperbacks, 1971–74.

Macleod, David I. *Building Character in the American Boy: The Boy Scouts, YMCA and Their Forerunners, 1870–1920*. Madison: University of Wisconsin Press, 1983.

Macoun, John. *Manitoba and the Great North-West*. Guelph, Ont.: World Publishers, 1882.

Macoun, John, and James Macoun. *Catalogue of Canadian Birds*. Ottawa: Government Printing Boreau, 1909.

Mair, Charles. *Tecumseh, A Drama, and Canadian Poems*. Toronto: Radisson Society, 1926.

Major, Mabel, and T. M. Pearce. *Southwest Heritage: A Literary History with Bibliographies*. 3rd ed. Albuquerque: University of New Mexico Press, 1972.

Marchand, Ernest. *Frank Norris: A Study*. New York: Octagon Books, 1964.

Martin, Chester. *"Dominion Lands" Policy*. Edited by Lewis H. Thomas. Toronto: McClelland and Stewart, 1973.

Marx, Leo. *The Machine in the Garden: Technology and the Pastoral Ideal in America*. New York: Oxford University Press, 1964.

McCraye, Walter. *Pauline Johnson and Her Friends*. Toronto: Ryerson, 1947.

McCulloch, Joseph B. *Hamlin Garland*. Boston: Twayne, 1978.

McIlwraith, Thomas. *The Birds of Ontario*. 2nd ed. Toronto: William Briggs, 1894.

McInnis, Edgar. *Canada: A Political and Social History*. New York: Rinehart, 1959.

McWilliams, Carey. *The New Regionalism in American Literature*. Seattle: University of Washington Bookstore, 1930.

Meinig, D. W. *Southwest: Three Peoples in Geographical Change, 1600–1970*. New York: Oxford University Press, 1971.

Middleton, Jessee Edgar. *The Municipality of Toronto: A History*. 3 vols. Toronto: Dominion Publishing, 1923.

Morgan, Lewis Henry. *Ancient Society, or Researches in the Lines of Human Progress from Savagery through Barbarism to Civilization.* New York: Henry Holt, 1877.

———. *League of the Ho-de-no-sau-nee, or Iroquois.* 2 vols. Rochester, N.Y.: Sage, 1851.

Morgan, Neil. *Westward Tilt.* New York: Random House, 1961.

Morris, Edmund. *The Rise of Theodore Roosevelt.* New York: Coward, McCann and Geoghagan, 1979.

Morton, W. W. *Manitoba: A History.* Toronto: University of Toronto Press, 1957.

Mott, Frank Luther. *A History of American Magazines.* 5 vols. Cambridge, Mass.: Harvard University Press, 1938–68.

Mowry, George E. *The Era of Theodore Roosevelt.* New York: Harper, 1958.

Mulvany, C. Pelham. *Toronto: Past and Present.* Toronto: W. E. Caiger, 1884.

Murray, Joan. *Ontario Society of Artists: 100 Years.* Toronto: Art Gallery of Ontario, 1972.

Murray, William D. *As He Journeyed: The Autobiography of William D. Murray.* New York: Association Press, 1929.

———. *The History of the Boy Scouts of America.* New York: Boy Scouts of America, 1937.

Nash, Gerald D. *The American West in the Twentieth Century.* Albuquerque: University of New Mexico Press, 1977.

Nash, Roderick. *Wilderness and the American Mind.* New Haven, Conn.: Yale University Press, 1967.

Nelson, Bruce. *Land of the Dacotahs.* Minneapolis: University of Minnesota Press, 1946.

New Mexico Writers' Project. *New Mexico: A Guide to the Colorful State.* New York: Hastings House, 1940.

Nichols, Frances S., comp. *Index to Schoolcraft's "Indian Tribes of the United States."* Bureau of American Ethnology, Bulletin 152. Washington, D.C.: GPO, 1954.

Osborn, Henry Fairfield. *Impressions of Great Naturalists.* New York: Scribner, 1924.

Palmer, A. H. *Life of Joseph Wolf.* London: Longmans, 1895.

Paytiano, James. *Flaming Arrow's People.* New York: Duffield and Green, 1932.

Pearce, T. M. *The Beloved House.* Caldwell, Idaho: Caxton, 1940.

———. *Mary Hunter Austin.* New Haven, Conn.: College and University Press, 1965.

Peterson, Roger Tory. *A Field Guide to the Birds.* Boston: Houghton Mifflin, 1939.

Preble, E. A. *A Biological Investigation of the Hudson Bay Region.* North American Fauna, No. 22. Washington: U.S. Department of Agriculture, 1902.

Pringle, Henry F. *Theodore Roosevelt: A Biography.* New York: Harcourt Brace, 1931.

Putnam, Carleton. *Theodore Roosevelt: The Formative Years.* New York: Scribner, 1958.

Resek, Carl. *Lewis Henry Morgan, American Scholar*. Chicago: University of Chicago Press, 1960.

Reynolds, E. E. *The Scout Movement*. London: Oxford University Press, 1950.

Rich. E. E. *Hudson's Bay Company, 1670 – 1870*. 3 vols. New York: Macmillan, 1961.

Roberts, Charles G. D. *The Kindred of the Wild*. Boston: Page, 1902.

———. *The Watchers of the Trails*. Toronto: Copp Clark, 1904.

Robinson, Edgar M. *The Early Years: The Beginnings of Work with Boys in the Young Men's Christian Association*. New York: Association Press, 1950.

Robinson, Elwyn B. *History of North Dakota*. Lincoln: University of Nebraska Press, 1966.

Rollins, Philip Ashton, *The Cowboy: An Unconventional History of Civilization on the Old-Time Cattle Range*. New York: Scribner, 1936.

Roosevelt, Theodore, *Hunting Trips of a Ranchman*. New York: G. . Putnam, 1885.

———. *The Letters of Theodore Roosevelt*, ed. Elting E. Morison. 8 vols. Cambridge, Mass.: Harvard University Press, 1950.

———. *Ranch Life and the Hunting Trail*. New York: Century, 1899.

———. *The Strenuous Life: Essays and Addresses*. New York: Scribner, 1900.

———. *Works*. Edited by Herman Hagedorn. 20 vols. New York: Scribner, 1926.

Rosa, Joseph G. *The West of Wild Bill Hickok*. Norman: University of Oklahoma Press, 1982.

Roth, Leland M. *A Concise History of American Architecture*. New York: Harper and Row, 1979.

Ruttenber, E. M. *History of the Indian Tribes of Hudson's River*. New York: Kennikat Press, 1872.

Samuels, Peggy, and Harold Samuels. *Frederic Remington: A Biography*. Garden City, N.Y.: Doubleday, 1982.

Sandoz, Mari. *Cheyenne Autumn*. New York: Hastings House, 1953.

Schmitt, Peter J. *Back to Nature: The Arcadian Myth in Urban America*. New York: Oxford University Press, 1969.

Schoolcraft, Henry R. *Historical and Statistical Information Respecting the History, Conditions and Prospects of the Indian Tribes of the United States*. 6 vols. Philadelphia: Lippincott, Grambo, 1851 – 57.

Schultz, Gladys D., and Daisy G. Lawrence. *Lady from Savannah: The Life of Juliette Low*. Philadelphia: Lippincott, 1958.

Seger, John H. *Early Days among the Cheyenne and Arapahoe Indians*. Edited by Stanley Vestal. Norman: University of Oklahoma Press, 1934.

Seton, Robert. *An Old Family; or, the Setons in Scotland and America*. New York: Brentanos, 1899.

Sewall, William W. *Bill Sewall's Story of T. R.* New York: Harper, 1919.

Shrive, Norman. *Charles Mair: Literary Nationalist*. Toronto: University of Toronto Press, 1965.

Smith, Henry Nash. *Virgin Land: The American West as Symbol and Myth*. Cambridge, Mass.: Harvard University Press, 1950.

Stanley, George F. G. *The Birth of Western Canada: A History of the Riel Rebellions*. Toronto: University of Toronto Press, 1961.

Stedman, Raymond W. *Shadows of the Indian*. Norman: University of Oklahoma Press, 1982.

Steffens, Lincoln. *The Autobiography of Lincoln Steffens*. New York: Harcourt, Brace and World, 1931.

———. *The Letters of Lincoln Steffens*. Edited by Ella Winter and Granville Hicks. 2 vols. New York: Harcourt, Brace, 1938.

———. *The World of Lincoln Steffens*. Edited by Ella Winter and Herbert Shapiro. New York: Hill and Wang, 1962.

Steiner, Stan. *The New Indians*. New York: Dell, 1968.

Sterling, Keir B. *Last of the Naturalists: The Career of C. Hart Merriam*. New York: Arno, 1974.

Stokoe, William C. *Semiotics and Human Sign Languages*. The Hague: Mouton, 1972.

Sullivan, Mark. *Our Times*. 4 vols. New York: Scribner, 1926–32.

Swanberg, W. A. *Citizen Hearst*. New York: Scribner, 1961.

Tassin, Ray. *Stanley Vestal: Champion of the Old West*. Glendale, Calif.: Arthur H. Clark, 1973.

Taylor, Joshua C. *The Fine Arts in America*. Chicago: University of Chicago Press, 1979.

Trotter, Reginald C. *Canadian Federation*. Toronto: J. M. Dent, 1924.

Turner, Frederick Jackson. *The Frontier in American History*. New York: Henry Holt, 1920.

Underhill, Lonnie E., and Daniel F. Littlefield, Jr., eds. *Hamlin Garland's Observations on the American Indian, 1895–1905*. Tucson: University of Arizona Press, 1976.

Van Steen, Marcus. *Pauline Johnson: Her Life and Work*. Toronto: Musson, 1965.

Wade, E. K. *Twenty-One Years of Scouting: The Official History of the Boy Scout Movement from Its Inception*. London: C. Arthur Pearson, 1929.

Wagenknecht, Edward. *The Seven Worlds of Theodore Roosevelt*. New York: Longmans, Green, 1958.

Walker, Franklin. *Frank Norris: A Biography*. New York: Russell and Russell, 1932.

Walker, James R. *The Sun Dance and Other Ceremonies of the Oglala Division of the Teton Dakota*. New York: Trustees of the American Museum of Natural History, 1917.

Waltrip, Lela, and Rufus Waltrip. *Indian Women: Thirteen Who Played a Part in the History of America from Earliest Days to Now*. New York: David McKay, 1964.

Ward, Lester F. *Psychic Factors of Civilization*. Boston: Ginn, 1897.

———. *Outlines of Sociology*. Boston: Ginn, 1898.

Warner, Charles Dudley. *Complete Writings*. Hartford, Conn., 1904.

Washburn, Wilcomb E. *The Indian in America*. New York: Harper and Row, 1975.

Weigle, Marta, and Kyle Fiore. *Santa Fe and Taos: The Writers' Era, 1916–1941*. Santa Fe: Ancient City Press, 1982.

White, G. Edward. *The Eastern Establishment and the Western Experience: The West of Frederic Remington, Theodore Roosevelt, and Owen Wister.* New Haven, Conn.: Yale University Press, 1968.

White, Lynn, Jr. *Dynamo and Virgin Reconsidered.* Cambridge, Mass.: MIT Press, 1973.

Wister, Owen. *The Virginian.* New York: Grosset and Dunlap, 1902.

Young, Samuel B. M. *Report of the Acting Superintendent of the Yellowstone National Park to the Secretary of the Interior, 1897.* Washington, D.C.: GPO, 1897.

INDEX

Index

Printed in the United States
130171LV00003B/36/A